Surveying Instruments of Greece and Rome

The Greeks and, especially, the Romans are famous for the heroic engineering of their aqueducts, tunnels and roads. They also measured the circumference of the earth and the heights of mountains with fair precision. This book presents new translations (from Greek, Latin, Arabic, Hebrew and Syriac) of all the ancient texts concerning surveying instruments, including major sources hitherto untapped. It explores the history of surveying instruments, notably the Greek dioptra and the Roman libra, and with the help of tests with reconstructions explains how they were used in practice. This is a subject which has never been tackled before in anything like this depth. The Greeks emerge as the pioneers of instrumental surveying and, though their equipment and methods were simple by modern standards, they and the Romans can be credited with a level of technical sophistication which must count as one of the greatest achievements of the ancient world.

M. J. T. Lewis is Senior Lecturer in Industrial Archaeology at the University of Hull. His publications include *Temples in Roman Britain* (1966), *Early Wooden Railways* (1970) and *Millstone and Hammer: the Origins of Water Power* (1997), and many articles in such journals as *History of Technology*, *Technology and Culture* and *Papers of the British School at Rome*.

D1557304

SURVEYING INSTRUMENTS OF GREECE AND ROME

M. J. T. LEWIS

UNIVERSITY OF HULL

CAMBRIDGE
UNIVERSITY PRESS

CAMBRIDGE UNIVERSITY PRESS
Cambridge, New York, Melbourne, Madrid, Cape Town, Singapore, São Paulo, Delhi

Cambridge University Press
The Edinburgh Building, Cambridge CB2 8RU, UK

Published in the United States of America by Cambridge University Press, New York

www.cambridge.org
Information on this title: www.cambridge.org/9780521110655

First published 2001
This digitally printed version 2009

A catalogue record for this publication is available from the British Library

ISBN 978-0-521-79297-4 hardback
ISBN 978-0-521-11065-5 paperback

To Hywel

CONTENTS

List of figures   *page* x
List of tables   xiii
Preface   xv
Explanatory notes   xvii

Introduction   1

PART I: INSTRUMENTS AND METHODS

1 The basic elements   13
   A. Precursors of the Greeks   13
   B. Measuring distances   19
   C. Orientation and right angles   22
   D. Measuring heights   23
   E. Levelling   27

2 Background to the dioptra
   A. The sighting tube   36
   B. Astronomical instruments   38
   C. The Hipparchan dioptra   41
   D. The measuring rod   42
   E. Gamaliel's tube   46
   F. Philo's level and staff   48

3 The dioptra   51
   A. The treatises   53
   B. The sources of the treatises   62
   C. The minor sources   66
   D. The plane astrolabe   67
   E. The standard dioptra   71
   F. Hero's dioptra   82
   G. Levelling   89
   H. Other surveys   97

CONTENTS

I. Chronological conclusions 101
J. Testing a reconstructed dioptra 105

4 The libra
A. The evidence 109
B. Testing a reconstructed libra 116

5 The groma
A. Grids 120
B. The groma and its use 124

6 The hodometer 134

PART II: PRACTICAL APPLICATIONS

7 Measurement of the earth 143

8 Mountain heights 157

9 Canals and aqueducts
A. Early canal schemes 167
B. Aqueduct surveying 170
C. The Nîmes aqueduct and others 181
D. The challenges of surveying 191

10 Tunnels
A. Categories 197
B. Alignment 200
C. Level 204
D. Meeting 206
E. Instruments 213

11 Roman roads
A. Basic principles 217
B. Interpolation and extrapolation 218
C. Successive approximation 220
D. Dead reckoning 224
E. Geometrical construction 232
F. Examples 233

12 Epilogue 246

CONTENTS

PART III: THE SOURCES

The treatises
Hero of Alexandria: *Dioptra*   259
Julius Africanus: *Cesti* I 15   286
Anonymus Byzantinus: *Geodesy*   289
Al-Karaji: *The Search for Hidden Waters* XXIII   298

Other sources
The basic elements (Chapter 1)   303
Background to the dioptra (Chapter 2)   305
The dioptra (Chapter 3)   308
The libra (Chapter 4)   318
The groma (Chapter 5)   323
The hodometer (Chapter 6)   329
Measurement of the earth (Chapter 7)   332
Mountain heights (Chapter 8)   335
Canals and aqueducts (Chapter 9)   340
Tunnels (Chapter 10)   345
Roman roads (Chapter 11)   347

Appendix: Uncertain devices
   A. The U-tube level   349
   B. The dioptra on a coin   350
   C. Dodecahedrons   350
   D. The 'cross-staff'   351
   E. Sagui's instruments   352
Bibliography   355
Index   369
Index of ancient authors cited   378

FIGURES

1.1   The *merkhet* in use   *page* 16
1.2   Similar triangles   25
1.3   Thales' demonstration of the distance of a ship   26
1.4   Height triangles of Vitruvius Rufus and the *Mappae Clavicula*   27
1.5   Egyptian A-frame level for horizontals and plumb-line for verticals   28
1.6   The chorobates   31
2.1   Hipparchan dioptra   43
3.1   Dioptra reconstruction in vertical mode   52
3.2   Dioptra reconstruction in horizontal mode   53
3.3   Types of sight   74
3.4   Foresight and object seen through out-of-focus slit backsight   76
3.5   The *karchesion* for catapult and for assault bridge   77
3.6   Hero's dioptra: Schöne's reconstruction   83
3.7   Hero's dioptra: Drachmann's reconstruction   84
3.8   Hero's water level: Mynas Codex drawing and Drachmann's reconstruction   85
3.9   Hero's water level: Schöne's reconstruction   86
3.10 Sketches of Hero's dioptra, after Mynas Codex   87
3.11 Diagram apparently explaining how water finds its own level in a U-tube, after Mynas Codex   88
3.12 Methods of levelling   90
3.13 Hero's staff: Schöne's reconstruction   94
3.14 Back and fore sights with dioptra inaccurately set   95
3.15 Measuring the height of a wall   108
4.1   Egyptian balance, c.1400 BC   111
4.2   Libra reconstruction with shield   117
4.3   Libra reconstruction without shield   117
4.4   Detail of suspension   118
4.5   Detail of sight   118

x

5.1	Schulten's reconstruction of the groma	127
5.2	The Pompeii groma as reconstructed by Della Corte	128
5.3	Gromas on tombstones from Ivrea and Pompeii	129
5.4	Reconstruction of supposed groma from Pfünz	130
5.5	Supposed groma from the Fayum	131
5.6	Supposed groma and stand as control marks on denarius	132
6.1	Reconstruction of Vitruvius' hodometer	135
8.1	Transects of Olympus	164
9.1	Nile–Red Sea canal	168
9.2	Map of Nîmes aqueduct	182
9.3	Nîmes aqueduct, simplified gradient profile	184
9.4	Nîmes aqueduct, map of valleys section	186
9.5	Map of Poitiers aqueducts	190
9.6	Poitiers, Fleury aqueduct gradient profile	192
10.1	Samos tunnels, plan	201
10.2	Sections of Samos tunnel, Lake Albano and Nemi emissaries	203
10.3	Samos tunnel, strategies for meeting	208
10.4	Briord tunnel, plan	209
10.5	Bologna tunnel, lateral mismatch of headings	210
10.6	La Perrotte tunnel, Sernhac, plan and section of south end	211
10.7	Al-Karaji's procedure for recording deviations	212
10.8	Chagnon tunnel, Gier aqueduct, geometry of setting out	213
10.9	Al-Karaji's sighting tube for qanats	214
11.1	Simple alignment by interpolation and extrapolation	219
11.2	Successive approximation	223
11.3	Surveying alignments by traverse and offset	225
11.4	Surveying alignments by angle	230
11.5	Surveying alignment by offset	231
11.6	Surveying alignment by geometrical construction	233
11.7	The Portway	235
11.8	Ermine Street	235
11.9	Watling Street	235
11.10	Stane Street	239
11.11	Stane Street aligned by geometrical construction	239
11.12	The outermost German limes	244

12.1	Surveyor's staff and water level with floating sights, 1044	247
12.2	Finding the height and distance of an island	248
12.3	The plumb-line *mizan* and variant	252
App.1	Control marks on denarius	350
App.2	Roman cross-staff (?) from Koblenz and a nineteenth-century example	352
App.3	Carving at Little Metropolis, Athens, and Sagui's surveying table	353
App.4	Sagui's mine inclinometer	354

TABLES

3.1	Terminology of the dioptra	*pages* 80–1
7.1	Circumference of the earth	156
8.1	Measurements of mountain heights	160–1
9.1	Gradients of Greek aqueducts	173
9.2	Roman aqueducts with the shallowest gradients	175

PREFACE

First, a few definitions. *Surveying* is the science based on mathematics which involves measuring any part of the earth's surface and any artificial features on it, and plotting the result on a map or plan drawn to a suitable scale. Often, though by no means always, it also involves *levelling* or some similar process to record relative heights. *Setting out* is effectively the converse process, namely locating intended boundaries, structures or engineering works on the ground, in the correct position in all three dimensions. The surveyor will often have to carry out both procedures, especially when linear features such as aqueducts or railways are to be built: first to record the existing shape of the terrain and then, in the light of this information, to decide the best route and to mark it on the ground.

Almost without exception, surveying with instruments that rose above the level of low technology began with the Greeks and Romans, and a proper understanding of their achievements entails straddling two very different disciplines. The present-day surveyor who is curious about the origins of his profession may not be deeply informed on ancient history or engineering, while the classical historian may not have a detailed command of the principles of surveying. The resulting challenge, constantly encountered by historians of technology, is to try to put across the background, the material and the arguments at such a level that no reader feels neglected or patronised. I have done my best to strike a happy mean. My credentials, such as they are, for accepting this challenge are an upbringing as a classicist and classical archaeologist and a lifetime spent on the history of technology. I am not a trained surveyor, but through fieldwork I have acquired a working knowledge of surveying techniques. Since the techniques and instruments of ancient surveying were essentially similar to, if simpler than, those that I have experienced, I hope that this is qualification enough.

I am indebted to Denis Hopkin for constructing a dioptra for me, to David Palmer for making a libra, to Dr Guy Stiebel of the Hebrew University, Jerusalem, for help over Talmudic references, and particularly to Dr Youcef Bouandel for translating al-Karaji's Arabic. I am grateful too to Pauline Hire of Cambridge University Press for suggesting improvements to the layout of this book and for seeing it through the press with such care. But I owe most to my family. The staffman's job is, at the best of times, tedious. To act as staffman for a surveyor who is struggling with the idiosyncrasies of totally strange instruments is more tedious still. This is what my son Hywel did for me, with exemplary patience, over the many days when I was testing the reconstructed dioptra and libra. His understanding of the principles and his sound common sense, moreover, helped me through many a difficulty. My debt to him is very great. So it is too to my wife, who has also held the staff on occasion and who has commented on my drafts with her usual perception.

EXPLANATORY NOTES

CROSS-REFERENCES

Part III contains translations both of the four major treatises and of extracts from other sources arranged in the same order and under the same headings as the chapters and sections of Parts I and II. References to these translations are in bold type: in the form **Dioptra 22**, **Africanus 4, Anonymus 10, Al-Karaji 2** to the treatises, in the form **Source 33** to the other sources. Thus the cross-reference **Source 33** in Chapter 3.D on the astrolabe should guide the reader to the extract in Part III from Severus Sebokht. Occasionally a source deals with more than one instrument, in which case a note at the end of one section in Part III draws attention to relevant material in another section.

TRANSLATION

Few of the sources have hitherto been translated into English. Where they have been, the results vary from the excellent to the downright misleading. All the translations from Greek and Latin used here are therefore my own, done for the purpose of this book. The major treatises are written in a bewildering jumble of tenses and persons, sometimes in the same sentence: *I turn the alidade*, for example, *one will turn the alidade, the alidade was turned*, and *let the alidade be turned*. All these, and comparable phrases, have generally (but not always) been standardised into the imperative, *turn the alidade*. Greek reference letters are retained. Otherwise all Greek, Latin, Hebrew, Syriac and Arabic is translated, except for occasional words which, because of their untranslatable connotations, are simply transliterated. Semitic words are transliterated without diacritical signs (may purists forgive me), except that Arabic Ḥ and Ṭ are differentiated from H and T when used as reference letters.

TERMINOLOGY

To avoid potential confusion, although the context normally makes the distinction clear, two sets of terms need explaining. In levelling, *back sight* and *fore sight*, each in two words, denote the sightings taken through the instrument looking backwards and forwards at the staff. *Backsight* and *foresight*, each in one word, are terms borrowed from the rifle to denote the actual parts of the instrument (holes or slits) through which sightings are taken.

GRADIENTS

Gradients can be given in different ways:

The vertical reduced to unity relative to the horizontal, e.g.	1 in 200 or 1:200
The vertical as a percentage of the horizontal,	0.5%
The vertical as so much per thousand horizontal	5‰
Metres per kilometre	5m per km
Vertical divided by horizontal	0.005

All of the above figures mean exactly the same thing. The form most widely used in engineering circles is 0.5%. But (at least in Britain) the most common form found in histories of engineering is 1 in 200; and I feel that by this system the non-engineer can most easily visualise a given gradient: in this case a rise or fall of one unit of length for every 200 units of distance. I have therefore adopted this form throughout, and engineers will have no difficulty in converting it to their own pre-ferred version.

MEASURES

Ancient measures are a minefield for the unwary. For our purposes the precise value of a particular unit is normally of no great importance; as a rule of thumb it is often sufficient to take the cubit as rather under half a metre and the stade as rather under 200 metres. Exactitude is desirable only when comparing ancient estimates of length and height with known modern equivalents; the problem is that it is often impos-sible to tell which of several different values was in fact being used. The units encountered in this book are listed below.

Greek

The relationships are constant, regardless of the actual length of each unit:

4 dactyls	=	1 palm		
12 dactyls	=	1 span		
16 dactyls	=	1 foot		
24 dactyls	=	1 cubit	=	1½ feet
4 cubits	=	1 fathom[1]	=	6 feet
100 feet	=	1 plethron		
100 cubits	=	1 schoinion	=	150 feet
400 cubits	=	1 stade	=	600 feet

The value of Greek measures, however, varied from place to place and from time to time. Four values of feet and stades which were widely used in Hellenistic and Roman times deserve mention here.[2]

	Attic–Roman	'standard'	Olympic	Philetaeran
1 foot	29.6 cm	30.8 cm	32.0 cm	32.9c m
1 stade	177.6 m	185 m	192 m	197.3 m
stades to Roman mile	8.33	8.00	7.71	7.50

Roman

16 digits	=	1 foot	=	12 inches
24 digits	=	1 cubit		
5 feet	=	1 pace		
1,000 paces	=	1 mile		

The values are well established: 1 foot = 29.6 cm, 1 mile = 1480 m.

Islamic

4 fingers	=	1 palm		
12 fingers	=	1 span		
24 fingers	=	1 legal cubit		
32 fingers	=	1 Hasimi cubit		
60 Hasimi cubits	=	1 cord (asl)	=	80 legal cubits
4,000 legal cubits	=	1 mil	=	50 cords
3 mil	=	1 farsakh		

[1] But 9¼ spans = 1 fathom for measuring cultivated land.
[2] Based on Hultsch 1882. There are useful summaries in KP v 336–7 and OCD 942–3. The calculations of Lehmann-Haupt 1929, though seemingly authoritative, need to be treated with caution. See also Dicks 1960, 42–6.

The value of Islamic measures was widely variable. The legal cubit was usually 49.875 cm and the Hasimi cubit 66.5 cm.[3]

[3] See Hinz 1955 and 1965. For corresponding Babylonian measures see Powell 1987–90.

INTRODUCTION

Engineering is one of the skills for which the Romans are most renowned. Some of their works, such as bridges carrying roads or water, are visually spectacular because of their sheer scale and daring. Others are equally impressive for the less obvious reason that they required very precise surveying. Examples which leap to mind are roads which cut across country as straight as an arrow, kilometre-long tunnels whose headings met deep underground without significant error, and aqueducts on gradients that can average 1 in 8000 for twenty-five kilometres or 1 in 20,000 for eight. Such feats of engineering would have been impossible without good surveying techniques and good instruments. That these existed has of course long been recognised, and many historians of technology have commented on them, although there has been no fundamental discussion of the evidence for many years. The regular conclusion has been that the standard instrument for laying out straight lines and right angles was the groma, that the standard instrument for levelling was the chorobates, and that Hero's dioptra was a non-starter. Constant repetition has almost sanctified this opinion into a dogma. But while it is partly true, it is also partly wrong, and it is very incomplete in that it is biased towards the Romans and ignores much of the evidence available in Greek.

One of my aims is to remedy the deficiency, and in the process to restore to the Greeks their rightful share of the credit. 'The Greeks had the brains, the Romans had good drains', runs the jingle, in tune with the perception, common to the ancient Romans and to more recent generations alike, that it was Rome which borrowed the bright but unrealised ideas of Greece and brought them to fruition. Yet the Greeks were engineers too, even if their achievements in this field were often more modest and less immediately obvious. In contrast to the wealth, peace and unity of the Roman Empire at its height, the geography of Greece was divisive and its political units were smaller and incessantly at loggerheads. There was therefore less opportunity for major undertakings. But this did not inhibit creativity; and in the realm

I

of instrumental surveying, as in so much else, it was the Greeks who developed not only the theory but much of the practice too, and their pioneering contribution deserves our wholehearted respect.

This book embraces a thousand years, from the archaic Greek tunnels of the sixth century BC to the Roman aqueducts which were still being built in the fifth century AD. During that time span, two major revolutions which altered the political map of the Mediterranean also increased the demand for surveyors and indirectly affected their instruments. First, the death in 323 BC of Alexander the Great ushered in the Hellenistic Age, when his huge empire was carved up by his generals into what, compared with the previous norm of small units, were super-states. Of these, Egypt, ruled by the Ptolemies, at first dominated the scientific and mechanical scene, with a profound input from the royal research institute, the Museum of Alexandria, founded about 300 BC. At the same time Archimedes was engaged in largely independent but equally mould-breaking work in Syracuse. After a hundred years or so the influence of Alexandria waned. Its scientific lead seems to have been assumed by the emergent kingdom of Pergamon in Asia Minor in the realm of surveying and by the city state of Rhodes in the related pursuit of instrumental astronomy. The Hellenistic Age was ended by the coming of Rome. But it had seen the foundations of geometry laid, most notably by Euclid, and it had also seen the rise, rooted in that geometry, of the theory of surveying and of precision instruments. Surveyors could now answer questions asked by natural philosophers, such as the size of the earth and the heights of mountains, and more practically they could serve the state both in its military and its civil role.

The second revolution was the rise of Rome and its acquisition between 146 and 31 BC, both by force of arms and by diplomacy, of most Greek territories. Its surveying instruments and even some of the uses (notably road building) to which it put them differed from those of the Greeks, but they evidently went back just as far in time. With the Roman take-over of the eastern Mediterranean these two largely independent traditions met and to some extent melded. Roman engineering expanded eastwards, Greek theory (but not perhaps Greek surveying instruments) was exported west: Vitruvius, for example, the major Latin source of the first century BC, derived his material on surveying almost entirely from Greek sources. Nor was Greek enterprise stifled. Alexandrian science experienced a revival, exemplified by Hero in the first century AD, by Ptolemy the astronomer in the second and by Theon in the fourth. With its empire established and for two centuries in relative harmony, Rome was at leisure to undertake its mightiest engineering works.

The profession of the ancient surveyor, whether Greek or Roman, may be divided into four distinct categories.

1. The land surveyor (*geometres* or *geodaistes* in Greek, *finitor*, *mensor*, *agrimensor* or *gromaticus* in Latin) carried out relatively localised work on the ground surface. He might record the exact shape of an existing expanse of ground such as a field or an estate and calculate the areas enclosed. He might divide land into plots, normally rectangular, whether in the country for distribution to settlers, or in a town for setting out a grid of streets, or in a military context for laying out a fort. His work is the subject of the Roman compilation known as the *Corpus Agrimensorum*. Land surveying was concerned essentially only with horizontal measurement, not with vertical.

2. The cartographical surveyor (*chorographos*, *geographos*) made maps, usually of larger areas than the land surveyor, for example of regions or provinces or even of the whole known world. At least in theory, this might involve establishing latitudes and, indirectly, longitudes by a combination of astronomical and terrestrial methods, and the sphericity of the earth had to be taken into account. A related pursuit was the enquiry, originally philosophical, into the size of the earth and the heights of mountains.

3. The military surveyor (*mensor*) supplied practical information to the commander and his engineers, who might call in particular for two precise dimensions that were highly dangerous to measure directly in the presence of the enemy: the height of a city wall in order to prepare ladders or a siege tower of the right height, and the width of a river in order to prepare a pontoon bridge of the right length.

4. The engineering surveyor (*mensor* or *librator*) investigated terrain with a view to imposing man-made features on it. Roads and aqueducts are the most obvious instances, but hand in hand with aqueducts went drainage and irrigation channels and navigable canals; and with them, on occasion, went tunnels and mine adits with their particular

problems of maintaining direction and gradient underground. Harbour works could also require the services of a surveyor.

These categories were by no means mutually exclusive. Surveyors in the different branches could employ the same instruments and similar techniques, and could even be the same men. Some of their instruments and techniques were also shared by astronomers who, especially with the rise of mathematical astronomy, wished to find the angular distances between stars and planets and the apparent diameters of the sun and moon, and to establish the celestial coordinates of stars and planets relative to the equator or the ecliptic.

The various branches of surveying will not receive equal treatment in this book. The work of the *agrimensor* has already been much discussed, and little can be added to our still imperfect understanding of its principal instrument, the groma. Nor can much new be said of map making, considerable though it evidently was.[1] Ptolemy, its greatest exponent, claimed (**Source 64**) that places could be accurately located by coordinates determined either by astronomical observation or by terrestrial measurement. In practice, however, the vast majority of the latitudes and longitudes which he gives are the result of nothing more than dead reckoning.[2] None the less, new light can be shed on the use of instruments in calculating the size of the earth and the heights of mountains. Astronomers and terrestrial surveyors shared the dioptra, which was one of the parents of that important and long-lived device the plane astrolabe; but otherwise astronomical instruments have little direct relevance to terrestrial surveying and will receive short shrift here. Part I of this book therefore concentrates on instruments for military and especially for engineering surveying. Since it would be nonsensical to discuss the instruments and not their application, Part II includes a number of examples of how different surveying tasks might have been undertaken. The subject, too, is one that cries out for experimental archaeology, and the results are presented here of trials with versions of the dioptra and libra which have never, as far as I am aware, been reconstructed before.

---

[1] Dilke 1985, Sherk 1974.

[2] Toomer 1975, 200. As Ptolemy himself admitted (*Geography* II 1.2), the apparent exactitude of his coordinates was merely to allow places to be plotted on a map: see Aujac 1993, 155.

As already remarked, most historians of engineering have hitherto focused their attention on three instruments. One is the groma, which was primarily the tool of the *agrimensor*, although it had a role to play in laying out roads. The second is the chorobates which, taking Vitruvius at face value, historians wrongly assume to have been the standard device for levelling. The third is Hero's sophisticated version of the dioptra, described in his treatise of that name, which they rightly regard as having been too complex and expensive to find widespread use. In concentrating on Hero's instrument, however, they have over-looked the evidence in the rest of his manual for a pre-existing litera-ture on surveying procedures. They have moreover been almost totally unaware that a considerable part of this literature survives in the form of other Greek treatises (or parts of treatises) on surveying. Compiled in their surviving form by Julius Africanus and the Anonymus Byzantinus, these contain much information about the 'standard' Hellenistic dioptra and its uses. The original of another such manual, part of which is embedded in an Arabic treatise by al-Karaji, is shown by new techniques of dating to be Hellenistic too. In Part III, therefore, Hero's *Dioptra*, Africanus, the Anonymus and al-Karaji are collected together, along with a host of lesser ancient references to surveying and surveying instruments, for the first time. In most cases, too, this is the first time they have been translated into English.

The evidence, however, is very uneven. While the literature is sur-prisingly extensive, and a great variety of engineering work survives as the end product of surveying, in between we are missing a great deal, most notably (with the exception of the groma) the instruments them-selves. If the Greek dioptra can now be reconstructed from the new sources with some confidence, we have no description or example of its Roman counterpart for levelling, the libra. In this case there is only its name and its achievements (in the form of the aqueducts themselves) to work on, and discussion of it must necessarily be much more specu-lative. Even the groma, despite the fact that it is the only ancient sur-veying instrument to be attested archaeologically, has clouds of uncertainty hanging over it. And the possibility always remains that instruments and techniques existed which are not on record at all.

Modern surveying is so highly developed a science that we need to exercise caution in our expectations of ancient surveying. Recent developments in satellite surveying and laser technology, needless to say, would be far beyond the comprehension of the ancient world, and when I speak of modern practice I use the phrase as a convenient shorthand for the equipment and techniques available to, say, the Victorian railway engineer, who confronted problems not dissimilar to those of the Roman aqueduct engineer, and who made use of instruments which in a sense were not dissimilar either.

There were of course some fundamental differences. We are dealing with a period before optics and before the spirit level, both of which were developments of the seventeenth century.[3] Optics markedly increase the distance at which accurate instrumental readings can be taken. The spirit level markedly improves the precision with which an instrument is set in the horizontal plane. Without it there are only two methods of finding a horizontal, namely the open water level and (by means of a line at right angles to the vertical) the plumb-line; a useful variation on this last theme is to suspend the instrument itself so that it acts as its own plumb bob. Another difference between the ancient and the modern is that trigonometry was then in its earliest infancy – in essence it began in the second century BC with Hipparchus and his chord tables[4] – and Greek and Roman surveyors worked entirely with simple Euclidean geometry, notably in the form of similar triangles.

All that, however, having been said, the principles of ancient surveying were basically and recognisably similar to the modern, and there is consequently a family resemblance between Greek surveying manuals and those of the nineteenth and twentieth centuries.[5] It seems entirely legitimate to make direct comparisons between the old and the new, and to reconstruct ancient instruments as faithfully as the sources allow and to test their accuracy in the field. But, to revert to the caution expressed earlier, we should not be disappointed if they do not all measure up to the performance of their modern counterparts. Without optics and the spirit level – and indeed without long experience on the part of the surveyor – they could not hope to do so. But an impressive advance in accuracy is readily discernible from classical Greece through the Hellenistic world to Rome, and the sophistication

[3] Kiely 1947. Although his section on the instruments of antiquity is brief and outdated, Kiely's magisterial survey, which extends up to the end of the seventeenth century, remains invaluable.   [4] Toomer 1973.

[5] They are numerous. Three entirely typical examples are Merrett 1893, Williamson 1915 and Clancy 1991.

of the engineering of each period was dictated by the capabilities of its surveying instruments. A Greek aqueduct of the second century BC would typically be a pipeline with an overall gradient of 1 in 200, and only the most massive of surveying errors with the dioptra would prevent the water from flowing. In contrast, a Roman aqueduct of the first century AD would be a channel with an overall gradient, sometimes, of 1 in 8000, and the smallest of errors with the libra might spell disaster. It is therefore reassuring that a reconstructed libra, even in preliminary tests, proved itself capable of working to this degree of precision.

It is widely accepted that practical engineering in the ancient world, whether (in modern terms) civil or mechanical, generally owed little to theoretical science. It was more a case of the theory, if any, being based on practical results. This may be seen as early as the third century BC in the pseudo-Aristotelian *Mechanical Problems*; and it may be seen later in such hydraulic theory as came to arise from observation of the working of water clocks, aqueducts and the like.[6] At first there would doubtless be little if any quantified data available for engineers to draw on; but, as time passed, experience and comprehension accumulated to assist later generations. Norman Smith has rightly remarked that 'design is achieved by one of three techniques: [1] theoretical analysis, [2] objective testing, [3] empiricism based on experience and intuition and more or less codified into sets of rules and procedures'. But while he can cite plenty of examples from the ancient world of the third category, he apparently finds none of the first, and of the second only a few such as

the calibration of catapults by a procedure which is more controlled than mere trial-and-error. The relevant parameters are identified and assembled into a quantitative relationship whose solution is intricate to the point of requiring the determination of cube roots. We can reasonably postulate the calibration of other pieces of equipment such as Vitruvius' hodometer, water-clocks and surveying instruments.[7]

While Smith's attribution of catapults and water clocks to this second category is undoubtedly correct, it is hardly fair to bracket surveying instruments and the hodometer with them, for these were devices whose design and application were founded wholly on theory.

6 Lewis 2000.   7 Smith 1991, 118.

7

They belong to a family of instruments generated directly by the sciences – mathematics, geometry and astronomy – in which the Greeks most excelled. Thus, thanks to the geometrical invention of the planisphere, the anaphoric clock could display the position of the sun in the heavens at any given time (see Chapter 3.D). Observation of the behaviour of the heavenly bodies, translated first into mathematical relationships and hence via the mathematical ratios of cog wheels into an enormously complex gear train, allowed the calendrical computer known as the Antikythera mechanism to display an even wider variety of astronomical information for any date and time set on it.[8] Similarly but more simply the mathematical gearing of the hodometer recorded the distance travelled as accurately as its construction allowed.

This is the category, ruled by theoretical analysis, to which other surveying instruments also belong. Both the instruments and the procedures for using them were designed strictly according to the rules of geometry. Their fallibility arose not from defective theory but from defective technology. This is most clearly seen in levelling, where the evidence is fullest. Four different procedures are recorded, all of them theoretically impeccable; but in practical terms some are better than others, and in the end the best one triumphed (Chapter 3.G). Surveying was therefore one of the relatively few areas where engineering and science rubbed shoulders. The relationship was fully appreciated at the time. According to Strabo, when discussing a survey of the intended Corinth canal, 'mathematicians define engineering (*architektonike*) as a branch of mathematics'.[9] So too did Hero define geodesy (*geodaisia*, surveying).[10]

Surveying instruments, moreover, ultimately achieved an accuracy which can only have come from a combination of intelligent design, of meticulous procedure in the field and of good workmanship. Technical limitations, of course, prevented them from approaching the precision of modern equipment. But, like the 95 per cent efficiency of a few ancient pumps,[11] their ability to level an aqueduct to 1 in 8000, let alone to 1 in 20,000, is a sign of something well above ordinary crafts-

---

[8] Price 1974.
[9] Strabo, *Geography* 1 3.11 (**Source 92**). *Architektonike* embraced not only (in modern terms) architecture but civil and sometimes mechanical engineering as well.
[10] Hero, *Definitions* 135.8; and see **Source 13**.
[11] Those from the Dramont D wreck: Rouanet 1974, 65.

manship. Needless to say, it took time to reach this standard, and earlier and cruder surveying instruments and methods survived alongside later and more sophisticated ones.

At some point along this path of development – it is hard to say exactly when – they moved out of the realm of low technology into that of high technology. The first of these useful descriptions embraces, in Price's definition,

the sort of crafts that all men in all cultures have used in all ages for building houses and roads and water supply, making clothes and pots, growing and cooking food, waging war, etc. [High technology, in contrast, means] those specially sophisticated crafts and manufactures that are in some ways intimately connected with the sciences, drawing on them for theories, giving to them the instruments and the techniques that enable men to observe and experiment and increase both knowledge and technical competence.[12]

Price is talking in particular of the Antikythera mechanism, which was emphatically a product of high technology. So, equally emphatically, were the more advanced surveying instruments and techniques, which thus formed another rare example of spin-off from science and of feedback to it in return.

This, then, is the theme of this book. It is divided into three parts. The first discusses the instruments and the methods of using them, progressing from the simpler and then the transitional devices to those pinnacles of ancient surveying, the Greek dioptra and the Roman libra, with the groma and hodometer calling for quite brief treatment. Second, a number of different practical circumstances are investigated, in an attempt to understand how surveyors applied their instruments in the field and what their results imply. This is of profound importance because these instruments, and consequently these results, comprise one of the most successful technical achievements of the ancient world. Finally, the literary sources which, alongside the archaeological evidence, supply the raw materials for this study are assembled in translation.

I hope that, by virtue of a certain novelty of approach and by drawing on largely untapped sources, my analysis will revive a debate that has largely ground to a halt. But I am fully aware that it is not exhaustive, and it is emphatically not the last word. There is much still to be discovered, and much to be argued.

[12] Price 1974, 52.

PART I

INSTRUMENTS AND METHODS

CHAPTER I

THE BASIC ELEMENTS

Surveying no doubt began at the humblest of levels, and for millennia evolved only slowly. Its functions would encompass the recording of the boundaries of plots of land, estimating their area and, if new-won land was being distributed, dividing it fairly; where irrigation or drainage was involved, ensuring that the gradient of water channels was adequate; in architecture, particularly of prestige buildings, establishing a reasonably horizontal level for foundations and sometimes, especially for religious monuments, the appropriate orientation. All these activities, as at every stage in the history of surveying, were based on geometry. At first this was doubtless entirely empirical and of the simplest kind; and at first the surveyors employed the simplest of tools. The real breakthrough to more complex requirements, to a deeper understanding of geometrical theory, and to procedures and instruments of considerably greater sophistication and precision, was due to the Greeks and Romans in the third and second centuries BC, and it is this revolution which forms the main subject of this book. But to understand its nature we need first to look at what it grew out of. A satisfactory investigation, unfortunately, is impossible simply because, before the treatises on the dioptra of Hellenistic Greece and the *Corpus Agrimensorum* of imperial Rome, our information is deplorably scanty.

For some topics, like measuring cords and plumb-line levels which hardly changed over centuries, the story is here continued to the end of the Roman period.

A. PRECURSORS OF THE GREEKS

The Greeks themselves always maintained that they learned the art of geometry – literally the measurement of land – from the Egyptians, who from time immemorial had recorded land boundaries so that, if obliterated by inundations of the Nile, they could be restored. The earliest record of this debt is found in the fifth century BC, when Herodotus wrote:[1]

[1] Herodotus, *Histories* II 109.

13

This king [Sesostris], they said, divided the country among all the Egyptians, giving each of them a square holding of the same size, and raised his revenue by levying an annual tax. Anyone who lost part of his holding to the river would come to the king and declare what had happened, and the king would send inspectors to measure how much land had been lost, so that henceforth the proper proportion of the assessed tax should be paid. This was the way, I think, in which geometry was invented and ultimately came to Greece; for the Greeks learned of the sundial and gnomon and the twelve divisions of the day from the Babylonians.

Five hundred years later the accepted story was little different:[2]

As the old report tells us, the first preoccupation of geometry was the measurement and distribution of land, whence the name geometry. The concept of measurement was discovered by the Egyptians; many plots of land disappeared in the floods of the Nile, and more when they receded, so that individuals could no longer identify their property. For this reason the Egyptians devised measurement of the land left by the Nile: they measure each side of the plot by cord or rod or other measures. Its usefulness to mankind being thus established, the practice spread everywhere.

Almost half a millennium later again, Cassiodorus repeats much the same tale.[3]

Such an origin for Greek geometry, at first in the literal and developing into the secondary sense, is inherently plausible. Significant contact with Egypt began when Greek mercenaries helped Psammetichus I recover his land from the Assyrians in about 660 BC, and increased with the creation of the Milesian trading post of Naucratis in the Delta in the late seventh century. At the same time Egyptian influence inspired Greece to adopt two artistic forms which were to have the profoundest consequences: architecture in stone and monumental sculpture.[4] The elements of practical geometry, later to generate equally revolutionary results, could very well have been transferred hand in hand with them.

Nobody could deny the proficiency of the Egyptians in some forms of surveying. It is well known how precisely the foundations of the Great Pyramid were laid out in terms of orientation, equality of sides and horizontal level – the latter achieved by cutting trenches in the

---

[2] This passage of Hero's survives in four very similar versions (*Geometry* 2, 23.1, *Geodesy* LXXII 9–18, CVII), the present translation drawing on all of them.
[3] Cassiodorus, *Variae* III 52.2. [4] Boardman 1964, chapter 4.

rock along each face and filling them with water.[5] Long distances could be measured with considerable accuracy: two lines of boundary marks on either side of the Nile valley, intended to be of the same length, differ apparently by only 54 m over a length of 15 km.[6] Techniques of land surveying were doubtless entirely adequate for the somewhat limited purpose required of them. But, that said, Egyptian surveying instruments, from what little we know of them, were extremely simple. As we shall see, there were the ubiquitous plumb-line, level and square for building, the cord and rod for measuring, and possibly a crude precursor of the groma for laying out right angles. Although much has been made of the earliest known sighting instrument, the *merkhet*, it was applied not to surveying as such but to the ritual purposes of measuring the time or orientating a temple. It consisted of a split-palm leaf used as the 'backsight' and a plumb-line for the 'foresight'; if both were aligned on the celestial pole, they lay on a north–south line.[7] But there were obvious limits to the accuracy that such a hand-held device could attain.

Staggering achievements have quite unwarrantably been ascribed to Egyptian surveyors. Borchardt suggested that they levelled the course of the Nile for 1200 km from the sea to the First Cataract to establish a datum for the nilometers, the calibrated scales at the larger towns which recorded the height of the floods. He deduced that the gradient represented by the zero points on these scales averaged 1 in 14,440, as compared with the 1 in 13,700 of the river surface at low water as surveyed in modern times.[8] This theory is nonsense, for such a survey would be not only forbiddingly daunting but quite unnecessary. The zero point on each town's nilometer would be established from observations of low water recorded locally over many years; small wonder if the overall gradient which they preserve resembles the modern gradient.[9] Levelling was nevertheless practised. The Nile floods automatically watered low-lying fields beside the river, but to irrigate higher land further from the banks the floods were tapped by long diversionary canals running parallel to the river but at a shallower gradient.[10]

[5] Lehner 1983.   [6] Montagu 1909, 80.
[7] Borchardt 1899; Lyons 1927, 135–6; Kiely 1947, 11–12.
[8] Borchardt 1906. 'Modern' of course means before the building of the Aswan High Dam.   [9] For technical details see Bonneau 1986.
[10] For a useful survey of Egyptian irrigation see Oleson 2000.

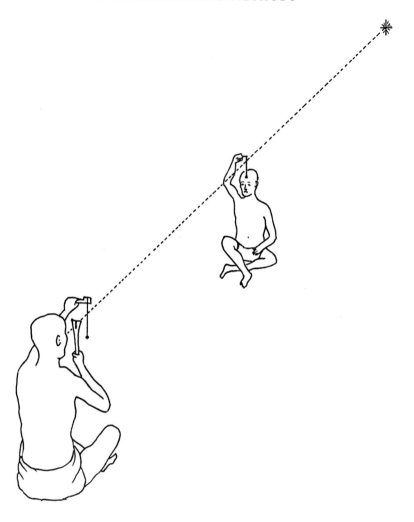

FIG. I.I. The *merkhet* in use (after King 1955, Fig. 2).

Quite possibly the levelling was originally done with the water itself, by digging a ditch approximately along the contour and realigning or deepening it until the water flowed. If any instrument was involved, the only known candidate was the simple builder's level.

On the theoretical side, Egyptian astronomy was crude and empirical, and mathematics (and even arithmetic) was equally primitive. It was adequate to solve simple problems of quantity surveying such as estimating the number of bricks needed to build a ramp of given dimensions;[11] but it could teach the Greeks little apart from a few useful formulae for measurement. While Greece may indeed have been indebted to Egypt for the basic concept of land surveying and the most basic of equipment, the evolution of sophisticated instruments, which ironically began in Ptolemaic Alexandria, seems to have owed nothing to pharaonic Egypt.

The second potential source of inspiration for Greek surveying was Mesopotamia: Assyria to the north and especially Babylonia to the south. Here a very high level of mathematics, both in arithmetic and algebra and to some extent in geometry, had been practised for millennia; and the same is true of astronomy, although its predictive nature contrasted with the numerical and geometric approach finally achieved by the Greeks. In these spheres Greece undoubtedly learned far more from Babylonia than from Egypt. But the pupillage was gradual, doubtless because, before Alexander's conquests, there was little direct contact between the two cultures. Indeed Babylonian mathematical astronomy reached its highest level under Greek and later Parthian rule, between 311 BC and AD 75. Herodotus remarks, in the passage quoted above, that Greece learned of the sundial, gnomon and twelve-hour division of the day from Babylon, which is likely enough; and the claim that the philosopher Anaximander (c. 610–545 BC) discovered the gnomon should no doubt be taken to mean that he merely introduced it to Greece.[12] Some Babylonian astronomical practices, we shall see (Chapter 2.B), were adopted by the Greeks in the course of the fourth and third centuries, but it was only in the second, when Hipparchus evidently consulted Babylonian records at first hand, that the link became close and the golden age of Greek mathematical astronomy began.[13]

The theory of surveying and its cognate sciences, then, at least as they evolved into more advanced forms, owed more to Babylon than to Egypt. As for the practice, little is known of Mesopotamian methods. In Assyria about 690 BC Sennacherib built a major aqueduct at least 50 km long for supplying water to Nineveh, which

[11] Neugebauer 1969, chapter IV.
[12] Kirk, Raven and Schofield 1983, 100–1, 103–4.
[13] For Babylonian mathematics and astronomy and their transfer to the Greeks see Neugebauer 1969, chapter II; Dicks 1970, 163–75; Jones 1991.

wound along the hillside and incorporated bridges just like its later Roman counterparts.[14] In Babylonia, with its need for perennial irrigation, the network of canals was even more complex than in Egypt.[15] For levelling, the medieval surveyors of Islamic Iraq used the *mizan* which, given that the region coincided with the former Babylonia and the requirements were identical, they may very well have inherited, like their units of length, from earlier civilisations. In essence – more detailed discussion must await Chapter 12 – the *mizan* consisted of a cord held between two graduated vertical staves. The ends of the cord were raised or lowered until a plumb-line device at the centre showed that they were level. Their relative positions on the graduated scales gave the difference in height between the bases of the two staves. Measurement was by cord and rod; and irregular plots of land on Babylonian survey maps, subdivided into right-angled triangles, rectangles and trapezoids whose dimensions and areas are indicated,[16] show an approach to land surveying similar to that of the Greeks.

The final oriental source of inspiration for the Greeks was very likely Persia, where there was a long-established tradition of tapping underground aquifers and conducting the water to the surface by means of qanats or tunnels. This technology spread to Egypt, and especially the Kharga oasis, at an early date. The first significant Greek aqueduct tunnel was built about 530 BC by Polycrates, the tyrant of Samos. It was closely followed by another at Athens, and at about the same time similar counterparts appeared in Etruria. Persia first impinged directly on the Aegean world with Cyrus' conquest of Asia Minor in the 540s BC. At this stage Polycrates was in close alliance with Egypt, but in 530 abruptly changed his allegiance to Persia. This period therefore seems much the most likely occasion for the transfer of the specialist technology of surveying and driving tunnels, whether before 530 indirectly via Egypt or afterwards from Persia. At least in later times the qanat was levelled by means of a suspended sighting tube, and it is possible, though very far from proved, that this gave rise in later generations to the standard Greek dioptra and the standard Roman libra. This difficult question is debated more fully in subsequent chapters.

[14] Jacobsen and Lloyd 1935.   [15] Oleson 2000.
[16] Kiely 1947, 12–13. On Babylonian maps and plans see Millard 1987.

B. MEASURING DISTANCES

Accurate measurements of length, and especially of long lengths, were surprisingly difficult to achieve, and figures worked out geometrically would inevitably reflect any inaccuracies in the measured distances on which they were based.[17] In Greek surveying the normal measuring device was the cord, made of a variety of fibres. The sort most commonly found was the *schoinion* which, according to the derivation of the name, was strictly of twisted rushes but, one suspects, was more often made of other substances.[18] Not only did the word denote a measuring line in general, but also the specific distance of 100 cubits,[19] which presumably reflects a standard length of cord. This was subdivided into 8 *hammata* or knots of 12½ cubits apiece, no doubt because it was knotted at those intervals.[20] The *schoinion* was well entrenched in Ptolemaic Egypt. The *aroura*, the standard unit of area for land, was one *schoinion* square, and the term *schoinourgos* was sometimes applied to the land surveyor.[21] Another fibre employed for cords was esparto, whence *spartos* (which is found in Hero, but only for cords whose precise length was not of importance, such as plumb-lines and for laying out straight lines on the ground) and *sparton* and *spartion* (words which are applied to measuring cords by other sources). The flax measuring cord (*linee*) is encountered in the second century BC in Boeotia[22] and in the Talmud,[23] and **al-Karaji I** specifies a 100-cubit cord of well-twisted flax or silk, the latter no doubt an Islamic alternative. We will meet hair and hemp cords in a moment.

The problem with any fibre cords is that, unless very well pre-tensioned and protected from damp, they are liable to shrink or stretch according to their moisture content. Official cord-keepers and

[17] For an overview of Greek measuring devices see Coulton 1975, 90–1.

[18] For references over and above those given in the notes to this section, see LSJ under the words in question.

[19] To be distinguished from the very much longer *schoinos* which varied between 30, 40, 48 and 60 stades.

[20] Shelton 1981, citing a number of papyri. Knots are visible on the surveying cord depicted in a well-known pharaonic fresco (reproduced by Lyons 1927, f.p. 132; Kiely 1947, Fig. 1; Dilke 1971, 49). The *amma* of 40 cubits mentioned by Hero, *Geometry* 4.12, 23.14 has not been found in papyri.

[21] As was the term *harpedonaptes*, 'cord-fastener'.   [22] *IG* VII 3073.128.

[23] Talmud, *'Erubin* 58a, and also rope made of palm fibre.

cord-stretchers are attested far back in pharaonic Egypt.[24] Hero was well aware of this failing, and several times insists on 'a cord (*schoinion*) that has been well tensioned and tested so that it will not stretch or shrink' (**Dioptra 20**).[25] Elsewhere he describes how to prepare cords for use in automata by a process that sounds equally applicable to measuring lines:[26]

The cords must not be capable of stretching or shrinking, but must remain the same length as they were to start with. This is done by passing them round pegs, tensioning them tightly, leaving them for some time, and tensioning them again. Repeat this a number of times and smear them with a mixture of wax and resin. It is then best to hang a weight on them and leave them for a longer time. A cord thus stretched will not stretch any more, or only a very little.

A Byzantine treatise on land surveying of uncertain date may also preserve features from an earlier period:[27]

The cord which you intend to make into a 10- or 12-fathom measure should not be of hair, because this has an unreliable quality and always gives a misleading measurement. If it is partially, or above all totally, soaked in dew it immediately shrinks and shortens by a fathom; then, on drying out again and stretching, the 10 fathoms, from the slackening and extending, becomes 11, and the cord's accuracy remains misleading. Instead, the cord for measuring should be of hemp, thick and firm. First make short pegs, one spade-shaped with a flat iron blade underneath to cut and mark the earth around each cord, the other a sharp iron for fixing and positioning in the mark left by the first. Both of these marker pegs have solid iron rings into which the ends of the cord are tied and sealed with a lead seal [to prevent fraud by shortening the cord]. At each fathom along the cord a thick tuft is hung to indicate the fathoms . . . If the pegs tied to the measuring cord are [too] long, they can be tilted by pulling on the cord, and each cord length can gain 5 spans or half a [fathom] or even more.

There were two alternatives to unreliable fibre cords. One was the measuring chain (*halysis*), which Hero twice mentions as a substitute (**Dioptra 34** and (not translated) 23). Again, Rabbi Joshua b. Hananiah, a contemporary of Hero, said, 'You have nothing more suitable for

[24] Dilke 1971, 21.   [25] Similarly in *Dioptra* 23 and 25, not translated in Part III.
[26] *Automata* II 4–5.
[27] Schilbach 1970a, 51.12–52.2; see also Dölger 1927, 83–4 and Schilbach 1970b, 28–9.

measuring than iron chains, but what can we do in the face of what the Torah said?',[28] referring to the Jewish law which specified that Sabbath limits must be measured only with ropes exactly 50 cubits long. From the paucity of these references, the chain was evidently much rarer than the cord, no doubt because of its cost and perhaps because of its weight.

The other alternative was the measuring rod (*kalamos*). Originally made of a reed, as its name implies, it could also be of wood and in Ptolemaic and Roman Egypt might be either 5 or 6⅔ cubits long.[29] The latter, also known as the *akaina*,[30] corresponds in length to the wooden ten-foot rod (*decempeda* or *pertica*[31]) of the Roman surveyor,[32] which was furnished at the end with bronze ferrules marked in digits or inches for small measurements and flanged to butt neatly against its neighbour.[33] Since wood expands and contracts very little along the grain, rods would give a much more accurate result than cords, and were evidently standard equipment for the architect and builder. But for the surveyor and the longer distances over which he operated, rods would be vastly more tedious to use. None the less, there is hardly any evidence that measuring cords were employed at all by Roman surveyors,[34] who seem rather to have relied on ten-foot rods used in pairs, one leapfrogging the other. The same Byzantine treatise also speaks of fathom rods of wood or reed with a lead seal at either end to deter malpractice.[35]

It is entirely feasible that Greece should have learned the techniques of land measurement from the Egyptians and, by way of their colonies in Italy, passed them on to the Romans. But, once again, the potential contribution of the Babylonians should not be ignored. A relief from Ur dating to about 2100 BC depicts a god commanding the king to build a ziggurat and holding what appear to be a coiled measuring cord

---

[28] Talmud, 'Erubin 58a.   [29] Hero, Geometry 4.11, 23.13.   [30] Hero, Geometry 4.12.

[31] Balbus, Explanation 95.6–7. The pertica might on occasion be 12, 15 or 17 feet according to local circumstances: Hultsch 1866, 136.6.

[32] Who was consequently sometimes known as the decempedator: Cicero, Philippics XIII 37.

[33] Examples found at Enns in Austria are illustrated by Lyons 1927, facing p. 140 and Dilke 1971, 67, others from Pompeii by Della Corte 1922, 85–6.

[34] The tombstone of an agrimensor from Pompeii does depict a cord alongside two rods, but it could be for setting out a straight line rather than for measuring (Adam 1994, 10).   [35] Schilbach 1970a, 51.29–32.

and a measuring rod,[36] reminiscent of the angel with a flax cord and rod whom Ezekiel saw in a vision in Babylonia in the sixth century.[37] The surveyor is referred to in land charters as 'the dragger of the rope'.[38]

For really long distances – too long to be measured by cord – there was the option of counting paces. On the staff of Alexander the Great during his campaigns were expert *bematistai* whose job it was to count their paces as they marched and to note the direction of travel and the names of places passed, so that from their records outline maps could be compiled and descriptions of the routes published. We know the names of a few: Diognetus, Baeton and Amyntas.[39] Their results were necessarily approximate but, as Sherk remarks, we should not underestimate their abilities.[40] It was probably their successors in the service of the Ptolemies who measured the overland distances required by Eratosthenes in his estimate of the circumference of the earth (Chapter 7).

Surveyors recorded their field measurements on wax tablets or papyrus (**Dioptra** 7), and for arithmetical calculations they no doubt used the abacus, which was well known throughout the ancient world.[41]

C. ORIENTATION AND RIGHT ANGLES

Temples and town grids and even land boundaries sometimes needed setting out to a particular orientation. It was not difficult to establish a north–south line. An approximation could be found by simply observing the stars, but not so easily as today because Polaris was then remote from the celestial pole (about 18° in 1000 BC, about 12° in AD 1). The nearest bright star to the pole was Kochab, β Ursae Minoris, about 6° distant in 1000 BC but moving further away. It was better to use the sun, observing the shadow of a vertical gnomon and marking the point where it appeared to be at its longest. Better still, a circle was traced around the base of the gnomon, the points were marked where the tip of the shadow touched the circle before and after noon, and the result-

---

[36] Woolley 1925, 398 and pl. xlviii.   [37] Septuagint, Ezekiel 40.3.
[38] Lyons 1927, 137.
[39] Pliny, *Natural History* VI 61; Athenaeus, *Learned Banquet* 442B.
[40] Sherk 1974, 535n.   [41] Dilke 1987a, 21–2.

ing angle was bisected.[42] Similarly, the directions from a stake of the rising and setting of a star could be marked by planting two poles and again bisecting the angle. Since the horizon is rarely entirely level, a more accurate result could be obtained by creating an artificial horizon in the form of a temporary circular wall whose top was levelled by water and, sighting from a pole at the centre, marking the points on the wall where a star rose or set.[43] This was very likely how the pyramids were orientated; as is well known, the sides of the Great Pyramid diverge from true east–west and north–south by a maximum of $5'30''$ and a minimum of $1'57''$.[44]

To set out a right angle without an instrument, various methods were possible with cords. The properties of the triangle whose sides are multiples of 3, 4 and 5 were well known (if not proved) long before Pythagoras. Euclid showed, as had probably been accepted earlier, that a triangle contained by a semicircle is right-angled, and that lines drawn between the centres of two overlapping circles and between the intersections of their arcs cross at right angles. These facts are mentioned by Balbus, though it is not clear if they were applied in the field.[45] A relatively small set square could be laid on the ground, its sides extended by cords and pegs, and the diagonals of a resulting rectangle measured to check that they were the same.

D. MEASURING HEIGHTS

Civilian surveyors, unless motivated by pure curiosity, rarely needed to discover the height of existing structures or objects; but in warfare it was often necessary for a besieging force to try to scale a city wall by ladder or by siege tower. To construct them to the right size, the height of the wall had to be discovered and, since it would normally be suicidal to attempt to measure it directly, more devious methods were developed. The simplest was to count the courses of brick or stone, estimate or surreptitiously measure a typical course, and multiply it out. We first hear of this ruse in 428 BC when the besieged Plataeans, wishing to break out, counted the bricks in the Peloponnesians' siege

---

[42] This method is described by Vitruvius I 6.6; Proclus, *Outline* III 23–4; and Hyginus Gromaticus, *Establishment* 152.4–22, who adds another complex method, more academic than practical, based on solid geometry.   [43] Edwards 1985, 246–7.

[44] Edwards 1985, 99.   [45] Balbus, *Explanation* 107.12–108.8.

wall.[46] In 212 BC Marcellus' long and hitherto fruitless siege of Syracuse was brought to an end when a Roman soldier escorting a conference party outside the wall of Epipolae noticed how low the defences were and furtively counted the courses; his information allowed Marcellus to construct ladders and attack this weak point when the Syracusans were distracted.[47] Later generations would normally use dioptras to obtain the height (Chapter 3.H), but at this date they were probably not available, and in any event the wall at this point was close to the sea, allowing no room to use them.[48] As late as AD 537 the Goths besieging Rome – who could hardly be expected to have dioptras at their command – counted the courses of the wall preparatory to building siege towers.[49]

Vegetius, the military source of the late fourth century AD, offers two alternative methods of finding wall heights. One, which he fails to explain properly, involves tying a fine thread to an arrow which is shot at the top of the wall, and somehow deducing the height from the length of thread. The other is to clandestinely measure the shadow of the wall and at the same time set a ten-foot rod vertically in the ground and measure its shadow.[50] The relationship between the rod and its shadow will be the same as that between the wall and its shadow. Polybius, writing about 150 BC on the same subject, says that 'the height of any object standing vertically on a level base can be taken from a distance by a method that is practicable and easy for anyone who cares to study mathematics'.[51] One might have expected both authors to mention the dioptra, for both wrote within its lifespan. In the case of Polybius his vague language might refer either to the shadow stick or to the dioptra; in the case of Vegetius there is, strangely enough, no good evidence that the Roman army ever used the dioptra.

The practice of measuring heights by the shadows they cast is of considerable antiquity. Its discovery (at least by the Greeks) is traditionally ascribed to Thales, the philosopher of Miletus (624–546 BC?), who is said to have been the first Greek geometer and to have visited Egypt. Miletus' close links with Naucratis make such a journey plausible enough. According to one later legend Thales measured the heights of the pyramids by their shadows at the time when his own shadow

---

[46] Thucydides, *History* III 20.3–4.   [47] Polybius, *Histories* VIII 37.2.

[48] For the site, Parke 1944.   [49] Procopius, *Gothic Wars* I 21.3–4.

[50] Vegetius, *Epitome* IV 30.   [51] Polybius, *Histories* IX 19.8.

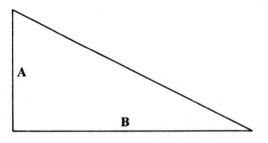
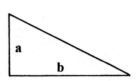

FIG. 1.2. Similar triangles.

equalled his own height, that is when the sun stood 45 degrees high. Another version makes him understand the wider truth that, wherever the sun may be, the heights of all vertical objects are in the same proportion to the lengths of their shadows at the same time of day.[52] The concept remained well established in the geometer's basic repertoire. Hero explains it simply and clearly: to find the height of a tall column, set up a 3-foot rod near by, and measure the shadows of the rod and the column. If the rod's shadow is, say, 6 feet long and the column's is 100, the column is 50 feet high.[53]

The principle involved, utterly simple but lying at the root of ancient surveying, is that of similar triangles. If the angles of two triangles are the same (in this case because the objects are vertical and the sun is at the same height), then the lengths of their sides are in proportion. Thus **a** is to **b** as **A** is to **B**, and since **a**, **b** and **B** are known, **A** is easily worked out.

Normally heights were found from distances, but it was equally possible to find distances from heights. This discovery, without shadows, was also attributed to Thales who 'demonstrated the distance of ships out at sea'.[54] Later Greek writers did not know exactly how he did this, but assumed that he used similar triangles. There are a number of possible methods which differ only in detail. If, for example, he stood on a tower of known height **A** above the sea, and positioned a vertical rod **a** so that the sight line from its apex to the ship's hull touched the edge of the tower, then **a** and **b** could be measured and the required distance **B** was found by multiplying **A** by **b** and dividing by **a**.

[52] Kirk, Raven and Schofield 1983, 76–86. [53] Hero, *Stereometry* 2.27.
[54] Kirk, Raven and Schofield 1983, 85.

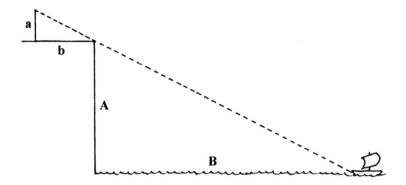

FIG. 1.3. Thales' demonstration of the distance of a ship.

This kind of straightforward geometry underlies most of the exercises later carried out with the dioptra. It also recurs in a pair of simple devices for discovering heights, recorded by late Latin sources, in the form of light triangular wooden frameworks where the base is held horizontal and the object is sighted along the hypotenuse. A snippet of Vitruvius Rufus preserved in the *Corpus Agrimensorum* (**Source 1**) deals with a right-angled isosceles triangle. Nothing is known of the author; but while it is very unlikely that he is *the* Vitruvius, it is curious that the former's phrase 'lie flat on your teeth' (*decumbe in dentes*) is almost exactly matched by the latter's instruction *procumbatur in dentes* when looking for mist rising from the ground as an indication of the presence of water.[55] A fragment in the *Mappae Clavicula* (**Source 2**), which might also derive from the *Corpus*, describes a more sophisticated right-angled 3–4–5 triangle.

Finally the shadow stick, or gnomon as it is more properly called in this context, was also used for measuring the altitude of the sun by the same process of comparing the height of the rod with the length of its shadow. This became a standard method of determining latitude, taking the reading at noon on the summer solstice. At first the result was given cumbrously as the ratio between gnomon and shadow; for example Pytheas in the fourth century BC recorded the latitude of Marseille as 120:41⅘. When from the second century BC the system of

[55] Vitruvius VIII 1.1; somewhat similar phrases are also found in Pliny, *Natural History* XXXI 44, Palladius, *On Agriculture* IX 8, *Geoponica* II 5.11 and Cassiodorus, *Variae* III 53.

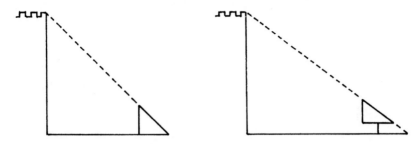

FIG. 1.4. Height triangles of Vitruvius Rufus and the *Mappae Clavicula*.

360 degrees was adopted (Chapter 2.B), this ratio could be converted into the angle of the sun below the zenith, and adding the obliquity of the ecliptic gave the latitude in degrees. Pytheas' ratio for Marseille works out at 43° 11′, compared with the modern value of 43° 17′.[56]

E. LEVELLING

Of the two fundamental methods of finding a horizontal, the water level was little favoured in the ancient world. It is true that, as we remarked, the Great Pyramid was levelled by water, and there are other instances where the Egyptians probably flooded a complete building site to establish an overall level; but this approach was hardly practicable in Greece.[57] Instead, for setting a vertical and hence a horizontal at right angles to it, the principle of the plumb-line ruled supreme. The tools which became traditional to the carpenter and builder in many cultures first appear in Egypt: the square, the rigid rule, the string, the A-frame level for horizontals and its counterpart for verticals. Of these it is the A-frame level which concerns us. A right-angled isosceles triangle with a cross-bar is made of bronze or wood (sometimes strapped with bronze at the joints), and a plumb-line is hung from the apex. When the line coincides with a vertical mark scribed on the centre of the cross-bar, the feet are at the same level.

The Greeks borrowed the device at an early date and used it extensively.[58] At first it was called the *staphyle* or 'grape', referring to the

---

[56] Strabo I 4.4, II 1.12, 5.8, 5.41. For discussion, see Dicks 1960, 178–9. This conversion into degrees uses the correct value of the obliquity for that period, not the approximation (usually 24°) then current. [57] Coulton 1982, 46.

[58] Martin 1965, 188–9.

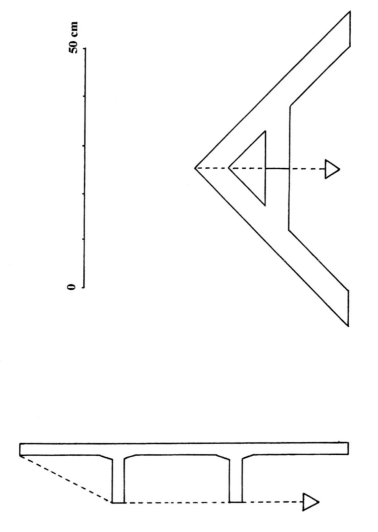

FIG. 1.5. Egyptian A-frame level for horizontals and plumb-line for verticals, c. 1300 BC (based on Glanville 1942, Pl. 22).

plumb bob, but it then acquired its usual name of *diabetes*, 'strider', after its two equal legs: for the same reason the term was also applied to a pair of compasses. Homer makes Admetus' horses identical in height 'according to the *staphyle*'.[59] A later scholiast explains this as 'the mason's *diabetes* which measures the horizontal and the vertical at the same time', a definition displeasing to another commentator who adds 'but the *diabetes* only measures the horizontal'.[60] *Pros diabeten*, literally 'by the level', became the standard term for 'horizontal' and crops up frequently in Hero's *Dioptra*. Theon of Alexandria (**Source 4**) mentions the same device under the alternative name *alpharion*, alpha-shape; and *alphadion* and *alpha* are also found in late sources.[61] The **A**-frame level was likewise extensively used by the Romans,[62] who called it the *libella* (for the derivation of which see Chapter 4, and for references **Source 44**); and *ad libellam* was the precise equivalent in Latin of *pros diabeten*, level or horizontal.

The **A**-frame level was clearly the standard tool for levelling the foundations and wall courses of buildings under construction. For most purposes it was no doubt entirely adequate, but for large structures its accuracy necessarily depended on four factors. If it was not very precisely made it could mislead. Even given precision of manufacture, the smaller it was, the less accurate the results. Its plumb was liable to sway in the wind. And even in a total calm it would be impossible to align the plumb-line with absolute precision over the mark on the cross-bar, given that both had an appreciable thickness. None the less, as the inscriptions attest, it was used on prestige buildings, where its deficiencies are only revealed by detailed measurement. The deliberate curvature of the stylobate of the Parthenon, for instance, is well known: the whole floor is convex, rising about 10 cm on the sides (69.51 m long) and 7 cm on the ends (30.86 m). The workmanship which achieved this refinement is properly admired. What is less well

---

[59] Homer, *Iliad* II 765.

[60] *Scholia in Iliaden* I 130. The *diabetes* is found not uncommonly in literature and in epigraphic specifications for public building works, e.g. *IG* II² 1668.10 for the Piraeus arsenal in 347/6 BC.

[61] From *alpharion* comes the modern Cretan *alphari*. For *alphadion* (whence modern Greek *alphadi*) and *alpha* see Eustratius, *Commentary on Nicomachean Ethics* 322.18 and 74.2.

[62] Adam 1994, 41–2, Figs. 48, 51–2, 79, 81–3 including variations on the basic theme.

known is the fact that the platform on which the stylobate rests, clearly meant to be horizontal, is not: it rises to a peak at the south-west corner where it is about 5 cm too high.[63] The fault presumably lay in the levelling devices employed.

The Parthenon was built in the fifth century BC when Athens was at the pinnacle of her greatness. Not only is it considered the acme of Greek architecture, but it was intended as a deliberate manifestation of her glory, and one may assume that its architects drew on all the best and latest technology. Yet its foundation slopes at an average of 1 in 1400. In architectural terms this failing, being quite undetectable to the observer, is hardly a serious one. But if the same instruments were used for levelling an engineering project, similar inaccuracies might not be so immaterial. The ultimate test would come with the extremely shallow gradients of some Roman aqueducts, for which inaccuracies of this order would be quite unacceptable. With Hellenistic aqueducts, as we shall find, gradients were very much steeper and such errors might be tolerable, as they would with most irrigation channels.

Any level like the *diabetes*, therefore, which depended on a simple plumb-line was fine for the builder and passable for the Greek engineering surveyor, provided he did not require shallow gradients; it was not adequate for the Roman aqueduct surveyor whose work demanded a precision instrument. In fact there is no certain evidence whatever – even in the *chorobates*, which we will shortly meet – that the ancient world used the simple plumb-line level for any purpose other than building construction. This is no doubt our ignorance, for it seems highly likely that, in the absence of anything better, such levels were indeed used for irrigation work at least.[64] It is not difficult to visualise the surveyor placing one on a plank, which he adjusts until the level shows it to be horizontal. He squints along the top of the plank at a pole held by an assistant, whom he instructs to mark the pole where his line of sight meets it. The difference in height between the mark and the plank represents the rise or fall of the ground. It sounds easy; but anyone who tries to sight a relatively distant object along a straight

---

[63] Carpenter 1970, 116.

[64] For the irrigation systems of the Negev and the Maghreb, more localised than in Egypt and Mesopotamia and originated by indigenous peoples even if further developed under Roman rule, see Evenari et al. 1982, Lindner 1987, Birebent 1964 and Shaw 1984.

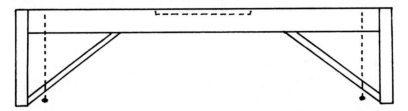

FIG. 1.6. The chorobates.

edge will discover how imprecise the operation is, although it is much improved by the addition of simple sights such as ring-headed nails driven into the plank. This scenario is purely speculative; but it does have something in common with our oldest description of instrumental levelling by Philo of Byzantium (**Source 10**).

If such a method might suffice for simple aqueducts, irrigation channels and drains, it would not suffice for more advanced aqueducts. These could only be surveyed with advanced instruments which likewise worked on the plumb-line principle, but differed from the **A**-frame level in two important respects. First, they had proper sights; and second (certainly the dioptra and probably the libra) they were suspended to act as their own plumb bobs, and could therefore be reversed to check the sightings taken. These matters will be explained in later chapters. For the moment, suffice it to mention the possibility that about 530 BC both the Greeks and the Etruscans inherited from Persia the suspended sighting tube for levelling tunnels, and that this was responsible for the survey, astonishingly precise for so early a date, of the famous tunnel on Samos and a few of its contemporaries.

This brings us on to Vitruvius and his famous – one is tempted to say infamous – chapter on the chorobates (**Source 3**). Whatever detailed reconstruction one prefers, notably in the cross-pieces bracing the legs, the broad outline is perfectly clear. Because Vitruvius describes the chorobates in detail, it was evidently a novelty to his Roman readers. Yet, because he claims that it was more accurate than the dioptra and the libra, it is almost universally assumed to have been the principal instrument for levelling Roman aqueducts. It must be said at once, however, that as a serious instrument for surveying shallow gradients it has very few qualifications indeed.

Firstly, at 20 feet long and on legs, it resembled a lengthy but narrow trestle table. To avoid sagging in the middle its straight-edge must have been of considerable depth and therefore weight. It can only have been levelled by adjusting wedges under its feet. It would be exceedingly, one might even say impossibly, cumbrous to use in the field, and especially in rough terrain.[65]

Second, the very length of the straight-edge ought to be an aid to precision: the further apart the sights the better. Yet Vitruvius does not even hint that it possessed sights at all, or that readings were taken on a calibrated surveyor's staff, both of which are essential prerequisites for accurate levelling and both of which were already known to Philo (**Source 10**) two centuries earlier. In view of this deficiency, Montauzan suggested that two or more instruments were set up touching each other end to end and made to leapfrog each other in continuous horizontal steps, the difference in height being recorded each time.[66] The theory may be appreciated, but the practice, on aqueducts of any length, is totally beyond belief.

Third, the chorobates is prey to the defects inherent in every plumb-line level: the impossibility of exactly aligning the string on the mark, and movement of the bobs in the wind. Vitruvius, recognising this latter problem, supplies a water level as well. But a wind that will swing the plumb bobs will also ruffle the surface of the water; and why is the trough only five feet long when it could be four times the length? Let us take the chorobates as 6 m long and 1.5 m high, and the trough as 1.5 m long. If the strings are in contact with the frame, friction will prevent them from hanging exactly vertical; if they are clear of the frame they are more liable to swing and more difficult to align to the marks. If at the lower end their centre line is half a millimetre to one side of the centre line of the mark, the top of the straight-edge (always assuming total precision of manufacture) will slope at 1 in 3000. If the water in the trough is half a millimetre higher at one end than the other the slope will be the same. If the error in either case is one millimetre, the slope is 1 in 1500. This point will be picked up again in Chapter 9.c in connection with aqueduct surveying. Adam constructed a quarter-size replica (1.5 m long) to which he added sights, and tested it in the field (using a staff) against a modern instrument. Over a traverse of 51.3

[65] Smith 1990–91, 60.   [66] Montauzan 1909, 166, followed by Callebat 1973, 140–1.

m the chorobates was in error by 4 cm, equal to a slope of 1 in 1282.5.[67] Even allowing for the relatively small scale, this is not an impressive result, especially with sights and staff.

In short, the chorobates was in essence a glorified builder's level. As Vitruvius himself says, it was fine for levelling a single position such as, we may imagine, a temple platform. But for projecting a level over a long distance, as aqueduct surveying requires, it was not good. As Ashby rightly remarked, 'Vitruvius may be guilty of an architect's prejudice in favour of an instrument more useful to a builder than to a field surveyor.'[68] But, even if Vitruvius was misled or simply wrong, the question of his source remains to be answered. Although it is always assumed that no further information on the chorobates is available, in fact something of its history can be recovered.

A Greek origin is proved by the exceedingly rare name, which translates as 'land-ranger' or 'land-pacer', a strange soubriquet for a levelling device. The associated verb, *chorobatein* (as rare as the noun), means to measure land by pacing.[69] It is found in this sense in the Old Testament as translated into Greek at Alexandria about 200 BC, where Joshua sends men to measure the Promised Land before it is divided among the Children of Israel.[70] It is used in a papyrus of 248 BC of workers who might be measuring or might merely be inspecting a vineyard.[71] It is found once in Hero (**Dioptra 12**) apparently in the sense of 'taking levels with a dioptra'.[72] From this flimsy evidence one might deduce that the meaning of the noun, originally 'land-pacer', was narrowed to 'leveller'.

This is undoubtedly the sense – builder's level – in which it was used by Theon of Alexandria (**Source 4**), who says that the *diabetes* or *alpharion* for levelling a foundation resembles Carpus' chorobates. Who was this Carpus, and when? Only one man of that name is known who had scientific and technical interests, and we may be sure that he is the right one. He was a mechanic from Antioch in Syria who wrote on

---

[67] Adam 1982, 1029; cf. Adam 1994, 18–19.   [68] Ashby 1935, 37.
[69] Hesychius, s.v. *chorobatein*.   [70] Septuagint, Joshua 18.8.
[71] *P. Cair. Zen.* 59329.
[72] The noun may also occur on a late (Christian) tombstone from Corycus in Asia Minor, describing the profession of one Sergius (*MAMA* III 694). He is usually taken to be a land-surveyor, but the word has a short *o*, not a long one, and, if it is correctly spelt, means that he was a chorus-dancer.

astronomy and geometry;[73] not a great deal is recorded about him, and even his date is not certain. Proclus reports that in his *Astronomical Treatise* Carpus discussed (apropos Euclid) whether problems come before theorems, a matter on which Geminus held contrary views.[74] It is sometimes assumed that Carpus was criticising Geminus, who lived (it is usually accepted: see Chapter 7) in the first century BC, and that therefore Carpus was contemporary or later.[75] If so, he might be too late for Vitruvius. But all Proclus is saying is that the two men held different opinions, and Carpus could just as easily be earlier than Geminus.[76]

There are indeed two suggestions that this was so. Pappus notes that, according to Carpus, Archimedes wrote only one book on practical mechanics (on the construction of a planetarium) because he refused to allow external applications to sully the purity of geometry and arithmetic. But, Pappus goes on, 'Carpus and some others did make use of geometry for certain practical techniques, and with good reason; for geometry, which by its nature can foster many techniques, is in no way injured by its association with them.'[77] It sounds as if Carpus was a pioneer in applying geometry to instruments. If so, it must have been not long after Archimedes' death in 212 BC and before about 150, by which time, as we will see, instruments for astronomy and for terrestrial surveying, all governed by geometry, were well established. The other indication is a short list of mathematicians who constructed curves for squaring the circle:[78] Archimedes (c. 287–212), Nicomedes (a little older than Apollonius[79]), Apollonius of Perge (probably c. 260–190/180[80]), and Carpus. Since the first three names are in chronological order, Carpus should have been younger than Apollonius; but not much younger, because squaring the circle was a preoccupation of earlier Hellenistic mathematicians, not of later ones.[81] On two counts, therefore, it is likely that Carpus was active in the first half of the second century BC.

[73] Pappus, *Collection* 1026; Proclus, *Euclid* 125.25, 241.19, *Republic* 218.22.
[74] Proclus, *Euclid* 241.19– 243.11.
[75] So Neugebauer 1975, 943; Aujac 1975, LXIII; Heiberg 1919.
[76] As Tannery 1887, 147n saw.   [77] Pappus, *Collection* 1026.
[78] Iamblichus quoted in Simplicius, *Physics* 60.15 and *Categories* 192.19.
[79] Fraser 1972, II 610.   [80] Fraser 1972, I 416.
[81] Heath 1921, I 220–32 knows of no mathematician after Apollonius/Carpus who contributed to the problem.

As I have tried to show elsewhere,[82] Vitruvius knew little at first hand about aqueducts or surveying, and his chapters on aqueducts are very largely derived from Hellenistic Greek sources which he by no means fully understood. His chapter on the chorobates is entirely typical; and it smacks, moreover, of the language an inventor might use in publicising his own work. It seems possible that Carpus in one of his writings had sung the praises of his chorobates as a builder's level and, at least potentially, as a level for the aqueduct surveyor; and that Vitruvius, who had never set eyes on the thing, merely translated or summarised his words. Carpus' evident interest in and knowledge of Archimedes' work would account for the reference to Archimedes' theory about water surfaces, and an advertising motive would explain the derogatory reference to the dioptras and libra, which we can well believe were less appropriate for levelling masonry but were assuredly superior in levelling aqueducts.[83]

Because Theon (or his source) clearly expected his readers to know what Carpus' chorobates was, we may assume that it had to some extent caught on as a builder's level. As a surveyor's level, we have no idea whether it remained merely a gleam in Carpus' eye or did find use on Greek aqueducts with their relatively steep gradients; it would no doubt be preferable to the A-frame level in terms of accuracy if not of portability, although the dioptra would be superior in both respects. Certainly there is no evidence whatsoever that the chorobates found any use at all on the gently graded aqueducts of the Roman West. In short, with its cumbrous bulk and its absence of sights and staff, it does not deserve to be considered a serious surveyor's level.

---

[82] Lewis 1999b.

[83] Comparable examples of inventors' puffs are **Dioptra 1, 33** and **34** where Hero dismisses existing dioptras, gromas and hodometers, and Philo, *Artillery* 59–67 on Philo's supposed improvements to catapult design.

CHAPTER 2

BACKGROUND TO THE DIOPTRA

A. THE SIGHTING TUBE

The dioptra evolved from the humblest of beginnings to become the surveying instrument *par excellence* of the Greeks. The word means simply 'something to look through', and as such it bears a number of connotations which are quite irrelevant to our purposes – a spy, a translucent mineral such as talc or mica for use in windows, a gynaecologist's vaginal speculum or dilator for internal examination.[1] In a catapult, the dioptra was the window in the main frame through which the arrow was discharged and through which, using it as a foresight, the operator took aim.[2] Dioptra could even be used figuratively, meaning 'perspicacity'.[3]

It was long appreciated that looking at a distant object through a tube clarifies the vision by cutting out extraneous light and unwanted parts of the field of view.[4] Aristotle remarked that

the man who shades his eyes with his hand or looks through a tube will not distinguish any more or any less the differences of colours, but he will see further . . . In theory, distant objects would be seen best if a sort of continuous tube extended from the eye to what is observed. The further the tube extends, the greater is bound to be the accuracy with which distant objects can be seen.[5]

[1] For all these see LSJ and Supplement under *diopt-*. The meaning of *diopteuterion*, quoted from Petosiris by the astrologer Vettius Valens, *Anthologies* II 41, is unknown.

[2] Philo, *Artillery* 64.9, 76.31. Hero, *Artillery* 86.7 likewise uses the verb *diopteuein* for sighting along the arrow groove of a catapult.

[3] As in Fragment 8 of George of Pisidia's *Heracliad* of the 620s. The Latin verbs *transpicere* and *perspicere* are in some sense equivalent, and are also used of sighting with the groma.   [4] For the whole history of such tubes see Eisler 1949.

[5] Aristotle, *Generation of Animals* 780b 19–22, 781a 9–12. Strabo, *Geography* III 1.5 might seem to imply that a tube magnifies images. He suggests that the sun when rising or setting over the sea is made to appear larger than when high in the sky by vapours arising from the water: 'the visual rays are deflected by them as they are by tubes, and therefore appear wider'. But the *aulon*, 'tubes', of the manuscripts is probably a corruption of *hyalon*, 'glasses' or 'lenses'.

He does not call the tube a dioptra. That name is first applied to the simplest of devices for sighting in a particular and precise direction, and if necessary in the reverse direction too, by Euclid, writing in the early third century BC: 'Let Cancer, at point Γ in the east, be observed through a dioptra placed at point Δ, and then through the same dioptra Capricorn will be observed in the west at point A. Since points $A\Delta\Gamma$ are all observed through the dioptra, the line $A\Delta\Gamma$ is straight.'[6] Similarly, as proof that the earth is the centre of the universe, Pliny cites the evidence of dioptras that at equinoxes one sees the sun set and rise on the same line, and that sunrise at the summer solstice is on the same line as sunset at the winter solstice.[7]

For a very different purpose, a system of military signalling in code was devised by Cleoxenes and Democlitus, presumably in the early second century BC, and perfected by the historian Polybius. The signaller, standing at a pre-arranged spot, displayed differing numbers of torches to left and right, while the recipient of the message observed them through a dioptra with two tubes which had been previously set up aiming at the positions of the torches. The tubes ensured not only that he looked in precisely the right direction, but that he saw the torches more clearly.[8] Later philosophers underline the same factors. Themistius (fourth century AD) speaks of 'the straight line from a dioptra';[9] Olympiodorus (sixth century) says that 'dioptras were invented by mechanics so that vision should be directed by traversing a narrow passage and should not stay wandering about'.[10] The tubular dioptra was also applied to scientific experiments. Hero of Alexandria mounted one in a window, transmitting outdoor scenes indoors via a mirror, rather as in a camera obscura,[11] and Ptolemy used a dioptra to demonstrate that light is reflected from a mirror at the same angle as it falls on it.[12]

[6] Euclid, *Phenomena* I. Plutarch's statement (*Moralia* 1093e) that Euclid wrote a treatise called *Dioptica* presumably refers to the *Phenomena*, where this passage forms the first theorem.   [7] Pliny, *Natural History* II 176.   [8] Polybius X 45.6–47.11.

[9] Themistius, *Paraphrase of Physics* 41.26.

[10] Olympiodorus, *Commentary on Meteorology* 265.29.

[11] Hero, *Catoptrics* 354.20. The treatise survives only in a medieval Latin translation, one manuscript of which has the gloss (Schmidt p. 413) 'dioptra, a sighting instrument for estimating distance or size'.

[12] Ptolemy, *Optics* III 10–11. Ptolemy also uses (II 65) the dioptra, along with the ruler and plumb-line, as an image of straightness.

Having painted in this workaday and unexciting background to the sighting tube, we should here note a possibility which must await Chapter 10 for fuller exploration. It seems that about 530 BC the Greeks picked up from the Persians the concept of driving tunnels for carrying water. We know nothing directly about the instruments with which they were then surveyed, but a good candidate is one that was certainly employed by the Persians in the early eleventh century AD, when al-Karaji describes it. This took the form of a brass tube about 37 cm long and 2 cm in diameter, which was suspended horizontally by a chain and through which the surveyor sighted at a fixed mark to ensure that a tunnel heading was being driven truly horizontally. If it really did go back to the sixth century BC, it could well be the ancestor not only of the sighting tubes just listed but also of the standard dioptra which, as we will find in the next chapter, evolved about 200 BC.

B. ASTRONOMICAL INSTRUMENTS

Beyond the straightforward gnomon and sundial, the Greeks ultimately developed a number of relatively simple but ingenious observational instruments which rank on a par with their instruments for terrestrial surveying. Doubtless developments in one category influenced developments in the other, and the purely astronomical equipment therefore merits brief discussion here. Most such devices are described by Ptolemy, but of their earlier history we unfortunately know little, just as we know little of the development of mathematical astronomy itself.[13] The reason is simple. As soon as Ptolemy's *Almagest* was published shortly after AD 150, it was recognised as the masterpiece that it is. It superseded all previous work, which therefore ceased to be copied and has very largely perished. Hipparchus, who observed between 162 and 126 BC, was clearly the first great mathematical astronomer and the real founder of the science.[14] Yet of all his mould-breaking output only one minor book has survived, and most of his work in this field is known to us only through the references and quotations in the *Almagest*.

In various of his books, Ptolemy describes or mentions seven instru-

[13] The indispensable guide to this subject, though it specifically excludes instruments, is Neugebauer 1975.   [14] For a good and recent assessment see Toomer 1978.

ments, of which the four-cubit dioptra and the plane astrolabe will concern us later.[15] Of the others, three worked by shadows, and two had alidade-type sights in the form of small plates pierced by holes.

1. The equatorial armillary, a bronze ring fixed in the plane of the equator, showed the time of the equinox when the shadow cast by the upper part fell on the inside of the lower part. Alexandria already had one when Hipparchus wrote, and in Ptolemy's day it had two, one of which had suffered from subsidence and become useless.[16]

2. The meridional ring was a graduated bronze circle mounted vertically in the plane of the meridian, and inside it there turned another ring carrying two small plates diametrically opposite each other. As the sun crossed the meridian, the inner ring was rotated until the shadow of the upper plate fell on the lower one, and the sun's noon altitude could be read off. The latitude and the obliquity of the ecliptic could be derived from such figures for the summer and winter solstices. Proclus gives the instrument sights rather than shadow-plates.[17]

3. The plinth served the same function but consisted of a graduated quadrant engraved on the vertical face of a stone slab set in line with the meridian. A peg at the centre of the quadrant cast a shadow.[18]

4. The parallactic instrument (or Ptolemy's rulers) was apparently designed by Ptolemy himself. It consisted of a vertical graduated post at least four cubits high (about 2 m), with an alidade of equal length pivoted to its top in the plane of the meridian and a wooden lath pivoted to its foot. When the zenith distance of the moon or a star was sighted with the alidade (which with the post formed two sides of an isosceles triangle), the lath was positioned as the base of the triangle and a mark made on it. This mark was then measured on the vertical scale, and by means of a chord table the angle was obtained.[19]

5. The armillary astrolabe was a complex nest of seven concentric rings, the inner one carrying a pair of sights, for taking the latitude and

---

[15] For general discussion and illustrations see Dicks 1954 and Price 1957.
[16] Ptolemy, *Almagest* V 1.
[17] Ptolemy, *Almagest* I 12; Theon, *Commentary* 513–22; Proclus, *Outline* III 5–29.
[18] Ptolemy, *Almagest* I 12; Theon, *Commentary* 522–5.
[19] Ptolemy, *Almagest* V 12; Pappus, *Commentary* 69–77.

longitude from the ecliptic of any heavenly body. The primary instrument used by Ptolemy for compiling his star catalogue, it is first recorded in the *Almagest* but is thought by some to date back to Hipparchus. If so, it would have to be in rather different form since his coordinates were equatorial ones, namely declinations and right ascensions.[20] A more elaborate version, the meteoroscope, with nine rings but possibly smaller in size – Pappus says that the largest ring was only a cubit in diameter – is mentioned in Ptolemy's later *Geography* and is described by Pappus and Proclus.[21]

Except for the armillary astrolabe, none of these instruments was very elaborate, but great skill and precision were needed in their making. Ptolemy expected calculated values and observations to agree within 10' of arc.

Finally there were sundials. Beyond the considerable variety of stationary types,[22] there were several different types of portable sundial. The more elaborate of them bore a family resemblance to some of the observational instruments listed above.[23] One of these portable versions may be the *pros pan clima* ascribed by Vitruvius to Theodosius and Andrias,[24] of whom the former was a Bithynian astronomer and mathematician (like Hipparchus, but a generation later) and wrote on spherics.

In this connection a word needs to be said about the division of the circle.[25] As is well known, it was the Babylonians who first adopted the system of 360 degrees together with their sexagesimal subdivisions; the earliest record is in the late fifth century BC. The Greeks ultimately inherited it, but not before they had borrowed from the Babylonians more basic systems such as the division of the equator into 60ths, as is found in Eratosthenes (mid-late third century BC), and the system of dactyls and cubits which will engage our attention before long. Of earlier Greek astronomers, Aristarchus (early to mid-third century) used fractions of the zodiac circle, Archimedes fractions of a quadrant

---

[20] Ptolemy, *Almagest* V 1.
[21] Ptolemy, *Geography* (**Source 66**); Scholiast on same (**Source 67**); Pappus, *Commentary on Almagest* 3–16; Proclus, *Outline* VI 2–25 and *In Euc.* 42; Simplicius (**Source 69**).   [22] Extant specimens listed in Gibbs 1976.
[23] Price 1969; Gounaris 1980; Field 1990; Arnaldi and Schaldach 1997.
[24] Vitruvius IX 8.1.
[25] For overall surveys, Neugebauer 1975, 590–3 and Dicks 1966, 27–8.

(for example one quadrant less $\frac{1}{30}$ of a quadrant $= 87°$). The system of 360 degrees was not adopted by the Greeks until the mid-second century BC. At roughly that date it is found in Hypsicles (though perhaps only for the ecliptic circle),[26] in the Keskinto inscription from Rhodes, and in Hipparchus himself, who had access to Babylonian records and transmitted them to the Greeks,[27] although traces of earlier systems such as Babylonian cubits and dactyls are still to be found in his *Commentary*. But outside purely scientific circles the system of 360 degrees took time to catch on. In the first century BC Posidonius still divided the circle into 48ths, in the second century AD the astronomer Cleomedes quoted angles (though no doubt only at second hand) in dactyls,[28] as did Heliodorus as late as 508–9 for planetary distances that he had personally observed.[29]

In the absence of all but the most basic trigonometry, however, the measurement of angles was not the most obvious of ploys, and it remained confined to astronomy. Terrestrial surveyors worked exclusively on the basis of similar triangles, such as had been used empirically by the earliest geometers and had been formulated by Euclid in the early third century BC.

C. THE HIPPARCHAN DIOPTRA

This type of dioptra was used, as far as we know, only for measuring the apparent diameters of the sun and moon, for the very small angle subtended did not encourage the application of the instrument to terrestrial surveying.[30] The earliest version that we hear of was not even called a dioptra, no doubt because it did not involve 'looking through'. Archimedes mounted on a vertical stand a long rod, which he aimed at the rising sun and to one end of which he applied his eye. He then slid a small cylinder along the rod until it exactly covered the sun's disc. Allowing for the fact that vision does not emanate from a single point in the eye, he found from the known diameter of the cylinder and its distance along the rod that the angular diameter of the sun was between

[26] Fraser 1972, I 424 shows that Hypsicles does not belong to a later century as is sometimes claimed.   [27] Toomer 1978.   [28] Cleomedes, *On the Heavens* II 3.18–20.
[29] Heliodorus, *Commentary on Almagest* xxxvi-vii.
[30] Full discussion in Hultsch 1899. See also Neugebauer 1975, 657–9.

one 164th and one 200th of a right angle.[31] According to one story of his death, he was carrying this device, amongst others, to the victorious Marcellus at Syracuse when he met his end.[32]

The later version was called the dioptra, the Hipparchan dioptra, or sometimes the four-cubit dioptra. The principle was exactly the same. The rod was four cubits (nearly 2 m) long and carried two square plates projecting upwards at right angles. The 'backsight' plate had a small central hole for looking through, while the 'foresight' plate could be slid along a dovetailed groove until its width appeared to cover the object being sighted. This plate was later enlarged to contain two small holes which, rather than the plate edges, were made to coincide with the rim of the sun. The Hipparchan dioptra was used both by Hipparchus and by Ptolemy. The latter mentions it only briefly, but Pappus (early fourth century AD) and Proclus (mid-fifth century) both give good descriptions.[33] It also features in a fragmentary papyrus of the first or second century AD which deals with taking the sun's diameter.[34] Ptolemy professed doubts about its accuracy; and because, on a four-cubit rod, the 'foresight' plate was little more than 15 mm wide, one can understand why. None the less, the sun and moon diameters which Hipparchus and he obtained with it are surprisingly close to the truth: $31'20''$ for the sun, for instance, compared with the actual figures of $32'4''$ (mean) and $31'32''$ (minimum).

D. THE MEASURING ROD

The Hipparchan dioptra for measuring very small angles had a plate of fixed size set at a variable distance from the eye. The reverse procedure is also found, with plates of varying size (or even a calibrated scale) at a fixed distance. This is nowhere described or even named, but it is implicit in the Babylonian system already mentioned of dactyls and cubits as units of arc (12 dactyls = half a cubit = 1°).[35] This presumably

---

[31] Archimedes, *Sand-reckoner* 1.12–13.
[32] Plutarch, *Marcellus* 19.6.
[33] Ptolemy, *Almagest* V 14; Pappus, *Commentary* 90–5; Proclus, *Outline* IV 72–3, 87–99.
[34] *P. Oslo* 73; Eitrem 1933.
[35] Powell 1987–90, 461; Neugebauer 1955, 39; see also Neugebauer 1975, 591–3.

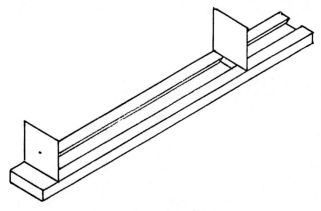

FIG. 2.1. Hipparchan dioptra.

originated in the angles subtended by given chords at a given distance, which can be worked out as 28.6 cubits or about 13 m. One wonders, in view of the predilection of the Babylonians for sexagesimal divisions, whether this was meant to be 30 cubits. Although the names of the units imply that at first the equipment was full-size, it must later have been miniaturised, with the units necessarily remaining the same. This was the way Pytheas of Marseille, the explorer of the end of the fourth century BC, recorded the altitude of the sun in northern latitudes, his figures going as high as 6 cubits.[36] While an instrument almost 30 cubits long is unthinkable on board ship, it is perfectly feasible to visualise a rod a few cubits long, which carried on its end either a transverse graduated scale or a selection of plates of varying diameter which could be slotted into place.

Likewise Ptolemy (borrowing from Hipparchus) cites a number of early observations of planets. Three of them, made by the Babylonians between 244 and 228 BC, are in the form 'Mercury was half a cubit above' or 'Saturn was 2 dactyls below' a given star,[37] which suggests a scale graduated in dactyls at a fixed distance. Similarly, five observations made apparently by one Dionysius at Alexandria between 271 and 240

[36] Strabo, *Geography* II 1.18, quoting from Hipparchus who in turn is quoting from Pytheas. For convincing arguments that these are Pytheas' units, not Hipparchus', see Dicks 1960, 185–8. Another record of a sun height of 9 cubits may also derive from Pytheas.   [37] Ptolemy, *Almagest* IX 7, XI 7.

BC are given in the form 'Mercury was three moons north' of such-and-such a star, which equally suggests a scale graduated in moon diameters of about 30′ each, at a fixed distance.[38]

Earlier still, in the mid-fourth century, Eudoxus had taken the approximate positions of a number of heavenly bodies and, from these observations, formulated his ingenious theory of homocentric spheres to explain their motions. The observational data in what survives of his work are few and crude,[39] and we do not know for sure what instrument he used. But a hint is offered by unexpected sources. While the Latin *radius* can mean the rod used by geometers for sketching in the sand,[40] Roman poets sometimes ascribe the *radius* to astronomers not as a mere drawing implement but as an observational instrument for recording heavenly bodies. Thus Virgil speaks of Eudoxus 'who defined with his staff the whole heavens for man', and makes Anchises prophesy that the Greeks would 'define with the staff the motions of the heavens'.[41] Avienus in the fourth century AD is yet more precise: Eudoxus' staff was 'pointed . . . at the stars'.[42] *Radius* could very well describe the measuring rod, whose comparative crudity is appropriate to Eudoxus' observations.[43]

In the early third century at Alexandria Timocharis (who observed between 294 and 271) and Aristyllus recorded the positions of at least eighteen stars.[44] Although we are not told what instrument they used, it is often assumed that it was similar to one of the relatively sophisticated designs described by Ptolemy four centuries later.[45] For so early a date, close to the beginnings of Greek mathematical astronomy, this

---

[38] Ptolemy, *Almagest* IX 7, 10. In one case it appears as '3° in advance of Spica according to Hipparchus' reckoning', which shows that Hipparchus had converted Dionysius' unit, no doubt 6 moons.   [39] Toomer 1996, 196.

[40] As by Archimedes: Cicero, *Tusculan Disputations* v 23.64.

[41] Virgil, *Eclogues* 3.41; *Aeneid* vi 849–50.

[42] Avienus, *Aratus' Phenomena* 53. Other possible usages of *radius* in this sense are Claudian, *Panegyric on the Consulship of Fl. Manlius Theodorus* 274–5; Servius, *Commentaries ad Ecl.* 3.41; Philargyrius, *Explanation of the Bucolics ad Ecl.* 3.41.

[43] The suggestion by Maula 1975–6 that he used a highly elaborate observational instrument may be discounted. Not only does it go far beyond the evidence but it is inherently unlikely.   [44] Ptolemy, *Almagest* VII 3.

[45] E.g. Tannery 1893, 80; Pannekoek 1961, 124 (who wrongly ascribes longitudes to them); Gounaris 1980, 11–12.

seems improbable. The only observations which Timocharis and his colleagues need have made were of meridional altitudes above the horizon or distances below the zenith, which Hipparchus, knowing the latitude of Alexandria, converted into declinations from the equator.[46] I suggest that, like Eudoxus', their only equipment was a rod of the kind under discussion, graduated either in moon diameters or, perhaps more likely, in cubits and dactyls.[47] Hipparchus, the originator of the chord table, could readily convert their readings into degrees. He remarked that 'the observations of the school of Timocharis are not to be trusted, since they were very crudely made'.[48] But they were accurate enough to stand comparison with his own and with Ptolemy's observations. Moreover the records of occultations made by Timocharis and others allowed Hipparchus, working from the known motion of the moon, to supply equatorial coordinates for the stars in question, which gave him the essential clue to his famous discovery of the precession of the equinoxes.

The principle of the rod evidently survived into Roman times. Plutarch in the early second century AD gave the apparent diameter of the moon at mean distance as 12 dactyls.[49] Sosigenes, a Peripatetic philosopher later in the same century, in demonstrating the varying distance (and therefore apparent size) of the moon from the earth, showed that 'on one occasion it is screened by an 11-dactyl disc, on another by a 12-dactyl disc placed at the same distance from the observer'.[50] If the discs were really of that size, they would have to be held, in order to cover the moon, at an inconveniently long distance from the eye – about 52 cubits or 24 m – and once again a miniaturised version of the instrument seems more likely. Two centuries later, Cleomedes remarks that 'the size of the sun and moon alike appears to our perception as 12 dactyls'.[51] By Roman times, it will be noticed, the units are about twice the size of the original Babylonian ones, of which 6 dactyls would cover the moon or sun.[52] But in both cases the principle is the

---

[46] Tannery 1893, 78.
[47] Heath 1913, 192 suggests that Eudoxus had only an elementary dioptra, which amounts to the same thing.   [48] Quoted by Ptolemy, *Almagest* VII 3.
[49] Plutarch, *Moralia* 935d.   [50] Simplicius, *Commentary on De Caelo* 504.33–5.
[51] Cleomedes, *On the Heavens* II 3.18–20.
[52] For this late Babylonian measure see Powell 1987–90, 463.

same as in the medieval Jacob's staff or cross-staff, which had adjustable crossbars of varying lengths and was applied to navigation and terrestrial surveying as well as to astronomy. Its invention is ascribed to Levi ben Gerson in the fourteenth century.[53]

A closer parallel, however, is to be found in an unnamed instrument employed for taking star heights by Arab and Indian sailors in the Indian Ocean. When first recorded in 1554 it was ascribed to 'the ancients', but its origin is unknown. On to a cord as long as the user's arm could be threaded any of nine discs which ranged in diameter from 4 to 12 fingers (the equivalent of Greek dactyls). The near end of the cord was held to the eye and the disc which best fitted the distance between the horizon and the relevant star was threaded on the far end.[54] This instrument differed from the postulated Greek version in that it used a cord rather than a rod, and the discs were labelled according to their actual size rather than a larger and nominal figure. But the family resemblance is clear enough.

E. GAMALIEL'S TUBE

We turn at last to our first certain instrument for terrestrial surveying. Although the writers of the Talmud, our only source, probably did not understand it, its nature is clear enough. While Jews were normally permitted to travel only 2000 cubits on the Sabbath, special rules applied on shipboard. If at nightfall when the Sabbath began the ship was more than 2000 cubits from shore, its passengers might not land until the Sabbath was over; but if, as in **Source 5**, it was less, they were allowed to. The commentaries (**Sources 6–7**) explain that Rabbi Gamaliel II, who was president of the Sanhedrin from about AD 80, knew the distance from the shore by means of a sighting tube (*mezupit*, 'viewer', or *sefoforet*, 'tube') which he used as a range finder.[55]

---

[53] For details see Kiely 1947, 83–7, 200–2.

[54] Hammer 1838, 771–2, 778–9; effectively the same device is recorded in Chinese sources from 1606 (Needham 1971, 573–5). Kiely 1947, 84–5 misrepresents this instrument. It is not the same as the *kamal*, in which the length of the cord is adjustable (Taylor 1956, 128–9). For not dissimilar instruments in the Mogul empire see also Prinsep 1836, 784–8.

[55] Eisler 1949, 320 and 329–30 nn. 49, 52 offers some very far-fetched etymologies of these Hebrew words. *Sefoforet*, he suggests, derives from a Greek loan-word, either

Suppose, for simplicity of calculation, the tube to be 50 cm long and 1 cm in internal diameter. When it was held against the eye, the field of view at a range of 2000 cubits would be 40 cubits in diameter. If Gamaliel knew that, say, a tower on the waterfront was 40 cubits high, and if its height when viewed through the tube more than filled the diameter, then he knew that it was less than 2000 cubits away.[56] By the reverse procedure, the tube would equally give the approximate height of an object provided the distance were known. The other texts (**Sources 8–9**) refer to the use of the tube for determining distances on land, although the precise details elude us. In the case of the ravine, Rashi's explanation is inadequate, for the observer must know the width of the ravine before he can determine its depth.

The tube was therefore a neat and handy if not particularly accurate instrument. It might seem surprising that we hear of no other example, because it would have military applications such as telling a besieging commander the height of the city wall. The drawback was perhaps that the distance to the wall would have to be measured directly, which was dangerous; and, as we shall find, there were methods of discovering this distance without venturing within bowshot of the enemy. None the less it is difficult to believe that Gamaliel's instrument was unique to him. It is recorded that, unlike some of his colleagues, he was tolerant towards matters Greek and was not unacquainted with Greek science.[57] The simple sighting tube existed by the time of Aristotle; the suspended tube was possibly used even earlier for levelling tunnels; and the standard surveyor's dioptra, as will emerge, seems originally to have had tubular sights which were later replaced by alidades. All this might suggest that Gamaliel's tube had a lengthy ancestry behind it; and as late as the third century AD Hisdai seems still to have been familiar with it (**Source 9**).

---

sphairophoros, meaning (he says) an astronomer's celestial sphere mounted round a tube and orientated by sighting on the Pole Star, or *sporophoros*, meaning a seed-drill funnel attached to a plough. *Mezupit* is sometimes translated as 'observatory' or 'landmark'; Eisler reads it as *mesudot*, 'nets', referring to the spider or *arachne* of an astrolabe. Others had earlier seen an astrolabe in Gamaliel's tube, but Sperber 1986, 108 refutes them.

[56] As Sperber 1986, 108 remarks, the same would apply if the tube were of larger diameter but had across the end a graticule of wires or threads, in this case 1 cm apart.

[57] *Encyclopaedia Judaica* 7 (Jerusalem 1971), 296–8.

F. PHILO'S LEVEL AND STAFF

Philo of Byzantium was one of the brighter lights of Hellenistic technology, but his career is obscure.[58] Although he had spent some time at the school of mechanics at Alexandria, probably in the 250s, and met its leader Ctesibius who diėd around 250, he was not a permanent resident there. His lifespan can only be deduced at something like 290 to 220 BC, which would make him a contemporary of Archimedes, whom he never mentions in his generally accepted writings. All the same, there are strong signs that, perhaps later in their lives, Philo edited some of Archimedes' work which the great man was reluctant to publish himself. This includes the water screw and the hodometer, descriptions of which were apparently borrowed from Philo by Vitruvius, and a clock which is described in a treatise that survives only in Arabic. Philo's *magnum opus*, however, was the *Mechanike Syntaxis* or *Compendium of Mechanics*. As internal evidence and other Greek sources show, this comprised at least eight separate books, which we might call the canonical ones. Apart from tiny fragments, only two of them survive in the original Greek, the *Artillery* and the *Siegecraft*, the latter being convincingly dated to 246–240 BC. The *Pneumatics*, however, survives (in several versions) in an Arabic translation of probably the ninth century and in a partial Latin translation done in the Middle Ages from the Greek rather than from the Arabic.

Prager, who made a careful study of the many manuscripts of the Latin translation, found frequent mention in their incipits of such titles as *De ductu aquarum* ('water conducting') and *De ingeniis* ('machines').[59] These books, as entities, are now missing from the corpus of Philo's works; but traces of them remain in the Arabic tradition. The contents of the Arabic versions of the *Pneumatics*, although essentially genuine Philo, are a hotchpotch, consisting of a core of descriptions of ingenious devices operated by air or water which are entirely appropriate to the title of the book, followed by a variety of more useful machines, mostly for lifting water, which have nothing to do with pneumatics. It is as if compilers, once the *Pneumatics* proper was safely copied, filled up the rest of their manuscript with a personal selection from other

---

[58] For a review of his work and influence see Lewis 1997, 20–48.

[59] Prager 1974, 47–51.

books of Philo which, from their subject matter, could readily have carried such titles as *Water Conducting* (*Hydragogia*) or *Machines* (*Mechanemata*).[60] Since there is no cross-reference to them in the canonical books, they were probably written late in the series, say in the 230s BC.

This is the background to **Source 10**, where Ibn al-'Awwam quotes from Aflimun's *Book on Water Conducting*. The title is right for Philo, and so is the author's name. While Philo was usually spelt Filun in Arabic, the historian Ya'qubi, writing in 891, refers to him as Aflimun. 'To the Greek scholars belongs Aflimun, who invented machines (*mahaniqa*). These are movements produced by water', he says, and proceeds to give an ill-digested or misunderstood account of devices that sound like the jackwork of an elaborate water-clock of exactly the kind that Philo published on Archimedes' behalf. It is clear enough that Aflimun is Philo; there is indeed no other candidate among known Greek mechanics.[61]

His procedure for levelling an irrigation channel is simple. At the cistern, an astrolabe is placed on a horizontal plank which, though Philo does not say so, was presumably levelled by means of an ordinary builder's **A**-frame level. The astrolabe is sighted on a crudely graduated staff held vertical at a distance. The height above the ground of the point where the line of sight meets the staff is the height of the astrolabe above the foot of the staff. How far is Ibn al-'Awwam quoting directly from Philo? Given the simplicity of the operation envisaged, it fits well with the undeveloped state of surveying in Philo's day, with one exception.

As Chapter 3.D will make clear, Philo certainly did not know of the astrolabe. But because the translation was made many centuries later, this raises no great difficulty: Philo could perfectly well have used the

---

[60] Of the many chapters probably borrowed from *Water Conducting*, the most obvious is *Pneumatics* 65, which concerns the well-known chain of buckets discharging water into an elevated aqueduct 'as has been described'. The text as we have it has described no such thing, which is a strong pointer to the chapter being abstracted from another book.

[61] The identification was first pointed out by Steinschneider 1896, 355, and confirmed by Wiedemann 1970, i 155–6 (first published in 1905) and by Wiedemann and Hauser 1918, 123–4, both of which give Ya'qubi's text. The name of Polemon the physiognomist was also rendered as Aflimun in Arabic (Rosenthal 1992, 43, 251, 254), but his subject matter can hardly be confused with Philo's.

word 'dioptra' instead. Although this came commonly to denote a complete instrument, it was already applied to the simple sighting tube and was sometimes applied to the alidade alone rather than the whole instrument (**Africanus 4, Source 32**). Arabic, however, had no word for the dioptra as a surveying device. Islam had not inherited it as such, but only in the form of the reverse of the astrolabe with its alidade, which was none the less used for surveying in much the same way as the Greeks had used the dioptra (Chapters 3.D and 12). *Asturlab* was therefore an entirely logical name for Arabic speakers to apply to the dioptra. Indeed when Ibn al-Nadim (**Source 27**) mentioned Hero writing on 'the procedure with the astrolabe' he almost certainly meant the *Dioptra*, for there is no other indication or likelihood that Hero wrote about the astrolabe proper. The only other mention in Arabic of a dioptra-like device for levelling is that by al-Karaji which, we shall shortly discover, is also copied from a Greek original.

Philo's dioptra or *asturlab* had at each end a vane sight with a hole in it. The Arabic word here translated as vanes is not the usual *al-'idada* (the original of *alidade*) but *stia*, which is otherwise unknown but can mean nothing else. It might be a transliteration of the Greek *histia*, 'sails', which would not be a bad description. This is the earliest evidence we have for a true alidade, namely a bar with upward-projecting vane sights at either end, as opposed to a sighting tube. We should envisage merely the alidade, attached to nothing else, being placed on the plank. Home-made substitutes are also mentioned, in the form of ring-headed nails and even hollow tiles, but it is not clear if they too came from Philo or were added by Ibn al-'Awwam.

Philo's procedure, which will be discussed in greater detail in Chapter 3.G, offers an invaluable insight into surveying practice before it blossomed into an instrumental science. Ancient references to the levelling staff are limited to Hero's sophisticated model, to al-Karaji's intermediate type, and to this exceedingly simple design which accords well with a very early date. The statement that the minimum gradient should be 1 in 200 is of profound interest, for (as will be argued in Chapter 9.B) this figure was picked up by Vitruvius and, by repeated miscopying, has caused untold confusion to later scholars.

CHAPTER 3

THE DIOPTRA

The dioptra became the standard surveying instrument of the Greeks and, although no actual example has yet been found (or at least identified), we can discover a surprising amount about its design and employment by tapping sources hitherto almost untouched. Apart from Hero's well-known manual, three treatises or fragments of treatises on the dioptra survive under the names of Julius Africanus, the Anonymus Byzantinus and al-Karaji, along with many passing mentions in other literature. To ease the difficulties of understanding these sources, it may help at this early stage to paint a brief preliminary picture of this very flexible device. Contrary to widespread belief, Hero's complex dioptra was not the only version. It was, rather, a one-off and probably fruitless attempt at improving on the earlier and much simpler dioptra, which already existed in a number of varieties that differed only in detail.

This simple type was a disc, engraved with two diameters at right angles and carrying an alidade or comparable sighting bar pivoted at its centre (Figs. 3.1–2). It could be mounted in two different ways. If it was suspended on edge by a ring from a suitable stand it acted as its own plumb, and hung vertically. A horizontal sighting line for levelling was obtained by aligning the alidade with the horizontal diameter. Altitudes could be taken by tilting the alidade, and a direct offshoot of the dioptra when used in this mode was the back side of the later plane astrolabe. Or, if the disc was mounted more or less flat on another stand by means of a kind of universal joint, the alidade could be rotated to sight right angles – or any other angles – on the ground. With the disc tilted appropriately, angular distances between heavenly bodies could be measured against a degree scale round the rim. Except for astronomical purposes of this kind, however, and in the absence of all but the simplest trigonometry, angles were never measured in degrees. Instead, calculations of heights and distances were made geometrically by the use of similar triangles or, in the case of levelling, by adding or subtracting differences of height.

FIG. 3.1. Dioptra reconstruction in vertical mode.

FIG. 3.2. Dioptra reconstruction in horizontal mode.

A. THE TREATISES

i. Hero of Alexandria

Hero is the last recorded member of the mechanical school of Alexandria, and the best known. His high reputation in later antiquity survived into the Middle Ages and persists today.[1] It is a justified reputation. He was not a great original thinker or even, it would seem, much of an inventor, and he was not deeply interested in theory. His virtues lay more in his practical down-to-earth approach and in his prolific descriptions of the scientific experiments and technical discoveries of his predecessors. His genuine works are the *Definitions*, *Metrics*, *Catoptrics*, *Mechanics*, *Pneumatics*, *Automata*, *Artillery*, *Cheiroballistra* and *Dioptra*, which all survive, and the *Water Clocks*, *Balances*, *Vaults*, *Barulkos* and *Commentary on Euclid*, which are lost, or largely lost. The *Geometry*, *Geodesy*, *Geoponics*, *Stereometry* and *Measures*, which all bear Hero's name, are rag-bags of Byzantine compilations, extensively

---

[1] For Hero's work the best overviews are Tittel 1913 (outdated in some respects but still valuable), Drachmann 1948 and 1963.

re-worked or excerpted from genuine works of Hero.[2] His date, once a matter of huge controversy, was finally established when Neugebauer showed that a lunar eclipse which Hero himself had observed (**Dioptra 35**) took place in AD 62.[3] His *Cheiroballistra* (whose genuineness there is no good reason to doubt) is the specification for a revolutionary design of catapult which is unlikely to have been introduced before AD 84[4] but which is attested on Trajan's Column as in service in 101–2. Hero was therefore alive after 84, and his working life fell in the second half rather than the middle of the first century AD.

The treatise on the dioptra is typical of his approach. He starts by extolling the useful applications of the instrument in military and civilian life, and dismissively criticising, in very general terms, all earlier writings on the subject (**Dioptra 1–2**). A literature of respectable size evidently existed already. So did a variety of different kinds of dioptra. All, Hero implies, were inadequate because individually their capabilities were limited. This, we may consider, was an exaggeration, for the basic dioptra is so simple an instrument as hardly to admit of significant variety of design. Perhaps he means that some could only be mounted vertically and some only horizontally; and, as we shall see, there were indeed different kinds of sights. Be that as it may, Hero claims to have made a single instrument which was able to perform all the tasks undertaken by his predecessors, and more. 'We have constructed it', he says, and there is no cause to doubt him. He implies that he had also designed it. Since Hero is not good at giving credit to others, this should be accepted only with caution. But it was hardly an old invention, for the tubes of its water level were of glass, necessarily both blown and reasonably transparent, which demanded techniques not available much more than a century before Hero's time. His instrument is ingenious; but as detailed discussion will later suggest, in some operations – notably levelling – it is unlikely to have exceeded its simpler predecessors in precision. As almost every commentator has remarked, it must have been extremely expensive to make, and for this reason, and in the absence (with one doubtful exception) of any hint that it was imitated, it is quite possible that only the prototype was ever built.

---

[2] See Heiberg 1914, LXVI–CXI and Tittel 1913.   [3] Neugebauer 1938–9.

[4] Frontinus, *Stratagems* II praef., written between 84 and 96, uses language which implies that no recent revolution had taken place in artillery design.

After a detailed specification (*Dioptra* 3–4), now somewhat marred by a lacuna, Hero proceeds to spell out the applications of his dioptra. The first description, and much the most valuable, is of how levelling was carried out with a staff (5–6). The bulk of the book consists of exercises or problems, some of them evidently designed for learners and of little practical value in the real world, some of them eminently useful for aqueduct engineers and the like. They are in exactly the same vein as those, many fewer in number, that are found in Africanus and the Anonymus. Africanus' exercises are entirely military in purpose; the Anonymus' are partly so; but Hero, despite the lip-service he pays in his introduction to military needs, has nothing at all that is specifically military, although such problems as **Dioptra 12** (finding a height) and **14** (finding the depth of a ditch) could have military applications. This civilian outlook may reflect the *pax Romana*, although Balbus (**Source 14**) reminds us that surveyors still had a military role to play.

These exercises appear to be representative of the repertoire of the ancient engineering surveyor. Whatever Hero's originality in the design of his dioptra, he seems to have inherited them from his despised predecessors and merely to have adapted their solutions to his own instrument. Some, as remarked, are very much more interesting than others. Yet all are disappointing in that they always focus on the relatively small problem and never on the larger challenge. How, for instance, did the engineer charged with surveying, laying out and building an aqueduct over dozens of kilometres of unpromising terrain actually organise the stages of what must have been a protracted, complex and demanding operation? We will return to this question in Chapter 9.B.

The treatise, having concentrated on the dioptra, ends with a few related oddments (31–5): measuring a flow of water, astronomical uses, the *asteriskos* or groma, the hodometer, and measuring long distances by observing eclipses. Here the original book probably stopped. The text as we have it, however, whose condition has begun to degenerate in **35**, carries on in considerable disorder. Chapter 36 is missing, **37** describes the *barulkos*, a theoretical haulage device that is quite irrelevant, and **38** (though unnumbered) describes a ship's log which is clearly cognate to the hodometer but is probably imported from some other source. The oldest and best manuscript, the 'Mynas Codex'

(Paris. suppl. gr. 607), dates from the eleventh or twelfth century. Most of the diagrams in it are geometrical ones, but a few are useful in showing details of the dioptra itself (Figs. 3.8, 10).

ii. Julius Africanus

Little is known of Sextus Julius Africanus. A Christian and a native of Jerusalem, he was involved in local diplomacy in Syria, and under Severus Alexander (AD 222–35) he set up a library in the Pantheon at Rome. He compiled two major works, the *Chronographies* down to 221 which provided the basis for Eusebius' *Chronicle*, and the *Cesti* (*Charmed Girdles*), written between 228 and 231, of which substantial fragments survive. This was a hotch-potch in 24 books that ranged widely in subject from medicine to tactics, but was especially concerned with magic in various forms.[5] Surprisingly, the brief section of interest to us has hardly ever been cited as evidence for ancient surveying.[6] It focuses on the two standard military requirements: how to discover the width of a river without crossing it and the height of a city wall without approaching it, in order to construct a pontoon bridge of the right length and a siege tower of the right height. The language is terse, clear and to the point. The material, which has much in common with the Anonymus', is certainly not original to Africanus, but its source is best deferred for discussion alongside that of the other treatises.

iii. Anonymus Byzantinus

Of this compiler we know even less: not even his name. He wrote two books that have survived, the *Siegecraft* and the *Geodesy*, and another on sundials known only from his own reference to it in **Geodesy 11**. Late manuscripts of the two extant works ascribe them to a Hero, or to Hero of Byzantium (possibly better translated as the Byzantine Hero), a name once widely used, along with 'Hero the Younger', in older publications.[7] But this is only a medieval example of hanging obscure works on the peg of a famous name, and should be consigned to obliv-

[5] See the introductions to Vieillefond 1932 and 1970.
[6] Kiely 1947 is an exception, but he fails to understand the nature of Africanus' dioptra.
[7] For general discussion see Dain 1933.

ion. The oldest manuscript leaves the books anonymous, and they have nothing to do with either Hero of Alexandria or the so-called pseudo-Hero who in the sixth century re-worked a few of the chapters in the genuine *Pneumatics*.[8] It is least misleading to follow current practice and call our man the Anonymus Byzantinus or (for our purposes) the Anonymus for short.

It is clear that the same man wrote both surviving books, for **Geodesy** 1 refers back to the *Siegecraft*. It is clear from his siting of several exercises in the Hippodrome and his references to the cisterns of Aspar and Aetius and the Bucoleon palace that he wrote in Constantinople. It is also clear that he belonged at least on the fringe of the circle of encyclopaedists who, under the aegis of the scholarly Constantine VII Porphyrogennetos (908–59), compiled 53 volumes of excerpts from ancient literature under a wide variety of headings.[9] When talking of the precession of the equinoxes (**11**, not translated in our extract) the Anonymus updates Ptolemy's star positions by adding 8° to the longitude which, according to Ptolemy's value for the precession of 1° per century, puts the date of writing in Porphyrogennetos' reign.[10] For the *Siegecraft*, he drew on very much earlier treatises on siegecraft and artillery – mainly Apollodorus of Damascus, but also Athenaeus Mechanicus, Philo's *Artillery*, Hero's *Artillery*, Biton and others unknown – which had first been assembled as a corpus probably early in the tenth century under Leo VI the Wise. For the *Geodesy*, as we shall find, his sources, though equally ancient, are less easy to identify.

The *Geodesy* is a short book, of only 16 folios in the archetype. It was originally half as long again, for there is a big and most unfortunate lacuna near the beginning, present in all the manuscripts, which must have included a description of the dioptra itself.[11] The archetype, Vatican Gr. 1605, was made in the mid-eleventh century, only about a hundred years after the original compilation. The text has been published only once, from an inferior manuscript at third remove from the archetype; but both (apart from the lacuna) are textually in a reasonable state with few obvious or important corruptions. They contain

---

[8] Drachmann 1948, 161–7.

[9] Lemerle 1986, 323–43, who does not however mention the Anonymus.

[10] Vincent 1858, 402–3.

[11] Dain 1933, 31–2 explains how the lacuna came about.

only a few uninformative geometrical diagrams. In his introduction (1) the Anonymus sets out his aims: to help students not only of the art of war by showing how to measure rivers and walls, but also of civilian surveying, as of aqueducts and harbours, and even of astronomy. To this end he will clarify the obscurities in his predecessors' writings, cut down their verbosity and their theoretical material, simplify their mathematical language, and reduce it all to a comprehensible and practical level.

Although we do not know quite how turgid and difficult his predecessors' works were, he may to some extent have achieved his aim. But if anything he went too far. Some of his exercises (such as 7) are so simple and banal as to be, in any practical sense, pointless. Others he tries to make more relevant to his age – surely his own idea, and in principle a good one – by setting them in the Hippodrome, which all his readers would know. The trouble is that he is not always very intelligent about it, and what is meant as clarification only confuses the issue. In 2 he combines the original problem of finding the height of a wall with his own parallel exercise of finding the height of the bronze chariot group (whose horses are now in Venice) mounted above the starting gates; and he combines two alternative ways of supporting the dioptra. The result is not satisfactory. Where he is at variance with other sources, as in 2 again where his use of the word *lychnia* is different from that of **Africanus 4**, it is undoubtedly the Anonymus who is wrong. Sackur remarked that 'the Anonymus Byzantinus is a very conscientious worker, but a genuinely practical idea . . . we should not expect of him . . . Apart from the fundamental wrongness of his observations, he has also totally misunderstood his sources.'[12] Sackur was talking of the *Siegecraft*, and the criticism is perhaps over-harsh if applied to the *Geodesy*; but it encapsulates the Anonymus' shortcomings. That said, he is none the less of enormous value, for he has preserved material that sheds more light than any other source on the construction and use of the standard dioptra. It is therefore astonishing that historians of surveying, or indeed of technology in general, have shown less interest in him than even in Africanus.[13]

---

[12] Sackur 1925, 106–7.
[13] Even the indefatigable Kiely 1947 gives him only one brief mention.

iv. Al-Karaji

Abu Bakr Muhammad ibn al-Hasan al-Karaji, to give him his full name, a native of al-Karaj in the Jibal in Iran, was by profession an administrator in Baghdad and by inclination a mathematician. His principal and highly important works on algebra, written about 1011–12, were based on, but much developed, the ideas of the Greek mathematicians Diophantus, Euclid and Nicomachus, which had long been available in Arabic translation. He later returned to al-Karaj where he died after 1019, when *The Search for Hidden Waters* was written.[14] This is a manual about the engineering of qanats or water-collecting tunnels. Some parts, which deal with underground survey-ing and describe a sighting tube which might be ancestral to the dioptra, will concern us later, especially in Chapter 10.E. Our present interest centres on three chapters about levelling on the surface. He first (XXI-II) describes traditional Islamic levels, which were variations on the theme of the *mizan*. A chain 30 cubits long, held between two vertical staves, is known to be level when a plumb line coincides with the vertical mark on a plate dangling from the centre of the chain (see Chapter 12 for further details). After specifying some improvements of his own, including the sexagesimal division of the staves and a version where the plate of the *mizan* is calibrated, **al-Karaji 1–2** describes and illustrates a better levelling instrument, which he does not seem to claim as his own invention.

A square or circular plate of metal or wood, engraved with two diameters at right angles, carries at its centre a pivoting sighting tube 1½ spans long and is suspended from a stand. There are two alternative procedures for levelling with it which will call for detailed discussion at a later stage. The first involves positioning the instrument and the staff 100 cubits apart as measured by a cord or chain; in the second – the closer to later practice – the staff can be held at any convenient distance and no cord is needed. In one case if not both the staff carries a cursor for sighting on.

The *mizan* and its fellow devices which relied on a cord and plumb-line were the Islamic surveyor's standard tool for levelling, and are well

---

[14] For a brief biography see Vernat 1978; for his algebra, Rashed 1973; for summaries of the *Search*, Krenkow 1947–9 (poor) and Hill 1993, 189–98 (admirable).

attested. But al-Karaji's tube sights are unique in medieval Islamic surveying, where there is no record of sights as such other than on the astrolabe. Not only does this instrument stick out like a sore thumb in an Islamic context but (apart from having a sighting tube rather than an alidade) it is identical to the Greek dioptra when suspended for levelling. Likewise al-Karaji's second method of levelling has, at the very least, points in common with Greek levelling as expounded by Hero. Again, al-Karaji prefaces his geometrical proposition with 'I say that . . .', and concludes his proof with 'which was to be demonstrated', that is, Q.E.D. These phrases are pure Euclid. While it is certainly possible that al-Karaji picked them up from his own reading, it is noteworthy that Africanus also employs precisely the same Euclidian formulae.

Yet another factor is the length of the cord or chain which determined the distance between staves, or between staff and instrument. For the traditional *mizan* the cord was 15 cubits or 30 spans long; in al-Karaji's improved version it was 30 cubits or 60 spans. Both lengths remind one of the sexagesimal system of the Babylonians, whose practices in this respect were inherited by Islam. There was indeed a standard Islamic measure, the *asl* (cord) of 60 large Hasimi cubits, the kind of cubit used by surveyors, which was clearly a descendant of the Babylonian *aslu* (cord) of 120 cubits.[15] But there was no Greek measure of 60 cubits, or of a subdivision or multiple of 60.[16] The *mizan* and its cords seem to be wholly Babylonian/Islamic. In contrast, for the first procedure with the tube level, al-Karaji specifies a cord 100 cubits long. There was no Babylonian or Islamic measure of this length; but as we have already noted the standard measure for land in Ptolemaic Egypt was the *schoinion* of 100 cubits. All these points raise strong suspicions: is al-Karaji's tube level really of Islamic origin, or did he discover it in some Greek source translated into Arabic?

A final test settles the matter. The reference letters to the diagram of the geometry of sighting (**al-Karaji 1**) run ABJDHZḤṬYKLMNS.

---

[15] Hinz 1955, 54; Hinz 1965, 232; Powell 1987–90, 464.
[16] The Greek *plethron*, normally of 100 feet, is once (and only once) defined as 90 feet or 60 cubits. This is in a table 'strikingly Babylonian in structure' (Powell 1987–90, 464) given by the 6th-century Julian of Ascalon (Viedebantt 1917, 126). Babylonian influence is hardly surprising in Palestine.

Like their Greek counterparts, Arabic geometers, astronomers and mechanics who illustrated their works with diagrams used an alphabetical sequence. The modern Arabic alphabet has the letters in a completely different order; but in the ancient Arabic and Greek alphabets, which both derived from a common Semitic source, the order of letters was identical (except for a divergence towards the end which does not concern us). But there was one crucial difference. Whereas the Arabs retained the sixth letter W, *waw* (و), its Greek counterpart, *vau* or *digamma* (Ϝ), survived in our period only as the numeral for 6, not as a letter. The letters, and the alphabetical sequence as far as is relevant, correspond like this:

Greek	A	B	Γ	Δ	E		Z	H	Θ	I	K	Λ	M	N	Ξ
Arabic	A	B	J	D	H	W	Z	Ḥ	Ṭ	Y	K	L	M	N	S

The practice was straightforward and obvious.[17] An Arab writing a new work would normally include W in his letter series. A Greek writer never did. An Arab translating from Greek, unless he was deliberately re-working the material, would follow the original and not use W. Any number of examples could be quoted for each of these three categories.

A contrary view has been expressed, that W and Y, as half-vowels, were sometimes consigned to the end of the Arabic alphabet, and that therefore their presence in, or absence from, their ordinary position in Arabic sequences has no bearing on their presence or absence in the Greek.[18] This may indeed be true, at least on occasion. But the fatal flaw in this argument is that W and Y stand or fall together: either they are both in their proper places in the alphabet, or both at the end. In the series under discussion in al-Karaji, the presence of Y shows that half-vowels were not banished to the end of the alphabet, and therefore the absence of W shows that the series is not an Arabic one, but Greek.[19] Exactly the same holds true of the *Pneumatics* of Philo of

---

[17] The matter is discussed more fully in Lewis 1997, 26–7, 135 n.61.

[18] Gandz 1933.

[19] Two other series of his, in the first part of XXIII and in XXIV (figs. 5 and 11 in the Hyderabad edition), neither of which is there any reason to suppose are Greek, do include both Y and W and are therefore of Arabic origin. The series in the last section of XXIII (fig. 9 Hyderabad) omits W but, because it also omits the adjacent Z and Ḥ, does not necessarily qualify as Greek. All three of these series deal with calibrated instruments, in which al-Karaji's claim to innovation seems to lie.

Byzantium, which is lost in Greek but survives in Arabic. The great majority of its letter series, when they reach far enough into the alphabet, exclude W but include Y. These too are clearly Greek sequences, and only those which contain a W are suspect as Arabic interpolations or re-workings.[20] The suspicions, therefore, that the dioptra is a stranger to Islamic surveying prove justified. Al-Karaji was drawing on some Greek work, no doubt translated with so many others in the great cultural borrowing of the ninth century. It does not necessarily follow that he was copying precisely; the sexagesimal division of his staves, for example, like the calibration of three instruments which we are not concerned with, is probably his own innovation. But the essentially Greek nature and origin of his level authorises us to consider it as a Greek dioptra.

B. THE SOURCES OF THE TREATISES

In their present form all four of our treatises are late, ranging from the first to the eleventh century AD; and they are all essentially derivative, not original. Can we deduce anything about their sources? Al-Karaji's, in the nature of things, are difficult to pin down. He is concerned solely with levelling, which does not feature in Africanus or the Anonymus. But while his affinities are thus more with Hero, his procedures – especially that involving a cord – are markedly less flexible and developed. His sexagesimal graduation of the staff, which he claims as his own innovation, may have been inspired by the Babylonian or Arabic tradition; it certainly does not sound Greek. His unit is the cubit, universally found among Babylonians, Greeks and Islam alike; but his use of a 100-cubit cord points, as we saw, to a Graeco-Egyptian source. His sighting tube is not paralleled on the dioptra in any Greek manual, but is found by itself in an early Greek context (Chapter 2.A) and might be a descendant of the tube for surveying qanats underground (Chapter 10). Overall, then, the sighting tubes and the use of cords suggest a source early in the history of the dioptra and of Alexandrian origin or at least under Alexandrian influence.

It is equally difficult to abstract directly from Hero any detail about his sources. He makes it quite plain that by the first century AD there

[20] Lewis 1997, 27–31.

was already a considerable literature on surveying in all its forms, much of which he found obscure, incomplete or plain wrong. There was variety, too, in this literature, in that different writers had used different versions of the dioptra; but he refrains from naming any of his fore-bears. Nevertheless, many if not most of his exercises were evidently inherited from them, even if the detail of their solutions was modified to suit his own instrument. This is implied by his own words and con-firmed by the correspondence between a number of his exercises and those of Africanus and the Anonymus. Hero's standard unit of length is also the cubit. Despite being based in Alexandria he uses no specifically Egyptian units at all, which rather suggests that his sources, unlike al-Karaji's, were not Alexandrian.

As for the Anonymus, he too says that he drew on the books of a number of predecessors. He too names few names: Archimedes and Hero and Euclid as geometers and authorities for measuring areas and volumes, but only Hero as a surveyor. Direct copying from Hero is evident in **Anonymus 10**, taken verbatim, with acknowledgement, from *Dioptra* **31**, and in the first part of **11** on astronomy, paraphrased without acknowledgement from *Dioptra* **32**. A number of his other exercises are clearly and closely related to Hero's. Whether these repre-sent direct borrowing, or borrowing from Hero's sources, is harder to tell. In their introductions, both writers adopt a supercilious attitude to those who had gone before, and both dwell on measuring wall heights. The Anonymus differs from Hero in that he gives lengths not in cubits but in fathoms, which were the standard Byzantine unit for land meas-urement;[21] no doubt he merely converted whatever units he found in his sources.

Apart from his debt to Hero, the Anonymus also shows a close corre-spondence to Africanus. Africanus' opening discussion of Euclid and the right-angled triangle with bisected sides may well be an example of the 'lofty theoretical concepts' which the Anonymus found in the old books and banished from his own. Their introductions share a specific reference to river widths and wall heights, and while the Anonymus' river exercise is lost, his wall exercise (**2**) is closely related to **Africanus 4**, which shares the same technical terms, found nowhere else, for the dioptra stand. **Anonymus 7** and **Africanus 2** are two very different

[21] Schilbach 1970b, 22–6.

exercises in which, as we shall later find, the Anonymus' dioptra also has a different type of sight from Africanus'. Yet these two chapters share an identical phrase: in both of them the surveyor sights on 'a rock or bush or some other distinctive object'. It does seem that Africanus and the Anonymus shared at least one common source, whether they drew on it directly or at second or third hand.

In putting a date on the exercises in al-Karaji, the Anonymus and Africanus, the principal weapon in our armoury is, once again, the reference letters. In lettering a diagram the great majority of Greek writers began with A and (with one very important exception which will be spelt out shortly) ran through the alphabet as far as they needed.[22] Hero is a prime example. So is the Anonymus (or his source), whose longest sequence runs from A to M, and al-Karaji's source went from A to Ξ. Sometimes a small clutch of letters is missing from the sequence. This is especially the case with geometers, as if they had amended a draft by rubbing out a line with its associated letters and, understandably, had not bothered to move the following letters back to fill the gap.

A very few writers, however, did not complete a straightforward alphabetical sequence but finished it off with letters selected apparently at random. Archimedes was particularly addicted to these, most notably in *On Conoids and Spheroids*, *On Spirals*, and the *Method*, where we find, for example, ΑΒΓΔΕΗΘΙΛΜΡΥΦ, ΑΒΓΔΕΖΗΘΡΣΤΨ, and ΑΒΓΔΕΖΘΙΝΥΩ.[23] In the same way Africanus, whose series in three cases run smoothly from A to E or Z, once (2) has ΑΗΘΙΚ-ΡΥΦ. Since this chapter is in a sense a continuation of 1, the absence of ΒΓΔΕΖ is understandable and paralleled elsewhere;[24] but the ΡΥΦ at the end defies any obvious logic. After Archimedes, much the closest parallel is Biton's *Construction of War Engines and Artillery*, addressed to an Attalus, a king of Pergamon whom he perhaps served as a military

---

[22] In a long series such as in **Dioptra 6, 18** and **20** which ran beyond the standard alphabet they would continue with the archaic letters Ϛ, Ϙ and ϡ, and then start the alphabet again with dashed letters (/A etc).

[23] Archimedes, *On Conoids and Spheroids* 20, 30, *Method* 12.

[24] Thus Apollonius of Perge, *Conics* II 52 has consecutive figures lettered A-Λ and M-X. There are plenty of similar examples in Euclid. Aristotle, *Physics* VI 2 has in one figure AB and Γ-K and in the next AB and ΛΜΞΠΡΣΧ, AB being common to both, as is the A in **Africanus 1-2**.

engineer. As I argue elsewhere, the addressee was Attalus II and the date 156/5 BC.[25] The book is a compilation of earlier specifications for catapults and siege engines, and the reference letters may be Biton's or may be the original authors'. The most relevant series run ΑΔΕΚΛΜ ΝΞΠΤΨ, ΑΔΕΖΘΜΝΦΨ and ΑΘΙΜΤΦΧ. While the irregularity resembles Africanus', in itself it proves nothing.

Another and more important factor, however, also comes into play. The series in **Africanus 2** (ΑΗΘΙΚΡΥΦ), **Anonymus 7** (ΑΒΓ-ΔΕΖΗΘΙΚΛΜ) and **al-Karaji 1** (ΑΒΓΔΕΖΗΘΙΚΛΜΝΞ when transliterated into Greek) all include the letter I,[26] which seems to be an infallible criterion for dating. To quote my own words from an earlier book,

Tedious perusal of hundreds of letter series . . . reveals that [the letter] I was only employed in such series before the time of Christ, not after. The earlier authors certainly did not use I as a matter of course: only in a few of Archimedes' works is it found in a majority of the diagrams, in a number of authors it is a rarity, and in others it is non-existent. The later writers, however, simply did not include it.[27] The presence of I, then, in a series which is long enough to reach it, tells us that it is early. Contrariwise the absence of I is no indicator of date.[28]

No letter I is to be found in the whole of Hero's works; he must meticulously have re-lettered every instance in the large volume of material that he borrowed from earlier centuries.

This dating technique immediately pushes al-Karaji's source, and

---

[25] Lewis 1999a.

[26] The other series in Africanus and the Anonymus do not extend far enough into the alphabet. Had they done so, they too might, for all we know, have included I.

[27] Users of I: Archytas, Aristotle, Euclid, pseudo-Aristotle in *Mechanical Problems*, Archimedes (notably in *On Spirals, Sand-reckoner, Quadrature of the Parabola, On Floating Bodies* II), Apollonius of Perge, Eratosthenes, Biton, Potamon as quoted by Simplicius, Asclepiodotus. All are of the first century BC or earlier. Where late writers such as Eutocius, Pappus or Alexander of Aphrodisias were commenting on earlier ones, they necessarily employed the same series and even the same diagrams which might well include I; but in original writings of the first century AD and later (Hero, Ptolemy, Theon of Smyrna, Diophantus, Serenus, Pappus, Proclus, Olympiodorus) I have not found a single example. Modern editions of Ptolemy, *Almagest* III 4 and Theon of Alexandria, *Commentary* 527 both have redrawn diagrams incorporating an intrusive I which is neither mentioned nor necessary in the text.

[28] Lewis 1997, 27–8.

the sources for at least these sections of Africanus and the Anonymus, back to the first century BC at the latest. It also brings us back to Biton, who remarks (**Source 11**) that the height of siege towers should be tailored to the height of walls by an unspecified method which he, as a specialist in dioptrics, had described in his *Optics*, a book sadly now lost. The disastrous consequences of failing to make towers the right height is also the subject of an anecdote of Athenaeus Mechanicus (**Source 12**), who may include a reference to Biton's *Optics*. The possibility is thus strengthened that Biton was one of the earlier authors on surveying whose unsatisfactory and turgid books are castigated by Hero and the Anonymus in their introductions.[29] What is more, the Anonymus knew and had read Biton's *Construction of War Engines*, which he cites in his *Siegecraft*.[30] Whether he had also read Biton's *Optics* we cannot prove. But we have two sets of facts. First, Africanus, the Anonymus and al-Karaji copied from their source or sources the lettering series which included I and must therefore have originated before Christ, while Africanus' series is very irregular. Second, before 156 BC Biton wrote a treatise on surveying and, in another book (known to the Anonymus), used lettering series which included I and tended to be irregular. It seems likely, though again beyond proof, that these two sets of facts are more than coincidence. Even if they did quarry Biton, the authors of all the manuals – and particularly the Anonymus – may of course have quarried other sources too. The important point is that at least some of their sources dated from before the Christian era.

C. THE MINOR SOURCES

These need not detain us long, for compared with the treatises they tell us little. Biton and Athenaeus have already been mentioned. Hero gives a general summary of what geodesy entails (**Source 13**), but outside the treatises and a brief and scathing remark by Vitruvius (**Source 3**) there is a general lack of references to the use of the dioptra for what we would call civil engineering. In addition to Hero, three sources talk of it for measuring mountain heights (**Sources 74–6**). Of the three men-

---

[29] This possibility was pointed out by Vincent 1858, 174–5n.
[30] Anonymus Byzantinus, *Siegecraft* 271.7.

tions of the dioptra in military service, two are unremarkable (**Sources 15–16**), although Anna's implication that the dioptra still existed in the twelfth century is interesting for the lateness of the date. Balbus' corrupt text, however (**Source 14**), is difficult to understand. He uses the word *ferramentum*, which is applied elsewhere both to the groma and to its stand (Chapter 5.B). But while the groma was entirely appropriate for Balbus' tasks of laying out straight lines and finding the width of a river, it was emphatically incapable of surveying heights as Balbus was also doing. Possibly, of course, he had both a groma and a dioptra with him. The curious fact, which will come in for fuller discussion later, is that there is no certain evidence for the use of the dioptra in the Roman army, nor even in the Latin-speaking half of the Mediterranean.

Further to *Dioptra* **32** and **Anonymus 11**, the use of the dioptra for astronomy is attested by **Sources 17–20**. Of these, Strabo refers to the simple taking of the midday altitude of the sun (**Source 20**), while Attalus and Geminus (**Sources 18–19**) talk of a rotary function which demands a full-blown dioptra, and could not be performed by the Hipparchan version. In connection with measuring the circumference of the earth, Simplicius mentions the dioptra for identifying stars at the zenith and the intervals between stars (**Source 69**). The remaining extracts (**Sources 21–4**) are all from late lexica and glossaries and tell us little.[31]

D. THE PLANE ASTROLABE

The principal descendant of the dioptra was the plane astrolabe, which, though applied in Roman times only to astronomy and astrology, deserves brief discussion here because of the light which it sheds on its

---

[31] The *astrabister* of **Source 21** is the same word as *astraphister* and is taken by LSJ and Supplement to be a levelling or surveying instrument. True, it is 'like a *dioptron*'; but as we saw in Chapter 2.A, *dioptra* can denote the window in a catapult frame through which the arrow passes. *Astrabister* is found only in Hesychius, *astraphister* only in lists of catapult components in 330–322 BC (*IG* II² 1627.349, 1628.522, 1629.998, 1631.229–30). It derives from *astraphes*, 'not turning back'. I suggest it was a 'rebound-preventer', some kind of funnel to guide the arrow through the window of the catapult, preventing it from hitting the frame and rebounding into the operator's face. If so, *astrabister* is irrelevant to surveying.

parent.[32] No ancient example has survived.[33] It is not to be confused with the armillary astrolabe already described, which was designed to take the ecliptic coordinates of a heavenly body and which is meant whenever the term 'astrolabe' occurs in Ptolemy's *Almagest*. The plane astrolabe, in contrast, had much wider application as a calculating device capable of working out many different kinds of problems of spherical astronomy.

While the astrolabe closely resembled the dioptra suspended in vertical mode, the intricacies of its front side hardly concern us except for the clues they offer to dating. It was very probably Hipparchus in the second century BC who first worked out how to project a spherical map, as of the heavens, on to a flat surface. Certainly, as Price remarks, 'Hipparchus was able to solve problems on the sphere without a knowledge of spherical trigonometry, and it is therefore very reasonable to assume that his method was that of stereographic projection.'[34] Its first practical application, certainly by the first century BC, seems to have been in the anaphoric clock. The kernel of this most ingenious device was a bronze disc engraved with a map of the stars in stereographic projection centred on the north celestial pole. The sun was represented by a movable marker placed on the ecliptic in its currently correct position relative to the constellations. This disc was rotated, one revolution a day, by water power. In front of it stood a fixed and concentric grid of wires, also in stereographic projection, representing the celestial coordinate lines and the horizon proper to the location of the clock. The position of the sun marker relative to these hour lines and to the horizon told the position of the sun in the sky, and therefore the time, even at night.[35]

The next step, it would seem, was to reverse the arrangement. The coordinate lines were now engraved on a stationary disc, and in front of

---

[32] The early history of the astrolabe is still a matter of some debate. There are three items of essential reading: Neugebauer 1949, Price 1957, 603–9, and Segonds 1981, which between them provide the background to much of this section.

[33] Fragments of clay discs found in Ashurbanipal's library are sometimes confusingly called Babylonian astrolabes. But they are only diagrams, not observational instruments. Likewise what is called a planisphere is merely a crude star map on a disc, with no grid (Weidner 1915, 62–112).

[34] Price 1957, 603. Dicks 1960, 194–207, however, is dubious about Hipparchus' role in stereographic projection.

[35] Vitruvius IX 8.8–15; Drachmann 1954; Noble and Price 1968.

it was a rotatable open-work grid (the spider or *arachne*), forming a map of selected stars (carried on pointers) and of the ecliptic circle. The stationary disc was the planisphere, the theory of which was described by Ptolemy in his treatise of that name, now surviving only in a Latin translation from an Arabic intermediary. In this he mentions the 'horoscopic instrument' and its spider (**Source 25**). What was this? One possibility is that it had other features which he does not name, and was already a true astrolabe. The other possibility is that it was a halfway stage consisting of only the front of the true astrolabe. The main argument for this is that the Latin text does not call the instrument an astrolabe and, because the word was perfectly familiar both to Islam and to medieval Europe, the original Greek very probably did not call it an astrolabe either. Since the name means 'star-taker', and was applied by Ptolemy to his armillary version which did sight stars, the horoscopic instrument of the *Planisphere* was therefore probably not an observational device but merely a desk-top calculator. If star or sun altitudes were needed for the problem in hand, they could no doubt be taken with an ordinary dioptra and the resulting figures fed into the planisphere.[36]

The true plane astrolabe was the result of the marriage of the planisphere and the dioptra. The disc was made to hang vertically from a ring, and its back was indistinguishable from the dioptra, with vertical and horizontal diameter lines, degree marks around at least one of the upper quadrants, and a pivoting alidade. The shadow square and other features found on the back of later astrolabes were an Islamic addition. Ptolemy's *Tetrabiblos* mentions the horoscopic astrolabe under that name (**Source 26**), which implies that, like his armillary astrolabe, it was used for observing star positions. So whatever the truth about the instrument in the *Planisphere*, we can be reasonably confident that with the instrument in the *Tetrabiblos* we have reached the true astrolabe. Unfortunately there is little indication which book came first, or exactly when: the middle of the second century AD is the closest date we can give.

The body of the later standard astrolabe was known (in Latin) as the

---

[36] Neugebauer formerly thought (1949, 242) that it was a full-blown astrolabe, but later changed his mind (1975, 866). At the same time he ignored the reference in the *Tetrabiblos* and assigned the first evidence for the true astrolabe to Theon.

mater or womb because it was recessed to hold a number of thin discs, each engraved with the coordinate lines appropriate to a different latitude so that the use of the instrument was not limited to one place. The *mater* (under the name *docheion*, 'receptacle') is first mentioned by Philoponus.[37] But, interestingly, the idea already existed in the mid-second century AD. A portable sundial from Aquileia in north Italy, whose lid is formed of a medallion struck in AD 140–3, consists of a shallow box similarly containing four plates engraved with hour-lines for various latitudes.[38] Price assumed that this sundial *mater* was copied from the astrolabe, which was therefore already developed; but the reverse could be equally true, that the alternative latitude discs in the astrolabe imitated those in the sundial.

As Table 3.1 (p. 80) shows, the back of the astrolabe shared much of the terminology of the dioptra itself, and it was used in much the same way. The only significant difference between the two was that the astrolabe was hung by the ring from the observer's finger, not from a stand, and the same precision of sighting could not be expected. As Philoponus clearly describes (**Source 32**), the altitude of a star was taken by direct sighting, and that of the sun by directing its ray through one sight on to the other. The resulting angle was set on the front of the astrolabe, where it was converted for a given date and a given latitude into the time; and it also depicted the whole state of the heavens at the time of observation, which provided information of great value, especially to the astrologer.

While Ptolemy's references supply little or no detail, it is quite clear that the lost treatise by Theon of Alexandria, written about 370 and attested by the Souda, al-Ya'qubi and the *Fihrist* (**Sources 27–9**), dealt in considerable depth with the true astrolabe. Its title, *Hypomnema*, implies, as was normal at this date, that it was a commentary on some earlier work. It formed the basis of the very clear descriptions by Philoponus in the early sixth century and by Severus Sebokht in the mid-seventh (**Sources 32–3**). Meanwhile, the astrolabe was used both by Paul of Alexandria (writing in 378) and by Heliodorus and his brother Ammonius, who was Philoponus' teacher, in an observation in

[37] It is conceivable that the *gaster*, 'belly', of the dioptra which Hero divided into degrees for astronomical work (**Dioptra 32**) corresponds to the *mater*; but much more likely it refers to the normal surface of the disc.

[38] Price 1969, 249–53. The sundial, now in Vienna, is very small, 38 mm in diameter.

503 (**Sources 30–1**): only the plane astrolabe would do the jobs which they specify. It was still in use, as pseudo-Stephen attests (**Source 34**), well over a century after the Arab conquest of Egypt. It was adopted very extensively by the Arabs, who, as a later chapter will show, employed it not only for astronomical and astrological purposes but also for terrestrial surveying in exactly the same way as the Greeks had used the dioptra; and from the Arabs it was passed to western Europe. Whether knowledge of the astrolabe continued unbroken in the Byzantine world is open to some doubt. Certainly Kamateros' poem of the eleventh century (**Source 35**) drew on ancient material and shows no sign of Arabic influence; yet the only extant example made by Byzantines, the Brescia astrolabe, dated by its inscription to 1062, is contemporary with Kamateros but has a number of Arabic features about it.[39] As with the dioptra, any surviving knowledge was probably lost with the Latin conquest of 1204, for with the revival of interest in the thirteenth century the oriental influence on Byzantine treatises on the astrolabe is very much more pronounced.[40]

E. THE STANDARD DIOPTRA

(Greek technical terms are listed in Table 3.1, p. 80.)

We have two reasonably detailed specifications of a dioptra. Hero's is quite untypical, and al-Karaji's is capable of being mounted only vertically. No doubt the Anonymus described the ordinary type, together with instructions for its use; but this is lost in the lacuna in his text. What does emerge from his book, however, and is confirmed by Africanus, is that the dioptra could be mounted on different stands for working either in an essentially horizontal plane (though without any means of being set precisely horizontal) or in a vertical one. For convenience, let us call these two fundamentally different positions the horizontal and vertical modes. For the latter, our prime sources are **Africanus 4** and **al-Karaji 1–2**, the one for taking altitudes, the other

[39] Dalton 1926, who thought it purely Byzantine; but cf. Neugebauer 1949, 249 n. 57.
[40] One fragment of c. 1300 or earlier is published in Heiberg 1912, xv-xvi. Five treatises of the fourteenth century, poorly edited by Delatte 1939, 195–271, either lean heavily on earlier sources or are translations from Arabic and Persian. See Segonds 1981, 69–88 for discussion.

for levelling. The dioptra was hung by a ring from a peg on a stand which Africanus called a lampstand. Al-Karaji says that, at least in his version, this was only about 4 spans (2 cubits, about 1 m) tall, so that the surveyor did not stand to take his readings, but squatted. Just like an astrolabe, it acted as its own plumb bob so that one arm of the cross engraved on the disc stood vertical and the other horizontal. When the alidade with its pointer was set to coincide with the horizontal diameter, the line of sight through it was horizontal. This was the arrangement for levelling. Al-Karaji is concerned with nothing else, and we will later consider the procedure in detail.

In contrast to al-Karaji, **Africanus 4**, though hanging his dioptra in the vertical mode, is concerned with measuring the height of a wall. He therefore ignores the horizontal setting, but tilts the alidade to take a sight line to the top of the wall in one direction and to project the same line down to the ground in the other. **Anonymus 2** follows the same procedure as Africanus but, because the beginning of the chapter is lost and because he also introduces the horizontal mode, he is not so easy to follow. But enough survives of the chapter to reconstruct the essentials of the lost part. Because the true horizontal is irrelevant, the angle from the wall top to the ground can be taken with the dioptra mounted either in the horizontal mode but with the disc tilted appropriately (ΓE), or in the vertical mode (HΘ) as explained by Africanus. The end result will be identical. Further confusion is caused by the Anonymus misapplying the word *lychnia* to the dioptra rather than to the stand. *Lychnia* can only mean a lampstand, an upright post with a bracket at the top for hanging the lamp from; and the Anonymus must be wrong where Africanus is right.[41] But he adds, quite correctly, that the vertical mode is essential for other forms of surveying such as levelling for aqueducts. This is because the horizontal mode offers no means of taking a truly horizontal line, and because in some versions of the dioptra the sights were of a design

[41] Earlier commentators (not that there have been many) have had trouble with these passages, being misled by the manuscript corruption of the word for 'sights' and by the Anonymus' misuse of the word *lychnia*. Vincent 1858, 351 and Kiely 1947, 27 thought that the stand was a surveyor's staff carrying a target like Hero's. Vincent 1858, 350–1 and 354n. thought that the sights were glass tubes for water levelling like Hero's. Kiely 1947, 285 and Stone 1928, 234–5 thought that the dioptra was merely a bar pivoting on a post. Vieillefond 1970, 154–6n. and 158n. saw it as two bars in the form of a cross which, in the vertical mode, could somehow be tilted.

that could be used only in the vertical mode for some purposes and in the horizontal for others. To this we shall return. The essential point to remember is that in the vertical mode the disc hung from the stand, as is clearly illustrated by the drawing in **al-Karaji 1**.

In the horizontal mode the dioptra was used for observing or setting out lines or points on the ground, rather as a plane table is used today, although nothing was actually plotted on the dioptra itself. There was no provision for setting the instrument precisely horizontal and, if occasion arose when that might be desirable, no doubt a few drops of water on the disc could serve as an *ad hoc* level. But it did not normally matter if an object being sighted was a few degrees above or below the horizontal. The Anonymus and Africanus differ on how to deal with this eventuality. **Anonymus 3–5** and **7** tell us to set the disc 'so that its plane coincides with the given points' (or words to that effect) or to 'tilt the disc a little' to bring the object into the sights. In contrast, **Africanus 2** and **3** mention nothing of the sort. They differ because they are using different sights.

This brings us to the alidade, a straight bar pivoted on the centre of the disc. Each end was pointed to align with the arms of the engraved cross or (in astronomical work) to set against the degree marks round the rim. Near each end was mounted a sight or pinnule, a small square plate or vane rising at right angles to the bar. The manuscripts of Africanus call this the *angeion*, a 'vessel' or 'container'; the manuscripts of the Anonymus call it the *augeion*.[42] Although it does not appear as such in the dictionary, *augeion* is a perfectly good word: its compound *diaugeion* is attested, denoting a hole in the sight of an astronomical instrument,[43] and it is surely the correct word for the dioptra's sight. In each sight was a hole; and it is here that the differences begin to emerge. Al-Karaji's tube served of course the same function, and its bore was large enough to insert a thick needle: say about 3 or 4 mm. The alidade probably replaced the tube sight because it was easier to make, lighter in weight, and could take a smaller aperture. **Anonymus 3** and **7** speak of sighting 'through the holes of the alidade' and **11** 'through the two holes'. For accuracy of sighting with an alidade, the

---

[42] Faced with the choice Vincent, followed by Vieillefond, unfortunately opted for *angeion*.

[43] Proclus, *Outline* III 16, 25, VI 11 on the meridional armillary and the meteoroscope. The terminations vary in the manuscripts between *-eion*, *-ion* and *-ia*.

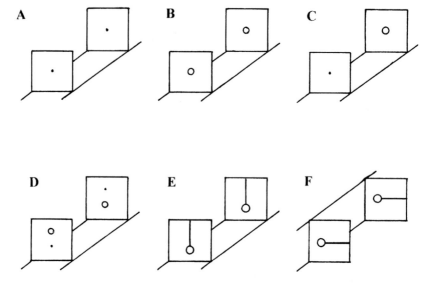

FIG. 3.3. Types of sight. Diagrammatic only. All except C bi-directional.

hole in the sight nearer to the observer – let us refer to it as the back-sight – needs to be very small: even one of 0.25 mm aperture, when the eye is close to it, gives a surprisingly wide field of view. But if the hole in the other sight, the foresight, is equally small (Fig. 3.3, A) it is impossible to see through it the object being sighted.

There are a number of solutions to the problem, some more satisfactory than others. Both holes can be made relatively large (Fig. 3.3, B), which makes it easier to find the object and centre it in the foresight but, because it is difficult to centre the eye exactly to a large backsight, such an arrangement leads to inaccuracy. The backsight can be left small and the foresight made large (Fig. 3.3, C), as in Ptolemy's parallactic instrument, which is fine provided that the alidade is used for sighting only in one direction; but this does not apply to the dioptra. On more recent alidades the problem is solved with two pairs of holes (Fig. 3.3, D), one for use in each direction, or even with very large openings in the foresights equipped with fine crossed wires to centre the object on, as in Schöne's reconstruction of Hero's dioptra (Fig. 3.6). Because there is no evidence for or likelihood of this arrangement in the ancient world, because C is not applicable, and because A is virtually unworkable, we must conclude that the Anonymus' sights were of type B, with relatively large holes. Al-Karaji's tube would fall into the same category. Yet the holes, or the tube, would still restrict the field of view, which is why the Anonymus had to set the disc so that 'its plane coincides with the given points' in order to see them, and when aiming at a new object had to 'tilt the disc a little' to bring it into sight.[44]

Africanus however does not tilt his disc, even in **2**, which, as we saw, must derive from the same source as **Anonymus 7**. Instead, his dioptra has a *schiste* sight. The very fact that this type is specified implies that other types which were not *schistai* were available and were mentioned in the same source. *Schiste* means 'split', 'divided' or 'slit': a *chitoniskos schistos* was a tunic slit up the side, like the present-day fashion in skirts. Africanus therefore used a slit sight, of the kind still common today: a narrow slit running for most of the height of the sight vane from a relatively large hole near the lower end (Fig. 3.3, E). When the instrument is in the horizontal mode it allows a very much taller field of view than any hole. The eye can look through the slit in the backsight at any point in its height, and find the object either in the hole in the foresight or even outside the foresight, but in both cases using the slit to align it on. Within reason, the taller the sight vane the taller the field of view. If the slits are of the right aperture and the sight plates are of the right width and at the right distance from the end of the alidade (and hence from the eye), the sighting can be extremely accurate. Although the backsight slit is out of focus, the foresight plate can be readily centred in it and the object accurately centred on the slit (Fig. 3.4). With the dioptra in the vertical mode, the slit of course lies horizontal (Fig. 3.3, F), which makes the accurate taking of a height very much easier. That is why Africanus with his slit sights hangs the dioptra vertically for taking heights, while the Anonymus with his somewhat crude hole sights gives the option of vertical and horizontal modes, for both of which they work equally well (or badly).

The need to tilt raises the question of how the dioptra was mounted when in horizontal mode. There is no direct information at all. The only parameters are that the disc must be capable of being rotated on the stand, and being tilted on it. This implies a true universal joint, which is not totally impossible. The basic idea is present in the Cardan

---

[44] Vincent 1858, 361 translates the phrase not as 'tilt' but 'look a little above the disc'. But the verb *ananeuein* cannot bear this meaning.

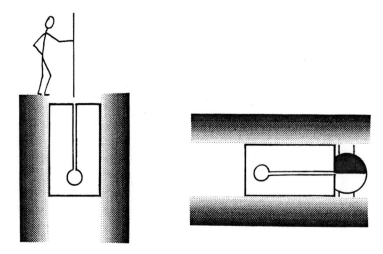

FIG. 3.4. Foresight and object seen through out-of-focus slit backsight.

suspension, twice recorded for the ancient world;[45] but there is no evidence that it existed in anything like the right form, and it might provide a somewhat unstable support for the disc. The next best device available, and surely the one employed, was the *karchesion*. This word is often translated as 'universal joint', but wrongly so because it could not turn in every direction. It was applied primarily to catapults, which were aimed by traversing in a horizontal plane and by elevating or depressing in a vertical one, but which did not need to be tilted sideways.[46] It was also to be found on cranes and similar devices whose jib had to be swung both sideways and up and down.[47] Illustrations survive from Hero's *Artillery* and from the Anonymus' *Siegecraft* (Fig. 3.5). The difficulty is that a *karchesion* allowed tilting in only one direction. If it was necessary to set out lines at right angles from a hill top, a dioptra mounted on a *karchesion* could be depressed towards, for example, the north and south, but not to east and west. This was perhaps another reason for the introduction of slit sights. But the strongest argument for the use of the *karchesion* is the fact that Hero's dioptra, with its semicircular gear for elevating or depressing the disc in one direction only, reproduces exactly the same effect.

---

[45] Philo, *Pneumatics* 56 (which seems to be genuine), *Mappae Clavicula* 288-O.

[46] See Marsden 1971, 51, commenting on Hero, *Artillery* 88.

[47] Polybius VIII 5.10, Athenaeus Mechanicus 35.4–36.5, Vitruvius X 2.10, 16.3.

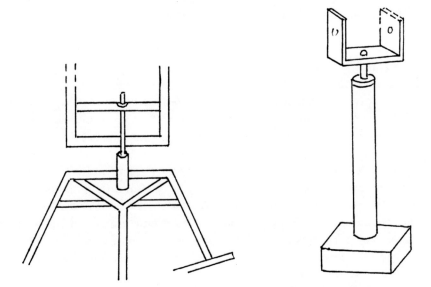

FIG. 3.5. The *karchesion*: left, for catapult (Hero, *Artillery*, after Wescher 1867, 90); right, for assault bridge (Anonymus Byzantinus, *Siegecraft*, after Wescher 1867, 271).

Anonymus 7 rotates the disc in horizontal mode 'by means of the socket which fits over the gudgeon, or of the screw (*styrax*) if there is one on the dioptra'. Although specific enough, this is not good evidence for the standard dioptra because the terminology of the socket and gudgeon and the idea of the traversing screw appears to be borrowed from **Dioptra 3**. While it must remain an open question whether Hero himself had borrowed the arrangement from some predecessor, the likelihood is that the Anonymus is updating what is undoubtedly an older source with a little Heronian sophistication. In either event the Anonymus has updated the standard classical word for 'screw' – *kochlias* – into its Byzantine equivalent, *styrax*, just as in the *Siegecraft* he has updated the same word when it occurs in Biton's *Construction of War Engines*.[48]

---

[48] Biton 58.12; Anonymus, *Siegecraft* 271.4 and diagram. In classical Greek *styrax* and *styrakion* denoted a spear-butt; to the Byzantines *styrakion* meant a spiral staircase or a column with spiral decoration: Constantine Porphyrogennetos, *De cerimoniis* II 151.14 and note on p. 230; *Patria of Constantinople* III 203, 213; Hippolytus of Thebes Frag. 7.1.

As to the dioptra's stand, only common sense can guide us. Al-Karaji's instrument, small and light, hung from a simple pole which was apparently held upright only by hand. But Africanus' and the Anonymus' 'lampstand', like the support for their dioptras when in horizontal mode, was self-standing. The main prerequisite was stability. The dioptra in **Africanus 2** and **4** is 'fixed' or 'mounted' (*pegnunai*), while the Anonymus 'stands' or 'positions' his dioptra. It is conceivable that a pole with a pointed iron-shod foot stuck into the earth might be sufficiently stable in the heavy soils of northern Europe or the silt of Egypt, but hardly in light and stony Mediterranean soils. The same considerations apply to any fairly heavy instrument, though the slender groma seems to have managed with only a single post. For everything else, including the dioptra in both vertical and horizontal mode, a tripod seems the only answer, then as now.[49] It would hardly resemble the modern version with telescopic legs that is neatly folded for transport, but would probably have shorter fixed legs supporting a vertical column, not unlike the arrangement for catapults (Fig. 3.5). Hero's dioptra was carried on a 'small column' – *styliskos* – and so were other astronomical instruments, although, since they were not used in the field, their columns rose from a flat base rather than from tripod legs.[50]

For astronomical work the requirements were distinctly different. With the dioptra in vertical mode, altitudes above the horizon of stars, sun or moon could be taken straightforwardly, like terrestrial altitudes. The apparent size of the sun and moon could in theory be taken (**Dioptra 2**, **Anonymus 11**), but because of the very small angular diameter the Hipparchan dioptra, designed for the purpose, would give far better results. The angular distances between stars could be taken by setting the disc in the appropriate plane, as both **Anonymus 11** and **Dioptra 32** describe. Finding the right plane would be a matter of delicate adjustment, yet it would have to be done, and the sightings taken, very smartly before the stars in question had moved out of the plane.

---

[49] In the only attempt at a graphic reconstruction of a pre-Heronian dioptra that I know of, Adam 1982, fig. 1 (= Adam 1994, fig. 1) supplies a sturdy tripod. His dioptra, while presenting a workmanlike appearance and not implausibly carrying very tall sight vanes, is designed for use only in the horizontal mode and incorporates a circular alidade, two plumb-lines and a water level, all of which are certainly wrong.

[50] Proclus, *Outline* III 19–20, VI 15, diagram to IV 74 (Manitius p. 122): the meridional armillary, meteoroscope and water clock.

Star coordinates relative to the equator (right ascension or declination) could be taken by setting the disc in the plane of the equator or meridian, and similarly those relative to the ecliptic (longitude and latitude) (**Anonymus 11**). Attalus and Geminus (**Sources 18–19**) talk of following the stars in their circular courses. To achieve this, the supporting column would have to be inclined to point at the pole. Stars on the greatest circle, the equator, could then be followed by setting the disc at right angles to the column and turning either the disc or the alidade. For those on lesser circles such as the tropics the disc would be inclined to the column at the appropriate angle – about 66° for the tropic – and rotated around the column by the pivot at the base of the *karchesion*, while the alidade remained untouched.

Given a solid tripod, the stability of the dioptra in horizontal mode would cause no trouble. A much more thorny question is the mobility of the disc when in vertical mode. The problem is wind. Even if the disc is suspended not by an ordinary narrow ring but by a long sleeve, fitting fairly tightly over the peg on the stand to prevent yawing, only a slight breeze sets it visibly swinging and foils attempts at a really accurate reading. The problem is endemic to any device that relies on the principle of the plumb. Penrose, for example, remarked of the building of the Parthenon and the precise measurements he took of it,

We may also fairly presume that none but an instrument on the principle of the water-level could have been used with precision in the usual state of the Athenian weather. I was obliged to seize every opportunity which the occasional lulls between almost constant and often strong breezes would allow me, to obtain the long plumbs of the columns and other delicate observations.[51]

In the absence of a water level in the dioptra, or indeed in any serious ancient surveying instrument other than Hero's version, the only alternative is to try to reduce the swinging of the disc. The only possible approach, entirely hypothetical in the absence of evidence (although the Anonymus may have mentioned it in the lacuna in his text), is to protect the instrument by means of a portable shelter, which need be no more than light cloth spread over the simplest skeletal frame. This has at least the confirmation of later practice. When in 1612 Edward Pond was surveying the line of the New River for bringing water to

---

[51] Penrose 1888, 33n.

Table 3.1 Terminology of the dioptra

		Africanus	Anon.	Hero	Philoponus astrolabe	Byzantine astrolabe★	Astron. instr.+
disc	tympanon				•	•	
	epipedon				•	•	
cross	chiasmos			○	○	○	
alidade	kanon	•	•	•	•	•	•
	kanonion					•	
	dioptra	•	•	•	•	•	
	pechys, kathetos					•	
pointer	moirognomonion	•	•	•		•	
	akron, oxytes						•
sight	augeion	•					
	diaugeion		•				•
	(sy)stemation				•		•
hole	ope		•		•	•	•
	trypema				•		•
	trype				•		•
to sight	diopteuein	•	•	•	•	•	•
	katopteuein	•					
	epistrephein			•			
to turn (alidade)	peristrephein	•	•				
	paragein				•		
	periagein				•		

to tilt (disc, in hor. mode)	*ananeuein*	
	enklinein	
	parenklinein	
to tilt (alidade, in vertical mode)	*epiklinein*	•
	kinein	
	enklinein	
stand (for vertical mode)	*kamax = lychnia*	•
stand (for hor. mode)	*pageus*	
	styliskos	
tenon/socket	*tormos/choinikis*	
	kochlias	
traversing screw	*styrax*	

Notes:

★ From Kamateros (eleventh century) onwards.

+ Astronomical instruments are armillary astrolabe, parallactic instrument, meridional ring and Hipparchan dioptra, in Ptolemy, Proclus and Pappus.

○ Mentioned, but not named as *chiasmos*.

London, the accounts record the purchase of '4 Ells of Canvas att xvjd [16 pence] the elle for to make a Shelter for Mr Ponde's leavell'.[52]

Finally, for the material and size of the disc, al-Karaji specifies wood or brass and a diameter of 1½ spans or roughly 37 cm. Metal seems more suitable both for durability and to provide weight to reduce swaying in the wind. Whether al-Karaji's diameter was typical is hard to say. According to **Anonymus 11**, the rim should be divided for astronomical work into degrees and *lepta*, which normally signifies minutes of arc. This is hardly possible here. Of medieval astrolabes, that with the finest divisions is the Brescia one which, with a diameter of 37.5 cm, is also among the largest. Here the rim is divided into degrees and thirds of a degree, the marks being at a pitch of slightly more than a millimetre.[53] To mark minutes of arc at this pitch would entail a diameter of nearly 7 m, which is ridiculous; and *lepta* in the Anonymus must denote unspecified subdivisions, not minutes.[54] Whereas astrolabes were hand-held, which imposes a limit on size and weight, one might expect a dioptra on a stand to be larger and heavier that the largest astrolabe, which is 50 cm in diameter. Certainly the longer the alidade, the greater the accuracy in taking sights, as Hero appreciated when he made his water level 4 cubits (nearly 2 m) long. But this is far too great for the ordinary dioptra. In fact astronomical instruments were surprisingly small: the diameter of the meridional armillary was not less than half a cubit or roughly 25 cm, of the meteoroscope one cubit or about 50 cm.[55] It may therefore be that the diameter of the dioptra was of the same order.

F. HERO'S DIOPTRA

Except, inevitably, for the lacuna, Hero's description is very clear. So too are Schöne's reconstruction drawings (Figs. 3.6, 3.9), although they tend to err in the direction of the modern rather than the ancient

---

[52] Gough 1964, 51. Hill 1993, 194 similarly suggests that a shelter would be useful with al-Karaji's level.   [53] Dalton 1926, 133.

[54] Proclus, *Outline* III 9 divides the ring of the meridional armillary into degrees and 'as far as possible into smaller units' which he then proceeds to explain as minutes, *lepta*. But if the ring has the minimum diameter which he prescribes, half a cubit or about 25 cm, the exercise is as impossible as the Anonymus'.

[55] Proclus, *Outline* III 5; Pappus, *Commentary* 6.

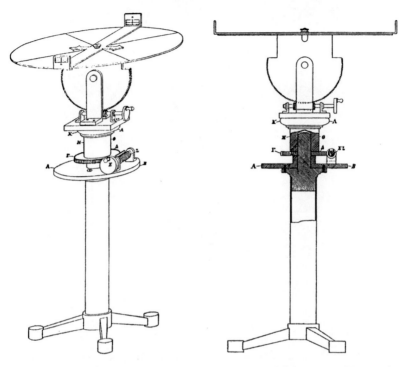

FIG. 3.6. Hero's dioptra: Schöne's reconstruction (Schöne 1899, Figs. 1–2).

engineer's approach to detail.[56] In places, Drachmann's drawings (Figs. 3.7, 3.8) and remarks improve on Schöne's.[57] Text and drawings together are self-explanatory, and need not detain us long, especially as Hero's dioptra was not in the main stream of development but a unique and perhaps misguided attempt at improving what, by its very simplicity, called for little improvement.

Hero's innovations were the gears for fine adjustment, and the water level in place of the alidade for levelling when the standard dioptra was in vertical mode. He was evidently, and rightly, proud of the gears, and especially of the tangent screws for slow motion with their groove to release the gear for fast motion; but one wonders if they were a really

[56] They were in fact drawn by an engineer, J. Neumann.
[57] The basic studies, apart from Schöne's text and translation, are still Schöne 1899 and Drachmann 1935. Venturi 1814 and Vincent 1858, though pioneering, are outdated.

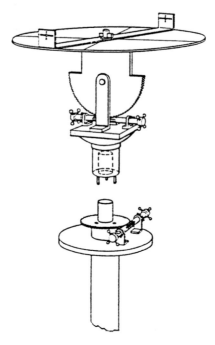

FIG. 3.7. Hero's dioptra: Drachmann's reconstruction (Drachmann 1957, Fig. 360, courtesy Oxford University Press).

necessary addition. The introduction of the water level meant that the new dioptra consisted of two alternative instruments sharing a common stand or column, in contrast to the old single all-purpose instrument with two different stands. Drachmann shows how both the dioptra proper and the water level were plugged into the column by three pins which fitted sockets in the traversing gear wheel.[58] He also points out that the word Hero uses for the stand (and found nowhere else) – *pageus* – is connected with *pegnunai*, which can mean 'to fix in the ground'. He therefore felt that the *pageus* was merely a spike stuck in the earth and, somewhat egregiously, that perhaps Hero's dioptra did not catch on because of the difficulty of supporting it in light Mediterranean soils. It is true that the manuscript diagrams illustrating the exercises show a single post (Fig. 3.10), but this is surely schematic.[59] *Pegnunai* in fact need mean no more than 'to fasten' or 'to mount': *pegmation* ('mounting'), another cognate word, is regular in Hero for the bearing of an axle. As with the standard dioptra, a tripod is

[58] Drachmann 1935.   [59] Drachmann 1969.

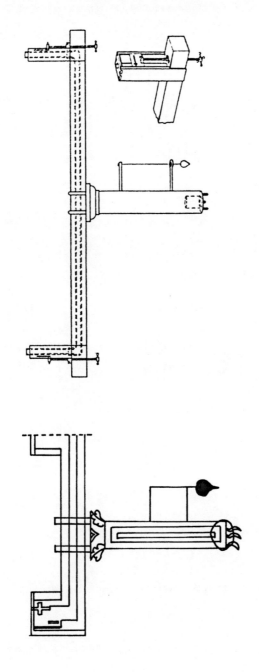

FIG. 3.8. Hero's water level: after Mynas Codex (Paris suppl. gr. 607 f. 64r) and Drachmann's reconstruction (Drachmann 1957, Fig. 361, courtesy Oxford University Press).

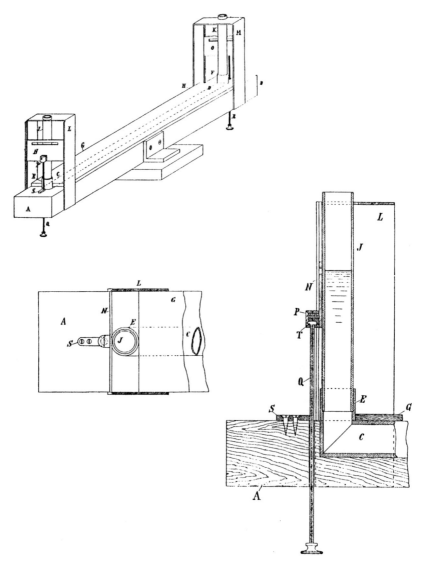

FIG. 3.9. Hero's water level: Schöne's reconstruction (Schöne 1899, Figs. 4–6).

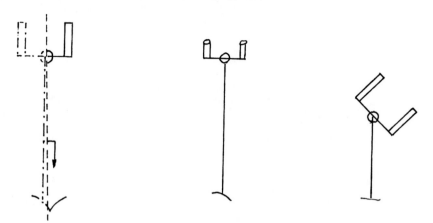

FIG. 3.10. Sketches of Hero's dioptra, after Mynas Codex. Left, chapter 12; centre, chapter 16; right, chapter 21 (Paris suppl. gr. 607, f. 69v, 71v, 74r).

necessary, if not quite so splay-footed as Schöne's. The manuscript drawings show that the column was set at least approximately vertical by means of a plumb-line. For another supposed illustration of the dioptra, see Appendix, B.

The Mynas Codex includes a sketch, evidently referred to in the text now lost in the lacuna, which appears to illustrate an experiment demonstrating how water rises to the same level at each end of a U-tube (Fig. 3.11).[60] If so, the water level is perhaps of Hero's own devising, and one wonders if he developed it in order to circumvent the effect of wind on the ordinary dioptra. At 4 cubits,[61] it is splendidly long, and should in theory provide very accurate readings. None the less the suspicion arises, as will shortly be spelled out, that it was no more infallible than the standard dioptra.

Hero's dioptra is sometimes described as a theodolite. This is hardly a justifiable label because a theodolite measures vertical and horizontal angles at the same time. In fact, despite Hero's boastful words in his introduction, his dioptra could do no more than its predecessors. Like

[60] Fully discussed by Drachmann 1968.
[61] Jones 1927, 140 complains that if the water level was 4 cubits long, Schöne's drawing (Fig. 3.6) shows the whole instrument standing over 3 m high, which would be unusable. The criticism is misplaced: the drawing shows not the water level but the dioptra proper, whose diameter is unknown.

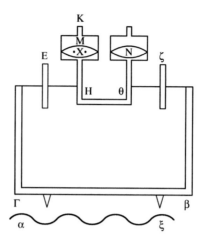

FIG. 3.11. Diagram apparently explaining how water finds its own level in a U-tube, after Mynas Codex (Paris suppl. gr. 607, f. 63v).

them, it operated in two modes, although the tasks it performed in each mode were rather different from before. With the water level attached, it levelled (**Dioptra 6** and probably part of **12**). In the horizontal mode it surveyed on the ground just like its forebears and, like theirs, its disc had sometimes to be tilted to bring the object into the sights (**8, 9**). Because these last two exercises, which are presumably based on an earlier source, have been updated with the phrase 'tilt the semicircle' (that is, the semicircular gear), they imply that the sights were holes, not slits. Still in the horizontal mode, Hero's dioptra also took altitudes (**12, 14, 21**). There is however a conflict here. All three chapters tell us to tilt or adjust not the disc or the semicircle, but the alidade on the disc. From this we might deduce that for altitudes the disc was turned to the vertical with the semicircular gear, and that the alidade was tilted as in the vertical mode with the standard dioptra. But the manuscript diagrams clearly show the dioptra is in horizontal, not vertical, mode (Fig. 3.10). The answer is perhaps that Hero drew for the exercises on different sources, and was not consistent in adapting them for his dioptra. We might thus guess that **8** and **9** were designed in the original for hole sights, and that therefore the disc had on occasion to be tilted, an operation which Hero updated by tilting the semicircle. On the other hand **12, 14** and **21** were perhaps originally designed for slit sights, the necessary corollary being that the disc was in vertical mode and that it was the alidade that was tilted. Hero should have amended it so that the disc was in horizontal mode and the semicircle was tilted; but he overlooked the anomaly and the alidade remained tilted, to our confusion.[62]

All this may shed a little light on the mysterious use of the word *chorobatein* in **Dioptra 12**. In the original exercise the dioptra would be in vertical mode throughout, with the alidade first tilted to sight on A and the rods ZH and ΘK and then turned to the horizontal to level to the rods. If Hero had fully adapted the exercise, one ought first to set the dioptra in horizontal mode with the disc tilted to sight on A, K and H, and then replace the disc with the water level for taking a horizontal sight to the rods. If the centre of the disc and the surface of the water were at exactly the same height, this would work. *Chorobatein* therefore, at least in Hero, means simply 'to take levels with the dioptra', and there is no reason to suppose that the chorobates was involved.

G. LEVELLING

Of all the functions of the dioptra, levelling – that is, determining the difference in height between two or more places – must have been among the most important, notably for irrigation channels and later for aqueducts. Three sources tell how it was carried out, and between them they give four different methods. The first three are relatively crude, and agree in placing the instrument at the starting point of the survey, which means that the height of the instrument above the ground has to be taken into account. In theory this height could always be the same, but with a tripod in soft or uneven terrain, and still more with a spike stuck to a greater or lesser depth into the earth, it would in practice be variable, and the resulting readings would not be exact. Only with Hero do we reach the more advanced (and still current) practice of placing the staff at the starting point, which renders the height of the instrument irrelevant. The only stations that matter are those of the staff, which rests on a single and preferably firm spot. Fig. 3.12 shows these methods in diagrammatic form, concentrating for the sake of simplicity on a single stage. For longer surveys (except in the case of Philo who does not seem to contemplate them) the process is

[62] Jones 1927, 140 can see no real use for the semicircle; but this taking of altitudes provides one.

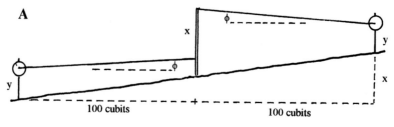

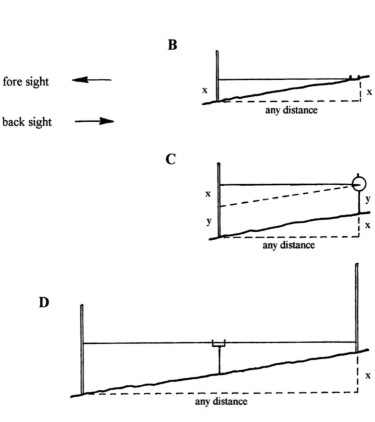

FIG. 3.12. Methods of levelling.

x = difference in height   y = height of instrument

A. Al-Karaji 1:   x = fore sight reading minus back sight reading
B. Philo: x = fore sight reading
C. Al-Karaji 2:   x = fore sight reading
D. Hero: x = fore sight reading minus back sight reading

90

continued by alternating the stations of the staff and the level. The final point is occupied by the instrument in A, by the staff in D, and by either in C. The surveyor records all the readings, finally adds up all the back sights and all the fore sights, and subtracts one total from the other to obtain the overall difference in level between the two terminal points.

It is difficult to be sure in what order the various methods were devised. Possibly the first three were of very much the same period, thought up in the study rather than in the field as alternative geometrical solutions to a given problem, and subsequent practice weeded out the inferior methods and suggested improvements to the better ones. They are given here in what seems to be a logical order, although hindsight may admittedly play a part in the sequence chosen.

Al-Karaji is concerned only with levelling for irrigation, and both his methods employ the same suspended dioptra with sighting tube, pointer and diameter lines. He specifies that the staff should be divided into 60 divisions, each subdivided as far as possible. Hill suggests that this was to facilitate calculations in relation to the distance between the staves,[63] which with al-Karaji's improved *mizan* was 30 cubits or 60 spans. This may well be true, provided that the divisions on the staff were also in recognised units such as fingers (i.e. dactyls). But the logic breaks down with al-Karaji's methods for the dioptra, in which the distance between the staves (where it is defined) is 100 cubits. For his first method the staff is 9 spans or $4\frac{1}{2}$ cubits long, with a length of one palm left blank at top and bottom. Since there are four fingers to a palm and six palms to a cubit, the length of the graduated section is $4\frac{1}{2} \times 24$ fingers less 2×4 fingers, or 100 fingers. Dividing this by sixty gives units of $1\frac{2}{3}$ fingers each, not very useful for calculating relationships to 100 cubits, whereas 100 fingers against 100 cubits makes perfect sense.[64] One therefore suspects that al-Karaji simply transferred his own sexagesimal division of the staves for the *mizan* to those for the dioptra without thinking out the implications.

To the modern mind Al-Karaji's first method of levelling seems unnecessarily cumbersome (Fig 3.12, A). The surveyor sets up the dioptra at one of the given points: in the example in **al-Karaji 1** the higher one. The staff is the kind just discussed, $4\frac{1}{2}$ cubits tall and with a

[63] Hill 1993, 190.
[64] The Hasimi cubit of 32 fingers used by Islamic surveyors gives the still less convenient total of 136 fingers.

red circle painted on the top and bottom graduation lines. It is held vertically by an assistant at a distance of 100 cubits as determined by a cord with a ring at each end, one held by the surveyor and the other attached to the staff. The surveyor sights with the tube at the top circle on the staff and, without moving the tube relative to the disc, he transfers the dioptra to a point 100 cubits beyond the staff. Sighting back with tube still at the same angle, he signals to the assistant who moves a cursor carrying a red circle up or down the staff until it coincides with the line of sight. Either the assistant on the spot, or the surveyor coming back, records the position of the cursor on the graduations. Its distance from the top circle is the difference in height between the two stations of the dioptra. It is noteworthy that this method cannot be used on a slope that averages more than 100 fingers in 200 cubits, or 1 in 48. By shortening the length of cord it could cope with steeper gradients, as indeed he says; but as first specified the method is designed for relatively flat land rather than hilly terrain.

This method perhaps gave rise to a simpler variation on the theme, which came with the realisation that it is more reliable and accurate to aim the tube horizontally than at a fore sight angle which has to be preserved for the back sight. Angled sighting is thus obviated; and the distance between instrument and staff is thereby no longer restricted by a cord of specific length, but can be anything that visibility permits. Of this method we have two early versions. The more basic is Philo's (**Source 10**; Fig. 3.12, B). His purpose is to build up a plot of land until it is level and suitable for irrigation. The surveyor lays beside the outlet of the water source a plank which he makes as horizontal as possible with, one presumes, a builder's level. On it he places what seems to be a plain alidade. At the far end of the plot an assistant holds vertical (and the importance of verticality is properly emphasised) a staff that is not graduated as such, but merely painted with coloured circles or other marks easily distinguishable from a distance. No distance, however, is specified: it can be whatever is convenient and practicable. The surveyor, face on ground, sights a horizontal line with the alidade and notes the mark where it meets the staff. He measures the height of the mark from the ground – this is the difference in height between the two points – and proceeds to build up the ground, and the staff with it, until the base of the staff is level with the alidade. The same operation carried out to the sides will eventually produce a level plot. If the equipment and the procedure are basic, the circumstances do not demand any high degree of precision. Al-Karaji's second method (Fig. 3.12, C) is the same as Philo's except that he has to take account of the presence of a stand for the dioptra. The height of the sighting tube above the ground is marked on the staff with a red circle, and the distance between this mark and the point where the line of sight meets the staff is the difference in height. As with Philo, no interval between dioptra and staff is laid down. Al-Karaji likes this method because of the flexibility it gives the surveyor, liberating him from his bondage to fixed intervals between the stations. Although he does not make it clear, the staff probably also has a cursor. The success of the method depends on the circle on the staff being at exactly the same height from the ground as the centre of the tube, which would not be easy to achieve with any great precision, but it seems likely that Philo's version is earlier than al-Karaji's simply because it is more primitive and inconvenient.

Finally somebody realised that if, instead of the instrument, it is the staff which is placed at the terminal point of the survey, and if all sightings are horizontal, the height of the instrument above the ground can be ignored as an irrelevance (Fig. 3.12, D). All that needs to be done, as **Dioptra 6** very clearly explains and as current practice maintains to this day, is to take the first back sight to the staff at the terminal point, the first fore sight to the staff at the next station, and subtract one from the other to find the difference in height. For longer traverses it speeds up the proceedings, as Hero knew, if there are two staves that leapfrog each other. Hero's staff is tall (10 cubits or nearly 5 m), is divided in cubits, palms and dactyls, and has a plumb-line to ensure that it is not tilted forwards, backwards or sideways (Fig. 3.13). Like al-Karaji's, it has a cursor with a pointer at the side to allow the assistant to take the reading, but unlike al-Karaji's staff, whose top was within the staffman's reach, the cursor has to be moved by a string. It has a target on the cursor for the surveyor to sight on, just as was to be found on staves until the middle of the nineteenth century.

Every instrument has limits to its accuracy, and every instrument is liable to error on the part of the surveyor. Modern instruments are of such quality that significant errors nowadays are almost invariably surveyors' errors. A word, however, needs to be said on the accuracy of levelling. This depended, then as now, on four factors: precision in

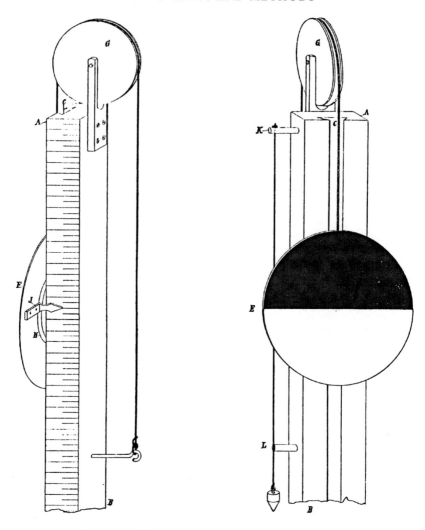

FIG. 3.13. Hero's staff: Schöne's reconstruction (Schöne 1899, Figs. 7–8).

manufacturing the instrument, accuracy in setting it up, exactitude in taking the reading on the staff, and care in recording the readings and calculating from them. Al-Karaji emphasises the need for meticulous attention. The first factor cannot be assessed beyond observing that absolute precision was neither likely nor possible; the limitations inherent in the third will be discussed later; the last, assuming a responsible

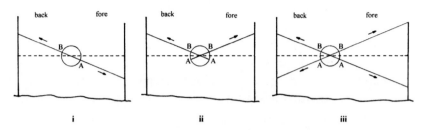

FIG. 3.14. Back and fore sights with dioptra inaccurately set.
Diagrammatic only.

surveyor, should cause no problems. But the second factor deserves comment. Let us assume that the horizontal arm of the cross on the disc really does lie precisely horizontal and that the sights, pointers and pivot lie precisely on the centre line of the alidade. If the alidade pointer is set only 0.1 mm off the true horizontal – an error undetectable by eye, given that the engraved line must have a reasonable thickness – and if the radius of the disc is 300 mm, then the reading on a staff 30 m away will be wrong by 10 mm: the alidade will be lying at a gradient of 1 in 3000. Let us suppose that it slopes upwards from sight A to sight B (Fig. 3.14.i). The back sight reading taken from A to B is too high by 10 mm and, if the dioptra is not touched and the second staff is also 30 m away, the fore sight reading taken from B to A is 10 mm too low. If the procedure is repeated in the same way, the error accumulates at the rate of a third of a metre per kilometre. With even less accuracy in setting up, which is entirely likely, the error is greater.

There are two very simple solutions to the problem. The first is to take a back sight on the staff, sighting from A to B. There is almost inevitably an error, though it is not immediately apparent: let us suppose once more that the staff is 30 m away and the reading is 10 mm too high. Without moving the alidade or stand, take the dioptra off the peg, turn it front to back, and replace it. Now take the fore sight to the second staff, which is likewise 30 m away. Because the sighting is again from A to B, the reading is also 10 mm too high, and the two errors cancel out (Fig. 3.14.ii). This method, however, in demanding that the dioptra is always exactly half way between any pair of staves, compromises the flexibility of the system. The second alternative preserves the flexibility. Take a back sight, the reading (A to B) being too high by 10 mm. Reverse the dioptra without touching the alidade and take another back sight (B to A), which is too low by 10 mm. Splitting the difference between the two gives the true horizontal. Repeat the operation for the fore sight, the second staff being at any distance, and again the true horizontal is found. No ancient author speaks of these manoeuvres, unless they were in the Anonymus' lacuna; but they seem precautions which any thoughtful surveyor could have worked out had he felt the need.

Hero's water level was probably less satisfactory. One doubts if the horizontal slits in the sights could be aligned precisely with the water surfaces, where a meniscus would inevitably be formed against the glass by capillary attraction. In this case a true horizontal could be found by reversing the level without altering the slits and by taking the mean of two readings if, but only if, the supporting column was absolutely vertical and there was no wobble between column and level: an unlikely circumstance. This is why Hero's dioptra was potentially less accurate than the standard type.

Nowadays, when the primary levelling is completed, its accuracy is checked by taking 'flying levels' back to the starting point. In theory this will bring the cumulative height difference back to zero; in practice a closing error is tolerated, provided it falls within strictly defined limits. If ancient surveyors had done the same, they too could have found how accurate or inaccurate their survey had been; but there is complete silence in the sources about any such check. This may seem surprising; but our expectations are liable to be coloured by the modern need for precision. The simple truth, most likely, is that what the Greek world required of its surveyors was, for the most part, nothing like so stringent as now. With the dioptra, the error mentioned above – the alidade sloping up or down at 1 in 3000 when it was meant to be level – might never matter. It certainly would not matter if the minimum gradient aimed at in a water channel was 1 in 200, the figure given by Philo (**Source 10**) and commonly found on Greek aqueducts (Chapter 9.B). Even an error three times as great, 1 in 1000 either way, would not matter either.

At this point, however, a sharp distinction must be drawn between the Greeks, whose water channels and pipelines generally had a relatively steep fall, and the Romans whose aqueducts could follow an extremely gentle gradient. There are plenty of later examples where a surveying error of 1 in 3000 could turn a potential success into an abject failure. If, as seems likely, the steeper gradients were surveyed by dioptra, its inaccuracies might be immaterial. But if, as again seems likely, the later and gentler gradients were surveyed by libra, we have to look for a much higher degree of precision in that instrument, even if it worked on the same basic principle (Chapter 4). Moreover, for all we know (which for Roman procedures is very little), Roman surveyors may have taken flying levels to check their results. Having said all this, there still remains the unsolved question of how levelling was carried out on what must have been, to judge from the results, a very sophisticated system at the tunnels of Samos, Lake Nemi and Lake Albano as early as the sixth century BC. This question will be examined, if not fully answered, in Chapter 10.E.

H. OTHER SURVEYS

It has already been noted that for terrestrial surveying the dioptra neither needed nor had degree graduations. When on occasion it was necessary to record the vertical inclination of a sight line, it was a matter not of measuring the angle as such but of marking on a pole the point where the line of sight intercepted it (**Dioptra 21** and probably **12** and **14**). The basic principle of dioptra surveys lay, rather, in setting out right angles by means of the cross on the disc, in projecting lines by sighting through the alidade in both directions, and in constructing similar triangles by sighting on objects that were not at right angles to the base line. As we saw in Chapter 1.D, two triangles with parallel or shared sides have the same angles, and if the lengths of two sides of the first triangle are known, as well as the ratio of one side of the first triangle to the same side of the second, the dimensions of the second triangle can easily be worked out. Some of the exercises in the manuals are extremely simple, some are quite complex, but all rely on the elementary geometry practised long before it was formulated by Euclid in the early third century BC.

The simpler exercises mostly involve measuring the distance between remote points without approaching them (**Anonymus 3–5**, **Dioptra 10–11, 21–2**). If they have any practical application at all, it is for military purposes or for mapping in mountains; but more probably they are intended for training apprentices, or even for no more than proclaiming the ingenuity of an armchair theorist. **Anonymus 7**, in particular, is of such startling naivety that one doubts if it was ever practised in the field. But most procedures are more useful. Among the more fundamental is that for discovering the distance between two points, one of which is inaccessible. **Africanus 2–3** gives two different versions, and the Anonymus certainly gave at least one which is lost, specifically relating this method to the problem of finding the width of a river for the purpose of constructing a pontoon bridge. But *Dioptra* **8** gives another variant without mentioning rivers,[65] and it played an essential role in the next problem.

This is the other standard military exercise, finding the height of a wall without approaching it, which has to be tackled in two stages, one in the vertical plane and the other in the horizontal. It is represented by **Africanus 4**, by **Anonymus 2**, by *Dioptra* **12** (though not labelled as such) and mentioned by a number of other authors (**Sources 11–16**). The same procedure can be applied to finding the height of mountains as also, specifically, can *Dioptra* **13(b)**. How accurate the operation might be is difficult to tell. Both **Anonymus 1** and *Dioptra* **2** say that the survey should be taken out of bowshot of the wall. Although the reasoning is obvious enough, it is by no means clear, as so often, what 'bowshot' means in terms of distance. If one takes it as what the Byzantines called 'moderate bowshot', which probably means the range beyond which an arrow has no power to disable, it equates to 328 m.[66] If one follows Philo in taking the minimum height of a reasonably strong city wall as 20 cubits or say 10 m,[67] then the apparent height of the wall at that range is very small. A 10 m wall at 350 m subtends an angle of about 1.6°, at 300 m about 1.9°. This very small apparent height had to be measured with sufficient accuracy to construct a siege tower that would match the wall's height within reasonable limits. Neither **Africanus 4** nor **Anonymus 2** inspires confidence, because both rely on projecting a line of sight from the dioptra to the ground. Only if E, Γ and B (see diagram to **Africanus 4**) lie in the same plane will any accuracy be achieved. Later, however, this exercise progressed to taking readings on a staff

[65] *Dioptra* **9** is a different matter, the very elementary process of laying out a line to cross a river by the shortest route, which might be of some use for establishing the line of a permanent bridge. [66] *Sylloge Tacticorum* 43.11. [67] Philo, *Siegecraft* 1 11.

(*Dioptra* 12), whereby irregularities in the ground surface do not matter. We shall see in Chapter 3.J that this improved method gives very good results.

For the rest, we are left with a number of Hero's exercises which are for the most part highly pertinent to civil engineering projects. *Dioptra* 7, plotting a straight line between two points that are not intervisible, might be used for establishing on the surface the line of a tunnel below, and thereby indicating where the shafts should be sunk, were it not that *Dioptra* 15 deals in a simpler manner with the same problem. In any event, unless the terrain is extremely rugged, it might well be more accurate to stake out a straight line by interpolation as described for roads in Chapter 11.B. Consideration of *Dioptra* 15–16 and 20, which specifically deal with tunnels and shafts, is best left until Chapter 10. *Dioptra* 14, on finding the depth of a ditch, could well have military connotations; but 17, on setting out a harbour wall by projecting the profile of a template, has an obvious relevance to engineering. None the less, this procedure smacks somewhat of the armchair invention, if only because it presupposes that, instead of the walls being built up in the sea, the harbour is to be excavated in the dry. This was rarely practised in the ancient world, and the most obvious exception, Trajan's great hexagonal basin at Portus at the mouth of the Tiber, would surely have been laid out geometrically on the ground. Similarly the self-evident way of setting out the foundations of an amphitheatre is to drive in two posts at the foci and trace the concentric ellipses with loops of rope. The outside of the amphitheatre at Pola in Italy (129.9 by 102.6 m) proves to be a true ellipse with a mean error of only 15 cm,[68] and it is hard to see how this accuracy could have been achieved by instrument. Other chapters with relevance to engineering, though the motive is not clear, are *Dioptra* 18 and 19 on building up earth into a mound or a ramp. *Dioptra* 31, though hardly a matter of surveying, is of profound interest as proof that the ancient world did not, as is often misrepresented, imagine that the discharge of water by an aqueduct was governed solely by the cross-section of the channel, but also recognised the velocity of the current as a factor.

A final and possible use for the dioptra was in mapping. Ancient maps of the world or even of whole countries hardly involved surveying

[68] *Nature* 88 (30 Nov. 1911), 158.

in anything like the true cartographical sense of the word; but complex plans of limited areas necessarily did so. Interest centres on the plans of the city of Rome inscribed on marble. Of one, commissioned in AD 73,[69] only a few fragments have been found. Much better known is the *Forma Urbis Romae* made between 203 and 208, for which we have more substantial evidence.[70] It occupied a marble-covered wall 18.3 by 13.03 m, and its scale was intended to be 1:240. There is much uncertainty because of the fragmentary nature of what survives. The longer distances between monuments are very accurate, to the order of 1.0 to 2.1 per cent in error, whereas shorter distances are less accurate and may be as much as 13 per cent out. The largest errors are not in the relative position but in the orientation of monuments, whose axes can be wrong by up to 21°. The leading authority on the *Forma Urbis* suggests that a basic triangulation was first carried out using dioptras with precise graduations, working both horizontally and vertically to cater for uneven terrain; hence the accuracy over longer distances. The topographical detail was then filled in, he suggests, in a less precise way,[71] conceivably by groma, laying out straight lines and measuring the offsets to buildings.[72] While these explanations are feasible, they do run counter to two impressions: that the dioptra was not, or was barely, used by Rome, and that the dioptra for terrestrial work was not provided with degree graduations. Both impressions may of course be wrong; we are talking of a period much later than that of most of our sources, and changes could have occurred. We simply do not know. And while maps played a substantial part in Roman life, hardly any others survive to be compared with reality. For the most part we can only judge from reports. Thus Frontinus says that as Commissioner for Aqueducts he had maps made of the aqueducts supplying Rome, which showed heights and distances;[73] but whether they were true to scale or were merely schematic diagrams is more than we can say.[74] However, a fragment survives of another map on marble, to the same scale (1:240) as the *Forma Urbis*, which does mark distances and was quite possibly made for Frontinus' counterpart, the Commissioner for the Tiber Channel and Banks.[75]

[69] Pliny, *Natural History* III 66–7.   [70] See in general Dilke 1985, 103–6.
[71] Rodriguez Almeida 1980, 45–8, 52 n.1, Figs. 10 and 11.
[72] Adam 1994, 14.   [73] Frontinus, *Aqueducts* 17.   [74] Hodge 1992, 172.
[75] Rodriguez Almeida 1988.

I. CHRONOLOGICAL CONCLUSIONS

It is unfortunate that, all the major sources being derivative, we have very little contemporary evidence for the dioptra. But enough hints emerge (some of which we will only meet in a later chapter) and enough deductions can be made to allow a tentative picture to be drawn – and it must be emphasised that it is tentative – of how, when and where the dioptra was developed for surveying. It was surely not invented out of the blue in fully-fledged form, but evolved over a period of time.

What may be the earliest ancestor of the standard dioptra is the sighting tube for surveying qanats, described by al-Karaji and to be examined in detail in Chapter 10.E. This seems to have been a Persian invention, for, unlike his dioptra proper, there is no suggestion that he derived it from some Greek source. It was nothing more than a simple tube suspended horizontally, with no disc, and it may have been transmitted to Greece in the sixth century BC. But its very existence at so early a date is only hypothetical.

Philo's instrument and his method of levelling for irrigation, being very simple (again there is no disc), seem to lie near the beginning of the dioptra's evolution. Because he was in Alexandria for a while, perhaps in the 250s BC, an Egyptian source for his information is perfectly feasible. From the dates known and deduced for his career, his *Water Conducting* can hardly have been written after the 230s, or at latest the 220s. This was the period when new irrigation projects of huge extent were afoot in Egypt. The Fayum depression lies west of the Nile and about 45 m below sea level. It had been partially brought under cultivation by the pharaohs of the Twelfth Dynasty, who installed sluices to control the channel now known as the Bahr Yusuf, which tapped floodwater from the Nile and delivered it to irrigate the Fayum. Over a millennium later Ptolemy II Philadelphus (285–46 BC) and Ptolemy III Euergetes (246–22) set about a further massive reclamation, perhaps trebling the area under cultivation, to provide land for their militia and food for a rapidly expanding population.[76] This was done by diverting water from the Bahr Yusuf through a complex network of trunk and branch canals to irrigate the new fields. In the process, Lake Moeris (Birket el Qurun) on the floor of the depression was starved of some of

---

[76] Butzer 1976, 36–8, 47.

its supply and its level was lowered by eight to ten metres, which in turn liberated a large area of new land.[77] From 262 BC at the latest the chief engineer of this project was one Cleon, a substantial part of whose papyrus archive has been found. About 252 he retired or was sacked, but his successor Theodorus remained in post until at least 237.[78]

While it is quite impossible to prove that the dioptra for levelling was first devised for the setting out of these irrigation channels in the Fayum, the context seems entirely appropriate. The Ptolemies had their tame scientists at the Museum in Alexandria to whom they could well have presented a problem which was in need of solution. Until his death, perhaps around 250, the leading light among the Alexandrian mechanics was Ctesibius, who was succeeded (as I have argued elsewhere[79]) by a man with the Semitic name of Abdaraxos. Whether or not either played a part in the early development of the dioptra, the middle of the century saw a great outburst of invention at Alexandria, including, it seems most likely, all the water-lifting machines (except the age-old shaduf) ever used in the Greek and Roman world.[80] Here too the needs of the Fayum may well have been the stimulus.

Al-Karaji's version of the dioptra was used only in vertical mode for levelling irrigation channels. One of his procedures was evidently intended for relatively flat terrain and (within the parameters first stated) could not work in hilly country. His source, with its mention of the *schoinion* of 100 cubits, seems to be Egyptian, which chimes with employment in irrigation works and quite flat country, and can be dated by the reference letters in the diagrams to before the Christian era. His instrument and procedures are more advanced than Philo's, but he still uses the sighting tube rather than the alidade. We may therefore place him very approximately, around 200 BC or a little before. By this date Alexandrian science and technology, which for a hundred years had led the world, was already in decline, and by the mid-second century the flower of its scholarship was sadly wilted.[81] There is no suggestion that the city, or Egypt, played any further role in the dioptra's evolution. The action took place elsewhere.

---

[77] For the history of Moeris see Caton-Thompson and Gardner 1929, and especially 49–51 on Ptolemaic canals.

[78] Cleon's archive is published in *P. Petrie*. For a summary of what is known of his life and work see Lewis 1986, 37–45.   [79] Lewis 1997, 60–1.

[80] Lewis 1997, especially 126–7.   [81] Fraser 1972, I 318–19, 422–3.

During the third century there is no sure sign of the dioptra measuring heights or working in the horizontal mode. Philo's *Siegecraft* of 246–40 BC, for example, which gives detailed instructions on how to lay siege, makes no mention of measuring the height of walls. Marcellus did not use a dioptra in 212 to measure the walls of Syracuse (Chapter 1.D). Such a widening of the dioptra's function evidently came later; indeed the earliest direct reference to a survey which sounds as if it involved the dioptra for anything other than levelling is the calculation by Xenagoras of the height of Olympus above Pythion as 6096 feet (**Source 84**). However imperfect this may have been – and we shall see in Chapter 8 that it was perhaps quite close to the truth – it implies a precise calculation and an instrument which at least held the promise of precision. This survey was made at some unknown date before 168 BC. Not so very long afterwards the height of Kyllene above, probably, Pheneos was quoted by Apollodorus of Athens in similarly precise terms as 5320 feet (**Source 85**). At much the same time – before 156 BC – Biton wrote his *Optics* which included a section on measuring the height of walls. By roughly the middle of the century Attalus and Hipparchus could talk without further explanation of the dioptra's astronomical role (**Source 18**). Its military applications, underlined by Africanus and the Anonymus, make no sense after the coming of the *pax Romana* – Hero pays only lip service to them – and not much more during the first century BC when Greek military activity was largely restricted to rearguard action against the advancing power of Rome. But what might be called proper warfare, with Greeks attacking Greeks, fits the second century and especially its earlier years.

The first half of the second century was indeed a time ripe for such a development. The dioptra was akin in concept and construction to purely astronomical instruments, and Hipparchus, the first truly instrumental astronomer, was observing in Rhodes from at least 162.[82] It was apparently in the first half of the century that Carpus invented his chorobates which, despite its drawbacks, he perhaps described as an instrument capable of surveying aqueducts (Chapter 1.E). It may well be no accident that this was also the time when long-distance urban aqueducts first appear in Greek lands, for which reasonably accurate

---

[82] Some feel that the observations which can safely be attributed to Hipparchus begin only in 147; but I am persuaded by Dicks 1960, 2–5 that the earlier ones were really his too.

surveying would be more essential than for almost any previous engineering project. The pioneer was apparently the wealthy and rising state of Pergamon, which during the second century BC and perhaps a few years before built no fewer than five pipelines to supply the city. They included the great Madra Dag aqueduct of the reign of Eumenes II (197–159), no less than 42 km long and with a monstrous inverted siphon 201 m deep.[83] All the evidence thus points to a date for the development of the dioptra, from little more than a level into a much more flexible instrument, somewhere around or very soon after 200 BC.

We have no hope of putting a name on the man or men responsible, but it is worth hazarding a guess about where it might have come about. One of the chief beneficiaries of Alexandria's intellectual decadence was Pergamon, where the Attalids fostered culture as assiduously as the earlier Ptolemies; and Pergamon is a good candidate for the development of the dioptra. Biton was evidently based there, and in the Attalids' service. Apollodorus spent a number of years at Pergamon en route from Alexandria to Athens, and could have picked up there the information on the height of Kyllene. It was Pergamon that, first of all Greek states, found the engineering skill to survey long aqueducts through mountains. This evidence, to be sure, is circumstantial and tenuous, and appearances may be misleading. But whatever the truth, during the last two or two and a half centuries before Christ surveying clearly spawned a literature of technical manuals, just as artillery inspired books by Ctesibius (the real author of Hero's *Artillery*), Philo and Biton, and just as siegecraft generated monographs by Philo and Athenaeus Mechanicus. But whereas all of these books survive, those on surveying are lost and we have to be content with secondary extracts from them preserved in the later treatises. Except for Philo, whose contribution was perhaps small, and for Biton the very names of their authors have perished too.

In the Greek world the dioptra evidently remained the normal surveying instrument, though it seems not to have been exported to Rome. It was presumably still available, if little used, when the Anonymus wrote in the tenth century; and whether or not Bohemond had a dioptra at Durazzo in 1107 (**Source 16**), it was apparently still

---

[83] For a summary, Garbrecht 1987; further discussion Lewis 1999b.

current enough at Constantinople for Anna to know about it, unless, of course, she was really thinking of the astrolabe. Knowledge of the dioptra, if it had survived that long, was no doubt lost, like so much else, in the sack of 1204. Although it retained its terrestrial functions, most of its astronomical ones had been passed on to its offspring the astrolabe. But when the astrolabe was borrowed from Byzantium by Islam, and was later passed by Islam to Western Europe, the dioptra as such did not go with it. If we except al-Karaji, the dioptra was unknown in Islam, and when the Arabs carried out exercises just like those in our Greek treatises, they used the astrolabe (see Chapter 12).

J. TESTING A RECONSTRUCTED DIOPTRA

To obtain some idea of the performance and accuracy of a dioptra, one was made to the design suggested by the sources (Figs. 3.1–2). It comprises a plywood disc 60 cm in diameter and 14 mm thick and weighs 2.35 kg complete. It is inscribed with diameter lines at right angles and a degree scale around one quadrant. A hole at the centre carries the pivot of the wooden alidade, which is equal in length to the diameter and is fitted with slit sights each made of two pieces of plastic sheet. The width of the slit was adjusted, after much trial and error, to what seemed the optimum: too wide and it is difficult to centre the foresight in it, too narrow and the view is blurred. The optimum is about 0.25 mm, which is equivalent to rather more than two thicknesses of 80 g/m² paper. The sights have a 5 mm hole near the base of the slit. One looks through the slit of the backsight, centres the foresight in it, and observes the staff or other object either through the hole of the foresight or at the outside edge of the vane. In either case the foresight slit is aligned on the centre of the object or gives the reading on the staff.

A purpose-built tripod was not attempted. Instead, for the horizontal mode, the central hole in the disc is screwed to a plate on the ball joint of a fairly sturdy photographic tripod. For the vertical mode, a brass sleeve on the rim at the top of the vertical diameter fits over a horizontal brass peg attached to the ball joint, loosely enough to allow the disc to hang freely but tight enough to avoid undue wobble. Nevertheless, the major problem is wind which, even if gentle, sets the disc visibly swinging or vibrating. Without a shelter, accurate levelling can be done only when the air is virtually still. The diameter and therefore the windage of the reconstruction is perhaps greater than it should be; and metal rather than wood would increase the weight and thereby reduce swinging.

Because, as explained, setting the alidade to the horizontal diameter cannot guarantee that it is perfectly horizontal, all readings when levelling were taken in duplicate: one from sight A to sight B, the other from sight B to sight A after taking the dioptra off the peg without touching the alidade, turning it through 180 degrees and replacing it. The mean of the two figures thus obtained gave what should be the true horizontal.

A distance was chosen, 173 m in length between two immovable stones, and was levelled with a modern quickset level which was carefully tested for accuracy. Repeated checks in both directions established the overall difference in height as 13.005 m.[84] With the dioptra, the same modern staff was used, on the face of which, instead of the circular target specified by Hero, the staffman slid a coloured piece of wood up or down at the surveyor's direction, and when its top coincided with the line of sight he took the reading. The considerable difference in height between the two ends of the survey required six stations of the dioptra and seven of the staff, or 24 readings over the whole distance. Six surveys were made in each direction. The first attempt gave a height difference of 12.359 m, far from the real figure. But results improved with practice, and the final three surveys showed a certain consistency at 13.173, 13.108 and 13.100 m. The mean of these three figures, compared with the true 13.005 m, represents an error of 1 in 1418, the best an error of 1 in 1821. These errors arose, no doubt, from a variety of causes: movement of the disc in the wind (slight though it was), the relative shortness of the alidade, and inexperience on the part of the surveyor. But if the gradient to be derived from the levelling was intended to be of the order of 1 in 200, they would make little practical difference. This matter is discussed more fully in Chapter 9.B. For the moment, it seems that the dioptra was quite adequate for surveying the typical steep Greek aqueduct.

---

[84] At first a metric staff was used, but its graduation in centimetres proved too coarse for precision, and an imperial staff more finely divided in hundredths of a foot was found preferable. All figures given hereafter were measured in this form and converted to metric; hence the horizontal distances which appear, improbably, to have been taken to the nearest millimetre.

Two more exercises were carried out with the reconstructed instrument. One, to measure the width of an (imaginary) river followed Nipsus' method (see **Source 55** and diagram), where the river width was deemed to be CF and was set out at an arbitrary 30.48 m. The base line CD, 117.80 m long, was laid out at right angles to CF and was bisected at E, and DG was set out at right angles to CD. Point H was located by sighting on E and F, and was found, as it should be, to be exactly 30.48 m from D. This is a simple exercise and, provided the right angles really are right angles, there is little scope for error.

More surprising (and pleasing) was the successful measurement of the height of a wall, as represented by the gable end of a house from the ground to the top of the chimney stack. In Fig. 3.15 (plan) the dioptra was placed in horizontal mode at A and sighted on the chimney stack at B. A line was then laid out at right angles to beyond F, and FB was aligned by eye and staked out for some way. The dioptra was moved an arbitrary distance to G and GH was laid out at right angles to AF. This intersected FB at H. AF and two sides of the triangle FGH were measured. Since FGH and FAB are similar triangles, AB could be worked out. This procedure corresponds to **Africanus 3**.

The dioptra was then returned to A and put in vertical mode (fig 3.15 (elevation)). **Africanus 4** was not followed, because it requires the ground to be level or at a constant slope, which it clearly was not. Instead, a simplified version of *Dioptra* **12** was employed, with a staff held vertically at D. AC was sighted to the top of the chimney stack and AB to the base of the wall, and where these lines of sight intersected the staff the readings were taken, which gave the distance DE. The length AE was measured, and since AB had been discovered in the horizontal mode and AED and ABC are similar triangles, this gave the height BC, namely 8.698 m. A siege tower or ladder built to that dimension would have fitted well, for the actual height as finally measured on the house itself proved to be 8.687 m.

So close a result was unexpected because on the most crucial of the stages, establishing DE, the staff was 48 m from the dioptra, which seemed rather far for comfort. True, al-Karaji was happy with distances of 100 cubits or 50 m, but experiment showed that at distances much over 30 m it was difficult to be precise over positioning the marker on the staff. In the levelling exercises already described, the quite steep slope meant that the distance from instrument to staff averaged only

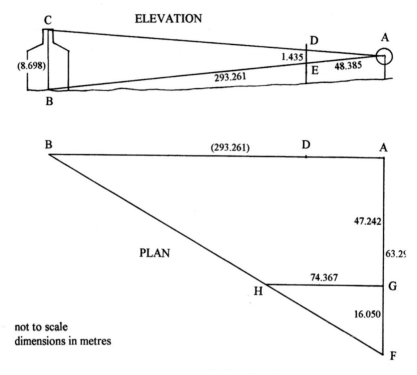

FIG. 3.15. Measuring the height of a wall.

about 14 m which, other things being equal, created no problems of visibility. There is no easy answer to the question of the optimum distance. If the ground is fairly flat, short steps, being greater in number, increase both the time taken and the opportunity for making mistakes. Long steps, though fewer, make accurate readings harder to take. It is a choice of evils. But at least the distances are always short enough for atmospheric refraction and the curvature of the earth, which have to be allowed for when taking long sightings with modern equipment, to play no significant part.

CHAPTER 4

THE LIBRA

A. THE EVIDENCE

The Greek dioptra served several functions. When self-suspended it took heights and levels, and when mounted horizontally it took angles in a more or less horizontal plane. For these purposes the Romans, in contrast, had not one but two instruments. The groma worked purely in the horizontal plane and was applied particularly to land surveying, while the libra worked purely in the vertical plane, most notably in levelling for aqueducts. *Libra* is therefore not a simple synonym for *dioptra*, as Vitruvius makes plain in distinguishing them (**Source 3**). Indeed it is quite clear from what the sources say – and from what they do not say – that Greek and Roman instruments differed markedly. No source written in Greek mentions the libra, or anything that might be interpreted as the libra, although it remains perfectly possible, and indeed likely, that the libra was used for surveying aqueducts in the Greek world once Roman technical influence had made itself felt there. Similarly there is a dearth of references in Latin sources from the western half of the Mediterranean to the dioptra as a surveying instrument. This dearth is not total, since Vitruvius is aware of it; but his words in no way prove that it was ever used by the Romans. We have twice had occasion, however, to wonder if the dioptra might have been applied in a Roman context: in mapping, as for the *Forma Urbis* (Chapter 3.H), and when Balbus found the heights of mountains (**Source 14**). To this last question we shall return; for the moment it is enough to draw attention to the deep difference between the instruments of the eastern and western Mediterranean.

As to the libra itself, we are gravely hampered by lack of direct information and by the lack of anything approaching a description. It does not feature in the *Corpus Agrimensorum*, which for all practical purposes is not concerned with altitudes. As a surveying instrument, the libra is in fact mentioned only once, by Vitruvius: 'levelling is done with dioptras or *librae aquariae* or the chorobates' (**Source 3**). It is often assumed that *libra aquaria* means a water level like that on top of the chorobates or on Hero's dioptra.[1] But as has already been remarked, there is no evidence for the water level, beyond these two instances, in the Greek or Roman world.[2] The adjective *aquarius* can occasionally refer to the role of water in a device,[3] but much more often it refers to the function of the object in question.[4] As was long ago observed,[5] this seems to be the case here: the *libra aquaria* was not a level levelled by water but a level for levelling water, or in other words an aqueduct level.

This is perhaps as far as Vitruvius' bald use of the term can take us in its own right. But considerably more light, fortunately, is shed by other uses of the word *libra* and by words derived from it (listed under **Source 44**), which refer to the taking of levels, to levels obtained by the libra and to men who levelled.[6] Perhaps the most useful passage is Pliny's account of surveying for mine aqueducts in the Spanish mountains (**Source 38**), where men hang from crags on ropes to take the levels (*librant*). This circumstance more or less rules out the water level and the plumb-line level which, to achieve any worthwhile degree of accuracy, need to be placed on a solid surface; and it very strongly implies a self-suspended level that can be held in the hand or even hung from a rope in front of the surveyor.

Such an interpretation accords with the history of the word *libra* itself. It basically meant a weight, and is cognate with the Sicilian Greek *litra*, both perhaps deriving from an early Italic **libra*, a weight. Hence *libra* came to mean a pair of scales or a balance, and sometimes merely the beam of the scales, for as a sign of the zodiac *Libra* is the Latin translation of the Greek *Zygon*, which specifically denotes a scale beam. We are concerned only with the traditional equal-armed version (*stathmos* in Greek, a word not found in any surveying context), and not with the steelyard (*statera*, a Roman innovation) where the beam is unequally

---

[1] So for example Callebat 1973, 138–9; White 1984, 171; Hodge 1992, 149.

[2] Saglio 1899 claims that a water level is shown on a late tombstone from Rome (Rossi 1857–61, 188 no. 443). It is not a level but a foot rule, almost identical to that labelled as such in *Inscriptiones Creticae* IV 411.

[3] *Cos aquaria*, a whetstone for use with water as opposed to oil, and *mola aquaria*, a mill powered by water.

[4] *Vas aquarium* and *urceus aquarius*, vessels for containing water; *sulcus aquarius*, a furrow for draining water; *fistula aquaria*, a pipe for carrying water; *rota aquaria*, a wheel for lifting water. So too with abstract nouns: *provincia aquaria*, the management of aqueducts; *res aquaria*, hydraulics. *Aquarius* as a noun is common from Cicero onwards as an aqueduct overseer or workman. For references, see *TLL* under *aquarius*.

[5] Michon 1899, 1230.   [6] These words are discussed by Callebat 1974, 317–18.

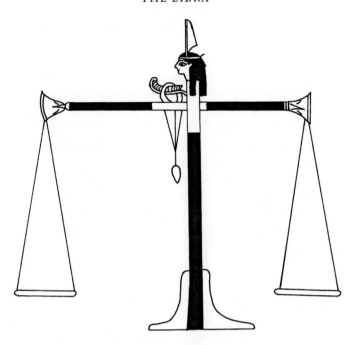

FIG. 4.1. Egyptian balance, *c.* 1400 BC. Beam *c.* 1.5 m long
(after Dilke 1987a, Fig. 45).

divided.[7] From this basic meaning of scales and weighing, the connotations of *libra* and its derivatives move on to embrace balancing and swinging or throwing: *librare* 'to balance', *libramentum* 'a counterweight', and *libratio* 'a balancing', as of the beam of a steelyard.[8] From balancing they shade gradually into setting horizontal (or even on a gradient) and, especially in Vitruvius, Pliny and Frontinus, into levelling in the surveying sense (**Source 44**).

This is the major clue to the form of the instrument. To weigh accurately, the weights in the pan of a balance are adjusted until the beam is exactly horizontal. This was often ensured on ancient scales, from Egyptian times onwards (Fig. 4.1), by incorporating a device called in Latin the *examen*.[9] When the balance was correct, either a suspended plumb-line coincided with a mark on a plate attached to the centre of the beam or, conversely, a pointer fixed at right angles to the beam coincided with a central mark on the stand.

---

[7] For their history and archaeology see Michon 1899. [8] Vitruvius X 3.4.
[9] For references see *TLL* under *examen*.

One may deduce that this emphasis on making the beam horizontal
was what prompted its adoption as a surveying instrument, and that the
libra for levelling consisted in essence of a scale beam, without the pans
and their chains, suspended from its centre. Possibly at first the *examen*
was retained to check the horizontal, and possibly there were no sights.
But because the libra became capable of levelling aqueducts on a very
shallow gradient, which demands a high degree of accuracy, we may be
confident that its design was ultimately refined. Slit sights as on the
dioptra would have to be added to the ends. The comparatively rough-
and-ready *examen* would have to be superseded by a more precise
method of balancing. Without the pans, the beam would always hang
in equilibrium; and its horizontality could be made as exact as possible
by taking a reading on a graduated staff, reversing the libra, using the
sights the other way round, and adding or removing metal from one
end until the reading was precisely the same from each direction.
Provided the bearing allowed free movement, and provided the centre
of gravity was a reasonable distance below it, the beam would always
return to the horizontal. In this form the libra would be the equivalent
of the dioptra in vertical mode: but only the partial equivalent, for it
was in effect merely an alidade suspended from its centre. Whereas the
diameter of the dioptra was limited by considerations of height, the
libra could be significantly longer than the dioptra's alidade, and
thereby gain in accuracy of sighting. Because a thin libra, even a long
one, offered a much smaller surface to the wind than did the disc of a
dioptra, it would be much less liable to swing, and (as we will find) it
was easier to protect from the wind.

The diminutive of *libra* is *libella*,[10] the standard Latin name for the
small A-frame builder's level with its plumb-line (Chapter 1.E; references under **Source 44**). Does this imply that, after all, the libra itself
was a large A-frame level? By no means necessarily. The diminutive
need not refer to the design but to the function, the libra and libella
being respectively a (large) device for levelling and a small device for
levelling.[11]

[10] Whence the modern words *level, niveau* etc.
[11] In two passages in Tacitus (*Annals* II 20 and XIII 39) the curious word *libritor* is
coupled with *funditor*, 'slinger'. It has been argued (Le Bohec 1987) that *libritor* was
the same as *librator*, a soldier who used a libra for surveying in peacetime and for
setting the angle of elevation of catapults in wartime. The latter function would

No example of the libra has been identified and no contemporary illustration is known. In the absence of any more precise information, the picture drawn above can only be hypothetical. Yet it is not, I feel, implausible. The libra's superiority over the dioptra explains why the Romans maintained two surveying instruments, one for levelling and one for horizontal plotting, where the Greeks could do everything with one. Its potentially greater length and its reduced tendency to swing in the wind explain its ability to level the shallow gradients of Roman aqueducts. The fact that it was evidently intended, as the *libra*-words imply, primarily for levelling does not, on the face of it, explain how the Romans handled the third function of the dioptra, namely taking vertical angles such as the height of mountains or buildings. The only Roman on record who did such a thing was Balbus, and it is possible that he used a dioptra. However, a libra could be made to do the job. The beam need only be tilted to the required angle by hand or, in a slightly less temporary and more stable fashion, by a string tied to the tripod.

In the absence of literary references to the libra before Vitruvius, any attempt to outline its history is risky. There is no direct clue whether the libra was a home-grown Roman device, inherited from the Etruscans, or borrowed from or influenced by the Greeks of southern Italy and Sicily. The frequency and variety of *libra-* words found in Vitruvius implies that they were well enshrined in Latin by 35–25 BC, when he wrote; which in turn implies that the libra itself was well established as a surveying instrument with, if one might hazard a guess, at the very least a century of use behind it. If its evolution from a simple scale beam, as suggested above, is at all correct, one is tempted to look at the gradients of early Roman aqueducts and comparable works in search of a visible improvement in precision of surveying.

The overall gradient of the 1600 m emissary tunnel dug in probably the sixth century BC to drain Lake Nemi is about 1 in 125, but was perhaps intended to be 1 in 160 (see Chapter 10.E). On the Albano emissary, dug according to legend in 397 BC but probably considerably

---

resemble that of the gunner of later ages who adjusted the elevation, and thus the range, of his cannon with a simple level, akin to a builder's level, consisting of a protractor and a plumb-line. But the context in Tacitus demands that the *libritor* throws missiles, and specifically sling-shot. The thorny question is considered by Goodyear 1981, 238–9, but seems irrelevant to the present discussion.

older, the gradient is 1 in 833.[12] That of Rome's first aqueduct, the Appia of 312 BC, is not known.[13] That of the Anio Vetus of 269 BC is about 1 in 370, of the Aqua Marcia of 140 BC about 1 in 350, and of the Aqua Virgo of 19 BC about 1 in 3670.[14] This progression might be taken as evidence of improvement in instruments or in technique, especially between 140 and 19 BC. But it is not. In practice no aqueduct was built on a constant gradient, and a given overall gradient necessarily embraces some stretches that are steeper and some that are gentler. Thus both the Anio Vetus and the Marcia include sections shallower than 1 in 1000. The Anio Vetus has at least four such, down to 1 in 5000; the Marcia has at least fourteen, down to almost 1 in 10,000.[15] It is rarely clear how long these stretches were, or whether they were intentional or accidental. As is not unknown on aqueducts elsewhere, the Marcia apparently had one short stretch on a reverse (i.e. uphill) gradient,[16] which was surely not deliberate; either the surveying was poor or the builders failed to adhere to the gradient staked out by the surveyors. If a section could be built sloping the wrong way, sections could be built on a gradient less than was intended. However, the stretch of the Anio Vetus between Romavecchia and Tor Fiscale fell 0.20 m in roughly a kilometre,[17] which is long enough to suggest that the resulting 1 in 5000, or something of that order of magnitude, was intended.

To anticipate the fuller discussion in Chapter 9.B, the overall fall of an aqueduct, once the source and the destination were decided on, was

[12] Castellani and Dragoni 1991, 55–6.

[13] The 1 in 2000 given by Ashby 1935, 54 and by those who copy him is founded on a false premise. The Appia's outlet was at about 15 m above the sea, lower, according to Frontinus, *Aqueducts* 18, than the outlet of the Aqua Virgo. Ashby evidently assumed that the Appia's source was also lower than the Virgo's source, which lay at about 24 m; hence a fall of about 8 m over the distance of 16 km. But outside the city no trace has ever been found of the Appia's channel, let alone of its source, which could be at any height. The gradient therefore is unknown.

[14] There is huge divergence in the figures variously cited for the gradients of the aqueducts of Rome. Those given here are based on the falls recorded by Ashby 1935 and the lengths worked out by Blackman 1979 or (Virgo) recorded by Frontinus. They can only be approximations. The Tepula of 125 BC and the Julia of 33 BC may be ignored because they tapped high-level springs and at first dropped very steeply to join the Marcia, on top of whose channel they then rode piggy-back to the city.

[15] Blackman 1978, fig. 7.   [16] Blackman 1978, 68–9.   [17] Ashby 1935, 79–80.

governed solely by the difference in their height, while its length depended on the terrain, which might permit a straighter and shorter route or demand a more circuitous and longer one. The point is that very gentle slopes were not deliberately aimed at. They were rather a necessity, and probably an unwelcome one, which was occasionally imposed by geographical circumstances but which could be accommodated provided the gradients fell well within the limit of error of the instruments available. The relatively steep overall gradients of the Anio Vetus and Marcia do not therefore mean that the instruments of the day were incapable of surveying more gently graded routes. It is not impossible that the stretches of 1 in 5000 on the Anio Vetus were deliberately set out by libra in the third century BC, and those of nearly 1 in 10,000 on the Marcia in the second. But all we can say with complete confidence is that by 19 BC the libra was accurate enough to set out the Aqua Virgo, nearly 21 km long, on an average gradient of about 1 in 3700. At Rome, however, the geography does not on the whole demand very gentle gradients, and no statistics are available for aqueducts of republican date in other parts of Italy.[18] Elsewhere in the expanding Roman world we shall find that overall slopes of 1 in 6000 are attested just before the birth of Christ, and even gentler ones, down to 1 in 8000 and even 1 in 20,000, not many decades after.

This historical enquiry, then, is quite inconclusive. While the dates of the first aqueducts of Rome – 312 and 269 BC – are early, the emissary tunnels of Lakes Nemi and Albano nearby are even earlier, both perhaps in the sixth century and contemporary with the earliest Greek tunnels on Samos and at Athens. The suggestion is put forward in Chapter 10.E that the Greeks borrowed from the Persians the sighting tube for levelling tunnels, and that the Etruscans borrowed it more or less at the same time from the Greeks. There is therefore the possibility that the libra grew out of the sighting tube. This is only hypothesis; but it does seem safe to claim that the developed Roman libra preceded the developed Greek dioptra as a levelling instrument of some capability. All the same, the additional possibility, in or after the second century BC, of influence from Greek levelling practices with the dioptra and of refinement of Roman ones with the libra should not be overlooked.

---

[18] Except the very steep one at Alatri which, as will later be explained, is a special case.

B. TESTING A RECONSTRUCTED LIBRA

With no hard evidence to base the design on, the reconstruction of a libra can only be tentative. The sole requirements are that (on the present argument) it should resemble a balance beam and that its manufacture should be within the capabilities of a Roman metal worker; and in order to survey the shallow gradients of Roman aqueducts it must also be more accurate than the dioptra.

A steel beam was therefore made, with each end bent at right angles to carry iron split sights as on the dioptra, projecting sideways because the instrument is used only for levelling. The overall length is 6 ft (1.829 m) and the weight 4.72 kg. From the centre rises a vertical member terminating in a transverse bar with a knife-edge underneath on each side. This rests in a slight notch on top of each arm of a deep U-shaped bracket carried on a heavy tripod intended for a modern level. The concave base of the bracket imitates that of the level, allowing it to be adjusted on top of the convex tripod head, and a small plumb-line indicates when the bracket is vertical in both directions.

The knife-edge ensures that the beam can swing with a minimum of friction; indeed it is so sensitive that a fly settling on one end affects the reading on the staff. Because its weight is twice that of the dioptra and its exposed surface is less than a fifth, it is much less liable to swing in the wind. As an extra precaution, a narrow and shallow case of thin wood was made, screwed to the inside of the bracket arms and leaving only a slot at each end for the sights to project through. This shields the beam and prevents movement even in a moderate wind. When made, the beam was slightly out of balance and did not hang truly horizontal. A small quantity of metal was therefore added to one end and pared away until the beam appeared to be in proper equilibrium.

The libra was tested over the same course as described in Chapter 3.J, 173 m long with a difference in height of 13.005 m. The procedure was the same as with the dioptra except that at first only one-way sights were taken. Early results, giving around 12.90 m, were little if any better than with the dioptra, and the suspicion arose that contrary to appearances the beam was not in perfect equilibrium and that one-way sightings were inadequate. As with the dioptra, two-way sightings were therefore adopted. The final three results were 12.999, 13.002 and 13.005 m, whose average differed from the actuality by only 3 mm.

FIG. 4.2. Libra reconstruction with shield.

FIG. 4.3. Libra reconstruction without shield.

FIG. 4.4. Detail of suspension.

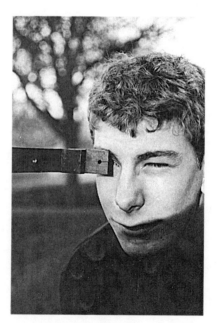

FIG. 4.5. Detail of sight.

This represents an error of 1 in 57,667, which would allow a gradient of 1 in 8000 or even 20,000 to be derived from levels taken with the libra. The best result was identical to that with the modern level. The implications are again discussed in Chapter 9.B. In a later demonstration for BBC television, the libra was given the task of setting out a 240 m stretch of aqueduct around a valley head at a gradient of 1 in 400. The total fall should therefore have been 60 cm. When the makeshift trough was installed and water was succesfully flowing, the actual fall was surveyed with a modern level and found to be 59 cm, an error of 1 in 24,000. This was probably due to the fact that, time being short, only one-way sightings were taken with the libra.

The libra's superiority over the dioptra seems to be accounted for both by the freedom from movement in wind and by the distance, three times as great, between the sights. As already observed, the design, though based on what can be deduced of the original libra, can only be tentative. That it works is no proof that it is correct. But the fact that it achieves the results postulated for it on quite different grounds makes it at least plausible.

CHAPTER 5

THE GROMA

A. GRIDS

The groma was an extremely simple instrument, possibly of Greek origin, which became almost the trademark of the Roman land surveyor. Because its function was limited to sighting and setting out straight lines and right angles, its use was restricted to surveying roads and the like and to establishing the rectangular grids of towns, military forts and, above all, land divisions. Since roads form the subject of Chapter 11, we may here confine ourselves to a brief outline of the history of surveyed grids.

An irregular street pattern was normal to early Greek cities; but in later times a regular rectangular grid became more widespread. Its introduction was generally attributed to Hippodamus of Miletus who rebuilt a number of cities in this way in the first half of the fifth century BC, and certainly it was a commonplace by 414 BC when Aristophanes lampooned the astronomer Meton as a town planner laying out Cloudcuckooland.[1] But while Hippodamus may have popularised the grid, he did not introduce it, for there are many Greek instances from earlier centuries, and even Egyptian and Mesopotamian antecedents.[2] It was most commonly applied to Greek colonies overseas, which often had the advantage of being built on virgin sites. The example of those in Italy was perhaps imitated to a limited extent by the Etruscans, to whom folk-memory ascribed a considerable ritual for the founding of new towns and an emphasis on correct orientation; but maybe their contribution was exaggerated, for archaeology reveals little planning of Etruscan cities. Beyond doubt, however, the Greek colonies of Italy inspired the Romans to adopt the regular urban grid.[3]

As for dividing agricultural land into a grid, Herodotus says that the Egyptians laid out square and equally-sized plots (Chapter 1.A); but in hard fact this seems to have been the exception, although there was

---

[1] Aristophanes, *Birds* 995–1009.   [2] Owens 1991, esp. 30–50.
[3] See Owens 1991, 98–120; Ward-Perkins 1974, esp. 37–40.

THE GROMA

certainly a complex system of land registration for tax purposes. In Greece the generally rough terrain militated against geometrical division of land; but once again it was around colonies, where land was distributed *de novo*, that a rectangular pattern of division is most evident, sometimes as an extension of and parallel with the town grid.[4] The best examples are in the Crimea, where huge areas of regular oblong plots of about 400 BC have been identified, and in southern Italy, where divisions of the sixth century tended to be in long rectangular strips, not in squares. The report of commissioners surveying land boundaries at Heraclea in Italy in about 300 BC survives on a bronze tablet;[5] and among the signatories is one Chaireas son of Damon of Naples, geometer (in the original sense of the word).

Nothing whatever is known about how these grids, urban or rural, were set out in Greek times. Orientation, as we have seen, would be no problem, and a straight line can quite easily be prolonged over considerable distances with nothing more than rods as markers. The bigger question hangs over the means of surveying right angles. The dioptra with its sights and engraved cross would serve very well; but as we have observed it appeared on the scene at a relatively late date. In Greek contexts we shall find that evidence for the groma, the standard instrument of the Romans, is slender though not non-existent, and possibly it was employed. If not, the set square or geometrical methods could have been used (Chapter 1.c). It is easy to check that lines are parallel by measuring the interval and that plots are truly rectangular by measuring the diagonals.

The regular division of land reached its ancient climax with Roman centuriation.[6] This was carried out, above all, around new colonies, which differed from Greek colonies in that their purpose, at least from the second century BC, was not so much mercantile as to provide for veteran soldiers or the landless. Territory conquered or confiscated or hitherto uncultivated was accurately divided up in systems that were often extensive and always carefully planned. Although there was much variation, the normal division was into squares of 2400 Roman feet on a side, containing 200 *iugera* or 50.4 ha. Each square was a *centuria*

[4] Dilke 1971, 25; Chevallier 1974; Isager and Skydsgaard 1992, 69; Saprykin 1994.
[5] *IG* XIV 645.
[6] The literature is huge. Useful starting-points are Bradford 1957; Dilke 1971; Hinrichs 1974; Behrends and Capogrossi Colognesi 1992; Campbell 1996.

which theoretically contained a hundred smallholdings of about half a hectare. It was demarcated by *limites* or roads at right angles, known as *decumani* (usually east–west) and *cardines* (usually north–south). Boundary stones were set up. When the system was complete and the land allocated, maps were drawn on bronze tablets with details of ownership and lodged in the record office. The surveyors were known originally as *finitores*, then as *metatores* or *mensores* or *agrimensores*, and ultimately (from their most distinctive instrument) *gromatici*. They not only laid out the divisions but were experts in such varied skills as measuring irregular plots and understanding the complexities of land law, and by the late empire had become judges in land disputes.

Centuriation originated at least as early as the fourth century BC in Italy; it increased dramatically in the second century BC and even more so in the early empire. Surveyors consequently grew in numbers, gained in status, and began to assemble a canon of manuals on surveying procedures which has come down to us as the *Corpus Agrimensorum*. In its present form this is a compilation of probably the fourth century AD, corrupt in text and desperately obscure, but our major source. Useful information also survives in inscriptions, notably the cadasters or maps on stone of land surveys at Orange in the south of France[7] and a newly-found fragment on bronze from Spain.[8] Above all there are the hundreds of square kilometres of centuriation still to be seen (most easily from the air) especially in northern Italy and North Africa.

To what extent Roman grid surveying was influenced by Greek practice is open to much debate.[9] Town plans could readily be imitated from Greek colonies in Italy. But the Roman tradition of centuriation, while it has some parallels with Greek practice, seems to be independent and early; and although land division utterly dominates the admittedly later *Corpus Agrimensorum*, it is almost totally ignored by the Greek surveying manuals. This is not to say that the Roman literature is innocent of Greek influence.[10] Some see connections between Hero's *Dioptra* and *Metrics* and some parts of the *Corpus*, notably in so far as Hero's methods of calculating the area of irregular plots are not unlike those of Frontinus and Hyginus. Balbus carried out such typically Greek exercises as measuring river widths and mountain heights, and

---

[7] Piganiol 1962.   [8] Sáez Fernández 1990.
[9] For a summary of the question see Hinrichs 1974, 107–12.
[10] Folkerts 1992 discusses parallelisms in mathematical procedures.

his parallel lines could have been set out by the methods in *Dioptra* 10 and 22. Hyginus' second method of finding south by gnomon is a very sophisticated one, dependent on solid geometry, which smacks strongly of Alexandrian scholarship,[11] and it is also one of the only two sections in the *Corpus* illustrated by a diagram with reference letters in the Greek fashion. The standard Greek practice of working by similar triangles is represented in the *Corpus* by two instances, which likewise stand out because they are the only ones. Hyginus' method (**Source 54**) of establishing parallel lines is in effect the same as that of *Dioptra* 8 and 10 and of **Anonymus 5**, and has the second example of a lettered diagram. Nipsus on measuring the width of a river (**Source 55**), although his method is not directly paralleled elsewhere, has an unlettered diagram and relies on similar triangles entirely in the Greek tradition. One sentence in particular, 'go to the other side of the *ferramentum* and with the croma remaining [unmoved] sight a line', might almost be a direct translation of *Dioptra* 21, 'without moving the alidade, go to the other side, [and] sight M'.[12] It has moreover been thought, and reasonably so, that Nipsus' *Podismus* is a straight translation from a Greek original.[13]

But these are the exceptions which prove the rule. The essential difference between Greek and Roman instruments, the difference between Greek and Latin terminology, and the idiosyncrasies of Roman land surveying all underline the basic independence of the Roman tradition. The Greek treatises, where the geometric theory which underpins them is readily visible, contrast strongly with their nearest Roman counterpart, the *Corpus*, which is utterly practical and virtually innocent of theory. They nicely illustrate Cicero's famous dictum: 'To them [the Greeks] geometry stood in the highest honour, and consequently nobody was held in greater esteem than mathematicians. But we have restricted these arts to utilitarian measurement and calculation.'[14]

Rome was undoubtedly tardy in acknowledging, let alone in imitating, the scientific attainments of Greece, and it was only in the second century BC that its awakening began. Two examples must suffice. The story goes that the critic, librarian and geographer Crates of Mallos,

---

[11] Hyginus Gromaticus, *Establishment* 153.1–154.11; Dilke 1971, 58; Dilke 1992, 340.
[12] Other close parallels are *Dioptra* 6, **Africanus 4** and **Anonymus 4**.
[13] Hinrichs 1974, 107.   [14] Cicero, *Tusculan Disputations* 1 2.5.

who constructed a terrestrial globe some 3 m in diameter,[15] came to Rome on an embassy from Pergamon in either 168 or 159 BC and broke his leg by falling into the manhole of a sewer. During his convalescence he gave lectures which first stimulated Roman interest in scholarship.[16] Similarly, the first public sundial in the city, brought back from Sicily as booty of war, was erected in 263 BC. But nobody appreciated that the change in latitude mattered, and for ninety-nine years it told the wrong time to a blissfully ignorant populace. Only in 159 BC did Rome acquire its first water clock, given by Scipio Nasica and conceivably designed by Crates.[17] It is against this background, and against the long-established Roman tradition of land surveying, that we may place the beginnings of Greek technical influence. Greeks now began to flock to a city which became more and more cosmopolitan, and some of them were surveyors. By the end of the first century AD Juvenal could utter his xenophobic outburst against the immigrants: 'Look, who do you reckon that chap is? He comes to us in any guise you care to name: teacher, public speaker, surveyor (*geometres*), painter, trainer, fortune-teller, tight-rope walker, doctor, magician. The hungry Greekling knows the lot. Tell him to fly, and he takes off.'[18]

While Greek surveyors clearly introduced snippets of Greek practice, as far as we can tell they had little effect on Roman land surveying. Nor, as we have seen, is there any sure sign of them greatly influencing Roman levelling techniques. Yet ironically, as we shall find in Chapter 11, an elegant method of setting out long straight alignments for Roman roads smacks more of Greek than Roman geometry.

B. THE GROMA AND ITS USE

It is a curious fact that, although the groma is the only surveying instrument of which actual examples and ancient illustrations survive, the details of its operation remain unclear. The principle is straightforward enough. A horizontal cross, its arms at right angles, was carried on a vertical support, and from the end of each of the four arms hung a cord or plumb-line tensioned by a bob. The surveyor sighted across one pair of these cords to project a straight line, and across another pair to set

---

[15] Strabo, *Geography* II 5.10; Geminus, *Introduction* 16.22; Aujac 1993, 91n., 135.

[16] Suetonius, *Grammarians* 2.   [17] Pliny, *Natural History* VII 214–15.

[18] Juvenal, *Satires* 3. 74–8.

out a right angle. He therefore worked only in the horizontal, or more or less horizontal, plane, and was not concerned with differences of height. If he encountered a steep-sided valley too wide to measure across in the ordinary way, he carried out the operation known as *cultellatio*. He held a ten-foot rod horizontal (presumably levelling it by eye, though we are not told) with one end resting on the ground at the start of the slope. From the other end he dropped a plumb-line and marked the point where it hit the ground. He moved the rod, still horizontal, so that its uphill end rested on this point, dropped the plumb-line again, and so proceeded down one side of the valley and up the other, counting horizontal ten-foot steps but ignoring the vertical difference.[19]

As Schulten showed, the name *groma* came to Latin from the Greek *gnoma*, not directly but via Etruscan.[20] Nonetheless the origin of the word remains somewhat mysterious. *Gnoma* and *gnome* are both by-forms of *gnomon*, which most frequently denotes the pointer of a sundial, but can be a carpenter's set square, a water clock[21] or, in a more general sense, any indicator or mark. Festus (**Source 50**) equates *groma* as an instrument with *gnomon*, for which no parallel can be found in Greek literature, unless a cryptic dictionary entry (**Source 24**) has this meaning. *Gnoma* and *gnome*, rather, seem to be words used of the central point of a camp or town, as in **Source 45, 46** and perhaps **47**. Possibly they reflect the setting up at such places of a stone or wooden marker bearing a cross, as might be implied by Strabo's description of Nicaea in Bithynia as laid out in the classic quadrilateral shape 'divided into streets at right angles, so that from a single stone set up in the middle of the gymnasium the four gates can be seen'.[22] The same usage is found for the Latin *gruma* and *groma* in the passages cited in **Source 46**. The instrument may therefore have derived its name from the starting-point of the survey. In Latin, when the word first appears in republican literature, it is spelt *gruma*, with the related verbs *grumare* and *degrumare* (**Sources 46–9**). Under the empire it is standardised as *groma* with the variant (in Nipsus, **Source 55**) of *croma*. It is twice given the generic name 'machine' or 'little machine' (**Sources 58, 50**).

---

[19] Frontinus, *Surveying* 18.12–16. Nipsus, *Resighting* 51–76 seems also to take account of slopes: see Bouma 1993, 120–6. [20] Schulten 1912, 1882.

[21] Athenaeus, *Learned Banquet* 42B quoting Theophrastus on Egypt.

[22] Strabo, *Geography* XII 4.7.

The instrument as such is mentioned only once in Greek literature, by Hero (*Dioptra* 33), under the name *asteriskos* or 'little star'.[23] Whether it had been imported from Rome or was a survival of an indigenous Greek instrument is more than we can say. The equation of dioptra and gruma in a glossary (**Source 48**) need mean no more than that both were used for the same purpose. If we take Hero at face value, he implies that in his day the groma was not much used in Greek-speaking lands, since the dioptra did the same job more effectively. Possibly, however, his derogatory remarks were aimed at Roman land surveyors, with the motive of persuading them to abandon their groma in favour of his dioptra.[24]

The authors of the *Corpus Agrimensorum*, to whom the groma was their everyday tool,[25] did not see fit to describe it, and what they incidentally let drop forms our only written evidence for its design. It clearly consisted of at least two parts, the *ferramentum* or 'iron' which was planted in the ground, and the groma proper which was placed on top (**Sources 52, 55**). More often, however, *ferramentum* is used of the whole thing. The groma proper comprised the cross with four arms, *corniculi*, from which hung the cords for sighting (**Sources 51, 57**). The centre of the cross, by the usual interpretation, had the strange name of *umbilicus soli*, the navel of the base or ground, or (if it should really be *solii*) of the throne. As it is normally understood,[26] the cross could pivot on a bracket which could itself pivot on top of the upright column of the *ferramentum*. If an existing line was to be picked up, the *ferramentum* was fixed in the ground one bracket-length away from the centre of the marker stone or stake and was plumbed vertical by reference to the hanging cords. The bracket was swung until its end, the *umbilicus soli*, was vertically above the marker as checked by another plumb-line, and the cross was then turned on the bracket until its arms and cords coincided with the desired alignment. The surveyor sighted across diago-

---

[23] *Asteriskos* does not seem to be a translation of the Latin *stella* which, though it appears in a surveying context, denotes not an instrument but a star-shaped bronze plate used as a marker on central or boundary marks. See pseudo-Hyginus (**Source 52**); Festus 476.26–9; Gaius 307.7 and 346.9.   [24] Hinrichs 1974, 108.

[25] It is interesting that Groma occurs once as a proper name, at Chester where a tombstone (*RIB* 503) to a legionary of the first century AD was set up by his heir Groma. Was he, or his father, a surveyor?

[26] Bouma 1993, 91–8 discusses the evidence of the texts at length.

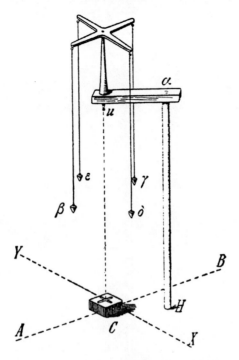

FIG. 5.1. Schulten's reconstruction of the groma (Schulten 1912, 1884).

nally opposite cords at rods placed exactly in line by assistants at his direction. If a new alignment was being established, the point vertically below the *umbilicus soli* was plumbed and marked. This is by far the best explanation of what the texts say. For geometrical precision the mark has to be directly below the centre of the cross, and the *ferramentum* therefore has to be significantly to one side. Schulten therefore reconstructed the groma as in Fig. 5.1, complete with bracket.

In the very year that he wrote, the metal parts of a groma were found at Pompeii and ten years later were published by Della Corte with a reconstruction (Fig. 5.2) which in essence followed Schulten's.[27] There was an iron spike for planting in the ground with a bronze bush on top to hold a missing wooden column, a long bronze bush for the top of the column, two small bronze bushes as pivots for each end of a missing wooden bracket 25 cm long and two strips of bronze for reinforcing it,

---

[27] Della Corte 1922.

FIG. 5.2. The Pompeii groma as reconstructed by Della Corte
(after Della Corte 1922, Fig. 13).

and a wooden cross sheathed in iron, with arms 46 cm long. Until very recently Della Corte's reconstruction ruled the roost, being reproduced countless times and accepted unquestioningly as fact. Now, however, Schiöler has cast serious doubts on its accuracy.[28] He points out that not all the components were found together (not even in the same room) and that, with the weight of the cross, 4.81 kg, cantilevered on a bracket from the top, a wooden column of the diameter dictated

---

[28] Schiöler 1994.

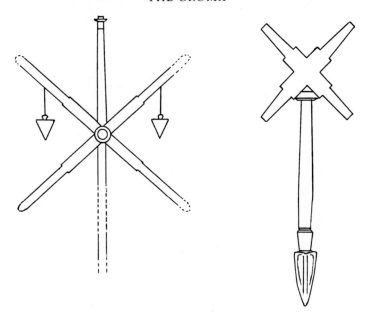

FIG. 5.3. Gromas on tombstones from Ivrea and Pompeii
(after Adam 1994, Figs. 3 and 4).

by the bushes will be bent markedly sideways. He argues that the bracket never existed (the original excavation report records one strip 50 cm long, not two of 25 cm) and that the cross was pivoted directly on top of the column.

Schiöler makes a very good case; and all the rest of the archaeological evidence seems to confirm it. Two tombstones of *mensores*, from Ivrea in north Italy and from Pompeii (Fig. 5.3),[29] show gromas, one dismantled and both with the cross depicted in plan. Neither has any sign of a bracket. An iron cross found before 1901 on the Roman frontier at Pfünz in Bavaria has a central iron column and rivets at the ends of the arms where wooden components were attached. Schöne interpreted it as a dioptra and reconstructed it as in Fig. 5.4,[30] although his interpretation has not found universal favour and some scholars see it rather as the remains of a military standard or as the iron strapping of a corn measure. But if it was a groma, it had no bracket. An extremely

---

[29] For photographs of the latter see e.g. Schöne 1901, Taf. II; Dilke 1971, 50; Schiöler 1994, fig. 3; Adam 1994, fig. 3; of the former, Adam 1994, fig. 4.   [30] Schöne 1901.

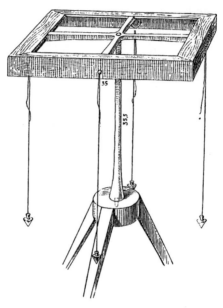

FIG. 5.4. Reconstruction of supposed groma from Pfünz (Schöne 1901, Fig. 3).

crude cross, found in 1899 in the Fayum in Egypt, is made of two pieces of palm-leaf rib, 35.2 and 34.2 cm long, tied together approximately at right angles and suspended from a central loop of cord (Fig. 5.5).[31] Four lumps of limestone served as bobs, and although no plumb-lines survived, the ends of the arms are notched to take them. If it was a groma (which Schiöler doubts) it would be almost impossible to use if held by hand as is usually suggested; and once more there is no sign of a bracket. Finally there are Roman coins minted by L. Roscius Fabatus in 50 BC which have control marks interpreted by Schiöler as a groma and its stand, again without a bracket (Fig. 5.6).[32] This is open to some doubt, for he does not explain why pairs of cords on the groma are looped together.

Whether or not the more debatable examples are accepted as gromas, the fact remains that archaeology has yet to provide any good evidence for the bracket. There are two possibilities. One is that all the archaeo-

[31] Lyons 1927, 138 and fig. facing p. 133; Wartnaby 1968, 7; Dilke 1971, 49.
[32] Crawford 1974, pl. LXVIII no. 85. Schiöler also claims that bronze castings from El Djem in Tunisia represent a simplified dioptra; but this is a very long shot which does not convince.

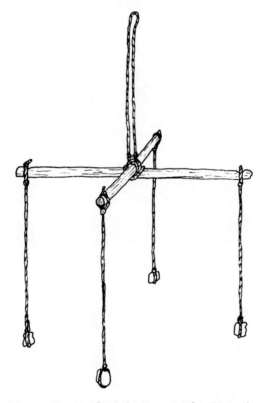

FIG. 5.5. Supposed groma from the Fayum (after Wartnaby 1968, 7).

logical specimens are of one type and all the texts are dealing with another, which does not commend itself. The other is that no groma had a bracket and that our reading of the texts is wrong. In this case two further possibilities arise. If the column was vertical, it would obstruct sighting across two diagonally opposite cords.[33] Both Nowotny[34] and Schiöler therefore suggest that the column was tilted slightly to permit the line of sight to pass beside it. Hero's chapter (**Dioptra 33**) explains how, if the cross is not horizontal, its arms cease to be at right angles in the horizontal plane, and Schiöler calculates that the error with the column tilted at 3° will be ± 1.4‰, which he regards as insignificant. Against this, the texts insist on plumbing the *ferramentum*. The alternative

---

[33] Grewe 1998, 30 claims that there is a slot under the bush at the top of the column on the Ivrea relief which would allow sighting *through* the column; but I can see no sign of such a thing.   [34] Nowotny 1923, 24, 28.

FIG. 5.6. Supposed groma and stand as control marks on denarius
(after Crawford 1974, Pl. LXVIII no. 85).

is that sighting was done not diagonally but along adjacent sides of the
square formed by the cords.[35] The problem here is the difficulty of positioning the *ferramentum* in exactly the right place. For turning a right
angle from an existing mark, not only does the cord at the angle have to
be vertically above it but the arms of the cross have also to point in
exactly the right directions, for in the absence of a bracket there is no
means of adjustment. Moreover the *umbilicus soli* has to be the end of
the arm rather than the centre of the cross, which seems a less plausible
explanation of the name. The Fayum groma, however, has arms of
different lengths so that a right angle could only be obtained by diagonal
sighting. Hero too (**Dioptra 33**) seems to envisage using the diagonals,
for it is they which he proves (in his instance) are not at right angles; nor
are adjacent sides, for that matter, but he shows no interest in them.
None of the alternatives, then, is satisfactory, and until more evidence
should emerge we have to admit that we do not know the answer.

Finally, the groma suffered from two limitations to its accuracy. First,
as Hero makes plain, its plumb-lines were all too liable to disturbance
by wind, and shielding them in tubes generated further problems.
Adam tried surveying with a reconstructed groma in Provence and
reported that, though it was accurate over short distances in a calm, his
experiments were much hampered by the *mistral*.[36] Secondly, if less

[35] As suggested by Schöne 1901, 131 and Dilke 1974, 572; discussed by Bouma 1993,
97–8 who claims that Nipsus (**Source 56**) used diagonal sighting. But 'go to the
other side of the *ferramentum*' could as well mean sighting across adjacent cords as
across diagonal ones. In either case the second sighting is at 180° from the first.

[36] Adam 1982, 1019n.; Adam 1994, 12–14.

importantly, the further cord appears to the user to be the thinner of the two and therefore cannot be centred exactly on the nearer one behind which, as Frontinus explains (**Source 51**), it is totally hidden. This contrasts with the slit sights of a dioptra which can readily be centred on each other. It has been calculated that with the Pompeian groma the resulting error is $\pm$ 1.5‰ or, when setting out the side of a *centuria* (2400 feet or 710 m), about $\pm$ 1 m.[37] But this figure depends on the distance of the eye from the nearer cord. For the uses to which the groma was put an error of this size or less would not matter much, and successive errors would be more likely to cancel each other out than to accumulate.[38] The marvellously straight alignment of the outermost German limes (Chapter 11.F(e)) bears witness to the accuracy of the groma.

[37] Schiöler 1994, 60 n. 22.

[38] Adam 1982, 1020–3 discusses the practical plotting of existing buildings with a reconstructed groma by measured right-angle offsets from a baseline. The results were impressively accurate.

CHAPTER 6

THE HODOMETER

The hodometer, as a vehicle provided with gearing to measure the distance travelled, cannot be reckoned among the more important surveying instruments of antiquity. But while its interest lies more in its mechanical complexities than in its contribution to the surveyor's work, it does deserve brief discussion.

We have two detailed specifications, by Vitruvius and by Hero. In Vitruvius' version (**Source 59**), which was 'handed down by our predecessors', the road wheel is one 400th of a mile in circumference. Attached to its hub is a disc carrying a single tooth. At every revolution of the wheel this tooth advances a vertical pinion, which carries 400 teeth, by one tooth. Similarly at every revolution of the vertical pinion a projecting tooth advances a horizontal pinion by one tooth. In the horizontal pinion is a series of holes, one corresponding to each tooth and each containing a pebble. After a mile, therefore, the road wheel has revolved 400 times, the vertical pinion has revolved once, and the horizontal pinion advances by one tooth. The first hole containing a pebble now coincides with a hole in the casing below, which allows the pebble to drop through into a bronze bowl, giving audible notice that a mile has been completed. At the end of the journey the number of pebbles in the bowl indicates the miles travelled.

The basic principle is clear enough, the rotation of the pinions being not continuous but intermittent; but the details long presented severe problems, most notably that the pinions would ostensibly have to be of impossibly large diameter. This led scholars such as Drachmann to write Vitruvius' hodometer off as an armchair invention,[1] until Sleeswyk made a number of brilliant suggestions which solve all the problems, shed a fascinating light on the origin of the machine, and are surely correct.[2] He pointed out that the device of balls falling through a hole to mark the miles was identical to that which marked the hours in

---

[1] Drachmann 1963, 157–9.   [2] Sleeswyk 1979, 1981, 1990.

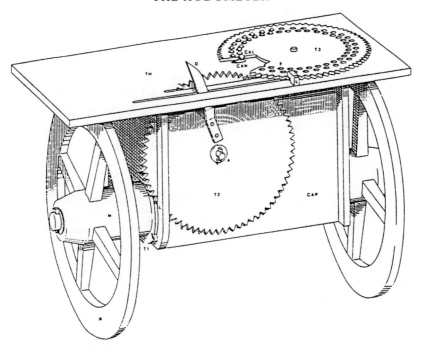

FIG. 6.1. Reconstruction of Vitruvius' hodometer. For clarity, the pinions are drawn with 72 teeth each rather than 400 (Sleeswyk 1979, Fig. 1; courtesy Prof. A. W. Sleeswyk).

an elaborate water-clock, also employing an intermittent drive, designed by Archimedes. He suggested that the hodometer was created by the great engineer about 240 BC, when Rome and Syracuse were in close alliance, to position milestones on the newly-completed Appian Way, the first and greatest of the Roman roads of Italy. He also proposed that the pinions were not ordinary spur or right-angle gears but skew or hypoid gears, which would overcome the difficulty of size and which are cognate to the screw gear known to have been invented by Archimedes. On this basis he built a scale model which worked well (Fig. 6.1).

A few points may be added in confirmation of Sleeswyk's arguments. Proclus (**Source 61**) includes devices 'to measure routes by land and sea' in a list which seems to reflect Archimedes' inventions, and so perhaps, if less clearly, does Tzetzes (**Sources 62–3**). Archimedes' screw gear first appears in 241–239 BC, the same time as Sleeswyk's suggested date for the hypoid gear.[3] The paddle wheel driving the maritime version of the hodometer is no more than a vertical waterwheel, which was invented, it seems, in the 240s BC at Alexandria[4] and no doubt came to Archimedes' attention when he was in Egypt (where he invented the screw) at the end of that decade. There are strong suggestions that Archimedes' mechanical work, which he famously refused to write up himself, was published by Philo of Byzantium, whom we know Vitruvius used as a source.[5] Thus an Archimedean origin for the hodometer seems extremely likely.

Hero (**Dioptra 34**) acknowledges that his predecessors have produced several designs for hodometers, of which Archimedes' was surely one, and invites comparison with what he seems to claim is his own version. The initial drive is by a single pin on the hub of the road wheel which advances a disc carrying eight pegs by one peg per revolution; thereafter the drive is by a series of screws and pinions.[6] The axles carrying these gears are alternately vertical and horizontal and terminate in pointers on dials – among the earliest on record[7] – on the top and sides of the box containing the gear train. Reading off the distance travelled would be rather like reading the dials on an old-fashioned gas meter. The whole design is neat and logical, and there seems no reason why it should not work.

Very strangely, however, Hero himself introduces qualifications. To turn a pinion through one revolution, the driving screw should rotate as many times as there are teeth on the pinion, as Hero was very well aware. But he considers a scenario where faulty manufacture prevents this smooth operation, giving as an example a screw which turns only 20 times to rotate a 30-toothed pinion once. Now Hero knew and wrote a great deal about the theory and practice of gear wheels, and used small screws and pinions for fine adjustment of his dioptra. Surviving examples show that by his time gear manufacture had become quite a fine art. The Antikythera mechanism, constructed probably in 87 BC, consisted of a nest of gear wheels, very much smaller than in the hodometer, the largest having a diameter of 126 mm and carrying 225 teeth at a pitch of 1.75 mm.[8] Gynaecological instruments

[3] Lewis 1997, 54–6.   [4] Lewis 1997, 56, 61.   [5] Lewis 1997, 37–9, 42–8.
[6] Technical discussion (with a few misplaced qualms) in Drachmann 1963, 159–65.
[7] They existed on the Antikythera mechanism of probably 87 BC: Price 1974, 47–50.
[8] Price 1974.

from Pompeii (and thus contemporary with Hero) have superbly-made screws with pitches as fine as about 3.6 mm.[9] One therefore wonders whether Hero's description of the hodometer, like Vitruvius', was drawn from a much earlier source dating from a time when the accurate cutting of screws and gear teeth had not yet evolved. The measurements, as befit a Greek origin, are in cubits and stades.

Hero's specification for a maritime hodometer (*Dioptra* 38), though sadly corrupted in the text, reveals a different arrangement.[10] It too has pointers and dials, but the drive, apart from a screw at the start, is entirely through spur wheels; and although stades are mentioned, so are miles. For this reason, and because it is separated from the chapter on the land hodometer by an intrusive and quite irrelevant section on the *barulkos*, it is usually and rightly considered not to be a genuine part of Hero's *Dioptra*. The remaining references to hodometers give no detail at all. Those belonging to Commodus (**Source 60**) are listed, interestingly, alongside what I have suggested elsewhere were the Roman (or Greek) equivalent of the Chinese geared south-pointing chariot carrying a human figure (or in Commodus' case a seat) which always faced the same direction no matter which way the chariot turned.[11] The hodometer mentioned by Simplicius (**Source 69**) evidently belongs, as will be explained in Chapter 7, in the first century BC.

It remains to ask just what the hodometer was used for. Vitruvius' answer, which may be his own rather than his source's, is that it was used to measure the length of a journey. By itself, this seems unlikely: travellers were more interested in how far they had to go than in how far they had gone. Hero's more useful answer is that the hodometer was a less laborious method of measuring long distances than the surveyor's chain or cord. While it could hardly travel across country unless the going was very smooth, it could readily find distances between towns by road. This would provide raw material for official or semi-official records such as Agrippa's great world-map (finished after 7 BC) and the later Antonine Itinerary and Peutinger Table, all of which included such information;[12] or for geographers like Marinus of Tyre and Ptolemy, who were concerned with coordinates for map-making; or

---

[9] Illustrated in Scarborough 1969, pl. 43.
[10] Discussed by Drachmann 1963, 165–7.   [11] Lewis 1992.
[12] Dilke 1985, 41–53, 112–29.

even for Simplicius' anonymous geographer, who required the length of a degree of latitude in order to estimate the circumference of the earth. But, from the mid-third century BC, Roman main roads were provided with milestones, and once they were in place the hodometer would merely duplicate, expensively and unnecessarily, information that was already freely available.

The implication, therefore, is that the hodometer was principally employed at a period when, and in regions where, Roman roads had not yet arrived or were in the throes of arriving. In newly-acquired provinces, it took time to install a network of good highways, and new roads were being built well into the first and even second centuries AD. One may thus visualise the hodometer both in a Greek context before the notoriously poor roads of the eastern Mediterranean were upgraded by Rome, and in a Roman context when new roads were being constructed and milestones needed to be positioned. One stone from the Peloponnese dated AD 114–15 records that Trajan 'ordered [milestones] to be set up, measurements having been taken of the roads'.[13] True, the intervals might have been measured by pacing or even by surveyor's cords or rods. But it remains entirely possible that sometimes and in some places hodometers were used for this purpose, just as in the seventeenth century John Ogilby measured all the main roads of England and Wales, before milestones were in place, with the waywiser or wheel dimensurator which was the lineal descendant of the hodometer.[14]

Why the notoriously dissolute emperor Commodus should own several hodometers, classified by his enemies as 'items appropriate to his vices', is a matter for conjecture. The same kind of machine also appeared in China (though distinctly later than in the west) where it often carried a regular band of puppet musicians, automatically striking drums or gongs according to the distance travelled. There is no record of these hodometers serving any useful purpose; it seems, rather, that they served as status symbols for emperors, being paraded in state processions.[15] Such a function sounds unlikely in the Roman empire, even under Commodus. The answer might lie, though this is pure guesswork, in that emperor's love of chariot racing. Another source,

---

[13] *Année Epigraphique* 1969/70, 589. [14] Ogilby 1675, preface.
[15] Needham 1959, 577–9; 1965, 281–6.

mentioning the sale of his assets, says that 'every article that Commodus had collected, whether as luxuries, for gladiatorial combat or for chariot driving, came under the hammer'.[16] Can it be that his hodometers were for marking out the length of informal racecourses?

Finally, measurement by hodometer of sizeable distances by sea was in the nature of things much less accurate than measurement by land. The paddle wheels could only record, and approximately at that, the movement of the ship relative to the water, and could not take account of currents or of leeway. But one can well believe that the results were better than dead reckoning. It may be that some of the distances recorded in the *Periploi* (volumes of sailing directions)[17] of the right period, on Agrippa's map, and in the Maritime Itinerary appended to the Antonine Itinerary were obtained in this way. Overall, then, the hodometer perhaps saw rather wider use both by land and sea than is often assumed, but the fact remains that its contribution to surveying in the usual sense must have been quite marginal.

[16] Dio Cassius LXXIII 5.5.   [17] Dilke 1985, 130–44.

PART II

PRACTICAL APPLICATIONS

CHAPTER 7

MEASUREMENT OF THE EARTH

The attempts by the Greeks to measure the circumference of the earth have generated much discussion. Two protagonists stand out among a cast of lesser actors: Eratosthenes, who produced a figure of 252,000 stades, and Posidonius, who is said to have produced one of 180,000 stades. Although both figures were variously accepted by later writers, it was the lower one that was adopted by Ptolemy. Backed by his immense authority, it came to rule the roost; and because it underestimated the size of the earth it was ultimately responsible for seducing Columbus into thinking that the Indies were readily accessible across the Atlantic. Eratosthenes' method is well known. What has not been clear, however, is how Posidonius, if it really was he, obtained his result. The answer can now in part be given.

The broad outline of the story, shorn of many of the much-debated details, must first be spelled out.[1] The earliest figure for the circumference is given by Aristotle in the 340s BC in his *De Caelo*, quoting unnamed mathematicians, as 400,000 stades.[2] A generation later this was refined, perhaps by his pupil Dicaearchus of Messana in Sicily, to 300,000 stades.[3] Whatever method Aristotle's informants had employed, we know that in this case the latitude difference between Syene (Aswan) on the Nile and Lysimachia on the Dardanelles was calculated by measuring the shadows of gnomons to be $\frac{1}{15}$ of the greatest circle (that is 24°, about 50 per cent too great), while the distance between them was estimated at 20,000 stades (about double the real figure); hence the circumference was $15 \times 20,000 = 300,000$.[4] The same figure is quoted, perhaps from the same source, by Archimedes.[5] These

---

[1] For the whole matter see Drabkin 1943; Dicks 1960; Aujac 1966, 170–6; Neugebauer 1975, esp. 646–54; Harley and Woodward 1987, 152–5, 168–70.

[2] Aristotle, *De Caelo* 298a 15–20.

[3] Wehrli 1944, 77. This attribution is disputed: see Harley and Woodward 1987, 152 n.30.   [4] Cleomedes, *On the Heavens* I 5.57–75.

[5] *Sand-reckoner* 1.8. This is not the place to discuss the figures for the earth's diameter and circumference ascribed to Archimedes by Hippolytus, which are fascinating but corrupt and therefore contentious, or those by Martianus Capella. Both are evidently

143

early attempts probably foundered on the difficulties of measuring both angles and distances. But techniques improved.

The first to achieve a result not far from the truth was Eratosthenes (c.285/280–c.200 BC), the librarian at Alexandria and a contemporary of Archimedes. Much under the influence of Dicaearchus, he adopted the same approach. Our major source is Cleomedes, a Stoic populariser of astronomy writing perhaps in the second century AD.[6] Eratosthenes, he said, found by gnomons at Syene (more or less on the tropic) and at Alexandria (which he took to be on the same meridian) that the difference in latitude was $\frac{1}{50}$ of the greatest circle or, by the later system of 360 degrees, 7° 12′.[7] His estimated distance of 5000 stades between the two places gave the circumference as 50 × 5000 stades = 250,000.[8] The exact value of the stade he used, a bone of great contention, does not concern us here. He evidently and properly regarded this result as only an approximation; and indeed it is just as often given as 252,000,[9] which suggests that he added 2000 stades to make the total readily divisible by 60, his normal division of the circle. When the system of 360 degrees was adopted in the time of Hipparchus it yielded the equation for Eratosthenes' circumference of 1 degree = 700 stades.

The next actor on the stage was Hipparchus, who was active at Rhodes between 162 and 126 BC. He provisionally accepted Eratosthenes' result until a more accurate one could be obtained,[10] but

footnote 5 (cont.)
　different from the figure that Archimedes himself gives in the Sand-reckoner. For details, see Neugebauer 1975, 647–51.
[6] Cleomedes, On the Heavens I 7.48–120. This is the date accepted by e.g. Aujac 1993, 21, although Neugebauer 1975, 960–1 argues for the fourth century AD. For discussion of Eratosthenes' method see Collinder 1956 and Fischer 1975.
[7] Syene is in fact at 24° 4′, not on the tropic, which was then at 23° 44′. Alexandria lies 3° west of Syene and (on a likely value of the stade) at a distance of some 4350 stades rather than 5000.
[8] Martianus Capella, Philologia VI 596–8 has the slightly different and possibly more accurate story that the observations were made at Syene and Meroe, which are more nearly on the same meridian, and that the distance was measured by the royal surveyors, no doubt by pacing.
[9] Eratosthenes Frags. II.B.1–42 Berger include all the many ancient authorities for both figures.
[10] Hipparchus Frags. 35–6, 39 = Strabo, Geography I 4.1, II 5.7, II 5.34. Pliny (Natural History II 247 = Hipparchus Frag. 38) states that Hipparchus added a little under 26,000 stades to Eratosthenes' figure. This is usually held to be 'an egregious blunder'

implied that other but similar figures had already been proposed: 'It makes little difference', he said, '. . . whether we adopt his [Eratosthenes'] measurement or that given by later writers.'[11] He also suggested, apparently for the first time, a terrestrial application of the figure. The difficulty of measuring long distances on earth with any accuracy was obvious, especially when the road between the places in question was indirect or non-existent. He therefore suggested identifying two stars, one at the zenith at each of the places, measuring their distance apart in degrees, and multiplying the result by the accepted value of a degree: in his case, 700 stades.[12]

After Hipparchus came the Stoic philosopher Posidonius (c. 135–c. 51 BC, also based at Rhodes), whose high reputation as a scientist is not in this case enhanced by his method, for he seems to have derived his data not from first-hand observation but from second-hand and distinctly crude measurements. At first, perhaps, he accepted Eratosthenes' circumference. Only fragments of his writings survive; but the very competent astronomer Geminus, who also worked in Rhodes probably during Posidonius' lifetime, was much influenced by him. Geminus, it can be argued, would reflect Posidonius' latest thinking; yet he shows no awareness of any circumference other than Eratosthenes'.[13] The dates traditionally ascribed to Geminus' *Introduction* centre on the 70s BC, although Aujac argues for one about 55 BC.[14]

But Posidonius then tackled the problem in a new way. He assumed that when Canopus was on the horizon at Rhodes, its altitude to an observer in Alexandria (which was deemed to be on the same meridian) was $\frac{1}{48}$ of the greatest circle, or $7\frac{1}{2}°$. The error is considerable, for the actual difference in latitude is about $5°$ or $\frac{1}{72}$ of the circle.[15] He also took the distance in question to be 5000 stades, which gave him 48 ×

(Dicks 1960, 153), though Fischer 1975, 155–6 defends it. For further and mysterious computations in Pliny see Pederson 1986, 187–8.

[11] Frag. 36 = Strabo, *Geography* II 5.7.

[12] Frag. 37 = Scholiast on Ptolemy, *Geography* I 3.3.   [13] Geminus, *Introduction* 16.6.

[14] The evidence is reviewed by Aujac 1975, xiv–xxiv. The complex argument of Neugebauer 1975, 578–81, which puts Geminus in the mid-first century AD, appeared too late for her to discuss; but she still favours her own dating (Aujac 1993, 28), and I think rightly so.

[15] Dicks 1960, 176. The exact size of the error depends on where on the island of Rhodes the latitude was taken.

5000 = 240,000 stades for the earth's circumference or 1 degree = 666.66 stades, a figure close to Eratosthenes', although he added the rider that if the distance was not 5000 stades then the circumference would be proportionately different. All this is clearly stated by Cleomedes, who acknowledges his overall debt to Posidonius' *On Ocean*.[16]

The next stage, where the problems really begin, heralds a more serious questioning of Eratosthenes' result and a more significant revision. It is attested by Vitruvius, writing about 30 BC: 'There are some who deny that Eratosthenes was able to obtain a true measurement of the earth.'[17] It is twice attested by Strabo (*c.* 64 BC – after AD 21), writing a few years before Christ. 'Whether the earth is as large as [Eratosthenes] said', he remarked, 'later writers do not agree';[18] and, more importantly, 'If of the more recent measurements we accept the one which makes the earth the smallest, such as Posidonius' estimate of about 180,000, it shows that the torrid zone is about half the space between the tropics.'[19] This statement is made quite categorically, and with no explanation of how Posidonius arrived at that figure. Taisbak, however, shows that this width of the torrid zone is incompatible with a circumference of 180,000 stades and is based instead on one of 240,000. He therefore rejects Strabo as evidence that Posidonius ever proposed a circumference of 180,000.[20] But he is wrong. Strabo confirms elsewhere that the figure of 180,000 stades *was* attached to Posidonius' name, just as that of 252,000 was to Eratosthenes'. The parallel of Athens (36°), he says, is less than 200,000 stades long according to Eratosthenes, 140,000 stades according to Posidonius.[21] These distances are approximately correct for equatorial circumferences of 252,000 and 180,000 stades respectively. The simple answer must be that Strabo was in a muddle and was copying figures indiscriminately from conflicting sources. It is well known that his interest in, and com-

---

[16] Cleomedes, *On the Heavens* I 7.8–47 = Posidonius Frag. 202, partially confirmed by Pliny, *Natural History* II 178.   [17] Vitruvius, *On Architecture* I 6.11.

[18] Strabo, *Geography* I 4.1.   [19] Strabo, *Geography* II 2.2.

[20] Taisbak 1973–4, 259–62.

[21] Strabo, *Geography* I 4.6, II 3.6. The modern method of calculating such distances (the ratio of a parallel to the equator is the cosine of the latitude) was not available to the Greeks; their approximation may be due to rough-and-ready measurement on a globe with a piece of string: see Dicks 1960, 151.

prehension of, the astronomical aspect of geography was limited, and elsewhere he states as a fact that the equatorial circumference is twice 126,000 stades, namely 252,000.[22]

Much ink has been spilled on attempts to explain, or explain away, this underestimate of Posidonius', and thus to vindicate his reputation.[23] Perhaps the standard assumption nowadays is that he changed his mind over the distance from Alexandria to Rhodes, and instead of 5000 stades adopted 3750, which, in conjunction with his erroneous $\frac{1}{48}$ of the greatest circle, gave $48 \times 3750 = 180,000$, or 1 degree = 500 stades.[24] No ancient source confirms this assumption. At first sight it is not unreasonable, because it was already known that the figure of 5000 stades was in fact too high. Eratosthenes had said that whereas some sailors put the distance at about 4000 stades and others at 5000, he himself had found it by gnomon to be 3750.[25] This can only mean that he found the latitude difference by gnomon: probably $\frac{1}{50}$ less a quarter of $\frac{1}{50}$ of the circle which, in conjunction with his equation of $\frac{1}{50} = 5000$ stades, gave the distance of 3750.[26] Hipparchus, moreover, had found the distance, presumably also by gnomon, to be 3640 to the centre of the island.[27]

Closer inspection, however, puts this assumption in dubious light. If Posidonius' revised estimate of 180,000 stades derived from multiplying his latitude difference of $\frac{1}{48}$ of the circle by the distance of 3750 stades, which itself derived from Eratosthenes' circumference of 252,000 stades, then it involved a glaring logical fallacy which a philosopher like Posidonius would be most unlikely to commit.[28] It is therefore

---

[22] Strabo, Geography II 5.6.

[23] See Dicks 1960, 150–2 for a critical evaluation of them, especially of Viedebantt's suggestion that the 180,000-stade circumference was merely an example employing fictional figures which Posidonius coined to demonstrate the principle to the layman but which later generations, notably Ptolemy, disastrously mistook for a genuine scientific estimate. Fischer 1975, 165 takes a similar line but argues that Ptolemy did not follow Posidonius in adopting the figure of 180,000, but arrived at the same result by pure coincidence.

[24] Originated by Heath 1921, II 220; followed, for example, by Dicks 1960, 150, Aujac 1966, 175–6, Kidd 1988, 723.

[25] Strabo, Geography II 5.24, confirmed by Pliny, Natural History V 132 (469 Roman miles = 3750 stades). [26] Taisbak 1973–4, 268. [27] Strabo, Geography II 5.39.

[28] Drabkin 1943, 509–10, Fischer 1975, 163, Kidd 1988, 724 and Aujac 1993, 132 all point out this fallacy.

probable that some other consideration, compelling but quite different, prompted Posidonius to revise his first estimate. This is the crux of
the matter, to which we will return later.

The next significant geographer was the great Ptolemy in the mid-
second century AD. Much of his raw material was drawn from Marinus
of Tyre, who wrote a generation or so earlier. Ptolemy was content to
follow Marinus and 'his predecessors' in taking the circumference as
180,000 stades and one degree as 500. This, he said, 'agrees with
accepted measurements' and 'has been found by the more accurate
measurements'.[29] He did not personally attempt to check these figures,
nor does he even mention Eratosthenes' rival figure, no doubt because
what mattered to him was distances in degrees rather than in stades. But
he did describe (**Source 66**) how his predecessors had chosen a distance on earth which lay due north and south (that is, along a meridian), observed a star at the zenith at each terminus,[30] and measured the
angle between the stars as a proportion of the full celestial circle. The
terrestrial distance bore the same proportion to the circumference of
the earth. This sighting of zenith stars proves conclusively that Ptolemy
was not referring to Posidonius' sighting of stars low in the sky.[31]

To this record of the old method Ptolemy adds his own contribution.
If the distance lay not on the meridian but at an angle to it, his meteoroscope (see Chapter 2.B) would supply the data necessary to work out
the ratio. Conversely, he goes on, once the circumference is known,
terrestrial distances can be worked out as a proportion of the circumference by measuring the angular distance of points at the zenith at the two
termini, which is precisely what Hipparchus had proposed. The scholiast on Ptolemy (**Source 67**) spells this out at greater length, with reference to a diagram which applies whichever way round the exercise is
performed. While Ptolemy does not say how his predecessors measured

---

[29] Ptolemy, *Geography* I 11.2, VII 5.12. Ptolemy also quotes a circumference of 180,000
stades in *Planetary Hypotheses* 7, where the text actually gives the earth's radius as
$(2 + \frac{1}{2} + \frac{1}{3} + \frac{1}{30}) \times 10,000$, which works out as 28,666.66. If $\pi = 3\frac{1}{7}$, the circumference is 180,190.

[30] He actually speaks only of a point at the zenith, but since the sun passes the zenith
only between the tropics, he must mean a star.

[31] Aujac 1993, 313n. claims that Ptolemy's procedure for establishing the circumference
was the same as Eratosthenes'. Because one used zenith stars and the other the sun's
shadow, she can only mean that both took the angular distance between two points as
a fraction of the greatest circle.

the land distance, an earlier passage of his (**Source 65**) underlines the difficulty. Although it is dealing with the plotting of relative geographical positions, it is equally applicable to the present problem.

At this point the comments of two scholars deserve mention. First, Taisbak claims that Ptolemy was not concerned with precision over terrestrial distances, but only with astronomical geography, that is with angular co-ordinates relative to the equator and a given meridian. He chose the equation of 1 degree = 500 stades as a convenient round number for the sake of argument, without pretending any exactitude. Taisbak even questions the genuineness of Ptolemy's reference to 'the more accurate measurements' on the grounds that 'no measurement in antiquity states directly the length of a degree'.[32] This approach will be dealt with shortly. Secondly, Fischer sees no conflict between Posidonius' first circumference and Ptolemy's, suggesting that Posidonius used a smaller, so-called Eratosthenean, stade (10 to the Roman mile) while Ptolemy used a larger one (7½ to the Roman mile). Thus the circumferences of 240,000 and 180,000 were in fact the same.[33] The case, however, for an 'Eratosthenean' stade of a tenth of a Roman mile had already been refuted before she wrote.[34]

So much for the background. What does not seem to have been investigated is who these predecessors of Ptolemy were who sighted stars at the zenith, and when they did their work. A new ray of light is shed by two passages hitherto overlooked by historians of astronomy and geography. Both were written in the 520s or 530s by Byzantine Neoplatonist philosophers who studied under Ammonius at Alexandria, wrote commentaries on Aristotle, and, though they never met, became bitter enemies. The Christian John Philoponus, based in Alexandria, was a brilliant if somewhat slipshod scholar who overturned many Aristotelian theories in favour of a Christian cosmology.[35] In contrast the pagan Simplicius, based in Athens, painstakingly followed the orthodox Aristotelian line. On Justinian's closure of the Academy in 529 he emigrated to Persia, but returned to the West in 532 and subsequently achieved renown for his scholarship.[36] His commentary on the *De Caelo* was written soon after his return.

---

[32] Taisbak 1973–4, 262–4.   [33] Fischer 1975, 159–60, 163.

[34] Dicks 1960, 42–4.

[35] See Sorabji 1987 and, for his relationship with Simplicius, Sambursky 1987, 154–75.

[36] For his life and *milieu*, see Hadot 1987.

Both Philoponus' commentary on the *Meteorology* (**Source 68**) and Simplicius' on the *De Caelo* (**Source 69**) annotate the Aristotelian themes that the earth is the centre of the universe and that its size is small relative to the sun and stars and the distances between them. Both make it plain that the 'ancients' who calculated the circumference chose a distance one terrestrial degree in length, as defined by two stars one celestial degree apart which passed the zenith at the termini. Simplicius adds that they identified these stars by dioptra. They then measured this terrestrial distance, according to Simplicius by hodometer, and found it to be 500 stades. This unqualified statement completely disposes of Taisbak's claim noted above, that Ptolemy's 500 stades to the degree was merely a notional and convenient round number chosen for illustration, and that 'no measurement in antiquity states directly the length of a degree'.

This statement, of course, did not originate with Philoponus or Simplicius. Their mathematical and astronomical writings being of limited originality, their enormous value to us resides in their frequent quotation of earlier writings now lost. The immediate source of this quotation, though not named, is easily deduced. Simplicius' *De Caelo* drew most heavily on the *Commentary on the De Caelo* by Alexander of Aphrodisias, and Philoponus' *Meteorology* drew most heavily on the same Alexander's *Commentary on the Meteorology*, and he was also familiar with Alexander's *De Caelo*, a different part of which he quotes extensively elsewhere.[37] Alexander was a Peripatetic at Athens who wrote around AD 200 and achieved renown as the most prolific, learned and inspirational of commentators on Aristotle.[38] His *Meteorology*, which survives, contains nothing on the earth's circumference, which is hardly relevant to it; his *De Caelo* has unfortunately perished.

More can be deduced about the lineage of the information on the measurement of the earth. Both Philoponus and Simplicius proceed in their ensuing paragraphs to deal with the diameter and volume of the earth and Simplicius proceeds to discuss the small height of mountains relative to the size of the earth (**Source 76**). Closely similar passages occur in the commentary on the *Almagest* by Theon of Alexandria, the famous mathematician and astronomer writing about AD 360–80

[37] Philoponus, *On the Eternity of the Universe* 212–22.
[38] Sharples 1987. Little is known of his *De Caelo* beyond what Simplicius and Philoponus tell us. On Simplicius' use of Alexander, see Théry 1926, 14.

(**Source 75**), and in the *Useful Mathematical Hints* of Theon of Smyrna, a Platonist who in the first half of the second century AD wrote an elementary book on arithmetic, harmonics and astronomy (**Source 74**). Whereas Philoponus, Simplicius and Theon of Alexandria all subscribe to the circumference of 180,000 stades, Theon of Smyrna envisages the Eratosthenean one of 252,000 stades. He is quoting, he tells us, from Adrastus of Aphrodisias, a contemporary Peripatetic philosopher and author of an otherwise lost commentary on Plato's *Timaeus* which evidently related contemporary astronomy to Plato's cosmology.[39]

It therefore seems likely that Alexander in his *Commentary on the De Caelo* took over from Adrastus (or from Adrastus' own source) the passage on the size of the earth and of mountains, which followed the Eratosthenean tradition, and adapted it to accord with the Posidonian tradition of how the 180,000-stade circumference was measured. Theon of Alexandria and Philoponus borrowed from Alexander different parts of the passage, Simplicius borrowed it all. To try to trace Alexander's source for the Posidonian tradition, however, is more a matter of guesswork. A good candidate – but no more than that – is Sosigenes, another Peripatetic working in Athens and one of Alexander's teachers, who was active in the 160s. He wrote extensively on logic, optics and astronomy and opposed the accepted theory of homocentric spheres,[40] and is cited, with approval, in some of Alexander's surviving commentaries. But in the absence of Alexander's *De Caelo*, to search any further back in the Posidonian tradition would lead us too deep into the realm of speculation.

Thus Simplicius (supported, though with less detail, by Philoponus), tells us the method by which the circumference of 180,000 stades was arrived at. Based on the zenith sighting of stars, it is clearly the same as in Ptolemy's sparse account, and is clearly different from Posidonius' method based on the supposed (low) altitude of Canopus. How, in practical terms, were the observations made? A vital point made by Ptolemy but omitted by Simplicius is that for the method to work the two stars in question must lie on the same celestial meridian and the two places must lie on the same terrestrial meridian. In what follows, place A is assumed to be due north of place B. Ptolemy's sophisticated

---

[39] On Adrastus, see Moraux 1984, 294–332.

[40] Moraux 1984, 335–60. This Sosigenes is not to be confused with the astronomer of the same name who assisted Julius Caesar with his calendar reform.

meteoroscope and his procedure with lines that do not follow the meridian are ignored because, being a later development, they are irrelevant to the earlier meridional observations of the 'ancients'.

By Simplicius' method, at place A a star α is selected that passes the zenith. It will do so every 24 hours and, darkness and weather permitting, can be observed to do so. A star β is found by instrument which lies one degree due south of star α. Place B_1 is selected and star β is observed from it to see if it passes the zenith. If it does not, but passes (say) to the north of the zenith, B_1 is abandoned and another observation is made at B_2 to the south; and so on until, by trial and error, place B_n is located where star β does pass the zenith. A and B_n are therefore one degree apart on the same meridian, and the distance $A-B_n$ is measured to give the number of stades to one degree. Ptolemy says, in effect, exactly the same, but does not specify the distance apart of stars α and β; whatever it may be, the difference in latitude of A and B will be the same. The scholiast on Ptolemy speaks only, as Ptolemy himself had mentioned, of the reverse procedure: measuring the arc between two stars, one at the zenith of each of the termini, gives the terrestrial distance as a proportion of the known circumference of the earth; which is just what Hipparchus had earlier suggested. The sightings must be taken either on the same meridian or at the same time. In all these proceedings the scope for error is of course considerable. If A and B are not on the same terrestrial meridian, or stars α and β are not on the same celestial meridian, or either star does not exactly pass the zenith when seen from A and B, or the measurement of either the celestial or the terrestrial distance is astray, the result will be inaccurate.

Ptolemy, Simplicius and the scholiast speak between them of four different instruments. The meteoroscope of Ptolemy and the scholiast may be disregarded as too late for the calculations of the 'ancients'. Ptolemy's statement that they used a sundial to identify a star at the zenith and measure the arc between two stars is simply incredible: how does one observe stars with a sundial, let alone establish what is at the zenith? The only possible solution to the problem is that his original text said something like 'by observing with the aforesaid instruments the points at the zenith', referring back to his earlier remark (**Source 64**) that the instruments of astronomical location were astrolabes and sundials; and that some zealous copyist changed the 'aforesaid instruments' to sundials rather than to the armillary astrolabes which Ptolemy actually meant. If these really did exist before Ptolemy's time, they would fit the bill. Simplicius, however, speaks of the dioptra both for sighting zenith stars and for measuring star angles. The Hipparchan dioptra might measure the angle, but could not find the zenith, while the standard dioptra would be entirely adequate for both purposes and is acceptable as an alternative to the astrolabe. As for the hodometer, Simplicius' reference is the only direct evidence for it performing serious work. There is no reason to disbelieve it, and there is indeed reason to wonder if measurement of this kind was one purpose for which it was developed in the first place.

The fact remains that in this case either the dioptra or the hodometer (or both) did not do the job with any great accuracy. The value of a stade generally accepted in and after the first century BC, for example by Strabo and Pliny and therefore most probably by Ptolemy also, was one-eighth of a Roman mile,[41] which gives 62.5 Roman miles or 92.4 km to one degree, compared with the reality of about 111 km. If the fault lay with the hodometer, we are reminded of two potential sources of error. First, even in areas where Roman roads were available it would be hard to find a straight stretch some 111 km long, and Ptolemy remarked, as we have seen, on the difficulty of allowing for deviations. Secondly, as we have seen in Hero's remarks, even hodometers were not to be relied on. But the fault – or the major fault – more likely lay with the dioptra and the practical problems of accurate observation outlined above.

This brings us back to the crux mentioned earlier. When did this anonymous geographer calculate the circumference with dioptra and hodometer? Assuredly before the time of Ptolemy, who describes virtually the same method and regards the results as the 'accepted' and 'more accurate measurements.' In other words Ptolemy, in adopting the equation of 1 degree = 500 stades, was following the anonymous geographer rather than Posidonius, whose data were blatantly inaccurate: it was well known by now that the latitudes of Alexandria and Rhodes differed not by 7½° but by about 5°.[42] The anonymous geographer was very probably one of the 'later writers' taking 'more recent

---

[41] Pliny, *Natural History* II 85, 247, VI 121; Strabo, *Geography* VII 7.4; see Dicks 1960, 43–5.   [42] Ptolemy, *Geography* IV 5, V 2.

measurements' to whom Strabo alludes, and therefore preceded Strabo.[43] Probably, however, he was not active before, or even during, the time of Hipparchus. If he was earlier, it would be very early for the dioptra which, as we have seen, evolved in the first half of the second century BC; and one would expect Hipparchus to have accepted the circumference of 180,000 stades since it was obtained by the same method of measuring the angle between stars at the zenith that he himself proposed. Most likely, then, the anonymous geographer worked in the period between Hipparchus and Strabo, roughly coincident with Posidonius' lifetime, when indeed the 180,000-stade circumference is first recorded.

Next, what was the relationship between the anonymous geographer and Posidonius, both of whom produced the same circumference? Did the one influence the other, or is it pure coincidence that 180,000 stades is the product of Posidonius' ¼₈ of a circle between Alexandria and Rhodes and Eratosthenes' distance of 3750 stades?[44] There seem to be three possibilities.

1. The anonymous geographer was contemporary with Posidonius. His findings cast serious doubt on both Eratosthenes' 252,000 and Posidonius' 240,000 stades, and caused Posidonius to abandon his original calculation and adopt the new measurement. Strabo made reference only to Posidonius, as being the more authoritative writer.

2. The anonymous geographer was actually Posidonius himself. Much the same considerations apply. This possibility receives some support from Posidonius' evident expertise in complex gearing such as was necessarily to be found in the hodometer. Cicero, who studied under him in Rhodes in 79–77 BC, records that he constructed a planetarium which showed the daily motions of the sun, moon and planets and, equally necessarily, had complex gears.[45] It is also worth remarking that the famous Antikythera mechanism with its sophisticated gearing (including the differential) dates from exactly this time and quite possibly originated in Rhodes.[46]

---

[43] Both Dicks 1960, 146–7 and Drabkin 1943, 512 point out that Posidonius was one of these writers, but that the plural leaves at least one other unaccounted for.

[44] As Fischer argues: see above.   [45] Cicero, *On the Nature of the Gods* II 34.88.

[46] Price 1974, esp. 61–2.

3. Posidonius did revise his original calculation of 240,000 stades by replacing his distance of 5000 stades with Eratosthenes' figure of 3750, which he had hitherto rejected or overlooked. The anonymous geographer came after Posidonius' death and by a quite different approach confirmed Posidonius' revised circumference. Strabo therefore gave the credit to Posidonius as the earlier and greater authority, while Alexander (or his source) understood the facts better and gave the credit to the anonymous geographer. This scenario leaves Posidonius guilty of logical sloppiness in using Eratosthenes' equation to formulate his own contradictory one.

Of these possibilities, the third seems much the least plausible. Either of the others, which are very similar, could be correct. Geminus' *Introduction* contains no hint of the new circumference, which might suggest that it was calculated after he wrote; but it contains no hint of Posidonius' earlier figure of 240,000 stades either. If Geminus simply ignored this aspect of Posidonius' work, his silence tells us nothing. If however he was interested in the subject but wrote before Posidonius had made either of his calculations, and if Aujac's date of *c.* 55 BC for the *Introduction* is correct, then both calculations must have been made in the very short interval before Posidonius' death in *c.* 51 BC, which seems unlikely. If, therefore, Geminus' silence has any relevance at all, the more traditional date for him is preferable, and the anonymous geographer worked between the 70s and about 51 BC.

Unless he was Posidonius himself, we can say little more about the anonymous geographer's identity. We do not even know whether he was a member of the astronomical school of Rhodes. The fact that his name disappeared from the tradition suggests that he was, compared with the dominant figure of Posidonius, a relative nonentity. At all events, Philoponus' and Simplicius' anonymous geographer who calculated the earth's circumference by zenith sighting of stars and by hodometer, and who first proclaimed it as 180,000 stades, is not a missing link in the story. He is, rather, the same individual whose existence has long been known if little recognised, and whose method is recorded by Ptolemy. We now know a little more of his method, and can deduce that he was active during the first half of the first century BC. The most important point is that the 180,000 stades, which for so long dictated the size of the world-map, was not plucked out of the air either by Posidonius or by Ptolemy, as some have suggested, for the

Table 7.1 *Circumference of the Earth*
in km (polar circumference actually 39,938 km)

Stade	Value	252,000 stades	Error %	180,000 stades	Error %
Philetaeran	197.3 m	49,720	+24	35,530	−11
Olympic	192 m	48,384	+21	34,560	−13
'Standard'	185 m	46,615	+17	33,296	−17
Attic	177.6 m	44,755	+12	31,968	−20

sake of argument or of illustration. On the contrary, it was actually measured, however imperfectly, by instruments.

What, it must at last be asked, of the accuracy of the two principal estimates? The question is of course bedevilled by our ignorance of the value of the stade used in each case; hence the long and acrimonious debate. Table 7.1 converts the two figures according to four of the more widely used values (see Explanatory notes), and gives the percentage error in each case. Because it originated in the first century BC the 180,000-stade circumference was most probably based, as remarked above, on the 'standard' stade of eight to the Roman mile, which would make the anonymous geographer's figure 17 per cent too small. If Eratosthenes used the same stade – which is a very much larger assumption – his figure was 17 per cent too big.

A postscript from Islam may be of interest. During the burgeoning of science under al-Mamun (813–33), the caliph read of the Greek estimate of a degree of latitude as 500 stades. Since, then as now, nobody knew the exact value of the stade, he commissioned his astronomers to make their own measurement. Whether or not they knew of our anonymous geographer, they used the same method. Repairing to the Iraqi desert they took the altitude of the Pole Star (or, according to a less probable tradition, the sun), presumably with an astrolabe. They then sent off two parties, one walking due north and one due south, who measured the distance with a cord and pegs until they found the altitude had increased or decreased by one degree. Comparing the results, they pronounced a degree to be 56 *mil* or 111.720 km.[47] We now know the value to be 110.939 km: they were in error by 0.7 per cent.

[47] Hill 1979, 4, quoting ibn Khallikan; Rosenthal 1992, 215–16, quoting al-Biruni.

CHAPTER 8

MOUNTAIN HEIGHTS

The interest shown by the Greeks in the heights of mountains was rooted in their desire to understand the nature of the earth.[1] There were two sides to it. First, it was commonly accepted by the fourth century BC, if not by the fifth, that the earth was a sphere; yet, since mountains very obviously projected above the general surface, it could not be a perfect sphere. By finding the heights of mountains it could be shown that relative to the diameter of the earth, whether the circumference was taken as 252,000 or 180,000 stades, they were insignificant and did not detract from the basic sphericity. The second consideration was the depth of the atmosphere: what height did clouds reach? The widespread acceptance that the highest peaks always rose above the clouds gave fuel to this debate. The earlier attempts to measure mountains, like those to measure the earth, were limited by the lack of adequate equipment, and philosophers had to be content with the roundest of round figures. But as surveying instruments improved, a more accurate assessment became possible. It is salutary to reflect that a selection of relatively modern atlases can ascribe to a particular mountain an equal number of different heights, which vary by several metres. Only now are the heights of some peaks, especially those far from the sea, being finally and definitively established by satellite surveying.

From the ancient world, two grossly excessive statements may first be cleared out of the way. Diodorus quoting Ctesias (**Source 72**) puts the height of the cliffs of Bagistanos at 17 stades or roughly 3000 m. In reality these cliffs of Bisitun near Ecbatana (Hamadan), famous for the reliefs and inscription of Darius I, do not rise to a third of that height.[2] In Ctesias' day, however, there were no means of surveying them and his figure is no doubt the merest guess. A more egregious error is committed by Pliny (**Source 73**) in putting the height of the Alps at 50,000 paces or 400 stades, an exaggeration which might be explained either

---

[1] For a pioneering study see Capelle 1916. For the ancient world, Cajori 1929 is a much slighter work.　　[2] Irving 1979, 30.

by the extreme difficulty of measuring in such a massif or by Pliny's mistaking the length of approach to a summit for its vertical height.[3] The Alps were recognised as being in a different class from the mountains of Greece, almost any of which, according to Polybius, an unencumbered climber could scale or walk around in a single day, whereas the Alps took over five days to climb and their length fronting the north Italian plain extended for 2200 stades.[4]

The first Greek to estimate heights was Dicaearchus about 310 BC, to whom is ascribed (**Source 70**) a work on *Measurement of the Mountains of the Peloponnese* which must in fact (according to Pliny, **Source 73**) have ranged further afield, and which was perhaps merely one section of his major geographical work, the *Circuit of the Earth*.[5] He thought that 10 stades was the maximum height of mountains, a figure which persisted for centuries (**Sources 73–9, 84**), long after new theories had been proposed and reasonably accurate measurements had been made. He exerted such profound influence on the geography of Eratosthenes that Dicaearchan material, its origin forgotten, was often ascribed to Eratosthenes instead. Yet Eratosthenes no doubt never measured a mountain in his life, and probably accepted Dicaearchus' findings without question.[6]

The next step was to raise Dicaearchus' maximum height of 10 stades to one of 15. This probably originated with Posidonius, the major source for Cleomedes, who gives this figure (**Source 82**). Like Eratosthenes, his involvement was more theoretical than practical, but he had perhaps two reasons for increasing the figure. One was a desire

---

[3] Thus Diodorus Siculus, *Historical Library* II 13.7 gives the length of approach to the summit of Orontes mountain (Elwend) near Ecbatana as 25 stades, and Pliny, *Natural History* IV 41 gives the journey to the summit of Haemus (Stara Planina or the Balkan mountains in Bulgaria) as 6 miles. These figures are credible.

[4] Strabo, *Geography* IV 6.12 = Polybius, *Histories* XXXIV 10.15. Even the highest peaks in Greece were regularly climbed in antiquity, but whether the Alpine ones were is another matter.

[5] For Dicaearchus see Wehrli 1944 in general, 35 for fragments on mountain heights, and 75–6 for commentary. The reference (**Source 71**) to a comparable book on the *Measurement of Mountains* by one Xenophon is too uncertain to make anything of, unless conceivably Xenophon is a mistake for the Xenagoras of **Source 84**.

[6] Wehrli 1944, 75–6 feels that Eratosthenes, while generally following Dicaearchus' measurement, was willing to raise some of his heights to 15 stades. This increase is however more easily attributed to Posidonius.

for symmetry, in that he seems to have found a maximum depth of 15 stades for the sea: the excrescences above the water should balance the hollows below.[7] This is attested by Pliny[8] citing Papirius Fabianus, a Roman Stoic who most likely drew on Posidonius, and by Cleomedes again (**Source 82**).[9] Posidonius' second reason was perhaps his belief, reflected by Geminus (**Source 80**), that the summits of high mountains were always above the clouds which, he thought, rose no higher than 10 stades; the summits were therefore higher. There are however difficulties. Geminus, in putting Kyllene at 'less than 15 stades, as Dicaearchus' measurements show', is perhaps trying to reconcile Dicaearchus' authoritative 10 stades with Posidonius' new maximum of 15. Possibly, too, Posidonius gave a range of 15 to 20 stades as the maximum, whence Strabo's doubt about the height of Kyllene (**Source 81**) and Arrian's figure of 20 stades (**Source 83**).[10]

How, it must now be asked, did Dicaearchus arrive at his figure of 10 stades? According to Theon of Alexandria (**Source 75**) and Simplicius who copied him (**Source 76**), by dioptra. Theon was surely mistaken, just as he was mistaken in attributing the 10 stades to Eratosthenes, and it is easy to see how his errors arose. He was drawing on Adrastus, either directly or through Theon of Smyrna (**Source 74**), who merely said that Eratosthenes and Dicaearchus (meaning Dicaearchus as reported by Eratosthenes) measured mountain heights. As an explanatory aside, Adrastus added that in his day (the second century AD), not necessarily in theirs, dioptras were used for this purpose. Indeed the developed dioptra appeared on the scene much too late for Dicaearchus.[11] So what was his method? He could have used a predecessor of the Hipparchan dioptra, or the measuring rod, to measure the apparent height of mountains; or he could have noted where the shadow of a peak fell and at the same time measured the shadow of a vertical pole of known height. In either case he would have to measure

---

[7] See Capelle 1916, 24.   [8] Pliny, *Natural History* II 224.
[9] Strabo, *Geography* I 3.9 says that the Sardinian Sea, the deepest of all, was found by Posidonius to be 1000 fathoms (10 stades) deep. Since this contradicts Pliny and Cleomedes, Capelle 1916, 24 suggested a simple emendation of the figure to 1500 fathoms or 15 stades.
[10] Pliny, *Natural History* II 85 reports Posidonius as putting the cloud tops at 40 stades, where XL may well be a corruption of X (Capelle 1916, 28).
[11] Collinder 1964, 476 agrees that he did not use the dioptra.

Table 8.1 *Measurements of mountain heights*

Source	Authority cited	Mountain	Height given	= height (m)	Actual height (m)	Error %
Grossly exaggerated						
72 Ctesias		Bisitun	17 st	3264	c. 1000	massive
73 Pliny		Alps	50,000 p = 400 st	76,800	4807	massive
Dicaearchan 10 stades						
73 Pliny	Dicaearchus	Pelion	1250 p = 10 st	1920	1547	+24
84 Plutarch	geometers	max.	10 st	1920		
74 Theon Smyrna	Dicaearchus Eratosthenes	max.	10 st	1920		
75 Theon Alex.	Eratosthenes	max.	10 st	1920		
76 Simplicius	Eratosthenes	max.	10 st	1920		
77 Cleomedes		max.	>10 st	>1920		
78 Apuleius	geometers	Olympus	<10 st	<1920	2917	−34
79 Martianus Cap.		Olympus	10 st	1920	2917	−34
Posidonian 15 stades						
80 Geminus	Dicaearchus	Kyllene	<15 st	<2880	2376	+21
		Atabyrios	<4 st?	<740 ?	1215	−37 ?
81 Strabo		Kyllene	15 st	2880	2376	+21
82 Cleomedes	Posidonius?	max.	15 st	2880		

Posidonian? 20 stades

81	Strabo		Kyllene	20 st	3840	2376	+62
83	Arrian		max.	20 st	3840	,	
Instrumental							
84	Plutarch	Xenagoras	Olympus	6096 ft = 10.16 st	1951	c. 1850 ?	+5 ?
85	Apollodorus		Kyllene	5320 ft = 8.87 st	1703	c. 1670 ?	+2 ?
86	Strabo		Acrocorinth	3.5 st	672	574	+17
87	Philoponus	experts	max.	12 st	2304		

Notes:

For comparability, all stades (st) are assumed to be Olympic ones of 192 m, as **Source 85** is specifically stated to be. If 'standard' stades of 185 m are applied in other cases, the error is smaller (e.g. **Source 84** Olympus + 2%?, **Source 86** Acrocorinth + 13%).

Pliny's figures in paces (p) are here converted to stades at his standard rate of 1000 p = 8 stades.

or estimate the distance to the peak – no easy matter, and a fruitful source of error – and from similar triangles to work out the height.

There is no doubt that Dicaearchus' and Posidonius' figures for mountain heights, like those of Eratosthenes and others for the circumference of the earth, were 'no more than crude estimates expressed in convenient round numbers';[12] and the very roundness of the numbers shows that they recognised the fact. I have so far deliberately refrained from translating them into modern terms. As Dicks very properly remarks, 'The Greek mentality cannot be judged correctly from the standpoint of the modern scientist, and any attempt to force a spurious accuracy on to ancient measurements and translate them into mathematically exact modern equivalents is bound to have misleading results.'[13] Nevertheless, some kind of yardstick is desirable against which to judge these ancient figures. Because of the variety of stades that might have been used, any result can only be taken as an approximation. Table 8.1 lists the figures in stades given by all the sources, and translates them into modern terms, for the sake of illustration only, according to the Olympic stade of 192 m. What emerges is that Dicaearchus' and Posidonius' findings, however crude their method and rounded their figures, were at least of the right order of magnitude.

All this having been said, what are we to make of the mountain heights given by Plutarch, Apollodorus and Strabo (**Sources 84–6**)? The first two of them, far from rounding a figure up or down to the nearest stade or five stades, purport to give the height to the nearest foot. It would be excessively cynical to regard them as examples of Gilbertian 'corroborative detail, intended to give artistic verisimilitude to an otherwise bald and unconvincing narrative'. They deserve to be taken at face value, as the result of genuine attempts to measure height by instrument; and it is legitimate to compare them with the heights of the same mountains as we know them today. The exactitude they claim is reflected by several of the sources which refer to instruments – notably the dioptra – for taking mountain heights: Adrastus (**Source 74**) and those who drew on him, Philoponus (**Source 87**), Hero (**Dioptra 13b**) and Balbus (**Source 14**).

The first of the more mathematical surveys of a mountain (**Source**

---

[12] Neugebauer 1975, 653. Similar sentiments in Wehrli 1944, 75–6.
[13] Dicks 1960, 45n.

84) introduces a complication. Olympus is the highest mountain in Greece, and its summit (or virtually its summit) can be seen from the coast. Yet in this case the height was measured not from sea level but from a point far inland. Since we know neither the precise height of that point nor which of the many peaks of Olympus was measured, it is hard to assess the accuracy of the survey. Scipio Nasica, in the course of Aemilius Paullus' campaign of 168 BC which culminated a few days later in the battle of Pydna, camped for the night at Pythion on the western flank of the mountain.[14] In a letter he wrote at the time he transcribed an inscription he saw there in the temple of Apollo. This recorded in verse that Xenagoras son of Eumelus had measured the height of Olympus above the temple as 10 stades (of 600 feet each) plus 100 feet less 4 feet = 6096 feet. With Olympic feet and stades, this makes 1951 m.

Xenagoras is otherwise unknown.[15] But he must have made his survey before 168 and, as Plutarch deduced, he must have made it with instruments which at least pretended to accuracy. Ancient Pythion is not the modern Pythio, the name given quite recently to the former village of Selos, but corresponds to the ruins now known as Avles or Topoliani about 4 km to the south-west.[16] The exact site of the temple of Apollo is not known, but it must lie between the 600 and 640 m contours, let us say at 620 m. The highest peak of Olympus, Mytikas, is 2917 m above the sea and lies over 13 km to the north-east. But it cannot be seen from Avles, for four other peaks or ridges intervene (Fig. 8.1),[17] and a survey would have to be done in several stages. Because, as we shall see, every stage would demand a sizeable area that was roughly level, a requirement not met by the intermediate points, a multi-stage survey seems improbable. More likely Xenagoras measured not Mytikas but a lower, nearer and visible peak. Looking east from Avles, the view is dominated by the north–south ridge of Flambouro. The only other significant peak that can be seen is Kakovrakas, 2618 m

[14] See Walbank 1979, III 378–83 on the campaign and Nasica's movements.
[15] Capelle 1916, 21 thought he might be the shadowy Xenagoras who wrote chronicles and a work on islands (*FHG* IV 526), but Müller thought not. In any event, since nothing is known of this Xenagoras either, it does not help.
[16] Kurz 1923, 160; Arvanitopoulos 1924, 142.
[17] I rely on the Greek Alpine Club's excellent 1:50,000 map of Olympus, undated but based on the Hellenic Army map of apparently 1995.

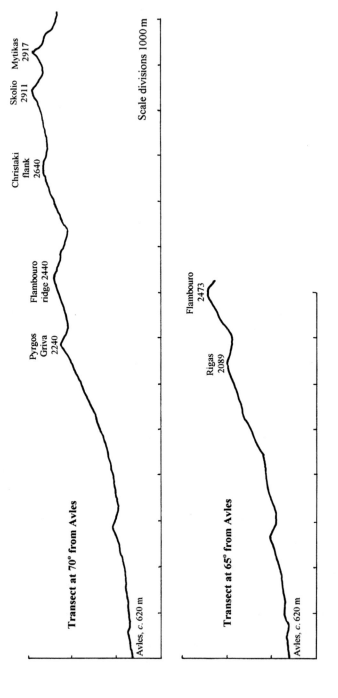

FIG. 8.1. Transects of Olympus.

high, 14 km away slightly south of east, and partly hidden by the end of the Flambouro ridge. But Flambouro itself, 2473 m high but only 8 km away, would appear much the higher. It seems probable, therefore, that Xenagoras measured Flambouro.[18] If so, its height above Avles is about 1850 m, which is not wildly different from Xenagoras' 1951 m.

If he measured Flambouro under the illusion that it was Olympus proper, he can hardly have done so by marking the shadow cast by the peak and by pacing or even measuring the slope from that point to the summit. This operation would have brought him to the top of Flambouro from where, to the east, he would have seen further peaks that were clearly higher. But it was perfectly possible to measure the mountain without climbing it, by using the dioptra and the routine described by **Dioptra 12** and **8** and specifically mentioned as appropriate for taking mountain heights at the end of **Dioptra 13b**. The same exercise appears in **Africanus 4** and **2** and in **Anonymus 2**. The main physical requirement was an area of reasonably level ground on which to lay out the base lines and the triangle for finding the horizontal distance as in **Dioptra 8**; the larger and the more level this was, the more accurate the final result would be. This method, evidently well known, is much the most likely to have been adopted by Xenagoras, by the anonymous surveyors of Kyllene and Acrocorinth, by the experts mentioned by Philoponus, by Adrastus' geometers, and by Balbus with his similar triangles (**Source 14**).

Less can be said of the survey of Kyllene (**Source 85**). This height is reported through Apollodorus of Athens, who was born around 180 BC and studied at Alexandria, from which he fled about 146 in the persecutions of Euergetes II. He took refuge at Pergamon, where he worked until the 130s when he left for Athens, to die there after 120.[19] He wrote on many subjects including chronology, mythology, and theology, and his commentary on Homer's *Catalogue of Ships*, heavily indebted to Eratosthenes' geographical writings, was in turn extensively quarried by later geographers.[20] The information on Kyllene, a mountain which features in the *Catalogue*, probably comes from this commentary. Apollodorus was certainly not a man who measured

---

[18] This was first suggested by Kurz 1923, 160, who also canvassed Kakovrakas (his Skamnia) as a possibility. Oberhümmer 1939, 260–1 suggested Hagios Antonis, 2813 m; but it is close to Mytikas and equally invisible friom Avles.

[19] Fraser 1972, II 683 n. 232.   [20] Fraser 1972, I 471.

mountains himself. But the figure he gives seems too precise to have originated with Eratosthenes, and more probably it dates, like Xenagoras' report, to the middle or shortly before the middle of the second century. Quite possibly Apollodorus heard of it during his stay at Pergamon, which seems to have been a nursery of surveying. Kyllene is not visible from the coast, and this is apparently another case of measurement, no doubt also with the dioptra, from an inland and level starting point. There are two obvious candidates for this point: the plain of Stymphalos to the south-east and the flat Pheneos valley to the south-west. From the former, however, the summit is not visible, while it can be seen from the north end of the Pheneos valley.[21] This lies at about 700 m above the sea, the summit about 10 km away rising to 2376 m, or some 1670 m above the valley floor. This is about 2 per cent less than the 9 Olympic stades less 80 feet or 1703 m of Apollodorus' record.

Still less can be said of Strabo's report that Acrocorinth was 3½ stades high (**Source 86**). Because he cites other unnamed authorities, it is quite unnecessary to attribute his information to either Hieronymus or Eudoxus,[22] who seem much too early. In this instance the height is surely taken from sea level, the mountain being close to and easily visible from the coast, and it smacks of an instrumental survey even though the result – 672 m against the reality of 574 m – is not particularly close to the truth. Finally Philoponus' statement (**Source 87**) deserves inclusion here not for its accuracy – a number of mountains in Greece alone exceed his 12 stades – but for the categorical reference to mechanical experts and their instruments.

Two general conclusions emerge. First, reasonably reliable mathematical surveying was not available to Dicaearchus in the fourth century or to Eratosthenes in the third; but it was available to Xenagoras before 168 BC and to the surveyor of Kyllene at about the same time, even if later in the century Posidonius preferred the older theoretical approach. Secondly, if our deductions about the surveys of Olympus and Kyllene are at all correct, a very respectable degree of accuracy could be achieved with the dioptra even in terrain which does not favour the surveyor.

[21] Contour map in Kalcyk and Heinrich 1986, Abb. 1.
[22] As does Wehrli 1944, 76.

CHAPTER 9

CANALS AND AQUEDUCTS

A. EARLY CANAL SCHEMES

The canal from the Nile to the Red Sea at Suez had a long, complex and uncertain history. Its origins go back far into the pharaonic period, and it remained in intermittent use until over a century after the Arab conquest.[1] Precisely what work was done by which ruler is largely irrelevant to us. What concerns us is the persistent tale (**Sources 88–91**) that until the Ptolemies the canal was not completed because it was reported that the Red Sea was higher than the Nile and, if the land were cut through, would either drown Egypt or pollute the river. This report need not detain us long because, as Strabo saw, it was total nonsense.

The canal was approximately 120 km in length and originally left the Nile near Bubastis (though the take-off was later moved upstream to near Cairo) and ran east down Wadi Tumilat to Lake Timsah, where it turned south through the Bitter Lakes to Suez (Fig. 9.1). Its purpose was no doubt primarily for irrigation and to supply fresh water to the settlements along its course, ending at the various towns that have existed in the Suez area; the sweet-water canal completed in 1863, which largely follows its route, has exactly the same function today. Navigation was probably a secondary consideration. Wadi Tumilat was once an arm of the Nile discharging into the Red Sea, and the Bitter Lakes were once an extension of the Gulf of Suez, but even in historical times the isthmus itself has been subject to tectonic uplift. The simple fact is that the normal river level at Cairo in the Ptolemaic period (it is higher now) was roughly 10 m above the Mediterranean, while floods raised it to some 17 m. At Suez the maximum tidal range, which is much affected by winds, is 2.78 m.[2] The Mediterranean and the Gulf of Suez are, for all practical purposes, at the same level: the

[1] For an overall survey of its history see Oertel 1964; for its earlier days, Posener 1938; for the most detailed survey of the Suez end, Bourdon 1925.
[2] Bourdon 1925, 115–16, 125–6.

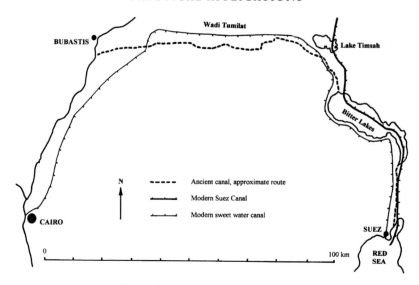

FIG. 9.1. Nile–Red Sea canal (after Bourdon 1925, Carte 1).

modern Suez Canal has no locks, and any current engendered by the tides at Suez is inappreciable.[3] There is therefore no question of the Red Sea flooding Egypt, although its tides would, if allowed, have run northwards for some distance up the canal, for at this end the gradient is insignificant. The lock of some kind installed at Suez by Ptolemy II was no doubt intended to keep the salt water out and to prevent the fresh water from running to waste in the Red Sea. Thus the survey, if there ever was one, which showed that the Red Sea was higher than the Nile was woefully wrong.[4]

Another canal scheme of antiquity is more debatable and more interesting. A succession of rulers had dreamt of cutting through the Isthmus of Corinth. It could never be an easy undertaking, for the isthmus is over 6 km wide and rises in a ridge of solid rock nowhere less than 79 m above the sea. But a canal would save ships which traded between the Saronic Gulf on the east and the Gulf of Corinth on the west (or even between the Aegean and western Greece, Italy and

[3] Marlowe 1964, 241.
[4] Ironically the first modern survey, carried out for Napoleon Bonaparte, was equally astray. The surveyors, pressed for time, deduced that the Red Sea was nearly 10 m higher than the Mediterranean (Marlowe 1964, 32).

Sicily) the long and dangerous journey around the Peloponnese, where Cape Malea in particular had a sinister reputation for gales and shipwrecks. The idea was first mooted by Periander, tyrant of Corinth about 600 BC; it was revived by Demetrius Poliorcetes the Hellenistic warlord, probably in 304–3 BC when he seized the Isthmus (**Source 92**), by Julius Caesar and by Caligula. Work was actually begun in AD 67 by Nero, employing convicts and prisoners from the Jewish war. He made considerable progress before giving up, and his abortive works remained visible until they were destroyed by the modern canal which was completed in 1893. After him the wealthy Herodes Atticus contemplated finishing the job in the second century AD.[5]

Three reports agree that the level of the sea was found to be higher to the west of the Isthmus than to the east, and claim that cutting was stopped, or not started, for fear that the resulting torrent would prohibit navigation and endanger the island of Aegina. The two later ones (**Sources 93–4**) ascribe this finding to Egyptian surveyors. But only the earliest (**Source 92**) seems reliable. The history in the works of Philostratus, both senior and junior, is muddled and unreliable, and almost certainly they picked up from Eratosthenes the story of Demetrius' engineers and applied it anachronistically to Nero's. Yet the Egyptian surveyors may be a survival from the earlier and genuine account. Nero, having plenty of expert military *libratores* at his command, would not need to rely on the services of Egyptians, whereas in Demetrius' day it might be that such skills were more readily found in Egypt than in Greece. On the other hand, Ptolemy I was at loggerheads with Demetrius and might be unwilling to loan him the necessary experts. Indeed it is worth asking (without being able to supply an answer) whether the whole story, including the Egyptians, might really belong to Periander three centuries before. In his time Greek links with Egypt were probably closer than at any time before the Ptolemies: he was a contemporary of the Necho who tried to cut the Nile–Red Sea canal, and his nephew was named Psammetichus after Necho's successor.[6] In both projects, does the similarity of the reports about the sea levels reflect a similarity of date?

So much for the historical side. The more interesting point is that the surveyors' report for the Corinth canal, unlike that for the

[5] For the history and a description of Nero's works see Gerster 1884.

[6] Salmon 1984, 225–7.

Nile–Red Sea canal, is correct. Tidal effects, exacerbated by winds, mean that the sea level west of the isthmus is always higher than that on the east, with a maximum difference of 51 cm. There is consequently a permanent current of up to 4.8 km per hour through the modern canal.[7] The canal being 6342 m long, its surface has a maximum gradient of 1 in 12,435. This is comparable with the gentlest gradients on Roman aqueducts which, we shall find in a later section, must have taxed the skills and the instruments of the surveyors to the limit. It is true that about 530 BC Eupalinus, in marking out the famous kilometre-long tunnel on Samos, succeeded in establishing one mouth only 4 cm below the other – presumably they were meant to be at exactly the same height – which gave a gradient of 1 in 25,900 (see Chapter 10.c). He had the luxury, however, of being able to level along the contour around the end of the mountain spur, whereas at Corinth the surveyors had no option but to traverse from sea level up to at least 79 m on the ridge and down again, at a date when dioptras, at least in their developed form, did not exist. While we do not know what instrument they had, we might guess that it was the suspended tube postulated in Chapter 10.E.

It is all too easy to hail their result as a triumph. But it is not recorded what they supposed the difference in level to be. If it were known that they found it to be a cubit, a triumph it could very well have been. But would so small a difference have raised fears for the safety of Aegina? Had the surveyors found it to be, say, 6 cubits (roughly 3 m) it would be a massive error which could just as easily have been in the opposite direction and made the eastern sea higher than the western. This would be written off by posterity as a failure, just as in the case of the Nile–Red Sea canal. We have to conclude, regretfully and at the risk of doing Demetrius' (or Periander's) engineers a grave injustice, that their survey was probably not very accurate, and that it was only chance which made them err in the right direction.

B. AQUEDUCT SURVEYING

Selecting a route for an aqueduct and setting it out on an appropriate gradient involved levelling, whether with the simple plumb-line level,

[7] Hadfield 1986, 18, 173.

the dioptra or the libra. Apart from a very few exceptions (to be noted later) where water had to be lifted by machine, the ancient world relied exclusively on gravity to bring water along pipes or channels to its towns. The gradient of such aqueducts depends, first and foremost, on the local geography, namely the height of a suitable source of water above the destination and its distance along a practicable route. In hilly and well-watered country the difference in height is likely to be generous, the distance short, and the gradient therefore relatively steep. In flatter terrain the source might well be further away, the fall less and the gradient shallower. Very much a secondary factor, but still a crucial one when the slopes are gentle, is the availability of instruments capable of levelling to the required degree of accuracy.

The student of aqueducts labours under two particular difficulties. One is that, except in the rare instances when Frontinus or a handy inscription gives the answer, they are notoriously difficult to date.[8] There is often only circumstantial evidence to go on, such as the overall history of a town's development, or the presence of Roman features like arcades. Even so, in the eastern Mediterranean, it is sometimes impossible to decide if an aqueduct is Hellenistic or belongs to the early days of Roman rule before thoroughly Roman influences were felt. Even self-evidently Roman examples can be difficult to date more exactly.

There are a few diagnostic features. The typical Roman aqueduct had an open channel: occasionally, in less important cases, literally open to the air, but much more often a built channel roofed with slabs or a vault, large enough to allow human access for maintenance, and open in the sense that it ran only part-full and not under pressure. In the Roman west, pressurised pipelines were generally restricted to inverted siphons which are a law to themselves and barely concern us here. It was the Romans, too, who introduced the raised arcade. This is a sure sign of Roman date in the eastern Mediterranean, where the earliest known example, at Ephesus, was built between AD 4 and 14.[9] Greek aqueducts, in the sense of those pre-Roman in date, are more variable. While they might have open channels, they are much more likely to have pipes throughout their length and not merely in the inverted siphons which the Greeks pioneered. Some, like those at

[8] On this problem see Wilson 1996, 12–19.　　[9] Coulton 1987, 73.

Pergamon and the earliest at Smyrna, were pressurised pipelines which ran full. But especially in archaic times the pipes might have removable lids for access to the interior, either for grouting the joints during installation or for subsequent cleaning. These were necessarily unpressurised and ran only part-full.

Nevertheless, sizeable urban aqueducts remained a comparative rarity in Mediterranean lands until the hitherto endemic political insecurity was ended by the peace imposed by Rome. Strabo, writing under Augustus, comments on the backwardness of the Greeks in building aqueducts.[10] While he was admittedly comparing them with the city of Rome which was exceptional in the early date and capacity of its supplies, his point remains valid. Coulton states it plainly: 'The absence of earlier Greek parallels for the aqueducts of Rome was not due to poverty, ignorance, or inefficiency, but to the very obvious dangers of dependence on a visible and vulnerable lifeline from outside.' Exactly the same is true, he says, of other parts of the nascent Roman empire, including Italy itself. 'The reign of Augustus, then, seems to be the time when, no doubt with some official encouragement, cities began to feel that the longed-for peace was sufficiently well-established to justify the more or less elaborate water supplies.'[11]

The second difficulty facing the student, although the situation is very slowly being remedied, is the lack of basic measurements. There are depressingly few aqueducts for which detailed gradient profiles have been produced by reliable modern surveys. For the majority, all that is on record is the overall fall and length from which an average gradient can be worked out; and even here the figures are often approximate and sometimes vary considerably between different publications. There remain quite a number where not even these bare facts are known. However, it is clear that in the Greek world, as has already been remarked, pre-Roman and even some Roman aqueducts tended to have quite steep gradients.[12] Examples, including a few from Hasmonean Judaea and from Nabataea, where Greek influence is likely, are set out in Table 9.1, which does not pretend to be exhaustive. The surveying of archaic tunnels presents special problems, and discussion of them, and of qanats, whose gradient was sometimes

[10] Strabo, *Geography* v 3.8.   [11] Coulton 1987, 73.
[12] So too the greatest pre-Greek aqueduct, Sennacherib's supplying Nineveh (Chapter 1.A), with its overall gradient of 1 in 80 (Forbes 1955, 158).

Table 9.1 *Gradients of Greek aqueducts*

	Length, km	Fall, m	Average gradient, 1 in	Minimum gradient, 1 in	Notes
Archaic, sixth century BC					
Samos, pipes in main tunnel	1	3.6	289		2T
Athens, to city	8	c. 188	40	250	T
in city	2		75	1650	2T
Syracuse, Paradiso			150		2T
Ninfeo			140		2T
Tremilia			35		2T
Galermi*	29		220		part T
Copais*	1.75		87		2T
Hellenistic, third–first century BC					
Pergamon, Madra Dag	42.5	855	50	250	P
Apollonius			100		P
Smyrna, Karapinar	11+	170	65		P
Antioch on Orontes*	11	150	75		
Alexandreion (Palestine)	5		80		
Dagon (Palestine)	0.5		100		
Humeima (Nabataean)	27		40	100	
Roman, from first century BC *(only relatively steep gradients)*					
Antioch in Pisidia	0.5	15	35		P
Oenoanda	6		200		P
Mytilene	26	250	100		
Laodicea ad Lycum	2	20	100		
Gadara lower tunnel			114		
Gadara upper tunnel			233		
Corinth			200		
Smyrna, Akpinar	19.5	55	355		

Notes:
T = in tunnel, 2T = double-decker tunnel, P = pressurised system. Many figures are approximate.
* Galermi possibly Roman (Wilson 1990; his suggestion that other Syracuse aqueducts are Roman is unlikely to be correct); the unfinished Copais tunnel is presumed archaic because it is a double-decker; Caligula's aqueduct at Antioch is probably an older one repaired (Downey 1951).
Sources: Burns 1974 (Syracuse), Garbrecht 1978, 1987 (Pergamon), Garbrecht and Peleg 1989 (Alexandreion, Dagon), Grewe 1998 (Gadara), Kambanis 1893 (Copais), Kienast 1995 (Samos), Koldewey 1890 (Mytilene), Oleson 1991 (Humeima), Stenton and Coulton 1986 (Oenoanda), Stillwell 1938 (Antioch on Orontes), Tolle-Kastenbein 1994 (Athens, Syracuse), Weber 1898 (Laodicea), Weber 1899 (Smyrna), Weber 1904 (Antioch in Pisidia).

considerably shallower, is best deferred to the next chapter. What emerges quite clearly is that the average or overall gradient of traditional Greek aqueducts was rarely gentler than 1 in 200. Their minimum gradient, at least in the few cases where the detail is known, was of the order of 1 in 250. As far as I am aware, the earliest supply aqueduct in the eastern Mediterranean (as opposed to pipelines within a city) to have an average gradient of less than 1 in 200 was the high-level one at Caesarea, built a few years before Christ for Herod the Great by Roman engineers (Table 9.2).[13]

The typical Roman aqueduct, in contrast, had a very much gentler overall gradient. True, if mountain springs were tapped, the initial descent to the plain might inevitably be steep compared with the rest of the route, as at Carthage, at Segovia and the Aqua Julia at Rome.[14] But the usual expedient, should a steep gradient threaten, was to kill the velocity of the water by introducing stair-like cascades separated by sections sloping much more gently, as at Lyon, where the Brévenne averaged 1 in 200 and the Yzeron (Craponne) 1 in 60,[15] and Geneva where the fall averaged 1 in 25 overall but only 1 in 1800 between the cascades.[16] In the whole of the Roman west only one aqueduct seems to be known where a really steep gradient cannot be explained, or was not mitigated, in these ways. This is at Alatri in Italy, where, although it has not been surveyed in detail, the open channel averaged roughly 1 in 80 for 9 km. But the early date (about 130–120 BC), the huge siphon which continued the aqueduct to the town, and the eastern connections of the builder all point to a strong Greek influence.[17]

At one extreme, then, Roman aqueducts were very rarely as steep as pre-Roman Greek ones. At the other extreme, very gentle slopes will shortly be discussed in detail. In between lie the vast majority of cases.

---

[13] The aqueduct of Ptolemais (Acre) in Phoenicia had, in the few places it has been traced, a gradient of the order of 1 in 1250–1500 (Frankel 1985). From Ptolemaic control the city passed in about 200 BC to the Seleucids and in 64 BC to Rome. On the basis of lamp fragments the excavators place it in the Hellenistic period with a preference for about 300 BC. It was not a pipeline. Except for a section in unlined tunnel with inclined shafts closely resembling those on the Herodian high-level aqueduct at Caesarea, it ran in a vaulted channel. A date of 300 BC seems much too early, and the shafts and vaulting suggest a Roman construction of the middle or late first century BC.   [14] Hodge 1992, 441 n. 13.

[15] Burdy 1991, 32–4; see further Hodge 1992, 161.   [16] Grenier 1960, 103.

[17] Discussed fully in Lewis 1999b.

Table 9.2 *Roman aqueducts with shallowest gradients*

	Length, km	Fall, m	Average	Minimum[a]
			gradient, 1 in	
Narbonne	14.2	5	2840?	5000 over 2.5 km
Poitiers, Cimeau[b]	10	3.5	2950	7450 over 4.5 km
Carhaix	27	<10	3000	
Pergamon, Kaikos	53		3200	
Termini Imerese, Cornelio	3	1	3300	
Rome, Virgo	21	6	3650	
Nîmes[b]	49.5	12.5	4000	20,000 over 8 km
Poitiers, Basse-Fontaine[b]	11	2	6000	10,300 over 8 km
Caesarea, High Level	8.5		6250	
Poitiers, Fleury	25	3	8100	13,700 over 3 km
Pergamon, Aksu	15		8300	
Caesarea, Low Level[c]	5.5	0	level	

Notes:
[a] Over a respectable distance.
[b] Excluding the initial steep section of 400 m (Cimeau), 180 m (Nîmes), 934 m (Basse-Fontaine).
[c] No measurable fall on the channel floor; flow generated by the head from the supply dam.
Many figures approximate and all rounded.
Sources: Andrieu and Cazal 1997 (Narbonne), Ashby 1935 (Rome), Belvedere 1986 (Termini Imerese), Duffaud 1854 (Poitiers), Fabre et al. 1991 (Nîmes), Garbrecht 1987 (Pergamon), Olami and Peleg 1977 (Caesarea), Provost and Lepretre 1997 (Carhaix).

Hodge puts the 'usual' gradient between about 1 in 333 and 1 in 666.[18] I would extend this to between 1 in 333 and 1 in 1000 or even 1 in 1500. One has only to glance for example at the gradient profiles of the Lyon aqueducts[19] to see that, apart from the cascades mentioned, the standard gradient aimed at there was roughly 1 in 1000. But this is not a matter worth quibbling over. The essential and undeniable point is that, by and large, Roman aqueducts sloped much more gently than Greek ones.

[18] Hodge 1992, 218.
[19] Hodge 1992, Fig. 126, and reproduced in many other publications.

This is the context in which to view Vitruvius' famous and much-debated remark (**Source 96**) that the minimum permissible gradient for an aqueduct was 1 in 200, with its inevitable corollary that the average gradient was steeper and the maximum steeper still. Outside Greek lands, this is simply inapplicable to the Roman aqueduct on which 1 in 200, so far from being the minimum, was more like the maximum. The snag has long been recognised, and the favourite explanation is that Vitruvius' figure has been corrupted in the manu-scripts. This line of argument finds support in Pliny's section on aque-ducts which in all other respects closely follows Vitruvius, but which states (**Source 97**) that the minimum gradient should be 1 in 4800, a figure much nearer to the truth for his own time. On the other hand Faventinus, who also copied Vitruvius, and Palladius, who copied Faventinus (**Sources 98–9**), go further in the opposite direction and recommend a minimum of 1 in 67 or even 1 in 40.

These apparent anomalies, as I argue at length elsewhere, are readily explained. First, Vitruvius drew almost all the material for his sections on aqueducts not from his own experience, nor directly from Roman sources, but from Greek ones.[20] Indeed the precise source for his statement about gradients has apparently survived in the fragment of Philo of Byzantium (**Source 95**) who prescribes a minimum slope for irrigation channels of 12 fingers in 100 cubits, which is 1 in 200. This origin is strengthened by the likelihood that Vitruvius also drew on Philo for descriptions of water-lifting machines.[21] Second, the contradictions between the four Roman writers are simply resolved if Vitruvius' figure was not spelled out in words but given as an abbreviation, which (as so often happened with this ever-fruitful source of confusion) was miscopied or misread by later generations. His *in centenos pedes S* (half a foot per hundred feet) was read by Pliny as *in centenos pedes Ɔ* (quarter of an inch per 100 feet) and by Faventinus as *in centenos pede S* (a foot and a half per 100). Thus there is only one statement from antiquity about minimum gra-dients. Originating with Philo, copied by Vitruvius, and miscopied by Pliny, Faventinus and Palladius, it really applies to unlined irriga-tion channels in the Middle East and has nothing whatever to do with built Roman aqueducts.

---

[20] Lewis 1999b.   [21] Lewis 1997, 24–5, 42–8.

At the other extreme, the average and the minimum gradients on Roman aqueducts could, on occasion and where the terrain demanded, be exceedingly small. Table 9.2 lists aqueducts where the average is below 1 in 2500; again it is not exhaustive, but it sufficiently illustrates the point.

These instances are of the greatest interest to us. It is not that there is any virtue in a very shallow slope. On the contrary, other things being equal, it is easier to lay out an aqueduct on a steeper gradient simply because surveying errors can be more readily accommodated, whereas with a very gentle slope an aqueduct can be rendered unworkable by the smallest of mistakes. But it is this factor which provides the best yardstick of the accuracy of ancient levelling instruments, a topic hardly ever considered by scholars, who commonly seem to assume that the Roman surveyor could level with perfect accuracy. In practice this is impossible. The sights will not lie precisely on the horizontal, and any reading on the staff will necessarily be an approximation; it may be close to the reality, but it is an approximation none the less. Gradients are established from levels. As a result a surveyor can only safely set out a gradient that is significantly greater than the error his instrument is liable to.

Let us spell out a simple example, in three different scenarios.

1. Suppose the surveyor wishes to set out a gradient of 1 in 1000 downhill between points A and B which are 100 m apart. Sighting with the level, he establishes that the reading on the staff is 10 cm greater at B than at A, that B is therefore 10 cm lower than A, and that the gradient is indeed 1 in 1000. At least that is the theory. Let us further suppose, however, that the readings are, or might be, in error to the tune of 1 in 1000, either too high or too low. What the surveyor fondly imagines to be a true level might therefore be anything between 1 in 1000 up and 1 in 1000 down. In subtracting 1 in 1000 from the supposed level he will end up with an actual gradient which at one extreme might be 0 in 1000 (i.e. genuinely level) and at the other might be 2 in 1000 (i.e. 1 in 500) down. This is not good enough.

2. If, in the same circumstances, his instrument is liable to only half that error, namely 1 in 2000, the gradient he ends up with will be between 1 in 2000 and 1 in 666 down. This is emphatically better, but would probably still cause problems.

3. If the instrument with the error of 1 in 2000 is used to establish an intended gradient 1 in 200 down, the resulting slope lies between 1 in 222 and 1 in 182 down.

In other words, the shallower the gradient the more crucial is the accuracy of the instrument. The instrumental error should be, at the very most, half the gradient intended, as in (2) above; ideally it should be no more than a tenth, as in (3). In a long series of readings, imperfections of instrument or technique might cancel each other out; but, depending on their cause, they might accumulate. We shall shortly see that the all-important first survey of a proposed aqueduct was to establish whether a spring really did lie higher than the destination, and if so by how much. It is perfectly possible to visualise such a survey carried out with an inadequate level and indicating a comfortably positive height where in reality the source lay below the town. It seems inconceivable that Roman engineers were unaware of these limitations and made no allowance for them. Conversely their visible results – very shallow gradients over considerable distances – reveal what accuracy could in practice be achieved. Moreover the trials with a dioptra (Chapter 3.J) show that an average error of 1 in 1418 is attainable. If the surveyor was aiming at a gradient of 1 in 200, it might on this basis end up between 1 in 175 and 1 in 233, which for a typical Greek aqueduct is acceptable. By the same token the libra can achieve an average error of 1 in 57,667 (Chapter 4.B) whereby an intended 1 in 20,000 might end up between 1 in 14,863 and 1 in 30,674, which is again probably within an acceptable range for a shallow Roman aqueduct. And when the instruments were in the hands of surveyors more experienced than the author these average errors would without doubt be less.

Aqueducts are sometimes likened to the canals and railways of the industrial revolution; and with justice, for their surveyors and engineers faced much the same problems in fitting the route to the landscape within the constraints of cost and of ease of operation and maintenance. Yet there were considerable differences too. A canal consists of a sequence of level stretches interrupted by vertical drops in the form of locks. Its engineer certainly required a good eye for country, but if one pound ended up, say, 30 cm higher than expected it hardly mattered, since he could easily adjust the depth of lock at each end. Railways can go, within certain limits, both up and down. But (apart from the quite exceptional cases where water was lifted by machine) aqueducts must run downhill the whole way and, in the instances we are now concerned with, at an exceedingly gentle gradient.

Both Hauck and Hodge have considered in some detail the likely plan of campaign by which aqueducts were surveyed and set out, and their words should be compulsory reading for all those interested in such matters.[22] To summarise very briefly, they emphasise that such an operation involved three distinct phases. First, springs of suitable volume and quality had to be located which seemed to lie high enough for their water to be fed by gravity along an aqueduct, and at the other end a site had to be chosen for the receiving tank at, ideally, a point high enough to supply the whole of the town. Second, the exact difference in height between these two points had to be discovered by very careful levelling; and if that difference in height, taken in conjunction with the likely length of the channel as demanded by the terrain, gave a reasonable gradient, then the surveyors could proceed to the third stage.

This was to set out the route on the ground in such a way that, in the interests of cost, it was as short as possible and demanded a minimum of expensive engineering works, and that the gradient was as constant as the shape of the land allowed. These requirements often conflicted. To save heavy engineering such as tunnels or arcades, the length might have to be greater. On a more devious route a gradient which would be acceptable on a more direct and therefore shorter line might become unacceptably shallow. This third stage was no doubt divided into several phases, the first defining a few key intermediate points, the subsequent ones progressively filling in more and more detail between. In every phase there would be alternative routes to be considered, advantages and drawbacks to be balanced, and compromises to be reached. The surveyors, moreover, no doubt had to build up their own maps as they went. On a long and difficult aqueduct the whole process would take a great deal of fieldwork and of time. One is reminded of Robert Stephenson who, in determining the best route for the London & Birmingham Railway in 1831, walked the full distance (181 km) more than twenty times.[23]

On this whole matter, Greek and Roman literature is virtually silent.

[22] Hauck 1988, 74–82; Hodge 1992, 184–91.   [23] Smiles 1862, 306.

Vitruvius describes aqueduct routes in channel and in pipeline but hardly how to select them. Hero (*Dioptra* 6, end) gives a few sensible words of advice: that the final route of the aqueduct will probably not be the same as that followed in the preliminary survey to establish relative heights, and that care should be taken to distribute the available height evenly along the final route, stade by stade. Nonius Datus' inscription (**Source 104**) tells us that the surveyor made plans of his proposals and (confirmed by **Source 100**) that the route was staked out for alignment.[24] Presumably the same or different stakes were also marked to indicate the levels;[25] Hero speaks (*Dioptra* 6) of recording the levels with cairns or inscribed stones, apparently at every station of the staff which, as we saw, is not likely to be more than 60 m from the next. But there is evidence from the Siga aqueduct in Algeria of a change of gradient every Roman mile,[26] which suggests that in a primary survey levelling stakes were planted at quite infrequent intervals, and that if necessary intermediate stakes might be added in a secondary stage.

But how accurately could or did the builders follow such marks? As Grewe[27] and Hodge suggest, although they acknowledge that there is no evidence, it seems likely that then as now the builders would use boning or sighting boards to project a given gradient. These consist simply of two pieces of wood nailed together in the shape of a T. Someone sights from one surveyed level mark to another and, in between, boning boards are driven into the ground along or beside the route until the top of each T coincides with the line of sight. The floor of the channel is then built up to this level. Constructional differences and changes of gradient on the Eifel aqueduct supplying Cologne suggest that contracts were let for lengths of about three Roman miles, and steps in the floor (the biggest is 35 cm) at each end of one such section show how gangs had failed to match their work with that of their neighbours.[28] It was clearly possible for careful work by surveyors to be marred by shoddy work by the builders.

---

[24] Staking out of boundaries by land surveyors is also attested by *CIL* VI 1268, XI 3932, and *Liber Coloniarum* 244.13.

[25] Two small sand-filled postholes were found on the Lincoln aqueduct, one under the pipeline and the other just alongside it. The first was interpreted as having held a stake for alignment, the second one for level (Thompson 1954, 113).

[26] Grewe 1986, 225–6.   [27] Grewe 1998, 27–8.

[28] Grewe 1986, 84, 102–3, 232.

C. THE NÎMES AQUEDUCT AND OTHERS

Of all the shallow-graded aqueducts, that supplying Nîmes has been most intensely studied. It was built not in or around 19 BC as tradition has long insisted, but in the first century AD, most probably around 50.[29] The springs at Uzès lie some 20 km north of Nîmes and about 14.6 m higher than the point in the town chosen for the receiving tank. On a direct line the gradient, if constant, would be 1 in 1370. How close the Roman surveyors got to this theoretical figure there is no way of telling. Nor can we be sure along what line they took their preliminary levels. For convenience, it would probably be along a road, either the more direct high-level one or the circuitous low-level one to the east which approximated to the route finally selected. But, assuming that their levelling and their estimate of the direct distance was accurate, they would know that in no circumstance could the overall gradient be steeper than 1 in 1370. In fact anything like a direct route is totally forbidden by the terrain. Between Nîmes and Uzès rises a massif of rough limestone *garrigue* which would necessitate tunnels of impossible length. The only practicable route skirts the *garrigue* to the east in a great bow which more than doubles the distance and therefore more than halves the overall gradient (Fig. 9.2).

Many writers have commented on the difficulties of setting out the Nîmes aqueduct with its extremely shallow gradients. Recent surveys, however, show that these were even shallower than had been supposed.[30] The overall gradient emerges as about 1 in 4000.[31] Ideally, it should lose height consistently: when for example the channel had run a quarter of the total distance, it should have lost a quarter of the height available. But the actual gradient is very far from constant. Locally, it changes frequently; and when these local variations are smoothed out

[29] Fabre et al. 1991, 319, who read perhaps more into the evidence than it can bear.

[30] Fabre et al. 1991, gradient profiles facing p. 94. The frequency of the modern survey points varies greatly: they are most numerous on the stretches either side of the Pont du Gard, while elsewhere there are no intermediate levels available on stretches of 6 or 8 km in length. More have been taken, but are not yet published. It is of course only by chance if changes of gradient on the modern survey coincide with original changes of gradient; but the closer the modern stations to each other, the more the profile will resemble the original.

[31] This ignores the first 180 m of length below the springs, whose exact level is not known.

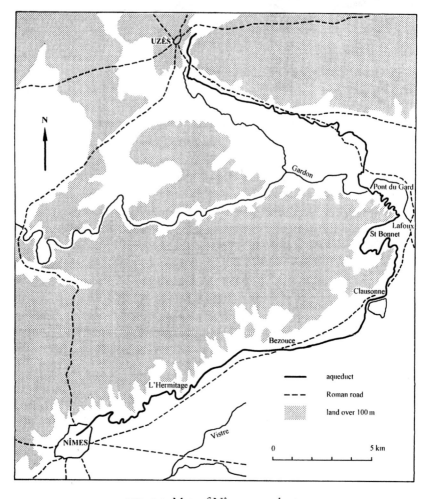

FIG. 9.2. Map of Nîmes aqueduct.

to emphasise the general trends (Fig. 9.3) the resulting profile shows a division of the whole into sections alternately steep–shallow–steep–shallow–steep (these words are used relatively, for what is steep at Nîmes is shallow by ordinary standards). At least some of these major steps were probably not accidental, but were demanded by geography or technology, and they repay closer investigation.

The aqueduct had to cross the Gardon somewhere, and one of the earliest and most fundamental decisions made by the engineers must

182

have been the choice of the site and whether there should be a bridge or an inverted siphon. For whatever reasons, they opted for a bridge. Hodge convincingly argues that the site of the Pont du Gard is in engineering terms the best available, and that, if the gradient were to be kept constant, the structure would have to be taller than in fact it is (see Fig. 9.3).[32] But the bridge as built, 47 m high above the river, is the tallest, as far as we know, ever undertaken by the Romans, and being long as well as high it must have been a daunting structure to design and build. The engineers, Hodge suggests, were willing to venture so far into unknown territory but no further. In fixing the height of the Pont du Gard well below the overall gradient, they gave themselves the luxury of a steeper gradient above it, but the penalty of a shallower one below. At the crossing, they had used up about half of the height available in only about a third of the distance. Put more starkly, they still had 34 km to go and only 6 m of height left to play with.

As a result of this decision and of moderately easy terrain, the gradient above the Pont du Gard is in fact fairly constant at an average 1 in 2542. One might therefore expect a fairly constant gradient below it. Indeed for nearly 5 km from the bridge to Lafoux it is not greatly less than the ideal. But then come the two steps which involve gradients much shallower than are ostensibly necessary. At the foot of the first step is survey point 38 at Bezouce, very close to this ideal gradient and, coincidentally or not, where the aqueduct crossed the Roman road. One might therefore suppose that point 38 was fixed soon after the height of the Pont du Gard was decided on.

The reason for point 37 at Clausonne being above the ideal gradient (if only by about 1.25 m) is probably geographical. Here the aqueduct crosses the low ridge between the Gardon catchment to the east and the Vistre catchment to the west. If it were set lower at this point it would have to traverse a swamp, the Etang de Clausonne, on the west side of the ridge.[33] Hence the necessity, one might deduce, for the steep slope below Clausonne to Bezouce and the gentle slope above Clausonne to Lafaux. But another reason for the small gradient below Lafoux may be the great loop described by the aqueduct around the St

---

[32] Working on the figures then available, he suggests 5 m higher. The new levels show that it would have to be only about 2 m higher; but the argument remains valid.

[33] Fabre et al. 1997.

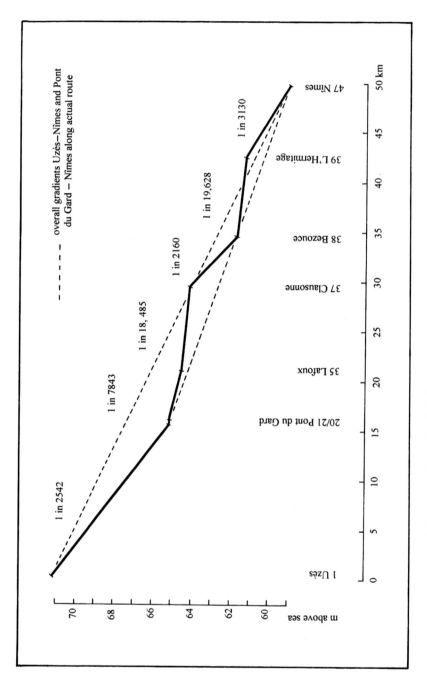

FIG. 9.3. Nîmes aqueduct, simplified gradient profile (based on figures in Fabre et al. 1991).

Bonnet valley. Possibly it was originally intended to span the valley mouth with a large bridge, which would markedly reduce the distance and steepen the gradient, but considerations of cost forbade it.

The other step, point 39 at L'Hermitage, although only a metre too high, has the same effect as that at Clausonne, but is not so readily explained. It raises the possibility of an alternative argument. Point 37 lies on, and point 39 lies close to, the *original* ideal gradient from the source to Nîmes. Perhaps both had been fixed *before* the height of the Pont du Gard was decided. For the reasons already given, point 37 could not be lowered to the new ideal gradient, possibly construction between point 39 and Nîmes had already begun, and both points were therefore retained. The problem on this scenario is why point 38 at Bezouce *was* lowered from the old level to the new. Only one of these lines of argument can be correct. Or of course, as a third possibility, maybe neither of them is right, and the major variations in gradient, like the minor ones, were the result of faulty surveying.

Certainly the variations had their effect on the working of the aqueduct. On a steeper gradient, water flows faster and shallower; on meeting a gentler slope it slows down, deepens, backs up and is liable to overflow. The shallow gradients below the Pont du Gard had exactly this effect. The channel, 1.8 m deep below the vaulting, was intended to run perhaps only half full, with plenty of built-in leeway for deepening due to shallow gradients. But in the event the water overtopped the lining and leaked out through the vault; and soon after completion a length of 6 km had to be heightened by removing the vault (or, on the bridge itself, the covering slabs), building the walls half a metre higher, and replacing the roof.[34]

Whether or not they contributed to the gross variations in gradient, on a more local scale the limitations of Roman instruments and techniques are made very plain by the modern survey. Immediately below the Pont du Gard a succession of small valleys descend from the *garrigue*, and the channel negotiates them by means of a series of re-entrants with hairpin bends at each end (survey points 21–35, Fig. 9.4). Presumably the cost of tunnelling through the spurs or bridging the valley entrances, which would have shortened the distance and helped the gradient, was considered too great. In this broken terrain, where the route is so tortu-

[34] Fabre et al. 1991, 60, 322–3; Fabre et al. 1992, 91–3.

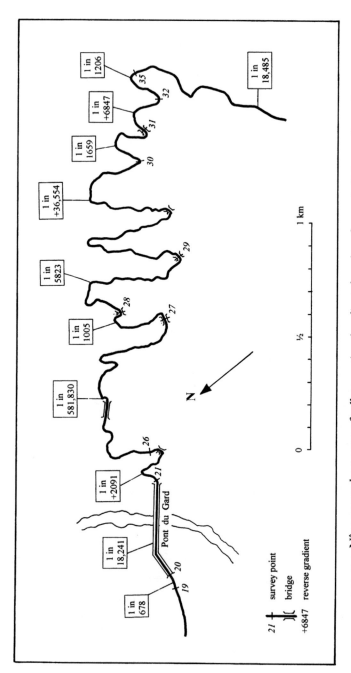

FIG. 9.4. Nîmes aqueduct, map of valleys section (gradients based on figures in Fabre et al. 1991).

ous that rarely can one see more than 100 m of it at once, surveying must have been a nightmare. Conceivably the difficulties were anticipated and allowance was made for them, for the average gradient here is not as gentle as it is on either side. Above, the Pont du Gard itself falls 2.5 cm in 456 m, or at 1 in 18,241; below point 35 the gradient is 1 in 18,485; while on the 4.8 km of the valleys section between points 21 and 35 it averages 1 in 7843. Within this section the variation is startling. There are short stretches as steep as 1 in 1005; between points 26 and 27 the fall is a mere 2 mm in 1164 m or for all practical purposes level; and there are a number of stretches where the bed of the channel actually climbs in a reverse slope.[35] Most of these are short and the rise insignificant, but that between points 29 and 30 is 1608 m long. The rise in this case is only 4.4 cm and the effect on the water flow little worse than if the channel were level. But whatever the reason for the variations in the downhill gradients, reverse slopes cannot have been intentional.

Two factors may have contributed to this unevenness. One, obviously, is inaccurate surveying which, especially in the valleys, is understandable. Let us suppose for the sake of argument that the first setting-out survey fixed the heights of the key points 21 at the end of the Pont du Gard and 35 at Lafoux. The intermediate stations on this initial survey would almost certainly not be on the line the aqueduct ultimately took. As the surveyors worked out this final route and set out its gradients, they presumably established spot heights along it in one of three ways: (a) by levelling longitudinally from 21 to 35 (or vice versa), (b) by levelling laterally from the intermediate stations, or (c) by lateral levelling checked by longitudinal levelling. If it was (a) alone, the scope for error is obvious. The second factor is failure on the part of the builders to follow the levels set out by the surveyors, as clearly happened on the Eifel aqueduct. Boning boards, if properly used, ought to give good results on a straight section, but are not so easy to use accurately around a hairpin bend. However, while the builders may have been responsible for some irregularities, it is hard to absolve the surveyors or their instruments from the blame for 1.6 km on a reverse slope.

[35] This assumes that there has been no movement of the earth or subsidence of the structure. The Carhaix aqueduct shows similarly startling changes of gradient which were later adjusted by adding a better-graded layer of concrete to the floor, and the worst 5 km, which included a reverse slope of 1 in 5000 for 500 m, was bypassed by a new route on a smoother gradient (Provost and Lepretre 1997).

Confronted by deficiencies like this, one is tempted to wonder if the Nîmes aqueduct succeeded more by luck than good management. Indeed Smith has asked if the topmost tier of small arches on the Pont du Gard was a last-minute response to a gross surveying error: that only the two large tiers were intended and had already been completed when it was realised that their top was much too low to maintain a practicable gradient. He points to the marked change of gradient at this point, and to what he sees as the Pont du Gard's uniqueness among aqueduct bridges in carrying a low third tier.[36] But this seems to be going too far. The change of gradient, as we have seen, has another explanation, and the Pont du Gard is not unique in its arrangement. The large bridge on the Roman Madra Dag aqueduct at Pergamon, though a little smaller, must have looked very similar.[37] Another, at 44 m almost as high as the Pont du Gard but with arches mostly of quite short span, is at Beirut.[38] The Kurşunlugerme bridge on the Strandja aqueduct supplying Constantinople also has a low third tier, although the spans are relatively wide.[39] An aqueduct bridge at Antioch, while only two-tiered, had a very large main arch capped with a row of small ones.[40] All these examples are admittedly later in date.

It is still possible, however, that the highest tier of the Pont du Gard (and even of the other bridges mentioned) was indeed added at a late stage, but deliberately so. The deck of the next tier down would be very useful as a bridge for carrying materials across the valley, and even more so for helping the surveyors. It must have been obvious from a very early stage that setting out the gradient was going to be touch-and-go, and accurate levelling across the Gardon gorge was imperative. Yet before the bridge was built (it was 360 m long at channel level, excluding the abutments), and in the absence of optics on the libra, there was no way a reliable reading could be taken directly across. The only alternative would be to level down one side and up the other, with all the risks of imprecision involved. But with two tiers of the bridge in place, the operation would be very much easier; and when the exact

---

[36] Smith 1990–1, 64–5.
[37] Gräber 1913, 390 Abb. 9. Although only the lowest tier survives, foundations in the valley sides demand restoration with a small tier on top.
[38] Lauffray 1977, pl. IV; Grewe 1998, 154.
[39] Dirimtekin 1959, Fig. 23 (drawing); Çeçen 1996, 155–64 (photographs).
[40] Stillwell 1938, 54 and Fig. 4.

level of the channel on either side was established the final row of arches could be built to precisely the right height. Did they, in short, serve the purpose of fine-tuning the ultimate height?

In the event, despite all localised hiccups, the system did work. And, all in all, the likelihood is that the (almost) 1 in 20,000 over 8 km below Bezouce and the 1 in 18,500 over 8.4 km above Clausonne were at least approximately what was anticipated. If so, they give a good guide to the overall accuracy of the libra, and they surely drive a final nail into the coffin of the chorobates as an instrument capable of fine work. We noted (Chapter 1.E) that if its plumb-lines were half a millimetre off the mark, or the water was half a millimetre higher at one end of the trough than the other, then the top of the plank sloped at 1 in 3000. We also noted above that the error an instrument is liable to should never be more than half of the gradient intended, and even that leaves the surveyor hostage to fortune. Developing these two points, we find that to set out a gradient of anything like 1 in 20,000 the top of a chorobates has to slope at no more than 1 in 40,000. To achieve even this slope, and assuming a quite impossible perfection of manufacture, the centre of the plumb-line has to be aligned to within 0.0375 mm of the centre of the mark. The impracticability of this is so obvious that no more need be said.

After the complexities of Nîmes, the three aqueducts supplying Poitiers are simple affairs (Fig. 9.5).[41] The low-level line from Le Cimeau was probably the earliest, of Augustan date. The high-level channel from Basse-Fontaine, which entered the city on arcades, followed soon after. Both came from springs to the south-west, falling quite steeply from the sources but flattening out to very shallow gradients of about 1 in 7450 and 10,300 respectively over long distances as they approached the town. But the Fleury aqueduct, probably built in the early second century AD, is the most impressive in terms of surveying. From springs to the west it followed the south side of the valley of the Boivre all the way, winding along the contour, crossing thirteen small tributaries on bridges, and also entering Poitiers on an arcade. Apart from a short section near the start where it dropped too rapidly and only recovered by means of a reverse slope, its overall gradient of 1 in 8100 is fairly constantly maintained. But it must be admitted that the challenge of setting out the channel along the contour beside a gently

---

[41] Their routes were traced and surveyed in detail in the mid-nineteenth century: Duffaud 1854, summarised in Grenier 1960, 164–71.

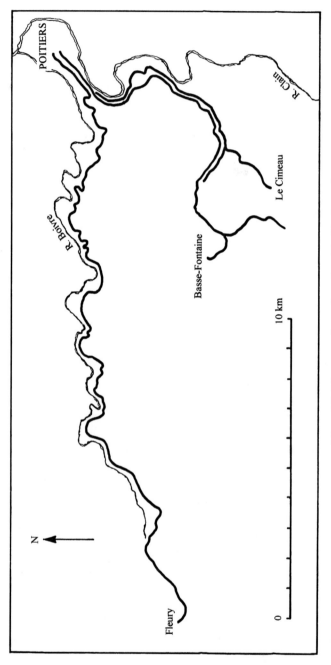

FIG. 9.5. Map of Poitiers aqueducts (based on Duffaud 1854).

sloping river was much less daunting than that faced by the surveyors at Nîmes. It might almost be true that longitudinal levelling could be replaced by establishing levels at intervals at a given height above the river, in the sure knowledge that since the river flowed downhill the aqueduct would do so too.

The Kaikos aqueduct from the Soma springs to Pergamon dated probably to the early second century AD, and ran for 53 km down the wide valley of the Kaikos, much further from the river and through very much rougher country than at Poitiers. It included no less than five tunnels (up to 1.65 km long) and 41 bridges, of which the greatest, over the Karkasos, was 550 m long and 40 m high. All the same, it maintained a very regular 1 in 3200. The bridges were destroyed probably by an earthquake in 178, but the aqueduct was soon restored in rather different form. The top section from Soma was abandoned in favour of a new one from springs at Aksu on which the gradient was steeper. But lower down the old line, to bypass destroyed bridges, two deviations were built which looped far up the tributary valleys to new and smaller bridges. Because the new routes were longer than the abandoned stretches but their fall was necessarily the same, the gradients were yet more shallow: 1 in 4750 on the Mentese loop and 1 in 8300 on the Karkasos loop, which was about 15 km long instead of the original 6 km. This too was heroic work.[42]

D. THE CHALLENGES OF SURVEYING

With these examples under our belt it seems right to address a question more than once raised by Smith: were very gentle aqueduct gradients set by instrument at all?

Instead, the engineer would let water into the channel as it advanced, and then build it level over lengthy stretches with small steps at intervals. After all, in setting a gradient of 1 in 10,000, say, it cannot be all that difficult to provide a step of 5 mm in every 50 m . . . Contrary to the conventional opinion, *very* shallow slopes may be the easiest of all to set out, which is not to say that a proving survey in very flat country is anything but quite the opposite.[43]

Water could indeed be used to establish a level or even a slope in an unlined channel dug in ordinary ground like an Egyptian irrigation

---

[42] Garbrecht 1987, 34–43.   [43] Smith 1998–99, 112; see also Smith 1990–91, 70.

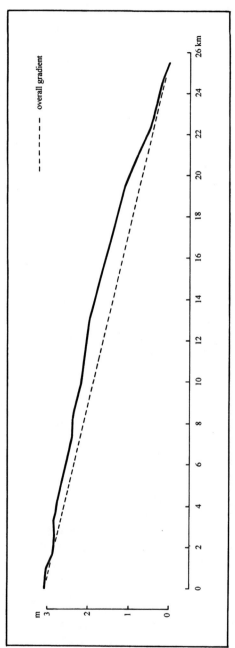

FIG. 9.6. Poitiers, Fleury aqueduct gradient profile. The ratio between horizontal and vertical scales being the same as in Fig. 9.3, the inclination is directly comparable (based on figures in Duffaud 1854).

canal (as was proposed in Chapter I.A) or the New River to London (which is Smith's subject in this passage). If when the water is admitted into a section it does not reach the end, the channel can be deepened until it does. The same applies to a pipeline which can readily be adjusted (if it matters) in height or depth. But this will not work for the built channels which were almost *de rigueur* for Roman aqueducts; or, rather, such a miscalculation can only be remedied by demolishing the structure and starting again. It is a chicken-and-egg situation: the channel cannot be built until there is water to level it, but the water cannot be admitted until there is a channel to receive it. Nor is it easy to imagine a small pilot channel levelled by water before the builders proper moved in. At Nîmes, through the *garrigue* and loose detritus, it would have to be clay-lined virtually all the way; and would it have permitted 1.6 km on a reverse gradient? For a built channel, levelling by water seems most unlikely, and setting out by instrument or (over relatively short stretches) by boning board seems inevitable.

Without levelling by water, and without an instrument which can be relied on to give a perfect level, very shallow slopes are extremely difficult to set out. Within limits, local variations do not matter. The irregular gradients of the valleys section at Nîmes – a switchback, in effect, with humps only a centimetre or two high – were tolerable. Quite possibly the engineers, while doing their best through this awkward terrain, expected something of the sort but knew that it did not greatly matter. What did matter were the long stretches on a very shallow average gradient. Point 37 on the Nîmes aqueduct is 8.5 km from point 35 but only 45.3 cm below it. It was this stretch which was responsible for backing up the water so that the channel had to be deepened. It was therefore the key points like 35 and 37 where there were major changes of gradient which demanded the greatest care and accuracy, and entailed the greatest risks. Whether the surveyors were aware how fine the tolerances were, how close they were to failure and shame, we shall never know.

While setting out shallow gradients, therefore, presents one challenge, the difficulty of working in rough ground presents another. Sometimes, as on the Kaikos/Aksu lines and on the valleys section at Nîmes, the two challenges come in tandem; sometimes only the second presents itself. This applies to the Strandja aqueduct supplying Constantinople, apparently begun in the late fourth century AD if not completed until later, which at 242 km was by far the longest of the ancient world. It traversed extremely broken terrain which necessitated a succession of very large bridges, but yet it maintained an astonishingly constant gradient, the top 10 km averaging about 1 in 250 and the remainder 1 in 1660.[44] Achievements like this or like the multiple aqueducts supplying Lyon, where the routes cross the grain of the country and the overall course of the aqueduct can never be seen from any one point, represent another triumph of surveying.

Today, with detailed maps readily available, it would be practicable to work out at least the outline route for a new motorway or railway or aqueduct from one's armchair. What is particularly remarkable is that, despite the lack of good maps, the ancient surveyors did not commit more irretrievable blunders. Smith has remarked,

It is worth noting that, so far as is known, route selection did not often go wrong. Roman engineers really did know what they were about and clearly had command of reliable surveying techniques. Here and there one finds evidence of errors, or at least changes of mind, but, to my knowledge, not a single case of an aqueduct that was ultimately useless due to faulty surveying.[45]

This is largely true. One apparent failure was at Lincoln, where there is no sign that water ever flowed along its pipeline; but Lincoln was very much an oddity in that its source lay 30 m *below* the tank in the city.[46] The intention must have been either to push the water up the pipes by force pump, or to raise it by machine at the source to a tower higher than the receiving tank and to use the intervening pipeline as an inverted siphon. It is possible that the surveyor thought the difference in height to be less than it really was. More likely the machinery simply proved inadequate for the task.[47]

There is however one case of aqueduct failure, recorded in literature rather than archaeology, where the finger of suspicion points at the sur-

[44] Çeçen 1996.
[45] Smith 1991, 123. Running parallel to much of the final Dorchester aqueduct is an abortive trench, evidently dug at too low a level (Putnam 1997).
[46] But it was not unique. The spring supplying the aqueduct at Cremna lies over 25 m below the reservoir in the city and mechanical lifting was certainly employed (Mitchell 1995, 141–50). At Lepcis Magna an inscription records that water was lifted to the aqueduct leading to the city (*CIL* VIII 11 = *ILS* 5754); for discussion of the circumstances see Vita-Finzi 1961, 16–17. Possibly the same happened at Leicester (Wacher 1974, 345).   [47] Lewis 1984.

CANALS AND AQUEDUCTS

veyor. Pliny the Younger reported to Trajan in AD 112 that Nicomedia in Asia Minor had made two attempts at building an aqueduct (**Source 102**), that both had been abandoned, and that what had already been constructed had been largely demolished. What went wrong? If money had simply run out, the works would surely have been moth-balled until more funds became available. Trajan, in his reply,[48] wondered if there had been profiteering on the part, one presumes, of dishonest contractors or town councillors. But the real reason emerges from Pliny's words: please send me a surveyor or engineer,[49] he asks the emperor, '*to prevent a repetition of what has happened*'. The problem, then, was not one of finance or fraud, but of engineering, and of engineering problems the most likely is bad surveying. Our confidence in the surveyors of Nicomedia is not improved by their claim (**Source 41**), at exactly the same date, that Lake Sophon nearby was 40 cubits or less than 20 m above the sea. In hard fact, the lake surface averages 32 m above the sea, which is about 20 km away.[50] If local surveyors were as inaccurate as that, one can readily believe that they were responsible for the fiasco of Nicomedia's aqueduct.

It seems wrong to close this section, which should be a record of, overall, resounding success, on this note of failure. Let us therefore finally note the inscription commemorating the benefactions of Lucius Betilienus Varus to his birthplace of Alatri just south-east of Rome (**Source 103**). He was responsible for the aqueduct already mentioned, built in or before 130–120 BC, which is very early for Italy. It is a curiosity. It incorporated an inverted siphon, almost the earliest known in the west, of huge size; it supplied a rather small hill town; and there are suggestions that Betilienus had links with Pergamon from which the technical know-how for the siphon might have come.[51] The inscription – a rare surviving record of a surveyed measurement – states that

[48] Pliny, *Letters* x 38. The sums spent on the aqueduct sound huge; but aqueducts were hugely expensive. Leveau 1991, 153 estimates that the 3½ million wasted would have built less than 2 km of conduit.
[49] *Aquilex* or *architectus*. *Aquilex* usually denotes a water diviner; but in this case, the source of water being already established, it must (as observed by Sherwin-White 1966, 615) be the approximate equivalent of *librator*. cf. **Source 41**, where Pliny requests a *librator* or *architectus* to survey his proposed canal. The military *aquilex*, alongside the *mensor* and *architectus*, features among those exempted from fatigues (Taruttienus Paternus in *Digest* i. 6.7, of about AD 175).
[50] Froriep 1986, 39 and Abb.17.   [51] For details and references see Lewis 1999b.

the siphon climbed 340 feet to the town. Much ink has been spilled on discussing the precise points between which this height was measured. Is it an exact or a rounded figure? Was it taken from the base of the siphon or from the stream which flowed beneath it? What exactly was the altitude of the receiving tank? Since none of the answers is certain, the argument seems futile. Suffice it to say that the figure is entirely compatible with such remains as survive, and that the aqueduct certainly worked. At this stage in our enquiry, we would hardly expect otherwise.

CHAPTER 10

TUNNELS

A. CATEGORIES

Surveying and driving tunnels must count among the most difficult of engineering projects. Not only are conditions of work underground unpleasant and dangerous, but to establish and maintain the required gradient and the required alignment through solid rock demand skills of a high order.

Tunnels could be of two basic kinds. One was the single-ended tunnel with only one mouth opening to the surface, the other end being underground in an aquifer as in the Persian qanat or in ore-bearing rock as in a mine adit. The other was the through tunnel for conducting water (or occasionally a road) through an obstruction such as a mountain ridge. This variety could be driven by two different methods.

The first, but certainly the second best, was the two-ended tunnel, where the depth of rock above was too great to sink shafts, except perhaps near each end for the purposes of alignment.[1] The best known example is that built about 530 BC for the tyrant Polycrates by Eupalinus of Megara to bring water to the town of Samos.[2] Its length was 1036 m,[3] but it was not the longest of its kind. The emissary tunnel driven at much the same date to drain Lake Nemi in Italy was over 1600 m, and that draining Lake Albano nearby, traditionally dated to about 397 BC but probably earlier, was 1400 m. The longest of all carried the Anio Novus to Rome under Monte San Angelo in Arcese. No trace of it has been found, but the terrain allows no alternative to the aqueduct passing under the mountain in a tunnel about 2.25 km long.[4] Two-ended tunnels permitted only two working faces, where

[1] Two-ended tunnels of course include very short ones where there is no need for shafts.
[2] Described by Herodotus, *Histories* III 60. For the date, Mitchell 1975, 82–3.
[3] All dimensions quoted for the Samos tunnel derive from Kienast 1995, who with his authoritative measurements and descriptions renders most earlier discussions obsolete.   [4] Ashby 1935, 271; Hodge 1992, 126.

the available space strictly limited the number of workers. Such under-takings therefore took a long time to complete, and the difficulties of ensuring that two long headings met were considerable.

In the much more common type, referred to hereafter as the shafted tunnel, a series of shafts was sunk from the surface and their feet were linked together by relatively short headings underground. This is the technique employed on the qanats of Persia, which surely provided the model. It too is first seen in Greece in about 530 BC at Samos, where the subsidiary tunnels bringing water from the source to the main two-ended tunnel and from its lower end to the town were both driven from shafts. This was the pattern followed wherever possible thereafter. The extreme cases in terms of length are the 7 km tunnel supplying Athens, built a decade or two after Samos; that completed in AD 52 to drain Lake Fucino in Italy, which is 5642 m long; and that bringing water to Bologna, built in the last years BC, which is 20 km long and entirely in shafted tunnel. The advantage of shafts is that each of them increases the number of working faces by two. Despite the extra material to be removed, they therefore speed up the work, and the headings, because they are shorter, are at less risk of missing each other. Shafts also provide for easy removal of spoil, for improved ventilation, and for access for maintenance once the tunnel is operational.

The tunnels of interest to us belonged to four distinct cultures. On the Iranian plateau the qanat was, and still is, the traditional method of bringing water for irrigation.[5] It tapped an underground aquifer, usually in the foothills, which was located by a deep mother-shaft. A string of often closely-spaced shafts was then sunk from the intended outlet towards the mother-shaft, each of an appropriate depth to main-tain a gentle gradient in the tunnel which was driven to join them at the bottom. The normal average gradient is said to be about 1 in 2000.[6] The length is usually several kilometres, one of 15 km is not rare, and in occasional (but perhaps relatively late) instances it can reach 35 km. The qanat was perhaps invented in Armenia, but made its home in Iran, where it was common by the eighth century BC. From there it

---

[5] The standard book, on which the following paragraph is based, is Goblot 1979; for briefer accounts see Hodge 1992, 20–4 and Hill 1993, 181–3.

[6] Goblot 1979, 27–8; but Hill 1993, 182 gives 1 in 1000 to 1 in 1500, and the qanats on the Varamin Plain were steeper still, between 1 in 400 and 1 in 1000 (Beaumont 1968, 176).

spread to Egypt, possibly with the Assyrian conquest of 671 BC, where it took particular root in the oasis of Kharga, and by Roman times it had reached modern Algeria. The relevance of qanats to Greek and Roman surveying lies in their role as potential ancestors of Greek and Roman tunnels. While we know nothing directly of how the early ones were surveyed, al-Karaji gives a detailed account of medieval methods. It is not impossible that techniques had changed little over two millennia, and that his information is applicable to earlier periods as well as to his own.

Examples of classical and Hellenistic tunnels being very few, the picture in Greece is dominated by archaic tunnels of (where they can be dated) the sixth century BC. These include a few curious double-decker tunnels, constructed in two layers linked by common shafts; those supplying water to Athens and Syracuse are the best known, but the unfinished example intended to drain Lake Copais presumably also belongs to this class.[7] In Greece, the whole concept of tunnels was probably borrowed from the qanat. It might have been brought back from Persia by Greeks who took service with Cyrus after his conquest of Ionia about 546 BC. It might have come from Egypt, with which Samos was in close alliance until 530;[8] Herodotus records the presence in about 525 of Samians at the Kharga oasis, where qanats abounded.[9] Or it might have been transferred directly by the Persian king Cambyses II, son of Cyrus, with whom Polycrates of Samos was in alli-ance between 530 and his death in 522, although this date seems a trifle late.

Around Veii in Etruria and in the Alban hills are scores of kilometres of *cuniculi* or small tunnels for supplying water in a domestic or urban context, and especially for draining waterlogged valleys and crater lakes.[10] Many are still at work today. Though often quite short, they can reach 4.25 km in length, and they are almost always shafted. Their

---

[7] The Copais emissary has been variously dated from Minyan to Roman times; for a summary of the arguments see Grewe 1998, 107–8. The purpose of double-decker tunnels is debatable: see Tolle-Kastenbein 1994, 36–7; Hodge 1992, 29 and note; Grewe 1998, 56–7. Although Eupalinus' tunnel on Samos is not a true double-decker, the end result is the same because it was driven on the level and the water pipes were laid on a gradient in a trench dug down from it to a maximum depth of 7.6 m.   [8] Burns 1971, 183–4.   [9] Herodotus, *Histories* III 26.
[10] For a general survey see Judson and Kahane 1963.

gradients, because they approximately follow those of the valleys they drain, tend to be steep, of the order of 1 in 40 to 1 in 80 and sometimes, if crossing from one valley to another, 1 in 25. In date they mostly seem to belong to the fifth century BC or before, and maybe as early as the ninth century. The question of their inspiration is imponderable.[11] While they may have been an indigenous invention, they have distinct similarities to the qanat. Possibly the idea came via Carthage; more likely, provided the *cuniculi* are not of too early a date, it came like other aspects of Etruscan culture from Greece, for there are obvious resemblances between the Samos tunnel and those built at the same sort of date to drain Lakes Nemi and Albano. Certainly there was extensive trade between Greece, especially Corinth and its colony of Syracuse, and Etruria.

'In hydraulic engineering, as in road-building,' said Ward-Perkins, 'it seems that Rome began where Etruria left off'; and 'this was a field of activity in which Rome was, and felt herself to be, deeply indebted to the Etruscans'.[12] Roman tunnels are far more numerous than Greek ones, and generally more ambitious than Etruscan *cuniculi*. They were dug to carry roads, divert rivers, drain lakes or swamps, and above all, as components of aqueducts, to supply water to towns or even villas. Another class of tunnel which, though it had a few earlier predecessors, first really appears in Roman times is the drainage adit for mines, often shafted and occasionally 2 km in length.[13] Tunnels for these various purposes ultimately spread to much of the Roman Empire, and together they provide most of the evidence for the methods of tunnel surveying. Ancient literature hardly mentions them.

<h3 style="text-align:center">B. ALIGNMENT</h3>

The difficulties inherent in tunnel surveying may be briefly summarised. Both the alignment and the level of the final route, which by definition is still invisible and inaccessible, have first to be established on the surface; both have to be marked in such a way that they can be projected underground once work has begun; and finally both have to be followed as driving proceeds. The scope for error is very great. It seems that a fairly standard set of procedures was developed, which can be

[11] See Hodge 1992, 21–2.   [12] Ward-Perkins 1962, 1643, 1637.
[13] Davies 1935, 24–5, 31–2; Domergue 1990, 434–40.

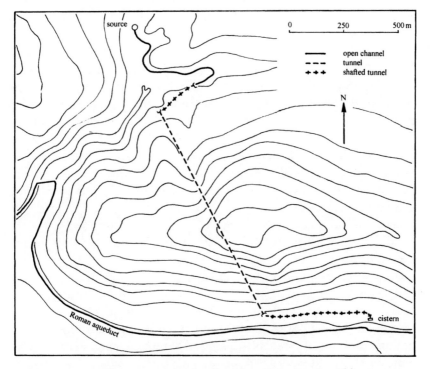

FIG. 10.1. Samos tunnels, plan (based on Kienast 1987, Abb. 1).

explained by reference to a few examples.[14] Alignment and level must have been decided and followed at the same time, but they are best discussed separately.

First, the alignment. Eupalinus' tunnel on Samos is an excellent example of the two-ended tunnel (Fig. 10.1). Because the ridge of the mountain rises about 165 m above its level, intermediate shafts were not realistically possible. The essential points to be fixed were therefore the two mouths and hence the alignment between them. It has been suggested that Hero's method of establishing a tunnel's alignment (*Dioptra* 15) by right-angled traverses around the mountain was actually based on the example of Samos; certainly the shape of the

---

[14] Grewe 1998 is not only the latest but by far the best (and splendidly illustrated) overview of the design of ancient tunnels, and I gladly acknowledge my debt to it. Unless otherwise stated all the information cited in the rest of this chapter is drawn from this book. Grewe does not however discuss in any great depth the instruments involved.

mountain in the diagram in the Mynas Codex is not unlike that at Samos.[15] It seems highly improbable, however, that a copy of the working drawing should survive from 530 BC to the first century AD. The western end of the mountain, moreover, is steep and awkward for such a survey, and it would be not only easier but more accurate to mark out the alignment directly over the hill. Indeed it has been noted that the sites chosen for the mouths align the tunnel under 'one of the few lines by which one can climb easily and directly up the rugged southern hillside and then down the gentler northern slope to the valley behind'.[16] The alignment between the mouths would therefore be obtained by successive approximation. In other and later cases in gentler country, both mouths might be visible from the ridge, in which case simple interpolation by dioptra or groma would be possible. These methods of alignment will be explained in Chapter 11. As at Saldae (**Source 104**) the line would be staked out.

To project the line underground two markers were needed at each end, and not too close together. At Samos, each mouth certainly acted as one marker, but both are on slopes too steep to place a second marker an adequate distance away. At the northern end, therefore, a sighting point was probably established on the alignment on the opposite side of the valley. At the southern end this was not possible, so a shaft was sunk on the alignment just inside the mouth. As the two headings were driven in, they were aligned by sighting backwards on the northern mouth and marker and on the southern shaft and mouth respectively (Fig. 10.2). Similar sighting shafts are to be found on the long and early crater lake emissaries in Italy: one near each end of the Nemi tunnel, and two towards the outer end of the Albano tunnel, which was driven in the uphill direction only.[17]

Whereas two-ended tunnels were almost always straight, shafted tunnels might be straight (e.g. **Dioptra 16**) but were often sinuous. In cases which pierced a ridge, for example, it was sensible to save unnecessary sinking by siting the shafts not on the direct line but along the lowest ground or rather, to avoid surface water flowing in, just to one side of the lowest ground. The interval between shafts was very vari-

---

[15] Van der Waerden 1954, 102–5; Burns 1971, 178–82. The suggestion is rightly rejected by Goodfield and Toulmin 1965, 49–52, Kienast 1995, 196–201 and Grewe 1998, 22.   [16] Goodfield and Toulmin 1965, 52.
[17] Castellani and Dragoni 1991.

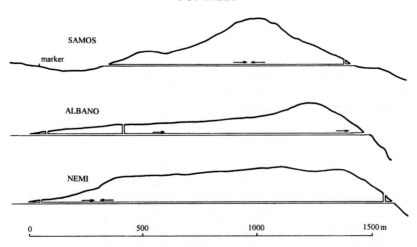

FIG. 10.2. Sections of Samos tunnel, Lake Albano and Nemi emissaries.

able: around 30 m was common, rising to 60 m in later times, but as little as 10 m and as much as 200 m were not unknown. It was at shafts that changes of direction took place because it was down the shafts that alignments were transferred. Al-Karaji xxvi shows that on medieval qanats a beam was laid across the shaft head on the alignment. Near its ends were tied two cords which reached down to the shaft foot, where they were tied to another beam which necessarily assumed the same alignment. If the alignment changed at that shaft, similar beams and cords also projected the new line down. The tunnellers normally dug from the shaft in both directions, following the alignments indicated by each beam or each pair of cords. Just the same principle was still employed on canal and railway tunnels in the Industrial Revolution, except that there the cords usually ended in heavy plumb bobs, with any movement damped in tubs of water or mercury.

In default of any real alternative, it seems well-nigh certain that the ancient world used a similar arrangement; indeed **Dioptra 20** transfers alignments by means of cords down adjacent shafts. Bessac proposes a sophisticated version in the form of a long metal rod with crossbars at top and bottom, parallel to each other and at right angles to the rod.[18] Such rods, all of the same length and plumbed for verticality, would be suspended down the centres of adjacent shafts. When their upper

[18] Bessac 1991, 306–7.

crossbars were adjusted to the same level and the correct alignment, the lower crossbars, reproducing the same alignment at the correct level, would direct the headings. While fine in theory, this seems altogether too fancy in practice. Such rods would only be feasible in quite shallow shafts, and more importantly their presence would prevent spoil being lifted up the shafts. Two simple plumb-lines on the alignment would be quite adequate.

Once the direction had been followed for a certain distance the workers knew that, as long as the tunnel mouth or the shaft foot could be seen from the face, the heading was straight. At Samos the southern heading zigzags slightly, but enough rock was chopped out of the inside wall on the resulting bends to maintain a line of sight to the mouth, and the essential straightness was not compromised.

C. LEVEL

The first step was to fix the relative heights of the mouths: identical if the tunnel was to be horizontal, one lower than the other by the appropriate amount if, as was much more usual, a gradient was intended. It is sometimes suggested that at Samos the levelling survey was carried out over the top of the hill above. But the circumstances were not the same as for the alignment survey. Levelling some 165 m up to the ridge and 165 m down again would open up huge scope for error, and it would surely be preferable to level along the contour around the western flank of the mountain, much along the line later followed by a Roman aqueduct (Fig. 10.1). The most impressive feature of Eupalinus' impressive undertaking is the accuracy of the levelling both on the surface and underground. The tunnel was clearly meant to be truly horizontal, for the northern mouth lies at 55.22 m above sea level and the southern at 55.26 m, only 4 cm different. Along the straight-line distance of 1036 m this represents an overall gradient of 1 in 25,900, but round the mountain, which is almost twice as far, about 1 in 50,000. How it might have been done will concern us later.

On shafted tunnels the process was more complicated, for shafts of variable depth had to be sunk to the correct horizon to meet the intended gradient underground. The surveyor therefore had to level the sites of the intended shaft heads on the surface, and from the heights thus obtained and the known distances along the line of the tunnel to calculate the depth required for each. Maybe he drew a longitudinal section to scale and measured the depths off. Maybe he made all the shafts of equal depth below some horizontal datum, while allowing for the gradient. The traditional method of sinking shafts on qanats to the right depth was of this kind. The surveyor measured one shaft with a knotted cord. He levelled from this shaft to the next one uphill, added to the cord the difference in height, and subtracted from it the height which the prescribed gradient should climb along that interval. The resulting length of cord was the depth of the next shaft.[19] In the Etruscan *cuniculi*, it has been suggested that the tunnellers obtained their levels simply by following the nearly horizontal bedding plane of the tufa.[20] But there could be no guarantee that this was on the required gradient. *Cuniculi* for land drainage, much the most common type, tend to run down valleys and approximately to follow their slope. It would be simple to mark the shaft heads with poles and, sighting down the valley, use them as boning boards. The tops of the poles would thus mark the datum line below which the shafts should be sunk to the same depth.

On the wall of the Samos tunnel are painted about 450 short horizontal lines, and maybe the same number again have disappeared. Thick lines at approximately floor level perhaps told the tunnellers where irregularities in the floor needed to be lowered. Finer lines are at such varying heights that interpretation is impossible, though the fact that all are on the east wall over the trench carrying the pipes implies that their purpose was to establish the gradient for the water, not for the main tunnel itself.[21] In Roman tunnels, once the pilot was complete, a level was occasionally marked on the wall for the guidance of the men enlarging the bore to its full size. At Bologna an arrow head pointing upwards, just like a benchmark, is incised on the wall every 17 or 18 Roman feet. The figure IIII is painted in red just above each arrow,[22] and sometimes a continuous red stripe is painted between the

[19] Hodge 1992, 205–6.   [20] Judson and Kahane 1963, 86.
[21] Kienast 1995, 161–3.
[22] Illustrated in Giorgetti 1988, Abb. 7 (printed upside down) and Grewe 1998, Abb. 221. I have not seen D. Giorgetti, 'L'acquedotto romano di Bologna: l'antico cunicolo ed i sistemi di avanzamento in cavo cieco', in *Acquedotto 2000. Bologna, l'acqua del duemila ha duemila anni* (Bologna 1985), 37–107.

arrow points. Arrows and stripes indicate the levelled datum (on a very regular 1 in 1000) below which the floor had to be cut down 4 Roman feet, which has been accurately done.[23] Similarly, though not in tunnel, the wall of the rock terrace carrying the Roman road towards the Little St Bernard Pass near Aosta is inscribed with a continuous line at 8 Roman feet above the road level. The terrace was evidently first roughly cut out, then the surveyor marked this line to indicate the ruling grade, and finally the road surface was cut down to 8 ft below it.[24]

Returning to the Bologna tunnel, occasional graffiti seem to be memoranda made by the surveyors (**Source 105**). *Resupinum*, 'sloping upwards', presumably indicates a reverse gradient for so many feet; *fastigium*, 'gradient', possibly means that the slope was too steep; *libratum*, 'levelled', no doubt implies that the gradient was satisfactory or had been corrected.[25]

D. MEETING

The preparatory planning of a tunnel therefore involved a great deal of work. Its construction also demanded very careful oversight and control by the engineer in charge, who needed at all times to know the exact state of the works. The most important information, in order to ensure that the headings met up, was how far they had progressed and to what extent, if any, they had deviated from the intended line. Occasionally, to save repeated measurement, the distance driven was marked at intervals on the tunnel wall, and once the tunnel was complete these marks might remain as a permanent record to help maintenance gangs locate themselves. At Samos there were distance marks every 19.45–21.85 m (average 20.65 m); at Bologna there was a painted or incised 'X' every 10 Roman feet (2.96 m), sometimes with a higher figure giving the distance from some datum point; the Fucine emissary had marble plaques every 100 Roman feet (29.6 m) and an aqueduct

[23] In some places the arrows are only 3 ft above the floor.

[24] Illustrated in Grewe 1998, Abb. 7. In the approach cutting to the Roman river tunnel at Çevlik (Seleucia) a horizontal line incised on the wall about 7 m above the floor might also be a datum line; but it might mark a flood level.

[25] Hodge 1992, 438–9 n. 49, curiously reads this as a signature: *Librat[or] Um[. . .*, 'Um . . . the surveyor'.

tunnel at Posilipo near Naples was similarly marked. But while the actual length of uncompleted headings could be measured directly, it was not nearly so easy to determine accurately on the surface, where tunnel mouths or shafts might be separated by rugged terrain, what the horizontal distance was going to be. Sometimes, therefore, the engineer would be uncertain how far the headings still had to go before they met. And despite all precautions he could never be completely certain that the headings were on the same alignment and the same level.

Thus his major worry, especially in two-ended tunnels, was that the headings would not meet at the expected point. This was precisely the fate that befell Nonius Datus' tunnel at Saldae (**Source 104**). Although it had a shaft close to one portal, it was effectively a two-ended one, 86 m deep below the ridge and at 560 m not particularly long. It had evidently been decided, whether by the provincial authorities or by Nonius himself or his superiors, that once planned, staked out and started it did not need his full-time supervision. His absence was no doubt what precipitated the crisis, and the inscription he set up afterwards reads like a self-defence against accusations of incompetence. The tunnel still exists, and indeed now carries water again, but unfortunately nothing seems to be on record of its interior and how Nonius retrieved the situation.[26]

While it was highly unlikely that long straight headings would achieve a neat head-on meeting, it was quite simple to adjust their alignment and ensure that they intersected. If one or both were deliberately angled so that their directions converged, they would be bound, provided the levels were correct, to meet each other. Samos offers an excellent example of the strategy. Whether or not Eupalinus had originally hoped for a head-on meeting, as the headings approached each other he opted for safety and made the northern heading zigzag to the west (Fig. 10.3.a). On its return eastwards it crossed the original alignment at an angle and should have met the southern heading. But, as we now know, this was still about 140 m away. Eupalinus had played his hand too soon, which implies that he had underestimated the total length of the tunnel.[27] He therefore continued the northern heading at

[26] Laporte 1997.

[27] This is another reason for rejecting the suggestion that the tunnel had been laid out by the procedure in **Dioptra 15**, which would have given an accurate length.

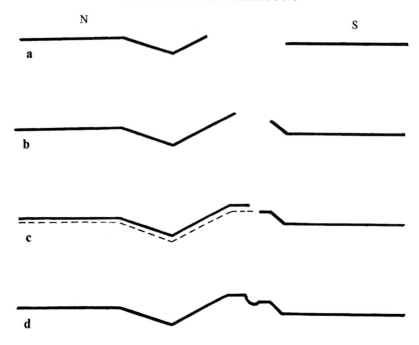

FIG. 10.3. Samos tunnel, strategies for meeting (based on Grewe 1998, Abb. 88).

the same angle and turned the southern heading eastwards too (Fig. 10.3.b). Still they did not meet. At this point he probably realised that his estimate of underground distances was astray, and turned both headings directly towards each other (Fig. 10.3.c). This should have been the final move, for he had clearly kept careful record of how far his deviations had departed laterally from the original alignment. What he still did not know was that the northern heading was out of line with the southern: over its whole length it pointed about half a degree too far to the east, either because of an error in staking out on the surface or because the heading did not follow the surface line. The northern face was therefore always further east than expected. But by this stage the tunnellers could probably hear each others' pick-blows through the rock, and by driving a final curved hook (Fig. 10.3.d) they were united.

A similar but more immediately successful plan was adopted in the 1600 m Nemi emissary. Its date and its sighting shafts were also very

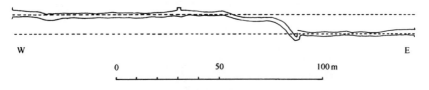

W   E

0   50   100 m

FIG. 10.4. Briord tunnel, plan (based on Grewe 1998, Abb. 261).

similar to those of Samos, which raises the suspicion that, remote
though the tunnels are from each other, a common hand or at least a
common school of engineering practice was at work. At Nemi the two
headings would have missed each other by 2 m sideways and 3 m vertically. As they approached and were no doubt within hearing distance,
each heading was turned equally to the left and then back sharply to
the right, while a steep step took care of the mismatch in level.[28] And
so they met. A variation on the theme was to drive the two headings on
different but parallel alignments, so that a traverse from one was certain
to hit the other, again provided that the levels were right and that the
turn was not made too early. This was the strategy in the two-ended
tunnel, only 197 m long, at Briord in France, where the traverse from
the western heading just overshot the end of the eastern heading (Fig.
10.4).

In shafted tunnels, it is often possible to tell from the horizontal or
vertical mismatch where the relatively short headings met. The smallest
bores were the *cuniculi*, which at around half a metre wide and 1.75 m
high were barely large enough for a single man to work. In one two-
ended *cuniculus* 200 m long the junction was 0.9 m out of line and 2.8 m
out in level, which left a waterfall at the step. But *cuniculi* normally had
shafts, most commonly set 33 or 34 m apart. The headings therefore
averaged about 17 m in length, and rarely met more than half a metre
out of line either vertically or horizontally; usually the mismatch was
only a few centimetres.[29]

While some aqueduct tunnels were not much more spacious, others
were 1.5 m or so wide and 2.5 m or more high. In these larger ones it
was normal to drive *cuniculus*-sized pilot headings, usually along what
was to be the roof, which were only widened and deepened to full bore
after they had met up. This enlargement might remove all evidence of

[28] Castellani and Dragoni 1991, 56.
[29] Judson and Kahane 1963, 86.

209

S   N

FIG. 10.5. Bologna tunnel, lateral mismatch of headings (after
Giorgetti 1988, Abb. 4).

the pilots; but there are plenty of cases where vestiges of them remain
visible, especially in river and road tunnels but also in larger aqueduct
ones. They reveal that the pilot headings were often more irregular in
alignment or in level than the finished tunnel. Indeed that was their
primary purpose: to achieve as rapidly and cheaply as possible a preliminary coarse link between shafts, which could then be refined laterally
and vertically into a more satisfactory finished product. Though usually
minor, mismatches can be quite spectacular: a horizontal one at
Bologna is seen in Fig. 10.5. In a drainage tunnel at Fontvieille in
Provence, between two shafts about 44 m apart, one heading strayed
some 6.5 m off line. In a 600 m tunnel at Walferdingen in Luxembourg,
probably supplying a villa, where the headings were apparently driven
only downhill from the shafts, there are lateral and vertical errors of up
to 3 m.

An especially instructive instance is the tunnel of La Perrotte at
Sernhac on the Nîmes aqueduct, where heading F from shaft III,
aiming to meet heading G from the southern mouth only 24 m away,
was not only driven wildly off course to the side but, where it (just) met
heading G, was also 1.45 m out in level (Fig. 10.6). Measurement shows
that G was 0.75 m too high and F 0.7 m too low. Indeed, although they
were ultimately hammered into reasonable shape and gradient, La
Perrotte and (to a lesser degree) its neighbouring tunnel of Les
Cantarelles were both shoddily surveyed and driven, and the engineer
in charge was clearly out of his depth. This is all the more strange
because, as we have seen, every millimetre of fall on the Nîmes aque-

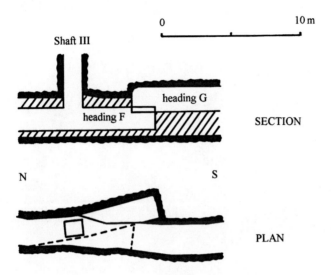

FIG. 10.6. La Perrotte tunnel, Sernhac, plan and section of south end
(based on Grewe 1998, Abb. 257).

duct was precious. We have no right, however, to be supercilious about errors like this, for even modern engineers are far from infallible. We need only to remember an instance in Norway in 1990 when, through a simple misreading of the instrument, a tunnel heading was driven on a bearing of 120 degrees instead of 130.[30]

However, irregularities were not necessarily due to mistakes. If the tunnellers struck a vein of unusually hard rock they might deliberately bypass it and try to regain the proper alignment beyond. An adit at the Sotiel Coronado mines in Spain zigzags between shafts, a feature easily attributable to bad surveying but more likely due to the geology: it is easier to drive alternately along the strike and dip of the rock than in a straight line diagonally across the strike.[31]

If a heading deviates from the straight line, whether by design or accident, the engineer needs to know on what relative bearing and for how far, in order to return it to the original alignment or to change his plans for the future. The easiest method of relating the actual to the intended state of affairs is to plot it on the surface. Two ways of doing this are on record. Hero (*Dioptra* 20) tells how to pinpoint the site for sinking a shaft to clear a blockage in a curved tunnel. He does it by

[30] Grewe 1998, 3.   [31] Davies 1935, 121–2.

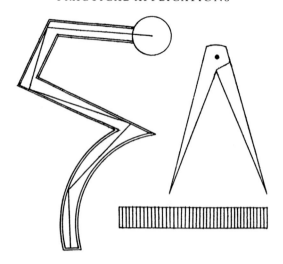

FIG. 10.7. Al-Karaji's procedure for recording deviations
(Hyderabad edition, Fig. 14).

establishing a base line with cords down adjacent shafts, by measuring the sides of triangles off the base line, and by transferring them to the surface. Al-Karaji XXVI gives a somewhat similar procedure for recovering the proper alignment if hard rock has driven a heading off course (Fig. 10.7). Fix cords to the roof of the tunnel, he says, and measure their lengths between the changes of direction. Measure each angle formed by the cords by adjusting the legs of a large pair of compasses to fit it, and record the angle not in degrees but according to the distance apart of the compass's points when set against a ruler, in other words the chord. Transfer these lengths and chord-angles to the surface.

Tunnels reveal other instances of applied geometry. The short 80-m tunnel at Chagnon on the Gier aqueduct supplying Lyon, though none too neatly built, was evidently planned as an isosceles triangle with a single shaft at the apex. The dimensions correspond to round numbers of Roman feet, and even rounder numbers suggest the layout of the markers to provide the alignments (Fig. 10.8). Again, some shafts were not vertical but inclined, which made it harder to determine the correct depths and to establish alignments from their foot. In one such case, the 'Roman Steps' on the Bologna aqueduct tunnel, the shaft was provided with a flight of 318 steps for access, 111 m long on the slope. It was dug at an angle of 36° 40′ to the horizontal, from the top down-

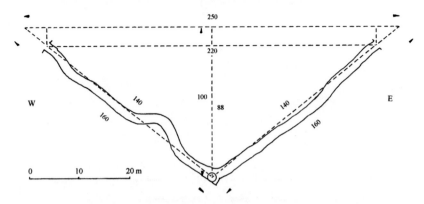

FIG. 10.8. Chagnon tunnel, Gier aqueduct, geometry of setting out.
Dimensions in Roman feet (based on Grewe 1998, Abb. 253).

wards.[32] At this stage the tunnel, which was here to run in a straight line
between a series of shafts, did not yet exist. Quite a complex geometrical calculation would be needed to ensure that the head of the steps was
located the right distance (actually 89.04 m) back from the intended
alignment and that the vertical fall of the steps (actually 66.28 m) went
down to the intended level.

E. INSTRUMENTS

In Hellenistic and Roman times there seems no reason why ordinary
instruments – the dioptra and libra – should not be used for levelling
tunnels, both to determine height differences between mouths and
shaft heads on the surface and (with short staves because of the limited
headroom) to maintain the gradient underground.

The much more thorny question is what was used before the standard dioptra evolved about 200 BC. If the assumption is correct that the
archaic Greeks and the Etruscans borrowed the very idea of tunnels,
directly or indirectly, from Persia, we might expect them also to have
borrowed the instruments for surveying qanats. For this early date we
have no direct information at all on their nature. But al-Karaji describes
the procedures and instruments used by Persian qanat builders in the
early eleventh century AD. Given that theirs was a highly conservative

---

[32] Giorgetti 1988.

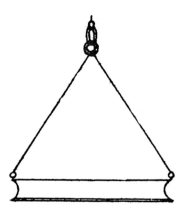

FIG. 10.9. Al-Karaji's sighting tube for qanats (Hyderabad edition, Fig. 13).

profession, handed down from father to son, it is not impossible that their instruments were much the same as their predecessors had always used.

On the surface, according to al-Karaji, height differences between shaft heads were levelled by *mizan* (see Chapter 12). Underground, the level of the floor was checked for every cubit advanced with a simple version of the builder's plumb-line level 3 cubits (about 1.5 m) long. He goes on (xxvi):

But the most appropriate instrument is a tube of brass with a bore large enough to insert one's ring finger without difficulty. It should be about 1½ spans [37 cm] long and carry a ring at each end. A light chain of iron wire is attached to each end and its centre is fastened by a ring to a wooden wedge in the roof. Each end of the chain should be 1½ spans long (Fig. 10.9). The tube when hanging must be horizontal. By means of this instrument one sights outwards from the working face at the qanat mouth or, better, at a ball suspended there . . . If one follows the guidance of this instrument, one may be sure to arrive precisely at the foot of the next ventilation shaft, whether it has already been dug or not.

The gradient should be gentle but steady, he says, around 1 in 1000, or exactly horizontal; but if the sections between shafts were dead level, the floor would be stepped, leading to turbulence in the water. This all seems to mean that because when digging it is easier to follow a horizontal than a gradient, the floor of each section should be made horizontal in the first instance, and then scraped or cut down to the required gradient. There is absolutely nothing to suggest, as there is for his dioptra, that al-Karaji drew his description of the sighting tube from some Greek source.

In most early cases in the west, like the Etruscan *cuniculi* (unless they were surveyed with nothing more than poles), the 7-km tunnel supplying Athens and the unfinished Copais tunnel, all of which are shafted and have quite steep gradients, these qanat procedures would be entirely adequate. The crux lies, rather, in the three major two-ended tunnels of the period, all of which were between 1000 and 1600 m in length. The Samos tunnel is virtually horizontal and the position of its mouths was perhaps established by levelling round the contour. At both the Albano and Nemi emissaries the surface levelling was necessarily done over the rim of the crater, some 120 or 130 m up and down again. The gradient of 1 in 833 on the Albano tunnel, which was driven from one end only, was no doubt approximately what was intended. At Nemi, with its presumably unintentional step of 3 m, either the surveyor set the outer mouth 3 m too low or the tunnellers, aiming at an overall gradient of 1 in 125, drove the headings on too shallow a slope (actually about 1 in 160). Of these three, the achievement at Samos is much the most impressive.

To the burning question of whether qanat instruments were capable of the accuracy required, the only possible answer, unsatisfactory though it be, is that we know of nothing else that was available at the time and could have done it any better. Both instinct and all the arguments hitherto deployed combine to suggest that the principle of the suspended sighting tube is more accurate than the principle of the plumb-line on which the *mizan* depended. If the horizontality of the tube were checked by turning it round and adjusting its balance until it gave the same reading in either direction, it would be more accurate still. It could readily be used outside the confines of a tunnel by hanging it from a stand. The *mizan*, as we have seen, was probably of Babylonian origin, and there can be no certainty that it was in use in Persia in the sixth century BC. It may have been a later addition to the qanat builders' repertoire, and there is no sign that it was ever borrowed in the ancient Mediterranean.[33] I therefore propose, and it can only be

[33] Kienast 1995, 196–201, in a somewhat superficial discussion of surveying instruments, assumes that the *mizan* was well known in Greek antiquity, but cites no evidence.

tentatively, that both the early qanats and the major archaic Greek and Etruscan tunnels were levelled by tube, both underground and on the surface.

It may be that in Italy the suspended sighting tube became the ancestor of the libra. It may be that in Greece it survived, unrecorded in literature until Aristotle, and ultimately, around 200 BC, evolved into the standard dioptra. In the absence of hard evidence we can only speculate. But, in the light of the Hellenistic developments explained in Chapters 2 and 3, this scenario does at least seem plausible.

CHAPTER 11

ROMAN ROADS

A. BASIC PRINCIPLES

Much the best-known feature of Roman roads is their straightness. Over long distances this is not, of course, by any means invariable. In hilly terrain the route necessarily meanders in search of reasonably gentle gradients, and although in such cases the engineer evidently used instruments to achieve a succession of short straight alignments he must have relied overall, as he did in setting out aqueducts, on his eye for the country. Nor, very probably, did early Roman roads follow such straight courses as did later ones. It seems likely that the first routes out of Rome, built in the wake of conquest and traditionally beginning with the Via Appia of 312 BC, were quite basic in alignment and structure and were merely improvements of existing trackways.[1] In just the same way, when Vespasian's army advanced into Galilee in AD 67, 'road-makers straighten bends on the highway, level the rough places and cut down woods that are in the way, so as to spare the troops the fatigue of laborious marching'.[2] The origin of straight alignment and solid structure is often ascribed on the basis of Plutarch's biography to C. Gracchus and his laws of 123 BC.[3] But Gracchus was probably in the main upgrading pre-existing roads, and Plutarch's words sound suspiciously like an echo of Galen's description in the second century AD of roads built by the emperor Trajan.[4] In any event, much of Italy is too mountainous for long straight stretches, although roads in the Po valley are generally (and not surprisingly) straighter than elsewhere. But it is in the provinces which came later under Roman sway that the best examples are to be found. This chapter will be largely limited to the intriguing question of how long straight alignments, sometimes not deviating from a direct line for scores of kilometres on end, were set out.

---

[1] Wiseman 1970, 149.　　[2] Josephus, *Jewish War* III 118.
[3] Plutarch, *C. Gracchus* 7.1.
[4] Wiseman 1970, 145 n. 186. Galen, *On the Therapeutic Method* X 632–3.

As with the levelling of aqueducts, ancient literature is virtually silent on the subject of road surveying, beyond revealing that (at least under the republic) the groma was employed (**Sources 46, 49**) and offering one possible procedure (***Dioptra* 7**). The only firm evidence to base our theories on is the roads themselves. Their planning, before ever spade or pickaxe was put to the ground, must have embraced three stages, of which the last two might overlap. First the specialist staff would reconnoitre the land between the prescribed termini. Doubtless they had, at best, only the crudest of maps, but they would have an accurate mental picture – probably better than we might imagine – of the countryside in question, derived from their own experience, from scouts or from native informants. They would already know the approximate direction required. This they could refine by observing the sun or the stars into something rather more precise[5] – a little north of west, say, or about half-way between east and south – and they would take note of potential sighting points and significant obstacles like marshes and rivers. Next, the surveyor would establish and stake out a straight line between the termini, or a series of slightly dog-legged straight lines, or even a choice of alternatives. Then the engineer (who might be the same man, but wearing a somewhat different hat) would look at these routes on the ground with a closer eye to gradients, river crossings, marshes and the like. If there were alternatives, he would make a choice, and if necessary he would order deviations past obstacles. If they were short, he might well bring the road back to the original alignment; if they were long, a new alignment to the destination might be needed.[6]

B. INTERPOLATION AND EXTRAPOLATION

The equipment required was simple: the groma (or the dioptra, which was equally capable of doing the same job, subject to the caveat about lack of evidence for it in the West), and a variety of targets and markers. Short-distance alignment was not difficult, and probably employed

---

[5] Rivet 1982 suggests, by no means tongue in cheek, that homing pigeons might have been transported from their loft at one terminus and released at the other, and the bearing noted on which they disappeared over the horizon.

[6] For an excellent and level-headed discussion of Roman road planning see Taylor 1979, 41–83.

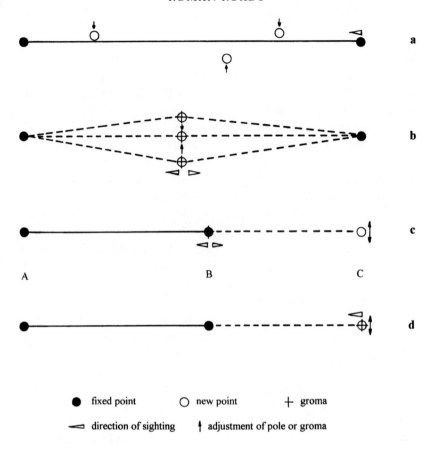

FIG. 11.1. Simple alignment by interpolation (a–b) and extrapolation (c–d).

standardised methods regardless of how long alignments might have been established. To stake out a straight line between two intervisible points up to, say, two or three kilometres apart the surveyor simply sights from one terminus[7] to the other and signals to an assistant to move a pole or stake sideways in one direction or the other until it is in line. The process is repeated until poles are planted sufficiently close together (Fig. 11.1a). If between the termini a single hill intervenes from which both termini are visible, the surveyor sets up a groma on it and aligns it on one terminus. He then sights on the other terminus,

---

[7] 'Terminus' is used from here on to denote the end of a straight alignment, not necessarily the town to or from which the road ran.

which will almost certainly necessitate turning the groma. He therefore moves the groma sideways and tries again until he finally locates the spot where the opposite cords are aligned on the termini in both directions (Fig. 11.1b). This is a matter of trial and error, but of a very simple kind as is attested for example by *Dioptra* 10a and 11, and it avoids the necessity of communicating over a distance. Both these procedures involve interpolation between two fixed points.

The opposite proceeding, extrapolation, involves projecting in one or both directions an alignment that has already been established by two fixed points A and B (Fig. 11.1c). The groma is placed at B and aligned on A behind it; sighting forwards establishes the alignment to the new point C; and so on. The limitations here are the distance (and therefore the visibility) of C from B and the surveyor's ability to communicate orders to his assistants at C. Both these last points will be discussed shortly. An alternative method of extrapolation is to place the groma at point C and adjust its position by trial and error until its cords are exactly in line with A and B (Fig.11.1d). This method again has the advantage that only the groma is moved and no communication is needed. It is attested by *Dioptra* 16 for locating shafts on a straight tunnel.

C. SUCCESSIVE APPROXIMATION

Over longer distances, the traditional view, still widely held, is that the major features of a Roman route reflect the method of its setting out. This has been defined as 'successive approximation, in which a rough solution is refined by trial and error, until sufficient accuracy is achieved'.[8] Margary summarised it in these words:[9]

The real purpose of the straight alignments was merely for convenience in setting out the course of the road, for sighting marks could be quickly aligned from one high point to another, with intermediate marks adjusted between, probably by the use of movable beacons shifted alternately to right and left until all were brought into line; it is noteworthy that Roman roads nearly always make important turns upon high ground at points from which the sighting could conveniently be done. In many cases where the road follows a major alignment for a long distance . . . it will be seen that very slight changes of line occur on intermediate hilltops, hardly to be noticeable as changes of

[8] Davies 1998, 4.   [9] Margary 1973, 17–18.

direction, and this presumably indicates the degree of latitude allowed in the sighting of major alignments . . . But in general the alignments of the main roads were laid out with rigid accuracy for very long distances. The alignment angles are very distinctive features, for the road follows each alignment right up to the angle, unlike the curving courses of later roads, and as the angle occurs upon a high point it is conspicuous.

Apart from a couple of points, this summary is an entirely acceptable statement of the traditional view. As we have seen, where a single hill interrupted the direct line of sight, there should be no great difficulty in filling in the straight line between two termini. But if a succession of hills intervened, Margary's claim that sighting marks on them could be quickly aligned into a straight line is surely wrong. He evades the question of exactly how it was done; and because the answer is nowhere recorded in ancient literature and is by no means obvious, few modern scholars address the question either.[10]

The first problem is the nature of the marks to sight on. At relatively short range, simple ranging poles would suffice. For distances up to a few kilometres, a large flag (if there was wind to spread it) or a distinctively painted target would serve, but beyond that sort of range, in order to be distinguished by the naked eye, it would be too large to be portable. Yet a sighting point, unless it chanced to be a peak readily identifiable from afar, must have been marked in a very positive way. As has often been observed, fire is the best method. Smoke by day is unsatisfactory, since wind or haze can make it hard to pinpoint the source. Flame by night is much more easily distinguished, even over very long distances, provided the fire is large enough. Herein lies the difficulty.

Albeit from a later period, an instructive example is the beacon system devised in the ninth century to bring warning to Constantinople of Arab attacks in the region of the Cilician Gates. Nine beacons spanned the total distance of about 725 km as the crow flies, so that the intervals averaged at least 90 km, although in fact they were longer at the eastern end than at the western.[11] These fires on high peaks under clear Anatolian skies were evidently visible

---

[10] A recent exception is Hargreaves 1990 and 1996, who favours successive approximation. His work, being unpublished, is not taken account of here; but it is to be hoped that it will be published as a valuable contribution to the debate. Another exception is Davies 1998, whose theories will shortly be discussed.   [11] Pattenden 1983.

enough. Even in the lower terrain and less certain climate of Britain, in the Jubilee celebrations of 1977 a beacon on Tiree was clearly seen from Rhum in the Hebrides, a distance of 65 km.[12] The interval between primary sighting points on Roman roads is rarely more than about 30 km and, weather permitting, visibility should be no problem. At distances of that order of magnitude, however, a fire has to be large and therefore stationary: a pyramidal bonfire about 5 m high is calculated for the Byzantine system.[13] Portable beacons as envisaged by Margary could be little bigger than hand-held torches, or at best a brazier carried on poles between two men. They would therefore be visible only at quite short range, of the order of 6 or 7 km at the most.

Equally crucial is the question of communication. If marks are to be shifted sideways to achieve a straight line, the surveyor must be able to instruct his men which direction to move. The longer the distance, the harder this will be. The practical difficulties inherent in sending comprehensible and variable messages by fire signal were well known in the ancient world.[14] In the absence of binoculars, daytime signalling is limited by the resolving power of the naked eye to a very few kilometres. At this distance it might be possible to instruct the target party to move their target laterally, by waving a flag on the appropriate side of the groma, whose own position would have to be marked distinctively enough to be seen by the target party looking back. Similarly by night, and over somewhat but not much greater distances, the groma's position might be marked by a brazier, and another brazier beside it might be alternately shielded and exposed to transmit a flashing signal ordering the target brazier to be moved sideways in the same direction. The only real alternative is the human messenger, who travels, even on horseback, extremely slowly.

Signalling in this kind of way might be possible over relatively short distances. The real challenge, however, for proponents of successive approximation is to explain how to bring into line primary marks on a succession of hilltops which might be 20 or 30 km apart, and where visibility extends only from one hilltop to the next (or to a terminus) in either direction. While it is straightforward to bring any three marks

[12] Pattenden 1983, 281 n. 35.   [13] Pattenden 1983, 297.

[14] Polybius, *Histories* x 43–7. Recent discussions in Donaldson 1988 and Southern 1990.

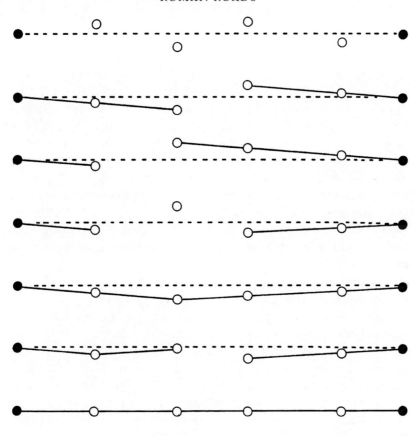

FIG. 11.2. Successive approximation.

into line by interpolating the third between two previously fixed ones, to align say four marks between two fixed ones is a problem of a totally different order. The three marks at one end can be brought into line with each other, and the three at the other; but how to align the two resulting alignments? It can be done, but only by laborious and lengthy trial and error (shown in simplified form in Fig. 11.2). Margary's comment that marks of this sort 'could be quickly aligned from one high point to another' seems wildly optimistic. This is the main reason for questioning the method of successive approximation along the line of the intended road. On the credit side of the balance sheet, however, a definite advantage (as will be explained) of this traditional method is that it involves only sighting, not measurement.

D. DEAD RECKONING

A quite different method has recently been proposed by Davies, whereby the surveyor builds up a map of the corridor through which the intended road is to run.[15] Davies adopts as a model Hero's *Dioptra* **15**, the exercise for aligning a tunnel; a better prototype might be *Dioptra* **7**, which, although the method is the same, is specifically designed to find the straight line between two places. A series of traverses at right angles to each other are set out by groma between two high points which lie roughly between the terminal towns (Fig. 11.3). It is convenient, though not essential, for these traverses to be orientated north–south and east–west. Each traverse is measured on the ground. By totalling the distances east–west and those north–south, the bearing and the length of the survey line between the high points are worked out. Features such as rivers, forests and settlements are located by setting out and measuring right-angled offsets to them from some known point. All this information is transferred to a temporary large-scale map laid out perhaps on the floor of a room. The same process is repeated between other high points until a continuous series of survey lines has been completed between the two towns and represented, true to scale, on the map. Once again the eastings and the northings are totalled to give the overall distance and bearing. From the information on the map the actual route is planned. When it has been decided, points along it are located by right-angled offsets from the survey lines, and the length of each offset and its distance along the survey line is measured and scaled up to full size. The surveyors must then mark out each survey line on the ground, though Davies does not say so, or how; presumably Hero's method is applied of laying out small triangles of the appropriate ratio. From the calculated lengths of the offsets and their distances along the survey line, the locating points are pinpointed in the field, and the line or lines connecting them mark the route of the road. Roman roads tend to be straight, Davies claims, as a result of the method: it is easier to compute offsets from a survey line to a straight line than to a curving one.

There are many problems with this proposal. Unless the map is fully contoured, any changes of direction will occur at points determined

---

[15] Davies 1998.

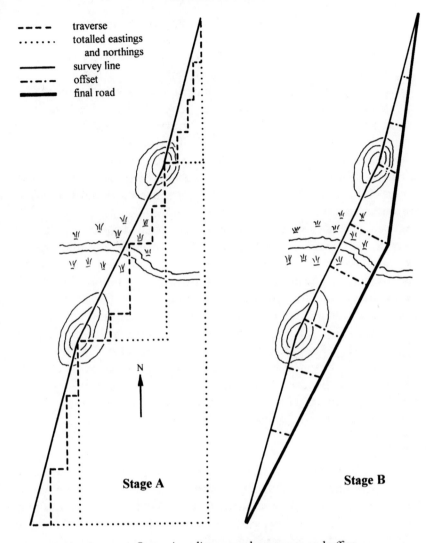

- - - - traverse
········ totalled eastings
          and northings
━━━━ survey line
─·─·─ offset
━━━━ final road

Stage A

N

Stage B

FIG. 11.3. Surveying alignments by traverse and offset.

only in plan, not according to height, and (except by chance) will not coincide with high points; which conflicts with observed fact. Since in practice a road normally respects natural features, to design it from a map which has been laboriously compiled by plotting natural features seems to introduce a quite unnecessary and potentially misleading intermediate stage. It divorces the engineer from the field. It is much more satisfactory for him to look at a route in its proper surroundings, in the form of a straight line or alternative straight lines marked at intervals by stakes on the ground. He can see in the field much better than in the office how well it fits the terrain.

But perhaps the major problem concerns accuracy of mapping. The hodometer would not be practicable across country. Cords or rods would give an accurate measurement but would be exceedingly time-consuming to use over long distances, and it would be virtually impossible to follow a straight line with them through forest. Finding the distance geometrically as described in the Greek treatises does not solve the problem, for in itself it involves considerable measurement on the ground. This leaves only pacing. In the hands (or feet) of an expert this might in general give a reasonably if not totally accurate result; but even the best pacer would find it hard to maintain a constant stride through bogs or up steep slopes, or a direct line through thick woodland. Accurate measurement of long distances, in point of fact, was inordinately difficult, which is a powerful argument against Davies' proposal. If measurement on the ground was flawed, then the survey lines, the calculated distances and bearings, and the whole map would also be flawed. The calculated offsets, on being scaled up and transferred back to the ground, would introduce scope for yet more error. It is very hard to believe that the finished product would be a road as straight as is found, with its bends normally on high points, and that Davies' dead reckoning would be any faster or easier than linear successive approximation.

A thorny question which also arises is how, if at all, the Greeks and Romans expressed the exact direction of one place from another. A well-known instance of a direct line surveyed between two towns is the Roman Stane Street from London to Chichester, which for the first 20 km out of London aims *precisely* at Chichester. Although thereafter it diverges for very good topographical reasons, the exact direction had clearly been discovered, and it is tempting to suppose that the Romans had some way of recording that direction other than by mere stakes (or ultimately a road) on the ground. We would nowadays say that Chichester lies south-west by south of London or, even more precisely, at a bearing of 213°. But the ancient world used neither of these systems.

In the first place, measurement of angles in degrees was apparently reserved solely for astronomy and science, as in celestial observations with the dioptra (*Dioptra* 32 and **Anonymus** 11) and angles of refraction in Ptolemy's *Optics*.[16] There is no evidence at all that in terrestrial surveying horizontal angles were ever measured in degrees. Hinrichs noted that Hero limited the use of his dioptra to setting out straight lines and right angles just as the groma did, and asked if he refrained from applying it to measuring other angles because his treatise was aimed at Roman land surveyors, whom he hoped to persuade to exchange their gromas for dioptras.[17] But the earlier manuals (of which Hinrichs was not aware) and indeed all other sources are equally silent on taking horizontal bearings, and we have to conclude that it was just not done. The practice seems to be a relatively modern one, engendered by the development of the magnetic compass.

Secondly, in the matter of direction, Greek and Latin vocabulary is poor. There were of course words for the cardinal points – north, south, east and west – which were defined either by celestial phenomena (e.g. *dytikos* and *anatolikos* from the setting and rising of the sun) or by wind-names (e.g. *Boreas*, 'north', or *Auster*, 'south'). These were widely used. In Egyptian property deeds of Roman date, for example, the orientation of a plot is expressed as *to kat' anemon*, the relationship to a wind.[18] But there were no combinations of cardinal points as in our south-west or north-east, let alone south-south-west or south-west by south, which have a very precise meaning. Instead, a wind-rose was built up, not unlike the card of a magnetic compass, by increasing the number of wind-names from the original four to eight, twelve, sixteen or even thirty-two.[19] But even when these were used in combination, they were only generalised directions, not specifically defined. Thus 'the tempestuous wind called Euroclydon' which nearly brought St Paul's ship to grief (actually a corruption of *Eurakylon*, the Greek version of the Latin *Euraquilo*) was a wind blowing from rather east of north-east.[20] Such names were coined by mariners, there is no sign of

---

[16] Ptolemy, *Optics* v 8–11.   [17] Hinrichs 1974, 109.

[18] *P. Oxy.* 100.10 of AD 133.

[19] Taylor 1956, 6–16, 52–5; Dilke 1985, 28, 110–11, 170. Aujac 1993, 126–7, 282 discusses Ptolemy's twelve-point wind-rose which named east and west as equinoctial sunrise and sunset and points 30° north and south of these as sunrise and sunset at summer and winter solstices, regardless of the fact that these were only accurate for the latitude of Rhodes, 36°. His other points were winds.

[20] Acts of the Apostles 27.14; Taylor 1956, 53.

them being employed by surveyors,[21] and they were not nearly precise enough for our purposes.

There are only two texts which are potentially relevant to the problem. The first, although it does not supply the full answer, is the passage in Ptolemy's *Geography* (**Source 106**) which speaks of finding the relationship of a direction to the meridian. Ptolemy makes it clear that the first step was to establish the meridian either by armillary astrolabe, which was surely never part of a surveyor's equipment, or by gnomon, which was in fact the only practicable means of finding south in the field:[22] the procedure is described in Chapter 1.c. Over the next step, however, how to measure the relationship of the required direction to north or south and how to express it, he leaves us guessing. But since it appears that the angle was not expressed in degrees, the next best alternative is that it was expressed in terms of the sides of the right-angled triangle which subtended it. Thus Chichester might be described as lying 20 units south of London and 13 units west of it, which represents a right-angled triangle aligned south and west with its hypotenuse linking the two towns. In modern terms, since $13/20 = \tan 33°$, Chichester lies $33°$ west of south relative to London, which is the same as a bearing of $213°$.

As we saw, the other text, **Dioptra 7**, prescribes how to draw a straight line between two distant points which are not intervisible. While Hero seems to be envisaging a very small-scale exercise within an area of only 82 by 70 cubits, there is no difficulty in applying it on a much larger scale. He relates his direct line not to a cardinal point but to an arbitrary base line, which it would be simple enough to align east–west or north–south with a gnomon. And he ends up with a right-angled triangle of just the same kind: 'the ratio of AM to AB is as 72 to 32', that is 9 to 4. He proceeds to set out the required line relative

---

[21] The only exception seems to be in late fifth-century deeds from Vandal North Africa which record plots of land as orientated, for example, *a coro et septentrione*, between north-west and north, i.e. north-north-west (*Tablettes Albertini* XXII 6 and several other examples).

[22] It has been suggested (e.g. Dilke 1987b, 214; Davies 1998, 13) that surveyors established a north–south line by means of portable sundials. Price 1969, 256 indeed claimed that one version acted like a compass in that it worked only when aligned north–south; but practical experiment clearly shows that he was wrong, and that portable sundials do not give direction except insofar as their shadow, like any shadow, points south at noon.

to the base line by means of small triangles of those proportions. Whether this system of expressing horizontal angles was applied to recording the direction of roads we do not know. But it does have the merit of being identical to the old system of expressing vertical angles – the altitude of the sun – as the ratio of the length of shadow to the height of a gnomon (Chapter 1.D).

Having reached this stage, let us return to Davies' method. If its totality is unsatisfactory in its complex cycle of moving from the field to a map in the office and back to the field, its first half, being based on Hero, may possess some virtue for aligning marks on a succession of hills. An alternative method, closer perhaps to what Ptolemy has in mind, is not to use right-angled traverses but to measure directly the distance between each pair of sighting points. At each point establish south by gnomon and observe the previous point by groma; record the angle between this sighting line and south in terms of the ratio of the right-angled triangle which, in conjunction with the measured hypotenuse, will give the easting and the northing; and, when the whole distance has been covered, add up, as in Davies' method, all the eastings and all the northings to find the overall distance and direction (Fig. 11.4). In both cases, because of the limitations of measurement, this direction will almost inevitably be inaccurate although, because less measurement is involved, the angle method may be less inaccurate than the right-angle one. But the direction might be good enough to be worth setting out. At one end, mark on the ground a triangle of the correct proportions, the bigger the better, and project the hypotenuse by groma in a straight line, leaving temporary marks on the intervening hills, until it hits, or more likely misses, the destination. By measuring the distance by which it misses, it is easy to calculate which way and how far to move the intermediate marks, because their distances along the line are at least approximately known.

This scenario, however, prompts another question. Would it not be simpler still to eliminate the bother of measuring right angles or triangles along the way? Why not set out from one terminus, marking out by groma a straight line in the direction which aims, by the best guess, at the other terminus, and measuring the distances along the way? Suppose it misses the destination by 4 miles to the east (Fig. 11.5). At the half-way point as measured, the alignment therefore needs to be moved west by 2 miles, at the three-quarter point by 3 miles, and so on.

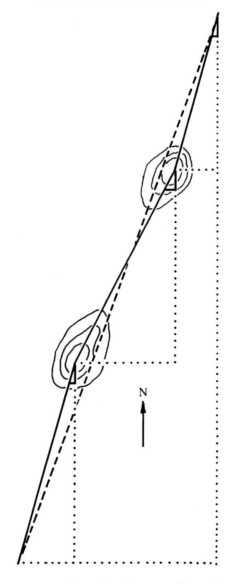

FIG. 11.4. Surveying alignments by angle.

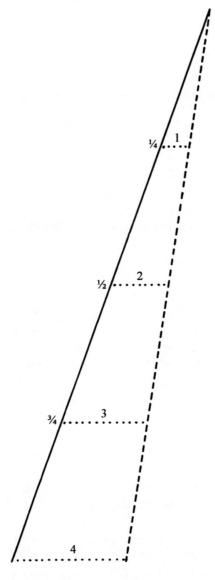

FIG. 11.5. Surveying alignment by offset.

The operation would probably be considerably faster than by successive approximation; but it is still unsatisfactory because it involves measuring the whole route.

E. GEOMETRICAL CONSTRUCTION

For establishing a straight line, then, between distant termini and across a number of intervening high points, the trial and error of successive approximation is laborious and slow, while the measurement demanded by dead reckoning is liable to be inaccurate. A third method may be suggested which reduces both measurement and trial and error to a minimum. It relies not on the interpolation of several marks between two fixed points but on the simpler process of extrapolation from one fixed point; it reflects Ptolemy's remarks (**Source 106**) on finding a direction relative to the meridian; and, like so many ancient surveying procedures, it is based on the geometry of similar triangles. The amount of trial and error involved depends on how accurately the required direction was estimated in advance. Let us take a hypothetical example where this estimated direction was somewhat astray.

Let A and B be the termini (Fig. 11.6). The meridian is very carefully established at each place. The best guess from available information is that B lies 1 unit north and 6 east of A. That angle is laid out relative to the meridian at A on as large a scale as possible, and on that bearing a line is projected by extrapolation from A to X. Once it becomes clear that it runs too far north and therefore misses B by a considerable margin, it is abandoned in favour of two new lines AY and AZ which aim further south and are designed to bracket B; let us suppose AY runs due east and AZ runs 1 unit south and 6 east. Once it is clear that they do bracket B, two lines are extrapolated from B on the reciprocal bearings, namely BD due west and BC 1 unit north and 6 west, until they intersect AY and AZ at C and D. AC is thus parallel to BD and AD to BC, and ACBD is therefore a parallelogram. The diagonal CD is measured and point E halfway along it is marked. Because ACE and BDE are identical triangles, as are ADE and BCE, AEB is a straight line. To fill in further points on this line, the same process can be repeated on a smaller scale, or marks can be interpolated in the usual way, as the terrain dictates.

A variation on the theme may be preferable if there is a prominent

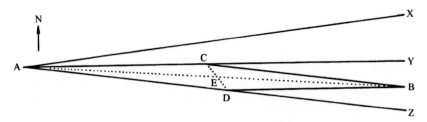

FIG. 11.6. Surveying alignment by geometrical construction.

high point in a suitable location to which bearings may be taken from A and from B without too much difficulty. Let us again call it C. The angle ACB will show if C lies reasonably near the direct line (the closer it is to 180°, the nearer it lies). Record the bearings, extrapolate the reciprocal of AC from B and the reciprocal of BC from A. Where these lines intersect is D.

As with the previous two methods, there is no proof that this one was employed. But it is argued in Section F(d) that it admirably suits the setting out of Stane Street. If the Romans did use it, it is interesting that it smacks of Greek geometrical surveying, even if it was not neces-sarily designed for this particular purpose; it would thus be one of the more important Roman borrowings of Greek procedures.

F. EXAMPLES

There is no reason to suppose that all long alignments were laid out in the same way, and it is worth citing a few examples from Britain (and one from Germany) to illustrate what seem to be different methods. It is also worth uttering a caution against reading too much into long and fairly straight roads such as the Foss Way, which in its course of 335 km from Axmouth to Lincoln never deviates more than about 12 km from the direct line. It is well known that it (or part of it) was planned as a temporary frontier road running diagonally across Britain once the first phase of the Roman conquest was complete, and it is often seen as a gargantuan feat of surveying. But it was not built all in one: the section south-west of Cirencester came later than that to the north-east.[23] Its relative straightness, moreover, resulted not from an overall

---

[23] Johnston 1979, 40–3.

long-distance survey but from the linking of places chosen for military reasons which happened to be, or because they were, in a more or less straight line. Almost all the settlements along it had either a pre-Roman or an early military origin. The Foss Way, therefore, is not so much a single long road as a succession of relatively short roads built to connect frontier forts and to pass close to important native strongholds.

(a) **The Portway.** The road from Silchester to Old Sarum, 58 km long, is a good example of basic surveying (Fig. 11.7). Between the two towns are two prominent and intervisible high points, Cottington's Hill (230 m) from which Silchester can be seen, and Quarley Hill (170 m) from which Old Sarum is visible. A groma on top of each would show that the four places lay in a nearly straight line which would serve as the route almost as it stood. To cross the two summits, however, would involve unnecessary ascents and descents, and Quarley Hill was already occupied by a hillfort. The primary sighting points were therefore moved down their southern flanks, by about 1 km at Cottington's Hill to a height of some 215 m and by ½ km at Quarley Hill to a height of about 130 m. From this new point on Quarley, however, where the alignment turned about 8°, Old Sarum was no longer visible and a secondary sighting point had to be introduced on the direct alignment by interpolation. From the new primary point on Cottington's, moreover, Silchester was no longer visible. The long alignment from the west was therefore projected eastwards beyond Cottington's Hill by extrapolation to a secondary point, where the road turned about 2°; and another secondary point was introduced between here and Silchester at which, by accident or design, the road turned another 2°. The Portway was thus a simple matter to survey and, as so often, it was clearly not considered worth the effort of establishing the direct line between the two towns. Nor was the survey complicated by the need to serve existing settlements *en route*: the only settlement on it, at East Anton, grew up later at the point where the Portway crossed the Winchester–Cirencester road.

(b) **Ermine Street.** The northernmost end of Ermine Street runs north for 51 km from Lincoln to the Humber ferry at Winteringham (Fig. 11.8). From just outside the north gate of Lincoln it follows a dead-straight alignment for 38½ km along the gently undulating eastern slopes of the Jurassic Ridge. At the point where it drops off the

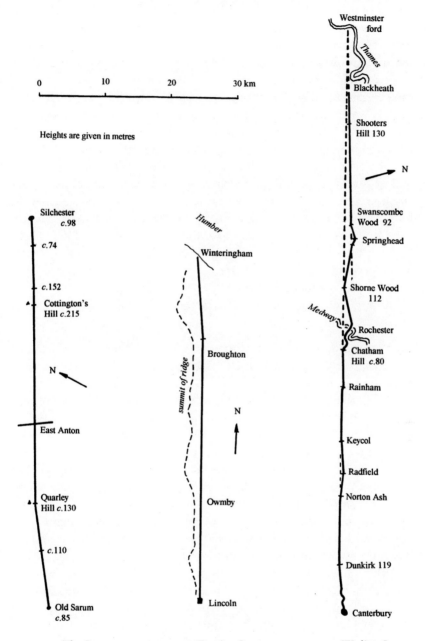

0   10   20   30 km

Heights are given in metres

FIG. 11.7. The Portway.   **FIG. 11.8.** Ermine Street.   **FIG. 11.9.** Watling Street.

Labels in figure 11.7: Silchester c.98; c.74; c.152; Cottington's Hill c.215; N; East Anton; Quarley Hill c.130; c.110; Old Sarum c.85

Labels in figure 11.8: Humber; Winteringham; summit of ridge; Broughton; N; Owmby; Lincoln

Labels in figure 11.9: Westminster ford; Thames; Blackheath; Shooters Hill 130; N; Swanscombe Wood 92; Springhead; Shorne Wood 112; Medway; Rochester; Chatham Hill c.80; Rainham; Keycol; Radfield; Norton Ash; Dunkirk 119; Canterbury

northern end of the ridge near Broughton it turns about 8½° to the west for the final alignment of 12 km to Winteringham. A cursory inspection along the summit of the ridge would show the surveyors that the required route ran very close to due north. They would not want to follow the ridge itself, which is sinuous and would involve unnecessary ups and downs over its peaks; but on the gentler slopes to the east, with no clear-cut high points and no long-distance sightings possible, one route was as good as another. It therefore seems likely that the alignment of 2° west of north was selected almost arbitrarily and was projected northwards from Lincoln by extrapolation until, at the end of the high ground, Winteringham came into sight and the final alignment could be set out by interpolation. If this was the case, the long straight stretch was in effect surveyed from one end only, from the fixed point of Lincoln, the exact location of the other end being relatively immaterial. There was indeed an Iron Age site at Owmby which developed into a Roman roadside settlement, but it is not clear whether it determined the route of the road. Even if it did, the principle of projecting the alignment by extrapolation still holds good to the north of Owmby.

(c) **Watling Street.** Watling Street between eastern Kent and London must have been the first Roman road in Britain, constructed immediately after the invasion of AD 43. We are concerned here with the major part of it, the 87 km between the native centre of Canterbury and the ford over the Thames at Westminster which preceded London Bridge (Fig. 11.9).[24] The general direction to follow would be obvious: west with a touch of north, roughly parallel to the Thames and its estuary, and below the northern edge of the North Downs but crossing some of the spurs emanating from them. Along the route there was a pre-Roman centre of some importance at Rochester beside the River Medway, and what was very probably a pre-Roman sanctuary at Springhead. Other settlements on the road were either contemporary Roman forts or later developments.

Although the western terminus was clearly Westminster ford, the route from there to Blackheath is uncertain. From Blackheath the road runs eastwards to Swanscombe Wood (92 m), crossing on the way Shooters Hill (130 m) which is the only actual hilltop, all the other

---

[24] For an interesting discussion of Watling Street see Hamey and Hamey 1981, 20–1.

points mentioned lying on side slopes. From Swanscombe Wood it deviates briefly north to Springhead, then south on two short alignments to a high point at Shorne Wood (112 m), and north again to descend to the Medway bridge at Rochester. Having climbed Chatham Hill (about 80 m) by a sinuous route, it then follows a basically straight alignment across relatively low and gently undulating land to the high point at Dunkirk (119 m) which, because the final length of 7 km down to Canterbury is somewhat tortuous, is the effective eastern terminus of the long-distance survey.[25] The devious sections between Shorne Wood and Chatham Hill and from Dunkirk to Canterbury are entirely understandable: they were the result of purely localised surveying where the engineers had to seek out reasonable gradients down steep valley sides and, at the Medway, the best crossing point. What concern us are the long-distance alignments.

There are two of these, each only partly followed by the road. The northern line runs direct from Westminster over the summit of Shooters Hill and via Swanscombe Wood to a point 1 km east of Springhead. Its first stage from the ford to Shooters Hill (which are intervisible) was no doubt projected onwards by extrapolation. If it were continued eastwards it would pass north of Canterbury. On the southern alignment, which runs from the ford to Dunkirk, the primary sighting point was probably at Shorne Wood, and a secondary point on the southern flank of Shooters Hill was interpolated by a groma sighting beacons at the ford in one direction and Shorne Wood in the other. This line would then be projected eastwards via Chatham Hill to Dunkirk. It passes south of Canterbury. As built, the road follows the northern alignment as far as Swanscombe Wood, and the change of direction 1 km east of Springhead also coincides with it. The southern alignment coincides with the change of direction at Shorne Wood; only between Chatham Hill and Dunkirk is it followed by the road.

It seems possible that Watling Street offers an incomplete example of the geometrical construction method of setting out a direct line as suggested in Section E above. If so, two lines were projected eastwards from Westminster to bracket the destination, but there is no sign that the counterpart parallel lines were ever projected westwards from

---

[25] There are other instances of major alignments starting (or ending) not at a town but at a high point some distance outside it, e.g. Worthy Down 5 km out of Winchester, where the long alignment towards Mildenhall began.

Dunkirk, let alone that the direct line was ever established. The road was doubtless built in a hurry – we shall shortly find other evidence for this – and once the first two alignments had been surveyed it was perhaps decided that, between them, they were entirely adequate without any further time being wasted on refining them. At the western end the northern alignment was adopted, the deviation north to Springhead being perhaps inserted as an afterthought; and between a point a kilometre east of Springhead and Shorne Wood the road was transferred to the southern alignment which, apart from the sides of the Medway valley, it followed to Dunkirk.

Even though the alignment from Chatham Hill to Dunkirk is clearly meant to be straight, it contains irregularities which are inexplicable in terms of the terrain and point to hasty or careless surveying. For 4 km from Chatham Hill the road aims about 2° too far north, necessitating a gentle zigzag at Rainham to bring it back to the proper orientation. A little further east, at Keycol, the line again deviates slightly to the north until at Radfield, where it is 250 m off-line, it turns south to rejoin the correct alignment at Norton Ash. It is interesting that, reckoning from Dunkirk, these minor changes of direction occur at whole numbers of Roman miles: Dunkirk to Norton Ash 7 miles, to Radfield 3, to Keycol 4, to Rainham 4. This tends to confirm the observation made on Roman roads in France that markers were installed at intervals of a mile and, where they were inaccurately interpolated, their sites are represented by slight changes of alignment.[26]

(d) **Stane Street**. The road from London to Chichester, the classic example of precise alignment, has been much discussed.[27] For the first 20 km from the south end of the Roman London Bridge it aims exactly at the east gate of Chichester (Fig. 11.10). Had it followed the direct line thereafter it would have entailed very steep gradients across the ridges of the North Downs and, after traversing the Weald, it would have had to climb the precipitous north scarp of the South Downs. In the event it left the direct alignment at Ewell to run roughly parallel to it for geological reasons: by doing so it could be built on chalk rather than on clay. A series of relatively short alignments then led it down through the Dorking Gap to near Ockley, whence it ran

[26] Ulrix 1963, 176.
[27] Bibliography and details in Margary 1965, 45–92; Margary 1973, 64–8.

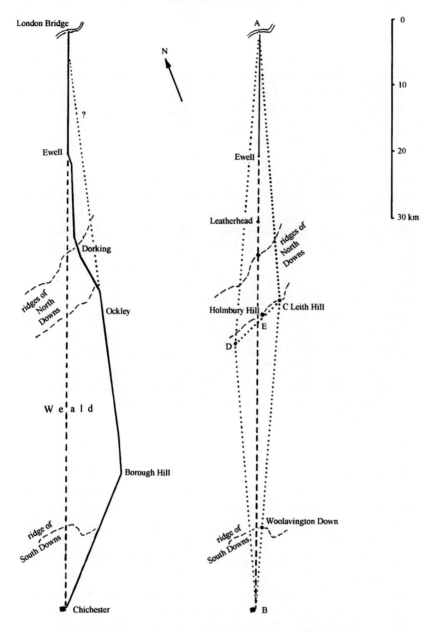

FIG. 11.10. Stane Street.

FIG. 11.11. Stane Street aligned by geometrical construction.

239

almost straight to Borough Hill near Pulborough. This section is said to be aligned on London Bridge, but in fact is not: it is actually composed of two different alignments, one of which, if extended, would meet the Thames about 400 m east of the bridge, the other about 1400 m west of it. It is difficult to tell whether there was some error in the surveying or, perhaps more likely, the apparent alignments are coincidental. From Borough Hill the road turns to the final alignment which takes it across the South Downs by an easy route to Chichester. For much of the way from Ewell, however, apart from short and understandable deviations crossing streams or bypassing rough ground, there are a number of irregularities which contrast with the precision of the direct alignment.

It is quite clear that the Romans worked out the direct alignment from London to Chichester and used it for part of the way, and it is in this that the main interest of Stane Street lies. As to the method employed, successive approximation, the usual assumption, seems improbable. Leith Hill (294 m) and a few other high points on the North Downs are visible from London, there is an unrestricted view across the Weald, and a few of the highest summits on the South Downs are visible from Chichester. An initial series of sightings could therefore be made in three stages. But the highest points are not in line with the termini, and as soon as they are abandoned in favour of a more direct line, the observers lose sight of London and Chichester and more stages become inevitable. The ridges of the South and North Downs are about 32 km apart, and communicating orders over that distance to move large beacons sideways seems beyond practical politics. Davies' method of right-angled traverses is likewise rendered unlikely by the difficulties of overland measurement in the forests of the Weald which intervened between the Downs.

In contrast, geometrical construction seems relatively straightforward. Let us suggest the method, repeating the lettering used in Fig. 11.6, with London Bridge at A and Chichester at B. Can the angle C of the parallelogram be identified? It might fall at some point on the supposed alignment from London Bridge to Borough Hill, in which case the diagonal CD had a length of at least 12 km to be measured. But the accuracy of this alignment is defective and its reality dubious. A far better candidate for C is Leith Hill, at 294 m much the highest point in the whole area (Fig. 11.11). As it is visible directly from London

Bridge, it was easy to measure the bearing AC. In the other direction, a groma on Woolavington Down on the South Downs, sighting on beacons on Leith Hill and at Chichester's east gate, interpolated an intermediate point which gave the bearing of BC. The reciprocal of BC was then extrapolated from London Bridge and the reciprocal of AC from Chichester. These two lines intersect at D, 8.6 km from Leith Hill. The point E, halfway along the diagonal CD, is also by definition the halfway point on the direct alignment between the termini. It falls at a height of about 150 m, less than a kilometre south of the southern ridge of the North Downs. By a lucky chance the point where the direct alignment crosses that ridge, at a height of about 244 m on the flank of Holmbury Hill, is visible from London Bridge, and could easily be established by interpolation by a groma sighting on beacons at E and at London Bridge.

By this stage it was obvious that it was a practical impossibility for the road to follow the direct alignment much further south than Ewell, and the southern half of the alignment was doubtless never staked out. The alignment from Holmbury to Ewell, which is about halfway to London, was not used for the road either, but points along it had to be located. Since Holmbury and Ewell are not intervisible, interpolation betweeen Holmbury and London Bridge established an intermediate point on the northern ridge of the Downs at a height of 188 m, and interpolation between here and London Bridge established another above Leatherhead. From this point the line to London, most of which was utilised by the road, was filled in in the usual way. Geometric construction therefore seems the most likely method for setting out the major alignment of Stane Street.

Marinus of Tyre, according to Ptolemy, recorded that Chichester was 59 (Roman) miles from London.[28] Much has been made of this as corresponding to the actual distance, not as the road runs but as the crow flies, with the implication that the Romans not only plotted the direct alignment but measured it as well.[29] There are two snags to this claim. First, the real distance is nearer 60 miles: to be precise, 59.84 Roman miles. Secondly, it is much easier to suppose that the distance was measured along the road as built, which from gate to gate was about 62 Roman miles. This sounds too great; but road lengths as

---

[28] Ptolemy, *Geography* I 15.7.   [29] Rivet and Smith 1979, 117.

indicated by milestones could be measured not from town centres or even town gates but from the edge of the 'town zone' outside.[30] Although we have no idea of the extent of the 'town zone' of either Chichester or London, it remains entirely possible that Marinus' distance was simply recorded from the milestones and has nothing to do with the direct alignment.

The direct alignment of Stane Street seems to be unique in Britain. Other instances have been claimed. It is said, for example, that Gartree Road, which runs south-east from Leicester, aims directly for Colchester, and that the distance as scaled off Ptolemy's map is correct at 108 Roman miles.[31] But while the alignment for the first 38 km from Leicester is at least approximately right, in hard fact Gartree Road then diverges from it to go to Godmanchester and Cambridge, and there is no evidence at all that it ever continued to Colchester. As with ley lines, it is all too easy to find illusory alignments of this kind. As for the distance on Ptolemy's map, his positioning of places is so haywire – this exactitude of distance is rare if not unique[32] – that the 108 miles (which should really be 109½) is almost certainly coincidental too.

(e) The outermost German limes. About AD 155 the German limes or frontier in the Odenwald east of the Rhine[33] was pushed 30 km forward to a new outer line, which between Walldürn and Haghof incorporated what must be the longest straight alignment of the ancient world.[34] In its length of 81.259 km it deviated only once, for a distance of 1.6 km, to avoid a steep valley. The limes consisted of stone-built watch towers at irregular intervals (which averaged about 400 m) and normally set 17 or 18 m behind a palisade, to which a ditch and bank were later added. Most of the towers stood on higher ground than their surroundings, in the interests no doubt of surveillance and intervisibility and probably of surveying too. It was most likely the positions of the towers, rather than the route of the palisade, that were pinpointed by the original survey, for at a number of them small postholes have been found in irregular patterns which have been interpreted as the sites of

[30] Rodwell 1975.   [31] Rivet and Smith 1979, 117.
[32] Rivet and Smith 1979, 119.   [33] It included a dead-straight section 35 km long.
[34] For full details see Fabricius, Hettner and Sarwey 1933, 33–44; for a more recent summary, Baatz 1975, 179–206; for discussion of the surveying method, Paret 1933.

scaffoldings or light platforms for raising surveying instruments above the trees. A very precise modern survey of the southern 29 km reveals that the mean deviation of the ditch from a truly straight line was ± 1.9 m, and available figures for the remaining 52 km show that an almost equal directness was maintained further north. Why the frontier was made so painstakingly straight when a series of connected alignments would surely have served equally well (was it military perfectionism run riot?) is perhaps hardly relevant to us. What does concern us is how it was set out. Because the country was probably even more heavily wooded in Roman times than it is now, geometrical construction would have been difficult, measurement and dead reckoning almost impossible, and successive approximation unthinkable.

The general line was determined by the three forts of Miltenberg-Altstadt, Welzheim East and Lorch which pre-dated the frontier (Fig. 11.12).[35] The precise location of the ends of the alignment, like that of the north end of the straight section of Ermine Street, was probably not of importance. All that was required was a northern terminus in the general area of Walldürn whence a diagonal link could be made to the River Main, and a southern terminus somewhere between Welzheim and Lorch whence a link could be made to the River Rems. If this was the case, much the easiest strategy was to start not at one end or at both, but at some intermediate point and to project a line north and south. Hertlein thought that a monstrous beacon near Walldürn was sighted from near Welzheim, which is rendered impossible over such a distance by the curvature of the earth. Fabricius, more reasonably, saw the starting point in the unique hexagonal tower 9/51 at Beckemer Ebene; but this stood relatively low and had poor visibility southwards. Paret, even more sensibly, looked at all the watch towers to see which lay on natural summits. While these could have determined the alignment, they could hardly have been determined by it. He found only two. One, 9/116 Spatzenhof, is not only the highest point on the whole line (561 m) but has the largest tower. The other, 9/83 Mehlhaus, is also high (536 m) and is visible from Spatzenhof. These, then, were surely the primary sighting points.[36]

---

[35] Schönberger 1969, 168–9 thought that the forts of Osterburken (500 m behind the limes) and Öhringen (200 m behind) also pre-dated it and fixed its direction.

[36] Baatz 1975, 180 agrees with Paret. Heights, distances and bearings quoted hereafter are from Fabricius, Hettner and Sarwey 1933, 38 and Taf. 1–2.

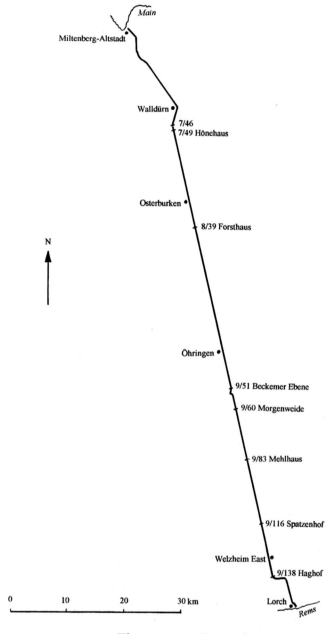

FIG. 11.12. The outermost German limes.

From them the alignment was projected southwards and northwards to secondary points by extrapolation.[37] The southern terminus, 9/138 Haghof, was visible from Spatzenhof, and the projected line passed about 130 m behind the existing fort of Welzheim East rather than in front of it as would doubtless have been preferred. From Mehlhaus northwards the first step would take the alignment to the ridge at 9/60 Morgenweide, perhaps three steps across lower undulating ground to 8/39 Forsthaus, perhaps one to 7/49 Hönehaus, and a final short one to the northern terminus at 7/46. The intervals between the primary and secondary sighting points would then be filled in by interpolation. How much trial and error went into establishing the primary and secondary points we will never know. Quite possibly other alignments derived from other pairs of primary points were tried and rejected before the final one was found. But once two satisfactory primary points and the seven or so resulting secondary points were established, the procedure, despite the distance and despite the nature of the country, would be quite straightforward.

From Haghof to Forsthaus the mean bearing of the alignment is 14° 9′ 4″, varying between the major high points by about 5′ either way. In contrast to this remarkable consistency hitherto, at Forsthaus the mean bearing suddenly changes to 14° 22′ 52″, which it maintains with a maximum variation between high points of only 14′ as far as Hönehaus, where it again turns slightly east to 14° 29′ 8″ for the final stage. These turns, small though they are, are presumably errors in surveying. So too are larger variations in bearing over the much shorter distances between the interpolated points at towers, such as 13° 33′ 47″ between 8/48 and 49 and 15° 28′ 33″ between 8/49 and 50. But overall the outermost German limes is wonderful testimony to the accuracy of the groma.

[37] My suggestions for secondary sighting points differ considerably from those of Baatz 1975.

CHAPTER 12

EPILOGUE

The foundations of instrumental surveying were laid down by Greece
and Rome. With the fall of the western empire in the fifth century AD
the science of engineering surveying, like so much else, seems to have
been lost; certainly little was built in western Europe over the next five
centuries or more which required anything like the same techniques. But
what happened in the East? How much survived in the Byzantine empire
and in Islam, and was that knowledge transmitted back to medieval
Europe? And did the contemporary or later practices of China display
any features which might suggest some interaction with the West?

To tackle this last question first, China, which in terms of technology paralleled Greece and Rome in so many ways and at the same kind
of period, had just as much need of surveying. Its system of major and
minor canals made up for the almost complete absence of urban aqueducts, cartography flourished, and agrimensorial and military needs
were comparable. Needham, however, the great authority, can give
little detail of instruments or techniques. Not surprisingly, the most
basic tools – gnomon, plumb-line, cord, chain and graduated rod or
staff – were much as in the West. His arguments for the existence in
China by the second century BC of the sighting tube and by the second
century AD of the groma are not very convincing, nor does he explain
how they might have been used. For levelling it seems that the norm
was the water level with floating sights, across the top of which the surveyor looked. They would be prey, once more, to disturbance by wind,
and accurate only if their tops were at exactly the same height above
the water. As late as about 1070 the survey of a canal with water level,
graduated staves and (as Needham interprets it) a sighting tube with a
graduated scale found the fall to be 194 feet 8 inches in about 175 miles;
but its accuracy being dubious it had to be checked by damming the
water into a series of horizontal pounds and measuring the fall at each
dam.[1] The overall impression remains that Chinese instruments were

[1] Needham 1959, 332–9, 569–79.

246

FIG. 12.1. Surveyor's staff and water level with floating sights, 1044 (*Wu Ching Tsung Yao*, reproduced in Needham 1959, Fig. 245).

not of high precision, and that they differed sufficiently from western ones to make any diffusion, in either direction, unlikely.

The same impression arises from the *Sea Island Mathematical Manual*, apparently the only surviving treatise on surveying, written by Liu Hui in AD 263.[2] Cast in much the same form as its Greek counterparts, its nine problems of measurement at a distance involve the use not of instruments but only of sighting rods. As in Greece, everything is based on similar triangles, but the calculations are done in an almost algebraic

[2] Needham 1959, 30–3. Translation and full commentary in Van Hee 1933.

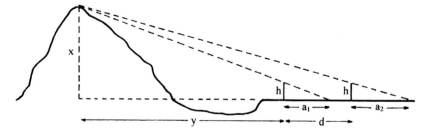

FIG. 12.2. Finding the height and distance of an island
(after van Hee 1933, 270).

way. The first problem reads (all dimensions are here reduced to paces
for clarity):

There is an island to be measured. The rods are set up, both 5 paces tall, one
nearer to the island and the other further from it, 1000 paces apart. Both rods
and the island are in a straight line. If the eye sights at the top of the first rod
from ground level 123 paces behind it, it just sees the highest point on the
island. In the same way, if one is 127 paces behind the second rod, the line of
sight to the peak of the island touches the top of the second rod. Find the
height of the island and its distance.

The solution, set out in modern algebraic terms (see Fig. 12.2), is as
follows:[3]

$$x = \frac{h\,d}{a_2 - a_1} + h = 1255 \text{ paces} \qquad y = \frac{a_1\,d}{a_2 - a_1} = 30{,}750 \text{ paces}$$

The process of taking two sights at the object in the same plane contrasts with the Greek method of taking one sight in each of two planes.
The other problems are in effect variations on the same theme, and the
complexities of the resulting mathematics also militate against a shared
origin.

During the Roman empire there is little likelihood that surveying
techniques were transmitted to any of its neighbours beyond the frontiers, with one exception. This was Sasanian Persia, long a thorn in
Rome's eastern flank. While we know nothing at all about Sasanian
surveying instruments and methods other perhaps than for qanats
(Chapter 10), we can confidently deduce that at least some were

[3] Van Hee 1933, 269–70.

acquired from Rome. In AD 260, in one of the worst blows ever to befall the empire, Shapur I captured the emperor Valerian, a large army, and many civilians.[4] They were put to work building a dam across the River Karun at Shushtar, a bridge on top of the dam, and long irrigation channels to distribute the impounded water. A number of similar schemes followed, no doubt with Persian rather than Roman labour but in all probability applying techniques which the Romans had passed on.[5] Certainly the army would include experienced engineers; and Firdausi's great Persian epic the *Shahnameh*, although composed centuries later when legend had accumulated, is plausible in having Shapur say to the emperor: 'If you are an engineer, you will build me a bridge as continuous as a cable . . . In this land and region apply all the science of the philosophers of Rum.'[6] The science surely included surveying. It is of interest, too, that the Arabic word for geometry, *handasah*, almost certainly derives from Persian *handazah*, which denotes measurement of water channels, or simply irrigation.[7] The Sasanians were far from hostile to Greek culture, and at times actively encouraged it. As a result their science and particularly their astronomy owed much to Greece. From the other direction, it also owed much to India, where the influence of Greek astronomy had already been felt.[8] But whether surveying had gone with it we do not know. How the great irrigation works of India and Sri Lanka[9] were surveyed is, unfortunately, a closed book.

With the fifth century and the end of the Roman empire in the west, the mantle of Mediterranean technology fell on the Byzantines, who for a thousand years preserved much of what their western neighbours had forgotten, and ultimately, in parallel with Islam, restored some of it to them. An early instance of such a return is the water organ, reintroduced to Merovingian France in 757; a late one is the force pump, which had to wait until the Renaissance.[10] The constant difficulty faced by students of Byzantine technology, however, is the paucity of information. It cannot be denied that the eastern empire produced little scientific or mathematical work of any originality; and

---

[4] For the meagre contemporary record see Dodgeon and Lieu 1991, 57–67, 282–3, 297–9.   [5] Smith 1971, 56–62.   [6] Levy 1990, 284.
[7] Nasr 1976, 210.   [8] Nasr 1976, 96–7; Pingree 1963.
[9] Conveniently described in outline by Needham 1971, 367–73.
[10] Lewis 1997, 117.

to the vast majority of Byzantine writers (except in the military field) practical and technical matters were of no interest at all. But their silence should not necessarily be taken to reflect a technical wilderness.

At first, land surveying continued to flourish,[11] and aqueducts were still being built well into the sixth century[12] although we have no idea whether they were surveyed by dioptra or by libra. But military needs became more urgent than ever before. From the seventh century, with continuous and growing pressure on the frontiers, most notably by Islam, the Byzantine world was fighting, back to the wall, for its life. For long periods it had neither the money nor the energy to spare for much more than survival. Yet there were respites and consequent revivals, as under the Macedonian dynasty in the late ninth and tenth century and under the Comneni in the late eleventh and twelfth. The very fact that the Anonymus Byzantinus could write about the dioptra suggests that it was still in at least limited use and was not merely an antiquarian revival. Anna Comnena (**Source 16**) implies that its military purpose of finding the height of walls had not been forgotten. Similarly the astrolabe remained current until at least the eighth century (**Source 34**), although it is uncertain how soon thereafter it was influenced by Islamic developments. Very probably all forms of surveying received a fatal blow from the crusaders' sack of Constantinople in 1204; but it is noteworthy that even later Byzantine treatises on the astrolabe, though exhibiting strong Islamic features, concentrate solely on its astronomical and astrological functions and completely ignore the surveying role which it had acquired in Islam.

On Islamic surveying we are much better informed, with a relative wealth of technical literature to draw on. Islam, by its early conquests of 632–41, became master of the thoroughly hellenised Syria and Egypt and the partly hellenised Persia, but at first it did not encourage study of the advanced cultures it had inherited. It was only after 750, when the Arabian Umayyads gave way to the Persian Abbasids and the capital was moved from Damascus to Baghdad, that Islam opened its doors to Greek learning. Translation of Greek scientific and technical texts into Arabic, at first mainly from Syriac versions but later direct, began in the late eighth century and reached a peak under the caliph al-

---

[11] Schilbach 1970a.
[12] As witness the many new aqueducts credited to Justinian by Procopius, *Buildings*.

Mamun (813–33).[13] This stimulated the great flowering of Islamic science, which included major advances in mathematics and astronomy, to name only the fields most relevant to us. Mathematics saw the development of algebra and trigonometry, and astronomy acquired new or improved instruments of which, from our point of view, the astrolabe was the most important.[14] While Islamic science was also influenced by Persia and India, the input from the Mediterranean came entirely from the Greek East. The Roman West was already ancient history, and in surveying, for example, the groma and the libra never reached Islam.[15] Alongside this Greek input, some local and no doubt age-old practices were also retained. In Iraq it seems likely that the practices of Babylonian land surveying were inherited by Islam. Details of setting out land divisions are scanty, but some literature survives on *misaha*, geometrical procedures for calculating areas.[16]

On levelling, at least from the eleventh century, we have much more information, and basic practice seems to have been much the same from Iran to Spain.[17] The builder's level was traditional, either the A-frame kind or a variant of it, and always set by plumb-line. There were three basic types of surveyor's level. The crudest consisted merely of a bowl set on a flat base and filled with water to the brim to ensure that it was horizontal, and a plank laid across the top to sight along. The most widespread type of level required two staves graduated in palms and fingers and a cord (its length variously given as 10, about 15, and 30 cubits) from whose centre point dangled a plate carrying a vertical mark. The staves were held upright a cord-length apart, the cord was stretched between the tops of the staves, and one end was lowered until a suspended plumb-line or weighted pointer coincided with the mark on the plate. This showed that the centre of the cord was horizontal and its ends were therefore at the same height, and the difference in readings on the staves gave the difference in height between their feet.

[13] For an excellent overview see Rosenthal 1992, 1–14.
[14] For Islamic mathematics and astronomy see Hill 1993, chapters 2 and 3.
[15] The only possible exception is in Spain, where Arabic writers on surveying use the word *qubtal* for a plank placed on a water-filled bowl as a primitive level (see below). *Qubtal* is said to derive from Latin *cubitale*, a cubit-long object (Wiedemann 1970, 1 281–2). Of all Islamic regions, Spain is of course the most likely for such linguistic survivals.   [16] Hill 1993, 26–7.
[17] What follows derives from al-Karaji; Cahen 1951; Ibn al-'Awwam, *Kitab al-Filaha* 1 130–1; Hill 1993, 187–91; Wiedemann 1970, 1 281–6; and Wiedemann 1993.

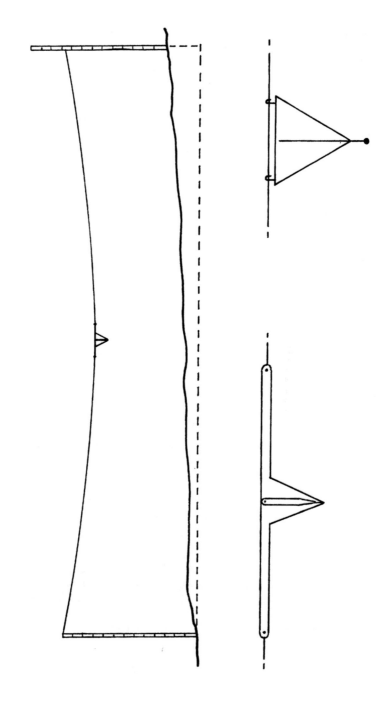

FIG. 12.3. The plumb-line *mizan* and variant. Not to scale.

Al-Karaji says the staves were 6 spans (3 cubits) long, and recommends dividing them sexagesimally. As an alternative, he describes how to calibrate the central plate so that the height difference was determined not by moving the cord down a staff but by the deflection of the plumbline. The third type of level, found only in the Middle East, was a hollow reed held against a staff at each end. Water was squeezed from a sponge into a hole at the centre, and if it emerged equally from either end the reed was deemed to be level. Al-Karaji, writing in 1019, also records that the reed had been superseded by a glass equivalent hanging from the centre of a cord or by a suspended glass tube, closed except for a hole in the top and half full of water.

The cord stretched between staves and made horizontal by a central level is not found outside Islam, and the emphasis on 15- or 30-cubit intervals and al-Karaji's sexagesimal division of the staff strongly suggest a Babylonian origin. But the Arabic names are interesting. The central level on the cord was known in Spain as the *murjiqal* or bat, presumably from its triangular appearance. But the generic name for the cord level was *mizan* (balance) if it had a plumb-line, and *qubba* (tongue or beam of balance) if it had a pointer, no doubt because of the resemblance to the device for ensuring that a balance beam was horizontal (see Fig. 4.1). We are therefore reminded of the libra and its similar derivation. But any closer connection is probably illusory: the libra represents the balance beam suspended from its centre, the surveyor's *mizan* the balance beam suspended from its ends. There is, to repeat, no evidence whatever for the use of anything like the *mizan* in the Greek or Roman world. Its accuracy, moreover, has very obvious limitations, and even if the *mizan* could be equated with the libra it is difficult to visualise it setting out Roman aqueducts on a gradient of 1 in 8000. We are in a different world. Ibn Lujun, a Spanish Muslim writing in 1348, gives the desirable fall for a channel surveyed with a *murjiqal* as the thickness of a finger-end in a distance of one cubit. Since there were 24 (or 32) finger *widths* of about 2 cm in a cubit, he would seem to be thinking of nothing shallower than about 1 in 100.[18] This accords with the comment of Ibn al-Saffar, another Spanish Muslim (see below), that water will not flow in a channel shallower than 1 in 100.

Except in the form of al-Karaji's revival, the dioptra as such never reached Islam. But the astrolabe did, and its role was broadened to

---

[18] Wiedemann 1970, I 281 optimistically suggests about 1 in 140.

perform not only the astronomical and astrological functions of the original but also most of the surveying functions of the dioptra.[19] It was first described by Masha'allah who died about 815, and a succession of treatises followed. In essence it retained the original Greek form, but one very important addition was made, first mentioned, and perhaps invented, by al-Battani (c. 850–929). This was the shadow square on the reverse of the instrument, which reproduced in miniature the triangle under survey. If for example the height and distance of an inaccessible point were required, two sightings at different distances gave enough data to work out the desired figures. While this could be proved trigonometrically or algebraically, the scale on the shadow square gave the answers on the spot with only the simplest of mental arithmetic. It was all very much easier than the more roundabout Greek and Chinese methods.

The treatises give endless exercises in finding inaccessible heights, depths, width of rivers and the like: exactly the same kind of problem which was standard in the Greek manuals, but now, in most cases, made easier by the shadow square. The astrolabe could be used for levelling too. The Spanish Ibn al-Saffar (died 1035) describes a method, comparable to the simpler methods with the dioptra, of finding the difference in height between two points when grading an irrigation channel. At one of the points, plant a pole with a mark at eye-level; stand at the other with the astrolabe suspended and the alidade horizontal, and sight at the pole. The distance of the line of sight above or below the mark is the difference in height. There were some very obvious limitations, however, in the usage of the astrolabe. In the horizontal mode it could be placed flat, though not fixed on a stand, but in the vertical mode it was suspended from the finger. The disc was generally small, the shadow square very small, and accurate divisions were difficult to make and to read. One solution was to enlarge the instrument in the form either of the quadrant, which was in effect only one quarter of the astrolabe's disc, first mentioned by al-Khuwarizmi (fl. c. 975),[20] or of the much larger open framework of the geometric square, first

[19] For general accounts of the Islamic astrolabe see Hartner 1960 and Wiedemann 1970, I 549–64. On its surveying functions, Wright 1934, 194–209 (translation of al-Biruni), Wiedemann 1970, I 577–96 and Hill 1993, 198–202.
[20] Price 1957, 599 wondered if the portable quadrant was an Alexandrian development, but there is no evidence pointing in this direction.

recorded by al-Biruni (died after 1050). But it would seem that the precision achieved by the dioptra firmly supported by its stand was not preserved.

Islam took the astrolabe to Spain, where it was encountered by western Christendom.[21] A special study of it was evidently made at the abbey of Ripoll in Catalonia where in about 1000 a certain Lupitus or Llobet, drawing heavily on Arabic sources, wrote a Latin treatise complete with surveying exercises. From 967, too, the Benedictine Gerbert d'Aurillac (later to become Pope Sylvester II) spent several years studying in Catalonia, and his subsequent writings, full of misunderstandings and of Arabisms, reintroduced the astrolabe to a wide audience in the West.[22] While it became popular, however, as an astronomical and especially an astrological instrument, medieval Europe did not show great interest in its surveying functions.

Some Roman (and hence Greek) methods of estimating areas survived into the Middle Ages.[23] The *Corpus Agrimensorum* was not entirely forgotten, and was copied in Merovingian and Carolingian monasteries. So was Vitruvius, though any influence he may have had on medieval practice is hard to identify. But instruments specifically for surveying were very few, the main exception being the cross-staff or Jacob's staff, first described by Levi ben Gerson in 1321, which ultimately became widespread.[24] Right angles were laid out by Pythagorean triangle or by bisecting a line geometrically. Levelling in architecture was done with variants of the old plumb-line level, which was no doubt also used for canals, mill leats and the like. It was only with the Renaissance that a plethora of new instruments appeared.

From our point of view, perhaps the most interesting were the levels. Most were water or plumb-line levels, sometimes of marvellous complexity, which were probably interpretations of the chorobates and *libra aquaria* (taken as a water level) inspired by the first printed edition of Vitruvius (*c.* 1486). Only a few were suspended levels essentially of the type here proposed for the libra.[25] The final step, the adoption of the

---

[21] On the transmission to the west see Hill 1984, 190–5; Hill 1993, 220–4.

[22] Which of the works attributed to Gerbert are genuine is much debated; see Struik 1972. Texts in Bubnov 1899. On Gerbert's Arabic sources, Würschmidt 1912.

[23] For a wide-ranging account of medieval and renaissance surveying see Kiely 1947.

[24] It had antecedents in China: Needham 1959, 572–6.

[25] Kiely 1947, 141–2.

spirit level and of optics, took place in the course of the seventeenth century. The details are obscure; but Smith, in a recent and penetrating paper, suggests a very plausible outline.[26] The New River, a 62 km aqueduct to supply London, was surveyed by Edward Wright and Edward Pond in 1609–13, too early for telescopic sights and spirit levels. We do not know the nature of their instrument, but it must have worked on a principle available to the Romans. Indeed in every respect, as Smith remarks, the New River was 'by any basic definition a water-supply in the Roman manner'; and it had an overall gradient of 1 in 12,500. In France, a feeder was built to the Canal de Briare in 1646 on almost exactly the same gradient, but a feeder to the Canal d'Orléans of about 1690 averaged less than 1 in 25,000. This doubling of accuracy in fifty years, Smith suggests, marks the change-over from Greek- and Roman-style open sights, with two millennia of service behind them, to modern telescopic ones.

[26] Smith 1998–99.

PART III

THE SOURCES

The four Greek treatises are arranged in the chronological order of the surviving versions. This is by no means necessarily the order of writing of the original material, which was much recycled. They were illustrated with diagrams, most of which were purely geometrical and which, where they survive at all, are usually corrupted. These are replaced by redrawn diagrams, and absent ones are supplied. Only a very few, in Hero's *Dioptra* (Figs. 3.8, 3.10) and in **al-Karaji 1**, tell us anything about the instruments themselves.

The other sources extracted from ancient literature and inscriptions include only those which deal with instruments designed for terrestrial surveying. Thus they exclude references to purely astronomical instruments and to simple devices like the builder's level (which might rather be described as a tool), but include references to the dioptra and astrolabe even when used for astronomy. They also include, especially for Chapters 7–11, cases which mention not an instrument but a circumstance which implies the use of an instrument. Illustrative diagrams are very few.

The edition from which each text is drawn may be found in the Index of Ancient Authors. Brackets and parentheses are used as follows:

< > text supplied which is missing from the original
[ ] editorial comment or explanatory material
( ) words belonging to original text, or equivalent words in another language.

THE TREATISES

Hero of Alexandria: *Dioptra*

Scientist and mechanic writing in late first century AD. Schöne's text, with a few readings adopted from Vincent. For reconstructions see Figs. 3.6–9, 3.13, for manuscript drawings see Figs. 3.8, 3.10–11.

1. Because the science of dioptrics serves many essential purposes and has been much discussed, I feel that those aspects omitted by my predecessors but which, as remarked, serve a useful purpose deserve discussion, that their ponderous writing needs elucidating, and their false statements correcting. But I do not feel it necessary here to expose our predecessors' fallible and difficult publications, or even their plain nonsense. Those who are interested can consult their books and judge the difference. Moreover, writers on the subject have not used for the purpose one and the same dioptra, but many different ones, and have solved few problems with them. This, then, is what we have striven to do, to solve the problems before us with the same instrument. Moreover, if anyone thinks up other problems, the dioptra we have constructed will not fail to solve them too.

2. That the subject serves many needs in life can be shown in few words. It is eminently useful for laying out aqueducts and walls and harbours and every sort of structure; it greatly benefits observation of the heavens by measuring the distances between stars, and the study of the size, distances and eclipses of sun and moon; likewise geography, by measuring, on the basis of their distance, islands and seas and every kind of interval between them. [Short lacuna introducing military applications.] Some impediment often keeps us from our purpose, whether the enemy has anticipated us, or the terrain cannot be approached or crossed because of some physical peculiarity or a river in rapid flood. Many, for example, who embark on a siege make their ladders or towers shorter than they should be, and when they move them up to the walls they are at the mercy of their opponents, because

in estimating the wall height they have been misled by their ignorance of dioptrics. Such measurements must always be taken, and out of bowshot.

First, then, we shall describe the construction of the dioptra, and then address its uses.

3. The construction of the dioptra is as follows [see Figs. 3.6–7]. There is a stand (*pageus*) like a small column, with a round gudgeon on top around which fits a concentric bronze disc. A bronze socket also fits loosely over the gudgeon, free to revolve around it, and has attached to its underside a toothed disc, smaller than the disc previously mentioned and resting on it. At its top, the socket ends in a plinth designed, for the sake of appearance, like the capital of a Doric column. There engages with the toothed disc a small screw whose thread fits the teeth of the disc, and the screw's bearings are fixed to the larger disc. So if we turn the screw, we also turn the toothed disc and the socket which is attached to it by three pins projecting from its base and fitting into the disc itself. The screw has along its length a groove as wide as the thread is deep. If, then, we turn the screw until the groove corresponds with the teeth on the disc, the disc can be turned by itself. So when we have set it as occasion demands, we will turn the screw a little so that the thread engages the teeth, and the disc therefore remains immovable.

Let the disc fixed round the gudgeon to the stand be **AB**, the disc fixed to the socket be **ΓΔ**, the screw engaging it be **EZ**, and the socket attached to the disc **ΓΔ** be **HΘ** with the Doric capital **ΚΛ** lying on it. On the capital let there be two bronze bearings like bars, set at such a distance apart as to allow the thickness of a disc to fit between them. On the capital between the bars let there be a revolving screw whose bearings <are fixed to the capital . . .>

[Here follows a long lacuna where four folios are lost from the archetype (Schöne xiii–xvi). The missing text clearly completed the description of the dioptra in its basic form. Passing references later in the treatise supply the outline. A toothed semicircle, adjusted in a vertical plane by the last-mentioned screw, carried the dioptra proper. This comprised a large disc and alidade which could be set in the required plane by means of the toothed semicircle. To measure angles for astronomical purposes, this plane might lie anywhere between the vertical and horizontal; but for terrestrial use the disc was normally set in a more or less horizontal plane for laying out right angles. For this purpose a right-angled cross was engraved on the disc, with which the alidade could be aligned in either direction. This section perhaps concluded with a note about the foot of the stand.

The next section dealt with an alternative attachment, a water level for taking levels, which could evidently replace the socket, vertical toothed semicircle and dioptra proper described above. This section also perhaps incorporated a passage demonstrating the principle of water finding its own level. The text resumes after the beginning of the description of the water level itself, and the gist of the missing part was perhaps on the following lines (see Figs. 3.8–9). Instead of the socket carrying the plinth shaped like a Doric capital and the dioptra proper, another socket carries a plinth (which the diagram suggests also took the form of a capital) on which are mounted two large brackets with vertical flanges. It has a plumb-line to ensure that it stands vertically. This socket, like the first one, is attached to the toothed disc by three downward-projecting pins as shown on the diagram, and like the first one it . . .]

. . . fits over the gudgeon. The large <brackets>, which are parallel to the gudgeon, project upwards about 4 dactyls. In the space between them is fitted a transverse bar (*kanon*) about 4 cubits long and of a width and depth to fit the space described. Let it be divided in two halves along its length.

4.   In the upper surface of the bar a groove is cut, either curved or angular, of such a length that it can accommodate a bronze tube whose length is about 12 dactyls less than that of the bar. At either end of the tube other vertical tubes are attached as if the tube had been bent up; their height from the bend is not more than 2 dactyls. After this the bronze tube is covered with a long strip fitting the groove, both to hold the tube in place and to make it look neater. In each of the bends of the tube is fitted a glass tube of a diameter to suit the bronze tube and about 12 dactyls high. They are sealed around with wax or some other sealant so that water poured into one of them can nowhere leak out.

Two small frames are attached around the transverse bar at the points where the glass tubes are, so that the tubes pass through and are enclosed by them. In these frames bronze plates are fitted, capable of sliding in grooves in the walls of the frames and in contact with the glass tubes. In the centre they have slits through which one can take sightings. Attached to the bottom of these plates are sockets about half a dactyl high which hold small bronze rods, equal in length to the height of the frame of one of the glass tubes, and passing through a hole in the bar which holds the bronze tube. In these rods are cut screw threads which are engaged by small pegs fixed to the bar. Thus if one turns the downward-projecting ends of the rods, one will move the plates with the slits up or down, since the knob at the plate end of the rod is enclosed in a hollow in the socket. [It is not explained until chapter 6 that levelling is achieved by filling the tube system with water and aligning the sighting slits with the water surface in the glasses.]

5. Now that the construction of the dioptra has been described, we discuss the staves (*kanones*) and targets supplied for it [see reconstruction, Fig. 3.13]. There are two staves about 10 cubits long, 5 dactyls wide and 3 dactyls thick. Down the centre of the wide side of each of them, the whole length of the staff, is a female dovetail, its narrow part on the outside. In this is fitted a small cursor that can run freely along it without falling out. To this cursor is nailed a round target about 10–12 dactyls in diameter. A straight line is ruled across the disc at right angles to the length of the staff and one of the two semicircles is painted white and the other black. A cord tied to the cursor is passed over a pulley on top of the staff to the other side. Thus if one sets the staff vertically on the ground and pulls the cord at the back the target will rise, and if one releases the cord the target will slide down under its own weight, for it has a lead plate nailed to its back so as to fall of its own accord. So if one lets the cord out, the target is positioned at any required point on the staff.

The staff is accurately divided from its lower end upwards into cubits and palms and dactyls, as many as the length will accommodate, and lines corresponding to the divisions are inscribed on the side of the staff to the right of the target. At its back, on the centre line, the target has a pointer that coincides with the lines on the side of the staff.

When a staff is stood on the ground, this is how to ensure that it is absolutely vertical: on the side where the division lines are not inscibed, a peg is fixed about 3 dactyls long, with a hole through its outer end from top to bottom to hold a cord with a weight hanging from it. Towards the bottom of the staff is another peg projecting as far as the hole above mentioned. On the outer end of the lower peg a central vertical line is inscribed. When the cord coincides with it, the staff is standing vertical.

Having described the whole construction of the dioptra, we will now as far as possible explain its use.

6. *To observe which of two given points, some distance apart, is higher or lower and by how much, or if both lie at the same height in a horizontal plane; and to observe how any intermediate points relate to each other and to the original points.*

Let the given points be A and B. We need to observe which of them is higher or lower; suppose point B to be a place where there is water, and A the place to which it is to be conducted. Stand one of the staves AΓ at A. Then, setting up the dioptra in the direction of B at a distance from A at which the staff AΓ is visible, turn the transverse bar carrying the glass tubes on top of the stand until it is in line with AΓ. By turning the screws on the bar, raise the plates until the slits in them coincide with the lines in the glasses created by the surface of the water in them. With the plates thus positioned, sight through the slits at the staff AΓ, whose target is raised or lowered until the central dividing line between the white and black appears <in the slits>. Without moving the dioptra, and going round to the other side, sight through the slits at the other staff which is set up as far from the dioptra as can be seen. Again the target is adjusted until the central line between the colours is sighted. Let the second staff be ΔE, the dioptra be Z, the points taken by the dioptra be Γ and E, and the position of the staff ΔE on the ground be Δ. Suppose AΓ when measured was found to be 6 cubits and ΔE 2 cubits. Write out two columns, heading one 'back sights' <and the other 'fore sights'>, as spelled out below, and put the reading of 6 cubits in the back sight column and that of 2 cubits in the fore sight one.

Leaving the staff ΔE in place, move the dioptra and set it at K. Turn the transverse bar until the staff ΔE is seen through it. When the plates have been positioned, place the staff AΓ ahead of the dioptra, that is in the opposite direction to staff ΔE. Once again, without moving the dioptra, set the target in line with the slits. Let the positions of the targets on the staves be H and Θ. Again note the height of H from the ground in the back sight column, and the height of Θ in the fore-sight column; suppose the back sight is 4 cubits and the fore sight 2 cubits. Once more, leaving the staff at Θ, move the dioptra and the other staff and set them up with the targets and slits in line as already described, and sight points Λ and M on the staves. The reading at Λ will be a back sight and that at M a fore sight; suppose the back sight is 1 cubit, the fore sight 3 cubits. With the staff at M remaining in place, move the dioptra and the other staff. Let the line through the dioptra be ΞO, the back sight at Ξ being 4 cubits, the fore sight at O being 2 cubits. Repeat the process until B is reached. Let the dioptra be T and the line through the slits be PΣ, the back sight 5 cubits, the fore sight 3 cubits. With the dioptra at X the line is ΥΦ, the back sight 1 cubit, the fore sight 3 cubits. With the dioptra at Ϛ the line is ΨΩ, the back sight 2 cubits, the fore sight 3 cubits. With the dioptra at ͵A the line is Ϙϡ the back sight 5 cubits, the fore sight 3 cubits. With the dioptra at ͵Δ the line is ͵B͵Γ, the back sight 2 cubits, the fore sight 1 cubit. With the dioptra at ͵Z the line is ͵EB, the back sight 3 cubits, the fore sight 1 cubit. Let the final staff be placed on the very surface of the water.

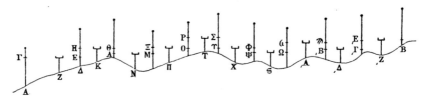

[i.e.	back sight	fore sight
	6	2
	4	2
	1	3
	4	2
	5	3
	1	3
	2	3
	5	3
	2	1
	3	1
	33	23]

Of the numbers noted in the columns, add up all the back sight figures, which make 33, and likewise the fore sight ones, which make 23, the difference being 10 cubits. Because the back sight total, that is in the direction of the place to which we want to lead the water, is the greater, the water will flow down: B will be 10 cubits higher than A. If the figures are the same, points A and B are at the same height, that is in a horizontal plane, and so the water can be led. But if the back sight total is the smaller, the water cannot flow by itself, and we need to lift it. If the spot is much lower, lifting is accomplished by a bucket-wheel or the so-called chain; if it is a little lower, either by water screws or by parallel wheels [see Oleson 1984, 52–3 for discussion of these machines].

To observe the relationship of intermediate places, through which we planned to lead the water, both to each other and to the original points, we use the same method, assuming that the intermediate places are the points originally given; it makes no difference. [The following sentence is perhaps corrupt, but this seems to be its meaning.] But one should also observe, having reckoned the total length, what proportion of the total fall will come in each stade <of length>; and for that reason, at the intermediate points, one should heap up or build marks and boundary stones with inscriptions, so that the workmen can in no way make mistakes. The water will not be led along the same route which we used for discovering the fall, but by another one that is appropriate for conducting water. For there is often some obstacle such as a hill that is of over-hard rock or too high, or soft ground, or sulphurous or similar land which would pollute the water. When we meet such obstacles, we deviate, so that the aqueduct is not impeded. But, to avoid incurring excessive expense through carrying the water over too long a distance, we shall next show how it is possible to find the straight line joining the two points, for that is the shortest of all lines that have the same ends. So whenever one of the obstacles mentioned above occurs on the line we have marked, we will avoid it.

7. *To draw a straight line by dioptra from a given point to another invisible point, whatever the distance between them.*

Let the two given points be **A** and **B**. At **A**, set up the dioptra to sight at right angles in a plane [i.e. with the disc and alidade, not with the water level]. With it lay out the straight horizontal line **AΓ**, of whatever length you like. Move the dioptra <to **Γ** and lay out **ΓΔ** at right angles to **AΓ**, of whatever length. Then move the dioptra> to **Δ** and lay out **ΔE** at right angles to **ΓΔ**, of whatever length. Move the dioptra to **E** and lay out **EZ** at right angles to any point **Z**; and **ZH** at right angles to **ZE** to any point **H**; and **HΘ** at right angles to **ZH** to any point **Θ**; and **ΘK** at right angles to **HΘ** to any point **K**; and **KΛ** at right angles to

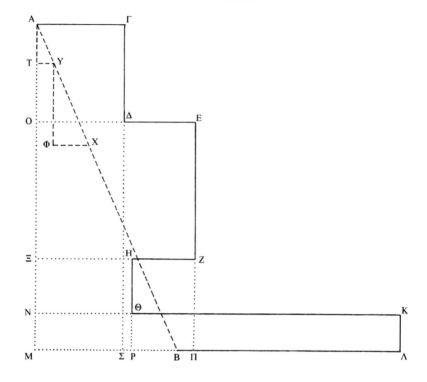

ΘK. Continue so until point B is visible. This now occurs. Move the dioptra along KΛ until B is visible along the other line on it [i.e. along the other arm of the right-angled cross engraved on the disc], which is the case when the dioptra is at Λ.

At the same time as taking the sights, write down on paper or tablet the plan of the sightings, that is the directions and lengths of the lines. Let for example AΓ = 20 cubits, $\Gamma\Delta$ = 22, ΔE = 16, EZ = 30, ZH = 14, HΘ = 12, ΘK = 60, KΛ = 8, ΛB = 50. With these data, imagine the line AM drawn at right angles to AΓ; and ΛB, KΘ, ZH and EΔ projected to <M>, N, Ξ and O; and EZ, HΘ and $\Gamma\Delta$ projected to Π, P and Σ. The figures therefore correspond: AO = 22 cubits like $\Gamma\Delta$, OΞ = 30 cubits like EZ, ΞN = 12 cubits like HΘ, MN = 8 cubits like KΛ. Therefore the whole of AM = 72 cubits. Again, MΣ = 20 cubits like AΓ, $\Pi\Sigma$ = 16 cubits like ΔE, ΠP = 14 cubits like ZH. Therefore PΣ = 2 cubits, and the whole of PM = 22 cubits. Again, PΛ = 60 cubits like ΘK, of which ΠP = 14 cubits; therefore $\Lambda\Pi$ = 46 cubits. The whole of

ΛB = 50 cubits, therefore ΠB = 4 cubits and BP = 10 cubits. PM = 22 cubits, therefore the whole of MB = 32. Because AM = 72 cubits, the ratio of AM <to MB> is as 72 to 32.

When you have worked this out, lay out the line AT, say 9 cubits long, <along AM>, and TY at right angles to it. As 72 is to 32, so 9 is to 4. <TY is therefore 4 cubits.> Thus Y is on the straight line joining points A and B. Again, lay out the line $Y\Phi$ at right angles to YT, say 18 cubits long, and ΦX at right angles to it. As 72 is to 32, so 18 is to 8. ΦX is therefore 8 cubits, and X is on the line joining points A and B. Thus by plotting <right angles> with the dioptra and working in the same way you will obtain successive points on the straight line AB that you want.

8. *To find the horizontal* (pros diabeten) *interval between two given points, one near us, the other distant, without approaching the distant one.*

Let the two points be A, near us, and B, distant. The dioptra with the semicircle is at A. Turn the alidade [lit. the bar on the disc] until B is sighted. Going round to the other end of the alidade, tilt the semicircle [if necessary to adjust the plane of sight] without moving anything else and mark a point Γ lying on our side in a straight line with A and B. Then with the dioptra lay out at right angles to $B\Gamma$ the line $A\Delta$ from A, and the line ΓE from Γ, and mark any point E on it. Moving the dioptra to E, set the alidade so as to sight on B, and mark the point Δ where $A\Delta$ crosses BE. The result is a triangle $B\Gamma E$ in which $A\Delta$ is parallel to ΓE. As ΓE is to $A\Delta$, so ΓB is to BA. But the ratio of ΓE to $A\Delta$ can be found by measuring both of them on the horizontal, as already indicated [presumably meaning because they are on our side]. If ΓE is say 5 times $A\Delta$, $B\Gamma$ is 5 times BA. So ΓA is 4 times AB. One can measure $A\Gamma$ on the horizontal, and can thus also find the length of AB on the horizontal.

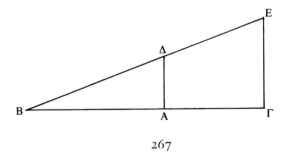

9.   *To find the minimum width of a river while staying on the same bank.*

Let the river banks be **AB** and **ΓΔ**. Standing the dioptra on the bank **ΓΔ**, say at **E**, turn the alidade until point **Δ** on the bank **ΓΔ** is visible through it. Lay out **EZ** at right angles to **EΔ** by turning the alidade. Then tilt the semicircle until some mark (call it **Z**) on the bank **AB** is seen through the alidade. **EZ** will be the minimum width of the river because it is so to speak perpendicular to both the banks, if we assume them to be parallel. When the horizontal distance from **E** to **Z** is discovered as we learnt above [chapter 8], it is defined as the minimum width of the river.

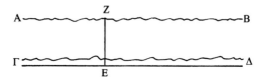

10.   *To find the horizontal interval between two visible but distant points, and their direction.*

(a). Let the points be **A** and **B**. Stand the dioptra on our side at **Γ** and turn the alidade until **A** is sighted on the straight line **AΓ**. Lay out **ΓΔ** at right angles to it, and move the dioptra along **ΓΔ** until **B** is visible through the alidade <when set at right angles>. The dioptra is now at say **E**. Because **BE** is at right angles to **ΓΔ**, **AΓ** is parallel to **BE**. Measure the distance **AΓ** in the way that we learnt above [chapter 8], and also **BE**. If **ΓA** is equal to **BE**, **ΓE** is also equal to **AB**, and **ΓE**, which is on our side, can be measured. But suppose they are not equal, and **BE** is say 20 cubits longer [Paris supp. gr. 607 wrongly has 'shorter'] than **ΓA**. In this case, starting from **E** on our side, subtract from **BE** 20 cubits, namely **EZ**. Because **AΓ** and **BZ** are equal and parallel, **AB** and **ΓZ** are also equal and parallel. Measure **ΓZ**, and so find **AB**. Since it is parallel to **ΓZ**, we have also located its direction.

[For the reverse exercise see chapter 22.]

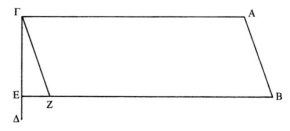

(b). There is another method of finding the distance **AB**. Stand the dioptra at any point you like, say **Γ**. Take lines **ΓA** and **ΓB** and measure both of them [as in chapter 8]. Starting from **Γ**, take some fraction of **ΓA**, say a tenth, namely **ΔΓ**, and the same fraction of **ΓB**, namely **ΓE**. **ΔE** is a <tenth> of **AB** and parallel to it. Measure **ΔE** which is on our side, and you have both the direction and length of **AB**.

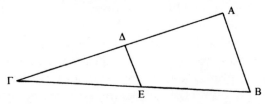

(c). There is yet another method of finding the distance **AB**. Stand the dioptra at **Γ** and project **ΓΔ** in line with **AΓ** and to a certain fraction of the length of **AΓ**, and likewise project **ΓE** in line with **BΓ** and to the same fraction of **BΓ**. **EΔ** is the same fraction of **AB** and parallel to it. Measure **ΔE**, and you have the direction and length of **AB**.

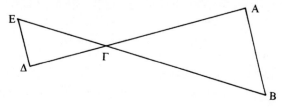

11. *To find a line at right angles to the end of a given line, without approaching either the line or its end.*

Let **AB** be the given line, and **A** be the end from which the line is to be drawn at right angles. Find the direction of **AB** from our side, as we learnt [chapter 10]. Let **ΓΔ** be a line <parallel to it>. Move the dioptra along **ΓΔ**, keeping the alidade trained on some mark on **ΓΔ** until, on turning it at right angles, point **A** is observed. The dioptra is now at say **E**. **AE** is at right angles <to **AB** as well>.

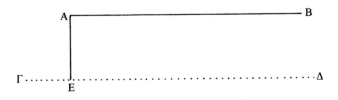

12. *To find the perpendicular height of a visible point above the horizontal plane drawn through our position, without approaching the point.*

Let the given high point be **A**, and the plane we are on be **B**. Stand the dioptra at **B**. Suppose its column to be **BΓ** and the adjustable alidade for sighting to be **ΔΓE**. Adjust the alidade until **A** is sighted through it. Without moving it, stand between the dioptra and point **A** two vertical rods **ZH** and **ΘK**, of different heights, the taller towards point **A**. Suppose the surface of the ground to be like **BZΘΛ**, and the horizontal plane drawn through our position to be **BΛ**. Move the rods **ZH** and **ΘK** until they appear in a straight line with point **A**, while the alidade **ΔΓE** remains unmoved. Point **H** is observed on the rod **ZH**, and point **K** on **ΘK**. Imagine **ZH** and **ΘK** are projected to **M** and **N**, and lines **HΞ** and **KO** are drawn parallel to **BΛ**. Discover how much higher **Z** is than **B** by levelling (*chorobatein*), both **B** and **Z** being on our side, and so find **ZM**; and likewise **NΘ**. Since both **HZ** and **KΘ** are already known, the height of **HM** and **KN** is evident, and the difference **KΞ** between them. And the length **HΞ** is also known, for it is the horizontal distance between **Z** and **Θ**. Therefore the ratio of **HΞ** to **ΞK** is known: suppose **HΞ** to be five times **ΞK**. Let a perpendicular **AOPΠ** be drawn from **A** to the plane through our position, that is to **BΛ**. **KO** is five times **OA**. Since the length of **KO** is known (it is the horizontal distance between **Θ** and **P**) the height of **AO** is also known. So too is **OΠ**, which is the same as **KN**. Therefore the whole height **AΠ**, the perpendicular to the plane through our position, is known.

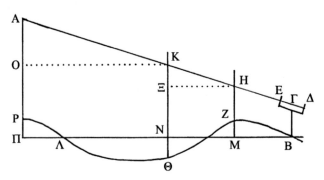

13 (a). *When two points are visible, to find the perpendicular height of one above the horizontal plane drawn through the other, without approaching either of the points A and B.*

As shown above, one can find the perpendicular height of **A** above the horizontal plane drawn through our position; imagine this perpendicular to be **ΓA**. Likewise find the perpendicular height from **B** to the plane through our position: let it be **BΔ**. And imagine a line through **A**, parallel to **ΓΔ**, namely **AE**, cutting **BΔ** at **E**. The required perpendicular is **BE** [i.e. **BΔ − ΓA**]. Moreover it is plainly possible to find the length of a line connecting two visible points, since the height of one above the plane of the other [= **BE**] and the horizontal distance between them [= **AE**] are both known, and these two lengths are at right angles to each other. Thus the hypotenuse [**AB**], which is the line connecting the two points, is also known.

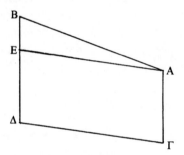

(b). *To find the direction of a line connecting two points, without approaching them.*

Let the points be **A** and **B**. It is possible to find the direction of a vertical plane passing through them, as we learnt in an earlier chapter [10]; in other words, if perpendiculars **AΓ** and **BΔ** are dropped <from the two points> to the horizontal plane, to find the direction of **ΓΔ**. Let this be found, and let it be **HZ**, and let the line **AE** be parallel to **ΓΔ** and therefore also to **HZ**. Thus **AE** and **BE** are also known, as shown previously. On **HZ** take two points, say **H** and **Z**. At **Z**, perpendicular to the horizon, raise **ZΘ** in the form of a rod or the like. It will be parallel to **ΔB**. As **AE** is to **EB**, so is **HZ** to **ZΘ**; and, as the parallel lines and ratios show, the connecting line **HΘ** is parallel to **AB**. The direction of **AB** is therefore found on our side.

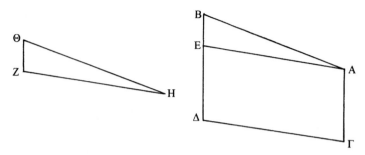

From the foregoing demonstrations it is clearly possible to find the height of a perpendicular dropped from the summit of a mountain to the horizontal plane through our position, without approaching the mountain, and to find the perpendicular height of any visible point on the mountain. We learnt how to find the perpendicular height of any visible point, and likewise the height of a perpendicular dropped from any visible <point> on the mountain to the horizontal plane through any other visible point on the mountain. In short we learnt, for any two points, how to find their perpendicular height and their horizontal interval and their direction, without approaching them.

14. *To find the depth of a ditch, that is the perpendicular height from its floor to the horizontal plane either through our position or through any other point.*

Let the ditch be **ABΓΔ** and the point on its floor be **B**. Set the dioptra at **Δ** or at any other point, say **E**. Let the <stand> be **EZ** and the alidade **HΘ**. Tilt the alidade until **B** is visible through it. Imagine the surface of the ground to be **ΔEKΛM** and the plane through our position to be **AΔΣO**. Stand on the ground, in line with the alidade **HΘ**, two vertical rods **KN** and **MΞ**. Sight point **N** on the rod **KN** and point **Ξ** on the rod **MΞ**. The problem is to <find> the height of the perpendicular drawn from **B** to the horizontal plane through **Δ**, that is to **AΔO**. Let the perpendicular from **B** be **BA**, which we need to find. Imagine the horizontal plane through **B** to be **BΠ**, the rod **ΞM** to be extended to **Π** and **NK** to **Σ**, and from **N** the line **NP** drawn parallel to **ΔO**. So **NP** is the horizontal interval between **K** and **M**, which can be found. So too can **KΣ** and **MO**, and also **ΞP** (i.e. the difference between **ΞPO** and **NΣ**), as we did when we measured the perpendicular dropped from any point by means of two rods [chapter 12]. If **NP** is found to be say 4 times **PΞ**, **BΠ** is 4 times **ΞΠ**. Thus **BΠ** can be found, which is the same as AO. This gives $\Xi\Pi$, namely a quarter of $B\Pi$. Because we know ΞO, we know $O\Pi$, which is the same as AB.

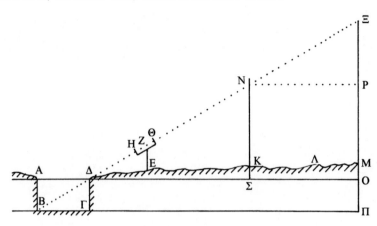

15. *To tunnel through a hill in a straight line, where the mouths of the tunnel are given.*

[This exercise is concerned only with horizontal plotting, and takes no account of vertical differences.]

Suppose the foot of the hill to be $AB\Gamma\Delta$ and the mouths of the tunnel to be B and Δ. Take a line on the ground from B, say BE. From say E take with the dioptra the line EZ at right angles to BE, from say Z take ZH at right angles, from say H take $H\Theta$ at right angles to ZH, from say Θ take ΘK at right angles to $H\Theta$, and $K\Lambda$ at right angles to ΘK. Move the dioptra along $K\Lambda$ <always keeping the alidade aimed at some point on $K\Lambda$> until the point Δ appears through the alidade when it is set at right angles. This happens when the dioptra is at M, and $M\Delta$ is at right angles to $K\Lambda$. Suppose EB to be projected to N, and ΔN to be perpendicular to it. From the lines EZ, $H\Theta$ and $K\Lambda$ the length of ΔN can be calculated, as we did when drawing a straight line from any point to another invisible one [chapter 7]. So too from BE, ZH, ΘK and $\Lambda\Delta$ the length of BN can be calculated. Suppose BN to be 5 times ΔN, and the line $B\Delta$ to be projected one way to Ξ with ΞO drawn perpendicular to BE, and the other way to Π with ΠP drawn perpendicular to ΔM. Thus BO is 5 times $O\Xi$, and ΔP 5 times $P\Pi$. Taking a point at say O on <a projection of> BE, and drawing $O\Xi$ at right angles to BO, make OΞ one-fifth of BO, so that BΞ inclines towards B. So too making ΠΡ one-fifth of ΔΡ, ΔΠ inclines towards Δ. Therefore we tunnel from B, driving along the line BΞ, and from Δ along the line ΔΠ. The rest of the tunnel is <aligned on> a stake planted on ΞB or on ΠΔ or on both. If the tunnel is made in this way, the workmen will meet each other.

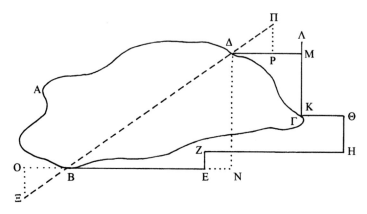

16. *To sink shafts for a tunnel under a hill, perpendicular to the tunnel.*

Let the ends of the tunnel be A and B. In line with AB, draw ΓA and BΔ in the way that we have just learnt. Stand two vertical rods ΓE and AZ at A and Γ, and set the dioptra a moderate distance away towards the hill so that the rods ΓE and AZ can be seen through the alidade at the same time. The dioptra is HΘ and the alidade KΛ. Without touching the alidade, transfer one of the rods ΓE and AZ to say point M ahead of the dioptra, where it becomes MN. Holding it vertical, move it around until it is visible through the alidade. M lies vertically above the tunnel. Transfer the dioptra ahead of rod MN to Ξ and move it around until both rods AZ and MN can be seen through the alidade at the same time; and again without touching the alidade transfer rod AZ ahead of the dioptra, and holding it vertical move it around at O until the rod OΠ is visible through the alidade. O also lies vertically above the tunnel. In this way, taking several more points over the hill, trace a line, all of which lies vertically above the tunnel. If we wish to do the same from the direction of B and Δ, it makes no difference. Take intervals of any size along the line over the hill, and shafts sunk vertically will hit the tunnel. In this demonstration one must suppose that the tunnel follows a single straight line.

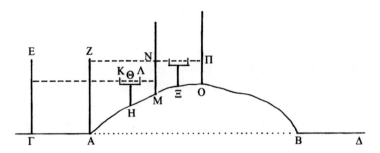

[It would be more logical if chapter 20, which deals with a shaft sunk to meet a curved tunnel, followed at this point.]

17. *To lay out a harbour wall on a given segment of a circle between given ends.*

Let the ends be **A** and **B**. Set in the horizontal plane the disc on the dioptra on which the alidade turns, and mark off on it points **Γ**, **Δ** and **E** corresponding to the segment of the circle on which the harbour wall is to be laid out. Stand a rod **ZH** close to the dioptra on the other side in such a way that the lines of sight from **Z** to **Γ** and **E** fall when projected at points **A** and **B**. This is achieved by moving the dioptra and the rod **ZH**, or one of them. When they are set up in this way, project the line of sight from **Z** through the line **ΓΔ** until it meets the ground at **Θ**. Point **Θ** lies on the perimeter line of the harbour. Taking the other points in the same way as **Θ**, lay out the perimeter line **BΘA**. It is important to make the ground as nearly horizontal as possible, so that the perimeter defined by the points taken on it is also horizontal.

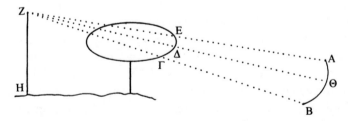

The line **BΘA** is clearly, like **ΓΔE**, the arc of a circle, for it is [part of] a cone whose base is the arc **ΓΔE**, whose apex is **Z**, and whose sides are the lines drawn from **Z** to the arc **ΓΔE**. It is cut in a plane parallel to its base on which lie **A** and **B**, and its sides are **ZΓB** and **ZEA**. So the line **BΘA** is, like **ΓΔE**, the arc of a circle. Likewise, if we want the perimeter to be the arc not of a circle but of an ellipse, or even a whole ellipse or parabola or hyperbola or any other shape, we make it in the same way with a plank. Cut the shape from a plank and fit it firmly to the disc ΓΔ so that it projects beyond its rim, and do the same as was described for the arc ΓΔE. In this way we can lay out a perimeter to any given line.

If we want the perimeter not on horizontal ground but in some other plane, set the disc parallel to the required plane and do the same thing. Once again it will be a cone cut in the plane of a line drawn parallel to the base. In the same way we can lay out the arc of a bridge [arch].

This is how to set the disc ΓΔE parallel to a required plane KΛMN. Find the inclination of KΛ and lay it out as ΞO on our side, and that of ΛM as OΠ. The plane KΛMN is parallel to that through ΞO and OΠ. Tilt the disc so that it lies in the plane of ΞO and OΠ and it is set parallel to the plane KΛMN.

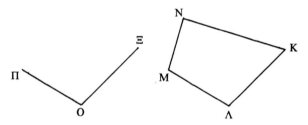

18. *To mound up the ground in a given segment of a spherical surface.*

Let the site be ABΓΔ and its centre be E. Through E lay out with the dioptra as many lines as you like, such as AΓ, BΔ, ZH and KΘ, and plant vertical stakes along them. Our instructions for one line apply to all the rest. Plant BΔ with stakes at ΛM, NΞ, OΠ, PΣ and TY. Set the disc of the dioptra vertical, with ΦXΨ corresponding to the segment of the mound. Stand a rod ΩϚ in the same way [as in chapter 17] so that the lines of sight from Ω to Φ and Ψ coincide when projected with B and Δ. Sight from Ω past the circumference ΦXΨ to the points M, Ξ, Π, Σ and Y on the stakes. These points lie on the segment of the curve. Plant stakes on the other lines, sight on them and, when the stakes have been marked, mound the site up to the marks. The mounding will correspond to the segment of the sphere.

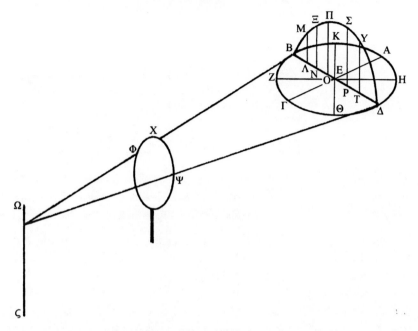

19. *To grade the ground at a given angle, so that on a level site with the shape of an equal-sided parallelogram its gradient slopes to a single point.*

Let $A B \Gamma \Delta$ be an equal-sided parallelogram, and let EZH be the angle at which the ground is to be graded. Raise verticals $A\Theta$, BK and $\Delta\Lambda$ from A, B and Δ on the underlying plane, and locate point Γ where the gradient is to begin. Make $ZH = A\Gamma$, and $EH = A\Theta$ and at right angles to ZH. Because EH is vertical, $A\Theta$ is to $A\Gamma$ as HE is to ZH. If Θ and Γ are joined, the angle $\Theta\Gamma A$ represents the gradient. Draw BM at right angles to $A\Gamma$, make $ZN = \Gamma M$, draw $N\Xi$ parallel to HE, and make BK and $\Delta\Lambda = N\Xi$. Join up ΘK, $K\Gamma$, $\Gamma\Lambda$ and $\Lambda\Theta$. The plane $\Theta K\Gamma<\Lambda>$ is inclined to $A<B>\Gamma\Delta$ at the angle $\Theta\Gamma A$, which is the same as EZH. If we consider MO is parallel to $A\Theta$ and extend OK to Λ, then $MO = N\Xi$. Now KO is equal and parallel to BM and at right angles to $\Theta\Gamma$. The plane is therefore inclined as required. But if the site consists of any quadrilateral whose diagonals are not at right angles to each other, draw BM at right angles to $A\Gamma$ and then, as before, make $NZ = <\Gamma M>$ and $BK = \Xi N$ [following Vincent's text, not Schöne's]. By the same process as on BM, find the length of $\Delta\Lambda$. Build the site up to ΘK, $K\Gamma$, $\Gamma\Lambda$ and $\Lambda\Theta$, and the resulting plane has the required gradient.

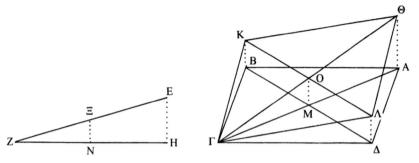

20. *To find the point on the surface above a tunnel where a shaft should be sunk to meet a given point in the tunnel so that, should there be a collapse there, materials for clearance and repair can be brought down the shaft.*

Let the tunnel be ABΓΔE, shafts connecting with it be HΘ and KΛ, and the point in the tunnel where the shaft is to be sunk be M. Lower cords with weights, NΞ and OΠ, down the shafts HΘ and KΛ. Without touching them, draw a line ONP on the surface through O and N, and another ΠΞΣ in the tunnel through Π and Ξ, meeting one of the tunnel walls at Σ. Make OP = ΠΣ. Taking a cord that has been well tensioned and tested so that it will not stretch or shrink, fix its end at Σ. Taking a point T on the wall ABΓ, extend the cord to T and thence to Π. Noting the lengths TΣ and TΠ, transfer them to the surface above making the triangle PYO, where PY = TΣ and YO = TΠ. Then taking another point X, extend the cord to make the triangle TΣX, and transfer it to the surface making the triangle PYΦ,

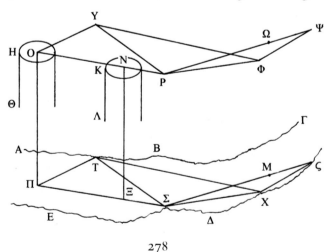

where $P\Phi = X\Sigma$ and $Y\Phi = TX$. Construct another triangle on the base ΣX and the same triangle on ΦP, <and so on> until near point M. To cut a long story short, mark ΣM with the cord, prolong it to ζ, and join ζX. Make the triangle $\Phi\Psi P$ on ΦP, where $P\Psi = \Sigma\zeta$ and $\Phi\Psi = \zeta X$, and let $P\Omega = M\Sigma$. Point Ω lies vertically above point M. If a shaft is sunk vertically from Ω it will hit M. This is clearly because the triangles in the tunnel and on the surface are equal and similar, and lie in the same plane. One should try to set out the triangles truly horizontal, so that the lines joining their corners are perpendicular to the horizon.

21. *To lay out with the dioptra a given distance in a given direction from us.*

Let the line along which the distance is to be laid out be <AB, and let the distance itself also be> AB, starting from A. Set up the dioptra EZ in a level area such as $\Gamma\Delta$, and in front of it stand a vertical rod $H\Theta$ about 10 cubits high at any distance from the dioptra, but say at 3 cubits. Measure from E on the level a line $E\Delta$ of any length, say 500 cubits, and leave a mark at Δ. Tilt the alidade on the dioptra until the mark at Δ is visible through it. Without moving the alidade, go to the other side, sight M on the rod $H\Theta$ and write '500 cubits' on the rod at this point. Then take other distances along $E\Delta$, for example EN at 400 cubits, leave a mark at N, and similarly go to the

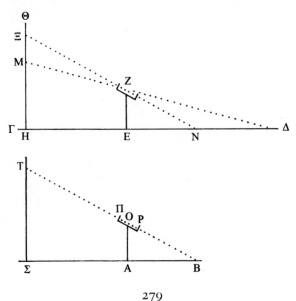

other side, sight Ξ on the rod, and write '400 cubits' on it here. Taking any number of such measurements will give you graduations inscribed on the rod.

Set up the dioptra at A and, standing the rod with graduations 3 cubits from A (the same distance as when the graduations were made), tilt the alidade on the dioptra until you see through it the graduation corresponding to the distance to be laid out. Go to the other side of the alidade and sight point B on the line AB. Thus the distance AB is laid out from the given place. Let the dioptra be AO, the alidade on it for sighting be ΠP, and the rod with graduations be ΣT.

22. *To lay out with the dioptra a given distance from another point, parallel to a given line, without approaching the point or having the line on which to lay it out.*

Let the given point be A. Set up the dioptra at B. Find the length of AB as we learnt [chapter 8], and on it mark off BΓ being any proportion of AB. Draw ΓΔ parallel to the required line and proportional to the required distance as BΓ is to BA. With the dioptra project the line BΔ to the distance BE, which is the same multiple of BΔ as BA is of BΓ. Thus AE is of the required length and parallel to ΔΓ. This is clearly because the proportions AB:ΓB, EB:ΔB, and AE:ΓΔ are all the same.

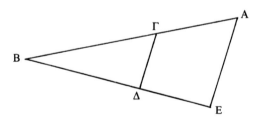

[This is the reverse exercise to chapter 10(b).]

23–30. [The first five of these chapters deal with the measurement or laying out of irregularly shaped plots of land, and the dioptra is used only to lay out straight lines or right angles, just as the groma is used by the *agrimensores*. The last three, on finding the areas of the resulting trapeziums and triangles, are pure geometry. Since all eight are more relevant to land distribution than to surveying for engineering purposes, they are not translated here.]

31. *To measure the discharge or outflow of a spring.*

It must be recognised that the outflow does not always remain the same: after rainstorms it increases because the excess of water on the hills is expelled with greater force, and in droughts the flow dwindles because the supply is less. The flow of good springs, however, is not much diminished. Having therefore entirely enclosed the water emerging from the spring so that it can nowhere leak away, make a rectangular lead pipe so designed as to be much larger than the outflow. Fit it to some part [of the wall] so that all the water from the spring flows out through it. To achieve this, it must be at a lower level than the spring itself, which can be determined by dioptra. The water flowing out through the pipe enters its mouth with a depth of say 2 dactyls, while the width of the mouth is say 6 dactyls. Since $6 \times 2 = 12$, <we find that the outflow of the spring is 12 [square] dactyls>. But it must be understood that, to discover the quantity of water supplied by a spring, it is not sufficient to know the cross-section [lit. size] of the flow, given here as 12 [square] dactyls, but [one must know] its velocity too. The faster the flow the more water is delivered, the slower the less. For this reason one should dig a pit below the spring's outflow and observe how much water flows into it in one hour as timed with a sundial, and from this [the known dimensions of the pit] calculate the quantity of water supplied in a day. It is not therefore necessary to look at the cross-section of the flow, because time is the factor which reveals the discharge.

32. We have now shown the advantages offered by the dioptra which we have constructed for solving dioptrical problems on the earth. It is also useful for many celestial observations such as determining the distance between fixed stars and planets, and we shall show how to take <these> distances with the dioptra. On the belly (*gaster*) of the disc on the dioptra, draw the circle, concentric with the disc, that is described by the tip of the degree-pointer (*moirognomonion*) on the alidade. Divide this into 360 degrees. To observe the distance in degrees between two stars, whether fixed stars or planets or one of each, take the alidade for sighting off the disc, and tilt the disc until both the specified stars are seen in its plane at the same time. Replace the alidade in its usual position and, without moving anything else, turn it until one of the stars is sighted. Note the degree indicated by the pointer, and

turn the alidade until the other star is sighted through it. Again note the degree indicated by the pointer, and you have the number of degrees between the two specified points, and know that the stars are the same number of degrees apart.

33. Because some people use the so-called 'star' (*asteriskos*) for a few purposes which are entirely within the realm of the dioptra, it seems sensible to indicate its peculiarities to those who try to use it, to save them from committing mistakes through ignorance of it. I think that those who have used it have experienced the inconvenience which arises from the cords with weights hung on them, which do not come to a rapid standstill but continue to swing for some time, especially when a wind is blowing. For this reason some people, wanting to remedy this inconvenience, have made hollow wooden tubes to put around the weights and shelter them from the wind. But if the weights rub against the tubes, the cords do not hang exactly vertical. What is more, even if the cords are kept at rest and vertical, the planes they hang in are not always at right angles to each other. If this is so, the required results are not accurately achieved [text corrupt, but this is the sense]. This we will demonstrate.

Let there be two horizontal lines **AB** and **ΓΔ**, not intersecting at right angles, the angle **AEΔ** being obtuse. Let **EZ** be a line perpendicular to the plane **ABΓΔ** and at right angles to **AE** and **EΓ**. The angle **AEΓ** between planes **EAZ** and **ΓEZ** is acute, so that these planes are

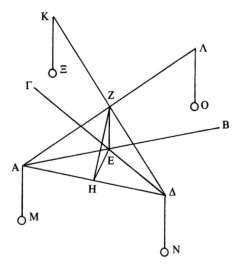

not at right angles to each other. Take two equal lines AE and EΔ, and join A to Δ. At right angles to it draw <E>H, so that AH = HΔ and both are longer than HE. From H, draw HZ equal to AH. Draw lines AZ and ΔZ and project them to K and Λ, making both KZ and ZΛ = AZ. From A, Δ, K and Λ draw AM, ΔN, KΞ and ΛO parallel to EZ; and because EZ is at right angles to the plane ABΓΔ, so too are AM, ΔN, KΞ and ΛO. Because AH, HΔ and HZ are all equal, ΛΛ is at right angles to ΔK. If we imagine that the arms of the star are AΛ and ΔK, that the plane ABΓΔ is horizontal, and that the hanging cords are AM, ΔN, KΞ and ΛO, then the planes of the cords, i.e. AMΛO and ΔNKΞ, are not at right angles to each other. This is proved because the angle between them is AEΓ, which is acute.

34. A matter which we feel is consistent with the practice of dioptrics is the measurement of distances on land by means of the so-called hodometer. Avoiding laborious and slow measurement with chain or cord, we travel by carriage and find the distance by the rotation of the wheels. Because our predecessors have proposed several methods of doing this, the machine described by us can be judged against theirs.

The whole of the machinery to be described is contained in a framework like a box. On the floor of the box <is mounted horizontally> the bronze disc ABΓΔ [diagram not reproduced here] with <8> pegs fixed to it. There is a slot in the floor of the box. A pin attached to the hub of one of the carriage wheels passes through this slot once every revolution of the wheel, and pushes forward one of the pegs so that the next peg takes its place, and so on indefinitely. Therefore while the carriage wheel makes 8 revolutions the peg wheel makes one. To the centre of the peg wheel is fixed a vertical screw whose other end turns in a crossbar attached to the walls of the box. Next to the screw is a cog wheel whose teeth are engaged by its threads; this is mounted vertically to the floor, and the ends of its axle turn in the walls of the box. Part of the axle is also spirally grooved to form a screw. Next to this screw is another cog wheel, lying parallel to the floor, one <end> of whose axle turns in the floor, the other in a crossbar fixed to the walls of the box. Part of this axle also carries a screw engaging another cog wheel, this time mounted vertically. This [gear train] is continued as long as we want or as space in the box allows; for the more wheels and screws there are, the longer the distance that can be measured.

Each turn of a screw advances the adjacent wheel by one tooth, so that one revolution of the peg wheel, representing 8 turns of the carriage wheel, advances the first cog wheel by one tooth. If then this wheel has say 30 teeth, one revolution of it results, by means of the screw, from 240 revolutions of the carriage wheel. One turn of this cog wheel and its attached screw turns the next wheel by one tooth. If this wheel also has 30 teeth (a reasonable number, which could be even greater), one revolution of it represents 7200 revolutions of the carriage wheel, which, if the carriage wheel has a circumference of 10 cubits, equals a distance of 72,000 cubits or 180 stades. This applies to the second wheel: if there are more wheels, and therefore more gears, the length of journey that can be measured increases correspondingly. But one should adopt an arrangement whereby the machine cannot indicate a much greater distance <than> the journey which the carriage can make in a single day. One can measure each day's journey by itself, and start the next day's journey afresh.

However, because the rotation of each screw does not turn the adjacent teeth exactly or mathematically, we turn the first screw by way of trial until the cog wheel next to it has completed one revolution, meanwhile counting the number of turns it takes. Suppose it takes 20 turns to rotate the cog wheel once. But that has 30 teeth. So the 20 turns of the peg wheel move 30 teeth on the wheel engaged by the screw. The 20 turns represent the moving of 160 pegs and the same number of turns of the carriage wheel, which makes 1600 cubits. If the 30 teeth indicate 1600 cubits, one tooth of the cog wheel indicates a distance travelled of 53⅓ cubits. So when the cog wheel begins to move, and is found to have moved 15 teeth, it indicates a distance of 800 cubits, that is 2 stades. We therefore write on the middle of this cog wheel '53⅓ cubits', and do the same calculations for the other cog wheels, and write the numbers on them, so that when each of them has advanced by a certain number of teeth, we know the distance completed.

When we want to find the distance travelled, to avoid opening the box to inspect the teeth on each cog wheel, we shall show how to find the distance from pointers (*gnomonia*) rotating on the outer face of the box. The cog wheels are so placed that they do not touch the sides of the box, but their axles project outside the walls. These projections should be square, to carry pointers (*moirognomonia*) with square holes, so that when the cog wheel and its axle revolves, it turns the pointer with it. Its tip as it turns describes a circle on the outside of the wall, which we divide into the same number of parts as there are teeth on the wheel inside. The pointer should be long enough to describe a larger circle, so that the divisions between the teeth are further apart, and the dial should have the same inscription as the wheel inside. Thus we see the distance travelled by looking at the outside.

If it is not possible for all the cog wheels to avoid touching the walls of the box because they get in each other's way, or because of the screws engaging them, or for some other reason, we must move them further apart so that they do not get in the way. Because some of the cog wheels are parallel to the floor and some are vertical to it, some of the dials will be on the vertical walls of the box and some on the top cover. For this reason one of the walls which does not have dials must be a [detachable] cover, so that the [top] cover can serve as a [fixed] wall.

(38). [If chapter 34 is reasonably straightforward, this unnumbered chapter, which should be 38 (the end of the treatise is in a confused state), is corrupt and probably interpolated into Hero's text.]

A screw **AB** [diagram not reproduced here] turning in bearings [meshes] with wheel **Δ** with <81> teeth. Fixed to **Δ** is <wheel **E**> with <9> teeth. Parallel to **E** is **Z** with 100 teeth. Fixed to **Z** is **H** with 18 teeth. Engaging with **H** is **Θ** with 72 teeth. Fixed to **Θ** is **K** with 18 teeth. Likewise **Λ** with 100 teeth, [*wrongly inserted*: next to it another with 30 teeth] on which is a pointer to show the number of stades. The paddle wheel **M** is made with a circumference under [= inside?] the paddles of <*figure missing*> paces, turned on the lathe and revolving in the same time as the ship [i.e. its circumferential speed is the same as the speed of the ship] . . . (*unintelligible*) able to advance one tooth on **Δ** for one turn of **M**. So it is clear that when the ship has sailed 100 miles the cog wheel **Λ** will have made one turn. So if a circle around the centre of **Λ** is divided into a hundred parts, the pointer fixed to **Λ**, moving round the circle, will show the progress of the ship division by division.

[The remaining chapters are irrelevant to us:
35 on finding the distance from Alexandria to Rome by observing an eclipse of the moon is purely astronomical: see Neugebauer 1938–9.
36 is missing.

37 deals with the *barulkos*, a geared machine for moving heavy weights, which is also found in Hero's *Mechanics* and does not belong here.]

Julius Africanus: *Cesti* I 15

Chronicler and encyclopaedist writing between AD 228 and 231, but using earlier sources. On surveying, only this fragment survives. Vieillefond's text.

1.   Those who are moderately advanced in general education have, I think, some acquaintance with Euclid's *Elements*. It is not difficult, with the help of Euclid's first book, to solve this problem: how to measure the width of a river whose further bank is inaccessible because it is in enemy hands, in order to build a bridge of the right length; and, by the same method, how to take the height of a wall from a distance in order to bring up siege towers of the same height. To make the demonstration comprehensible, let us start with this theorem:

> If in a right-angled triangle one of the sides adjoining the right angle is bisected, and from this point a perpendicular is raised, and from the point where it cuts the hypotenuse a line is drawn parallel to the first side, the other sides of the triangle are also bisected.

Let there be a right-angled triangle $AB\Gamma$, with a right angle at B. Let AB be bisected at Δ. Let a perpendicular be drawn ΔE. From E, let the parallel line EZ be drawn. I say that the other sides of the triangle are bisected, $A\Gamma$ at E, $B\Gamma$ at Z. Let Δ and Z be joined. Since $A\Delta = \Delta B$ and $\Delta B = EZ$, $A\Delta$ is equal and parallel to EZ. The lines joining the equal and parallel lines at the same points are also equal and parallel. So are

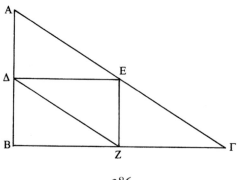

286

ΔE and ZΓ, which form the parallelogram ΓEΔZ. Therefore ΔZ = EΓ. But it was also equal to AE. <Thus EΓ = AE.> Again, since both BΔEZ and ΓEΔZ are parallelograms, ΔE is equal both to BZ and to ZΓ which are opposite to it. Therefore BZ = ZΓ. This demonstration applies to every triangle.

2. *To measure the width of a river from a distance.*

Let A be a point on the opposite bank which the enemy holds, and ΦH be the bank on our side. A dioptra with a slit sight (*schiste*) is fixed in place on our side at I, so that the distance from I to our bank of the river is greater than the river's width, which is easy to judge. Two points are sighted at right angles, one on the opposite bank – a rock or bush or some other distinctive object – at A, the other on our side, along the other arm of the cross, at Y. Moving the dioptra to Y, sight on A and make a right-angled triangle. Let IY be bisected at K. From K, let KΘ be drawn parallel to AI, and from Θ let ΘP be drawn parallel to IY. Since, in the right-angled triangle AIY, IY is bisected at K and ΘK is parallel to AI <and ΘP to IY>, AI is bisected at P. Measure IP, which also gives PA. Subtract PΦ, and the remainder will be the width of the river.

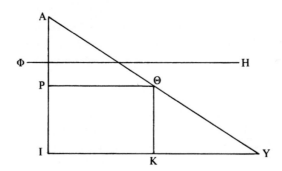

3. [Cognate with ***Dioptra* 8–9**]

To take the width of the river while standing on its very bank, if difficulties are foreseen in taking longer distances on our side because the line of sight is necessarily awkward and the marks confused.

Let the point taken on the opposite bank again be A. On our side let the point B be taken so that AB is perpendicular to the line BΓ along the bank. Point **Δ** is taken on **ΒΓ**, from which the rod (*kanon*) **ΔE** is laid [horizontally]. At the end of the rod let there be a vertical marker (*gnomon*) **E**, so that if the rod **ΔE** touches the surface of the water the marker is on top. Let the rod be advanced perpendicular to **ΒΓ** until, from a point **Γ** on the line **ΒΓ**, points **E** and **A** are observed through the dioptra. As **ΒΓ** is to **ΓΔ**, so **AB** is to **EΔ**. The ratio of **ΒΓ** to **ΓΔ** is known, and therefore the ratio of **AB** to **ΔE**. **ΔE** is known, and therefore **AB** is also known.

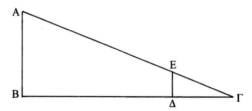

4. *To take the height of a wall in the same way, using the same diagram in a vertical plane.*

Let **A** be the top of the battlement, **B** its foot, and **ΒΓ** a line from the wall to our position out of range. At **Γ** a dioptra is set vertically, hanging from a stand (*kamax*) called a lampstand (*lychnia*). Let the line **ΔΓ** be the stand. Tilting the dioptra [i.e. the alidade], sight on the top of the wall at **A**. Go round to the other sight [reading *augeion* for the *angeion* ('vessel') of the MSS] and take, on the same line, the point <**E**, making the triangle> **AEB**. **ΓΔ** is parallel to one of its sides, namely **AB**. As **ΕΓ** is to **ΓΔ**, so **EB** is to **BA**. The ratio of **ΕΓ** to **ΓΔ** is known, because both of them are known. Therefore the ratio of **EB** <to **AB**> is also known. <**EB** can be measured> by the method demonstrated at the river. Therefore **BA** is also known. Q.E.D.

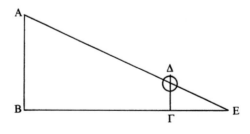

Anonymus Byzantinus: *Geodesy*

Byzantine compiler writing in mid-tenth century but copying much older sources. Vincent's text as emended by Müller 1883, checked against microfilm of Vatican Gr. 1605, which carries no title: *Geodesy* is a later but reasonable supposition.

1. Those who contemplate a siege are unable to use direct measurement to calculate the heights of walls from a distance, or the intervals between remote points, or the width of rivers. But those who are experienced in the use of diagrams and in direct sighting with the dioptra can, by making a survey, design siege towers which are of the same height as the walls, and bridges carried on boats which fit the width of rivers, so that an army may cross the bridge or the gangway in good order and unharmed. Engineers have often been deceived by false appearances and estimates into making and deploying engines that are larger or smaller than they should be, as has been shown in the foregoing treatise [the *Poliorcetica*]; and the result has been that the front ranks of those mounted on them have been slaughtered by the enemy. We have therefore investigated both the theory of the dioptra and its universally useful application, selecting the simpler examples from our most learned predecessors, clarifying them by straightforward illustrative methods, and demonstrating them a little with diagrams. As a result, while standing out of enemy range, we can exactly and unerringly determine heights, lengths and intervals. The investigation will not only serve the student of the art of war, but will prove eminently useful for laying out aqueducts, walls and harbours and contribute much to geodesy and to observation of the heavens. We must avoid the verbosity and repetitiveness of earlier scientists, pick out the obscure and difficult passages in their writings and adapt them to everyday parlance, render the diffuse mathematical language surrounding their demonstrations comprehensible at a glance, reduce their lofty theoretical concepts to a lower and more tangible level, and thus make the subject accessible to intelligent men and to amateurs alike, and especially to those who study geometry in any form.

[There follows a long lacuna where a whole quaternion of eight folios is missing (Dain 1933, 31–2). It included presumably (a) a description of the dioptra and certainly, as subsequent references make plain, (b) a section on basic arithmetic and (c) another on how to measure horizontal distances of which the further end is inaccessible. This section (c) probably took the form of measuring the width of a river by the method described by **Africanus 3**. Possibly a section on levelling aqueducts was also included. The text resumes part-way into the first surviving exercise. The content of the lost beginning of this exercise, if not its exact language, can be restored with confidence. Somewhat confusingly, the exercise not only deals with the military operation of discovering the height of a city wall, but as a practical example illustrates the method by finding the height of the bronze chariot which adorned a tower over the starting gates of the Hippodrome at Constantinople. For the plan of the Hippodrome on which my diagrams for Anonymus 3–5 are based see Mango 1949, 185.]

2. [Corresponds to **Africanus 4**. Akin to *Dioptra* 12. Set in the Hippodrome.]

<To take the height of a wall without approaching it.

Let A be the top of the battlements, B the wall's foot, and BZ a line from the wall to point Z on our side. By way of illustration, suppose that A is some point on the bronze chariot in the Hippodrome, and B is the threshold of the gates below it. Standing the dioptra at Γ, I tilt the disc E until I observe the top of the wall A, or the point on the chariot, through the holes of the alidade. Without moving the dioptra or the alidade, I go round to the other sight and take the line EΔ, in continuation of AE, and mark the point Δ. Sometimes, as will be explained, the dioptra is mounted in a different way, at ΘH. Thus we have three triangles, one larger one, ABΔ, and two smaller ones, EΓΔ and ΘHΔ. We can see that the ratio of the height ΘH to the base ΔH is the same as that of the height EΓ> to the base ΓΔ; so too is that of AB to BΔ. Again, as BΔ is to each of ΔΓ and ΔH, so AB is to <each of> the heights ΘH and EΓ. The vertical stand (*kamax*), sometimes planted in front [at ΘH] for surveying greater heights and aqueducts, must carry at Θ, hanging from a peg, a dioptra which is also called a lampstand (*lychnia*) [this last phrase is evidently a gloss which the Anonymus found in the manuscript he was borrowing from, and which he incorporated into his text at the wrong point: it should come after *kamax* above, as in **Africanus 4**]. Having measured ΔΓ and ΔH, i.e. the bases of the smaller triangles on our side, and having found their length, I also have the known distances

ΓE and HΘ, i.e. the heights of the dioptra and the stand. If I find the base is ten times the height, I show that the whole of ΔB is ten times AB. I can find the whole of ΔB by the method we learned in the [missing] section on lengths and widths. If I find it is 120 fathoms, I show that AB is 12, which is the height of the wall to the top of the battlements that we wanted; so too [in our case] from the threshold of the gates marked B to the point marked A on some part of the chariot. As to fractions and denominators, we have dealt with them sufficiently for the inquisitive in the section on arithmetical methods above.

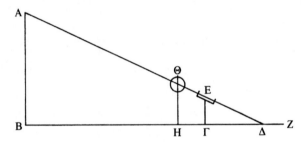

3. [Corresponds to **Dioptra 10(b)**. Set in the Hippodrome. See p. 292.]

To take the horizontal interval between two distant but visible points, without approaching them.

Let the observed points be A and B at the partitions between the starting gates [in the Hippodrome], A at the third, B at the ninth. Standing the dioptra at the upper turning-post at Γ and setting the disc so that its plane coincides with the given points, I take two lines through the holes of the alidade [*kanon*, lit. 'bar'], that is ΓA to the third gate and ΓB to the ninth. I measure one of them [this wrongly assumes that both are the same] by means of the alidade, as was described above [in the missing section]. Finding it to be say 80 fathoms, I divide it at whatever point I want, say at a tenth of the distance (i.e. 8 fathoms) from the turning-post, at Δ. Moving the dioptra to Δ, I take with the alidade a line ΔE, cutting the line ΓB at a tenth of its length, at E. So the line ΔE will be a tenth of the interval AB, since as AΓ is to ΓΔ and BΓ is to ΓE, so AB will be to ΔE. But also, as ΔE is to EΓ, so is AB to BΓ. When I measure EΔ, which is on our side, and find it to be 4 fathoms, I show that AB, which is ten times as long, is 40 fathoms. So the required distance between points A and B is found to be 40 fathoms.

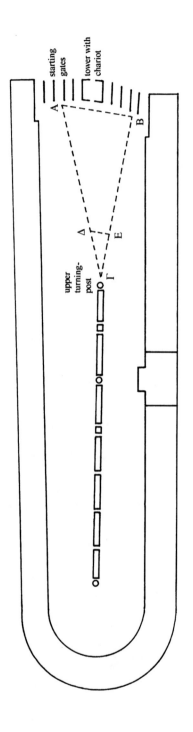

starting
gates

tower with
chariot

A

B

Δ

E

Γ

upper
turning-
post

Diagram to Anonymus 3

4.   [Corresponds to **Dioptra 10(c)**. Set in the Hippodrome. See p. 294]

Another method of determining the interval between two given points, according to the annexed diagram.

Suppose for example the observed point A to be on the left side of the curved end (*sphendone*) and B to be on the right, across the width of the track. I stand the dioptra at the straight end [reading *haploun*], at point Γ near and abreast of the upper turning-post, so that nothing impedes a direct sighting of the given points. Setting the disc in the same plane as the base of the *sphendone*, I take two lines with the alidade, ΓA to the left extremity and ΓB to the right. Measuring one of them [this again assumes that both are the same] as described above [in the missing section], and finding it to be say 126 fathoms, I go round to the other sight (*augeion*) of the alidade. Without moving anything else on the dioptra, I tilt the disc a little and project a line in continuation of BΓ, say one-eighteenth of its length, for 7 fathoms towards the left of the straight end to point Δ; likewise to the right on the line AΓ to E, and I join E and Δ. Since EΓ is one-eighteenth of ΓA and ΔΓ is one-eighteenth of ΓB, ΔE will be one-eighteenth of AB. As the sides of the smaller of the two triangles drawn with apexes touching are to those of the larger, so the base of the smaller will be to the base of the larger. Measuring ΔE, the base of the smaller triangle which is on our side, and finding it to be say 2½ fathoms, I show that AB is 18 times as long. Therefore the distance between points A and B, the width of the track at the base of the *sphendone*, is found to be 45 fathoms.

5.   [Corresponds to **Dioptra 10(a)**. Set in the Hippodrome. See p. 296]

To take the interval between two given points and also to find the orientation of the line joining them, without approaching either of them.

Let the observed points be A and B, A at one of the seven sections of the *euripus* (central spine) at the base of the balustrades, B at the base of the imperial box, or of one of the tents on either side for runners in gymnastic contests. Standing the dioptra on the track at the lower turning-post diagonally opposite B, at point Γ, I sight through the alidade until I observe A in a straight line at the end. Going round to the side of the dioptra nearest the turning-post, I tilt the disc a little and take a line ΓΔ across to the stairs of the seating tiers, say to the

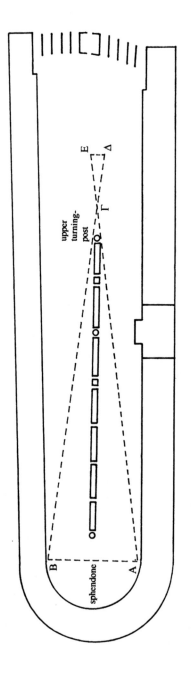

upper
turning-
post

E

Δ

Γ

B

A

sphendone

Diagram to Anonymus 4

base of the principal balustrades, perpendicular to AΓ with a right angle at Γ. I move the dioptra along ΓΔ until I observe point B <at right angles to ΓΔ>. Here let the dioptra be set, at E. BE is thus perpendicular to ΓΔ and parallel to AΓ. Then I can measure the distances ΓA and EB, as I have often done by means of triangles [in missing section]. If I find ΓA equals EB, I show that ΓE is also equal to AB. If one is longer than the other, I subtract the difference from the longer and join the [end of the] shorter [to the longer]. For example, if I find the width is 12 fathoms, ΓA is 90, and EB 81, I subtract the excess [by marking] point Z at 9 fathoms from Γ, and join it to the shorter line by means of ZE, which is equal and parallel to AB. If AΓ and BE are equal, the distance AB is 12 fathoms like ΓE; but because ΓA has been found to be 9 fathoms longer than EB, the line ZE subtracts this distance from it and subtends a right angle at Γ. The base ΓE is 12 fathoms, so that ZE is 15, because when squared it equals the [sum of the squares of the] two sides joined by the right angle. Therefore the distance AB will have the same number of fathoms. Thus one has found not only the length of AB but also its alignment, as shown in the annexed diagram.

6.   [Irrelevant. Very simple instructions for measuring plane surfaces. Those for rhomboids are drawn from Hero, *Metrics* 1.14. For trapeziums the Anonymus refers the reader to the works of Archimedes and Hero (*Dioptra* 28). Reference letters ABΓΔEZ. No dioptra involved.]

7.   [No counterpart elsewhere.]

To find the diameter of a circle, its circumference, and its area with a dioptra by standing at the centre and not approaching the circumference.

Let the centre of the circle be point A, at which I stand the dioptra. Setting the disc on it in the plane in which the circle is to be described by the dioptra, I take the point B by a line through the holes of the alidade. From this point I rotate the disc with its alidade by means of the socket which fits over the gudgeon, or of the screw (*styrax*) if there is one on the dioptra, until the rotation brings it back in the given plane to the point from which it began. In the course of this circular movement certain points will be seen demarcating the circle, such as rocks or bushes or other distinctive objects, e.g. B, Γ, Δ, E, Z, H, <Θ>, K, I, Λ, M, N, Ξ, O, Π. Having noted these points on the circumference, I

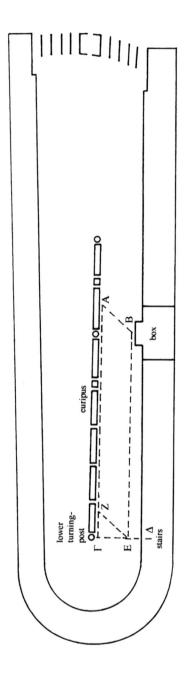

Diagram to Anonymus 5

measure the radius from **A** to **B** in the way that we have learned for lengths and widths [in the missing section]; and finding it to be say 105 fathoms, I have the diameter of the circle, namely 210, which is double the radius.

The diagram in Vatican Gr. 1605, f. 48v shows, around the circumference, rocks and bushes and the letters **B-N** in the right order.

[He then multiplies the diameter by 3⅐ to obtain the circumference, 660 fathoms; and, quoting Archimedes to the effect that the area of a circle is the product of the diameter and a quarter of the circumference, he obtains the area, 34,650 square fathoms. He then offers a simpler method of finding the same figures without using the dioptra: nothing more than describing a circle with a cord from a peg and performing the same calculations. In this case his reference letters are **ΑΒΓΔΕΖΗΘ**.]

8. [Irrelevant. Finding the volume of three-dimensional objects (cube, cylinder, cone, sphere, pyramid). The Anonymus mentions the Pythagoreans, draws on Archimedes' *Sphere and Cylinder*, and quotes from Euclid's *Elements*. No reference letters. Dioptra not involved.]

9. [Finding the volume of a water reservoir. He mentions the cistern of Aetius in Constantinople, which has irregular dimensions, but works on the example of the cistern of Aspar, which has a regular plan. No reference letters. Dioptra not involved. No counterpart elsewhere.]

10. [Measuring the discharge of a spring. Copied, with acknowledgement, almost verbatim from **Dioptra 31**, which see. No reference letters.]

11. [First paragraph paraphrased from **Dioptra 32**; for the rest, source unknown.]

Now that we have related above the applications of the dioptra on the ground, we will be ready, though based on the ground, to undertake observation of the heavens, thanks to the utility of such a dioptra. With it we can determine the size of the sun and moon, and observe the distance between stars, whether fixed stars or planets. We can define the required distance by marking on the disc the 360 degrees, with lesser divisions between them. When we wish to observe the distance in degrees between two stars, we depress our side of the disc and raise the other side until we see the two stars in the same plane. Without moving the dioptra, we turn the alidade on the disc until we see one of the stars through the two pinnules. Having noted the degree or fraction of a degree marked by the pointer (*moirognomonion*), we again turn the alidade until we see the other star through the two holes and likewise record the degree marked by the pointer. Counting on the disc the degrees between the two marks, we show the distance apart of the stars.

. . . If we want to observe a longitude or distance along the zodiac, we do not sight at random, but set up the dioptra parallel to the meridian [*sic*]; if we are in search of a latitude from north to south or vice versa, we set it up in the equator [*sic*: the Anonymus is in confusion here. He (or a copyist) reverses meridian and equator, but in any event if he wants longitude he should set up his dioptra in the ecliptic, not the equator]. We ourselves have engraved these lines in the green saloon of the magnificent imperial observatory south of the Bucoleon [in Constantinople]. We have described how to plot them in our *Laying out Sundials*.

[He continues at length on astronomy, with further references to the use of the dioptra for measuring distances in one plane or another, but adding nothing new about its construction.]

Al-Karaji: *The Search for Hidden Waters* XXIII

Iranian mathematician writing in Arabic in 1019 about qanats. Translated (fairly freely in the interests of clarity) from the Hyderabad edition.

I-XX discuss geology, water sources, prospecting for water, types of water, qanats in Islamic law, and qanats in general.

XXI-XXII describe traditional surveying instruments (the *mizan* etc: see Chapter 12) and procedures with them.

XXIII opens with 'some instruments I have invented', namely a calibrated plate for the *mizan* and its chain and staves. It continues with the following descriptions of a dioptra-like instrument, the only section (as argued in Chapter 3.A.iv) clearly of Greek origin. In the geometrical passage there is some corruption of reference letters. Confusions between J (ح) and H (ح) and between Z (ز) and R (ر) have been silently corrected, and only worse errors are noted.

[1. First method]

If you want a good level (*mizan*), better than anything already mentioned, easier to operate and more accurate, take a square or circular flat plate of wood or brass, and make a fine hole at the centre. Make a very straight copper tube 1½ spans long more or less, and with a bore wide enough to admit a large needle. Pivot it on the hole in the plate so that it can turn freely, like [the alidade of] an astrolabe. Fix a ring to hang the plate from at the top of an upright piece of wood [the stand], which is perfectly straight and about 4 spans long, so that, when you hang the plate on it and squat down, your eye is on the same level as the hole in the tube. If the dimensions are not right, shorten or lengthen it.

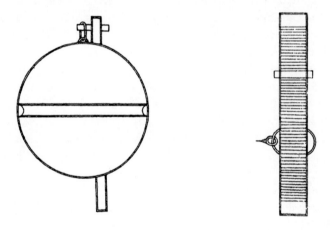

Then take another strong piece of wood [the staff] of square section and as tall as a man with his hand raised, that is about 9 spans. Carefully smooth it so that its sides are straight and parallel. Divide one of its sides lengthways into 60 parts, and subdivide each part as finely as possible. At the top leave a length of one palm which is not included in the divisions, and likewise at the bottom. Put a red mark (or black or white, as you wish) with its centre coinciding with the topmost division line. It should be clearly visible from a distance, and should be bigger than a *dirhem* (coin). Put another such mark on the bottom line. Make a cursor (*tuq*, lit. 'surround') for the staff, and put the same mark on it as on the staff.

Take a strong cord of well-twisted silk or flax, no thicker than a large needle and 100 cubits long, or more, so long as it does not exceed the distance at which the marks [on the staff] are visible. At each end attach a ring, one of which is fixed to the graduated staff and the other is held by the surveyor [lit. 'the man with the level'] so that he can stand the cord's length away from the staff.

If you wish to take a level, take the ring tied to the [loose] end of the cord and instruct the staffman to walk away to the length of the cord. Whoever finds himself the higher holds the ring on the ground while the other, who is standing lower, holds his end of the cord up until it appears to be horizontal; this can be checked by a third person at mid-cord. When the cord is horizontal, if you are the lower, drop a stone, and where it lands place the stand and hold it vertical, and allow the level to find its own balance by hanging free. Then sight through the tube at the staff, pivoting the tube on its centre until you sight the bottom mark on the staff. If you are the higher, stand the level at the end of the cord and sight at the top mark.

When you have done, move the level [without altering the angle of the tube] to the other side [of the staff], holding your end of the cord until it is extended horizontally to its full length. If it is in the air, drop a stone to locate the stand; if it is already on the ground, that is where the stand should be. Sight through the tube at the staff which has been turned to face you, and tell the staffman to move the cursor up or down until you see through the tube the mark on the cursor. Then measure on the staff the distance between the centre of this mark and the centre of the mark sighted by the tube [in the first operation]. This distance is the same as the difference in height between the two stations of the level. The two points which you have levelled with the first and second readings constitute one stage. Register the result, and instruct the staffman [text wrongly says 'the man with the level'] to move a cord's length away to discover the [next] rise or fall by the same method, [and repeat the process] until you arrive at your destination.

[Alternatively] put a mark on the centre of the staff. When levelling ground where there is little rise and fall and you sight on this mark through the tube [and then from the other side and with the tube at the same angle sight at the cursor], the height of the centre of the mark [on the cursor] above the central mark will equal the height of the first station [of the level] below the second. If the sighting [on the cursor] is under the mark, that will be the height of the second station below the first. But if the rise or fall is too great, you may not be able to see the staffman [from the second station], in which case reduce the length of the cord so that you can always see him.

To prove this, suppose the line YH to be the surface of the ground between the first and second stations of the level where the first and second readings are taken. BH [text has BY] equals the distance between the ground and the centre of the level. BA [text has BY] is the line of sight through the tube to the staff. SA is the staff. KY is the distance between the ground and the centre of the instrument when you place the stand at Y, and KD is the line of sight through the tube. I say that DA equals the height of H above point Y.

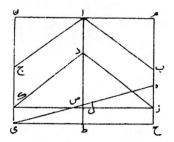 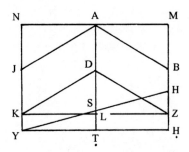

This is the proof. ḤY, projected horizontally from point Ṭ, is at right angles to the vertical lines YJ and HB which coincide with the stand for the level. AJ is drawn from A parallel to KD [text has KA]. The diagonal lines connecting BZ and JK to DA are parallel because BZ is parallel to JK and the distances between them are equal [because the cord extends equally either side of AS]. MA, which represents the level to which AD rises above BZ, is equal to AN, which represents the distance AD rises above JK. Hypotenuses on equal bases and sharing a common vertical are equal, and BZ, AD and JK are equal. Hence ZD = DK, DL being common to them. For this reason, and because angle ZDL = angle LDK, these triangles are identical. ZD and DK represent the angle which the tube makes with the horizontal. LṬY is a right angle and LK is parallel to ḤY. Therefore ZH = KY, each of which represents the distance between the ground and the centre of the level. ZḤ = BH and, because HZ is shared, BZ = HḤ. BZ [we have already seen] = AD. Therefore HḤ = AD. HḤ is the height of point H above point Y. AD, which is the same, is therefore the height required. Q.E.D.

[2. Second method]

This same level can be used in another way. Take the plate as described, install the tube at its centre, and use the stand as explained. On the graduated staff put a mark at the same height from the ground as the centre of the plate when suspended. To level by this method, set the tube on the diameter line that is horizontal and sight through the tube at the staff at any distance you like. If you see the centre of the mark, the two places are level. If you do not exactly see the centre of the mark, the distance of the point you do sight above the centre of the mark is the difference in height of the position of the level above the position of the staff; or, if below the mark, the other way round. By this method you can level as you please, for you can dispense with the cord, although if you are close enough [?] to the instrument you can use it as in the previous method. If you cannot see the mark on the staff, instruct the staffman to move closer to you, so that none of the ground remains unsurveyed and everything is taken into account. For your work to be trustworthy, you must level with extreme accuracy, and if [the tube on] the level is irregular or bent, you will have to sight on the staff from two sides [as in the first method] with always the same distance, be it long or short, between the surveyor and staffman.

[The rest of XXIII describes levelling with a similar instrument with calibration lines drawn on the plate.

XXIV deals with another calibrated variant, resembling the shadow square of an astrolabe, for working out the height and distance of a mountain (for the method see Chapter 12). The presence in the diagram to XXIV of the letter *waw* clearly points to an Arabic origin (see Chapter 3.A.iv). The last section of XXIII does not have *waw*, but no deduction can be made from this because it does not have the adjacent letters *za'* and *ha'* either. It seems that both calibrated variants, like the calibrated mizan of the beginning of XXIII, are of al-Karaji's own invention.

XXV discusses the construction of qanats.

XXVI-XXVII describe levelling instruments for tunnels and how to locate a shaft when the tunnel deviates; these chapters, though Arabic in origin, have a retrospective value for understanding Greek tunnel surveying and are discussed in Chapter 10.

XXVIII-XXX are about the maintenance of qanats and contracts for qanat building.]

OTHER SOURCES

The basic elements (Chapter 1)

1 **Vitruvius Rufus** 43
Some manuscripts of the *Corpus Agrimensorum* (notably the famous
Arcerianus of the sixth or seventh century) include 'the book of
Aprofoditus [Epaphroditus] and Bertrubius [Vitruvius] Rufus the archi-
tect', which is thought to be excerpted from two post-Heronian books.
For the authors, see Folkerts 1992, 319–22. The passage here quoted
stands in isolation; presumably the preceding sentences, now lost,
described the right-angled isosceles triangle for measuring heights.

To measure and tell the height in feet of a tree or tower or any tall
object without using the shadow of the sun <or> moon, do as follows.
Lie flat [lit. 'on your teeth'] and work backwards until you see the apex;
and at the point where you sight the apex and you see the sky, get up
and measure overland to the tree or tower or whatever it may be, and its
height in feet is the number of feet that you measure.

2 *Mappae Clavicula* 213
A Carolingian compilation of mostly chemical recipes, much of it clearly
of classical origin. This section, whose subject matter and consistently
clear and grammatical Latin are most untypical of the compilation, is
almost certainly from an ancient source. The Greek terms used for the
sides of a triangle are normal in classical Latin.

On levelling (planities) *or the measurement of heights.*

First, make a right-angled triangle in this way. Make three flat straight
rods, the first 3 inches or feet or cubits [long], the second 4, the third 5.
Set the rod 3 units long upright, the one 4 units long flat, the one 5
units long from the top of the upright to the end of the horizontal one.
These three rods when thus joined at the corners will make a right-
angled triangle. The upright rod is called the perpendicular, the flat

one the base, the one joining them the hypotenuse. Then take a stick whose height reaches up to your eye and fix the right-angled triangle to it at the middle of the base. Then put your eye to the corner between the base and hypotenuse and take a sight on the corner between the hypotenuse and perpendicular. Walk backwards and forwards until in your judgement you sight the corner between the hypotenuse and perpendicular in line with the apex of whatever the object is whose height you require. Having done this, measure the distance from where you are standing to the foot of the object. From this distance subtract a quarter; the remaining three-quarters, plus the height of the stick which you were holding in your hand, is established as the height. But take great care that the triangle with the stick beneath it does not incline in any direction. To detect any inclination, hang a plumb-line from the middle of the hypotenuse, and if it touches the centre of the base you know that the triangle is not inclined.

LEVELLING (CHAPTER I.E)

3   **Vitruvius, *On Architecture* VIII 5**
    Roman architect/engineer writing 35–25 BC.

1. I shall now explain how water should be supplied to dwellings and towns. The first step is the taking of levels (*perlibratio*). Levelling is done (*libratur*) with dioptras or librae aquariae or the chorobates, but it is done more accurately with the chorobates because dioptras and librae are liable to error. The chorobates is a straight-edge about 20 feet long. At the ends it has legs, identical and fixed at right angles to the ends of the straight-edge, and between the straight-edge and legs are cross-pieces joined by tenons. They have precisely vertical lines drawn on them, and a plumb-line hangs from the straight-edge over each line. When the straight-edge is in position and the plumb-lines uniformly coincide with the drawn lines, they show that the position [of the straight-edge] is level (*libratam*).

2. But if the wind intervenes and because of the movement [of the plumb-lines] the lines cannot give a definite indication, then have on top a channel 5 feet long, 1 digit wide and 1½ digits deep, and pour water into it. If the water uniformly touches the lips of the channel, it tells us that the instrument is level (*libratum*). So when the level has been

taken (*perlibratum*) in this way with the chorobates, we shall know how great is the slope.

3. A student of the works of Archimedes may perhaps say that true levelling (*librationem*) is not possible with water, because he argues that a water surface is not level (*libratam*) but part of a sphere whose centre is the centre of the earth. But whether the water surface is plane or spherical, it necessarily follows that the straight-edge must uphold the water equally at either end. If it slopes down from one end, the water will not reach the lip of the channel at the higher end. Wherever the water is poured in, it will necessarily assume a convex curvature, rising to the centre, but its ends to right and left must be level (*librata*) with each other. An illustration of the chorobates will be found drawn at the end of the book. [This is now missing.]

4   **Theon of Alexandria, *Commentary on the Almagest* 523.24–524.3**
Greek mathematician and astronomer writing *c.* AD 360–80. On setting up Ptolemy's plinth (see Chapter 2.B), which required precise positioning.

The plinth is set in an unshaded place, on a seating that does not deviate from the horizontal plane. This is achieved by the two-legged (*diabetes*) or A-frame level (*alpharion*) which resembles Carpus' chorobates, or even by pouring water on the surface and adjusting the base until the water is stationary.

See also **Dioptra 12**.

Background to the dioptra (Chapter 2)

GAMALIEL'S TUBE (CHAPTER 2.E)

Talmud. The *Mishnah* is the codification of the Jewish oral law, the *Gemara* the commentary on the *Mishnah*; together they form the Talmud. The Jerusalem Talmud was finished in its present form about AD 400, the Babylonian about 500. The translations are basically those of Sperber 1986, 107, with additions from Epstein.

5   **'Erubin IV 2**
Rabbis Gamaliel, Eleazar, Akiba and Joshua ben Hananiah were returning

from Brindisi by ship which made landfall, probably at Caesarea, on a Sabbath eve.

Mishnah. They did not enter the harbour until nightfall. 'Is it permissible for us to land?' they asked Rabbi Gamaliel. 'It is permitted,' he replied, 'for I observed [the distance from the shore] and we were within the [Sabbath] limit before nightfall.'

6   Babylonian *'Erubin* 43b
With annotation (Epstein p. 301) by Rashi, the eleventh-century commentator.

Gemara. It was taught: Rabbi Gamaliel had a [viewing-]tube (*sefoforet*) [through] which he would look and sight two thousand cubits on land and in the other direction two thousand cubits at sea. [Rashi adds: 'With a long instrument of this kind one can see but a small space but with a short one a far greater expanse.']

7   Jerusalem *'Erubin* IV 2.21d

Gemara. Rabbi Gamaliel had a viewing[-tube] (*mezupit*) with which he would sight by eye two thousand cubits on the land-horizon, and he would sight with it at sea.

8   Babylonian *'Erubin* 43b (Epstein p. 301)

Gemara. If a man desires to ascertain the depth of a ravine let him use a tube and by looking through it be in a position to ascertain the depth of the ravine. [Rashi adds: 'Having ascertained beforehand the distance his tube commands he takes up a position from which he can just see the bottom of the ravine, and by subtracting the distance between the brink of the ravine and his position from the distance the tube commands he obtains the depth of the ravine.']

9   Jerusalem *'Erubin* V 3.22d
Discussing methods of measuring the Sabbath limit across a river valley. Hisdai (*c.* AD 217–309) was a Babylonian interpreter of the law.

Gemara. If the river was twisted, Rabbi Hisdai says: He takes the viewing[-tubes] (*mezupot*) and sights by eye on the flat horizon, and then repeats the operation on the hillside.

10 **Philo of Byzantium,** *Water Conducting*
Quoted in Ibn al-'Awwam, *Book of Agriculture* (*Kitab al-Filaha*) i 131–3.
Greek technical author writing *c.* 230s BC. For Philo's authorship of this
passage, see Chapter 2.F. Ibn al-'Awwam was a Spanish Moslem writer of
the late 13th-early 14th century. His section on irrigation channels opens
by quoting Abu'l Khair of Seville, of whom nothing is known, on how to
survey the line with the *murjiqal* or *mizan*, the standard Islamic levelling
instrument (see Chapter 12). Adjust the level of the ground accordingly,
Ibn al-'Awwam continues, and then build the channel.

The smallest slope to give it is 12 fingers [i.e. dactyls] per 100 cubits.
That is the figure given by Aflimun in his *Book on Water Conducting*
(*Kitab fi Qaud al Miyah*).

One can also use the astrolabe [i.e. dioptra] to adjust and level the
ground. One proceeds in this way. Place at the mouth of the well or the
opening of the cistern a plank set quite horizontal. On it lay the instrument, so that the vanes are on top and the holes in its ends are level with
the opening of the well or the outlet of the cistern and are pointed in the
direction one wishes the water channel to follow. Then take a plank or
squared timber, and on one of its faces draw from bottom to top large
contiguous circles, of the same diameter but each in a different colour
from its neighbour, or else put markers on it of any sort you like that are
easily visible from a distance. Place this timber or plank vertically, not
inclined or tilted towards either side of the line you wish to level. The
circles face the astrolabe. A man then places his cheek on the ground
between astrolabe and cistern, close to the instrument. His line of sight
passes from the hole in the end of the vane which is nearest to him,
through the other hole, and in a straight line towards the coloured circles
on the staff. In this way, although his view encompasses all the circles, his
vision passes through the two holes in the vanes at the same time in a
straight line, and he can judge them and recognise which of the coloured
circles or the markers is at the end of his line of sight, to the exclusion of
all the others. He is careful to remember it, and returns to the staff to
check the height of the circle or marker above the ground. This height
is that of the cistern outlet above the [foot of the] staff. Then, where
there is excess [earth], he removes it to a place that is too low, and fills in
the depressions. The line of sight passing through the two holes in the

astrolabe must be brought to the first circle on the staff, the one which is in contact with the ground surface. [We would nowadays say that the foot of the staff is brought up to the line of sight.] When this is done, we can be sure that the intervening surface is level. Working in this fashion in front and to the left and right over a distance equal to the first, we complete the levelling of the earth, carrying it from areas that are too high to those that are not high enough, until the work is finished. Aflimun has explained this process in his *Book on Water Conducting*.

Sometimes the astrolabe is replaced by a plank about a cubit in length, along the centre of which a straight line is drawn. Both ends are bored with a hole in which is driven a ring-headed nail, each precisely equal in height and in aperture and with the holes exactly facing each other along the line. It is used like the astrolabe. Look through the hole in one nail, directing the line of sight through the other to reach the staff. Instead of the astrolabe, two hollow tiles are also used, one lying with its convex side on the ground, the other placed on top forming as it were a pipe. The observation is made from the highest point, that is the opening of the cistern, the sight is taken through the other hole to the staff, and the operation is carried out as stated above.

The dioptra (Chapter 3)

THE SOURCES OF THE TREATISES (CHAPTER 3.B)

11 Biton, *Construction of War Engines and Artillery* 52.5–53.3
Greek military engineer, writing shortly before 156 BC: for the date, see Lewis 1999a.

It should be appreciated that the size of siege towers must be specifically designed for assaults on walls, and that the towers should exceed the walls in height. This can be achieved by systematic observation, as I described in my *Optics*, for the subject of dioptrics is a preoccupation of mine.

12 Athenaeus Mechanicus, *On War Engines* 27.9–28.6
Greek military engineer, mid–late first century BC. Here he is discussing the *sambuca*, a ladder mounted on ships for assaulting walls or towers.

Those engaged in the siege of Chios committed some mistake and made their *sambucas* higher than the towers, with the result that those mounted on them could not step on to the towers and were wiped out by fire. Because it was totally impossible to lower the *sambucas*, the ships on which they were erected turned turtle when the loads overbalanced. For this reason and for others, technicians who want to use machines should not be ignorant of optics [this is the interpretation of Lendle 1983, 174; Wescher in his edition of Athenaeus takes it as a book, the *Optics*, whether by Biton (**Source 11**) or someone else].

> Athenaeus' account is copied by Anonymus Byzantinus, *Siegecraft* 268.2–9. Vitruvius x 16.9 gives a rather different version of this episode, and both he and Athenaeus are probably wrong in ascribing it to Chios. The details closely resemble those at the siege of Rhodes by Mithridates in 88 BC (Appian, *Mithridates* 26–7). Athenaeus and Vitruvius shared a common source in Agesistratus, who wrote about 60 BC on siege engines and artillery (Marsden 1969, 205–6; 1971, 4–5; Lendle 1975, 2–3; 1983, xix-xx). He was a pupil of Apollonius, an engineer active in Rhodes at the time of the siege (Athenaeus 8.9–13; Cichorius 1922, 273).

THE MINOR SOURCES (CHAPTER 3.C)

13 Hero of Alexandria, *Definitions* 135.8
Late first century AD.

Geodesy employs instruments for observing places: dioptras, staves (*kanones*), cords, sundials (*gnomones*) and suchlike for measuring heights whether by shadow or by line of sight. Sometimes, to solve these problems, it uses reflection of light. Just as the geometer often uses imaginary lines, so the geodeter uses tangible ones. The more precise of these lines are made by the rays of the sun, whether these are taken by sighting or by shadow, and the most tangible ones are made by laying and stretching strings and cords. By these means the geodeter measures remote points, heights of mountains, heights of walls, widths and depths of rivers and suchlike. Moreover, geodesy makes distributions [of land] not only in equal plots but by proportion, as the terrain merits.

14 Balbus, *Explanation and System of Measuring* 92.11–93.3
Roman surveyor writing in the form of a letter to Celsus, who is not certainly identifiable. His military work is usually thought to belong to Trajan's Dacian campaigns, but Dilke 1971, 42 convincingly ascribes it to Domitian's northern campaign of AD 89. The text is very corrupt and difficult; many of the points made by Hultsch 1866, 7–11 are fol-

lowed here. Military service has dragged Balbus away from his studies with Celsus, and he is apologising for the delay in completing his book.

Once we had entered hostile territory, Celsus, Caesar's military works began to demand surveying. Two straight lines (*rigores*) were specified, to be laid out a certain length of journey apart, along which a great mass of ramparts would arise to protect passage. These were laid out by using the *ferramentum* of your invention [reading, with MS J, *hos invento tuo*], with part of the work cut down [reading, with MS A, *operis decisa parte*]. As far as the planning of bridges was concerned, we could have told the width of rivers from the near bank even if the enemy had wanted to attack us. Then the venerable system of the triangle [reading, with Hultsch, *di*, i.e. $\Delta i = trianguli$] showed us how to find out the heights of mountains to be stormed.

15 Souda, *Lexicon*
Greek lexicon compiled *c.* 1000.

Diopter: a spy; a mechanical device whereby they used to measure the height of defences; the dioptra.
Dioptra: a mechanical device whereby geometers accurately measured the heights of defences from their distance.

16 Anna Comnena, *Alexiad* XIII 3
Byzantine historian writing in 1140s. Here she describes how Bohemond, Prince of Antioch, besieged the Byzantines in Dyrrhachium (Durazzo) in 1107.

A wooden tower was built on a four-sided base to a remarkable height. It was so tall as to overtop the city's towers by 5 or 6 cubits . . . It really seems that the barbarians besieging Dyrrhachium had a sound knowledge of the science of optics, without which they could not have measured the height of the walls. At least they understood, if not optics, the taking of measurements by dioptra.

17 Proclus, *Commentary on the First Book of Euclid's Elements*
41.24–43.6
Greek neoplatonist philosopher, *c.* AD 410–85. He is here quoting from Geminus' lost work on the divisions of mathematics.

The parts of astronomy are gnomonics [dealing with sundials] . . ., meteorology [rising of heavenly bodies] . . ., and dioptrics, which discovers the positions of the sun and moon and other stars by means of such instruments.

18 Attalus

Quoted by Hipparchus, *Commentary on Aratus* I 10.24. Greek astronomer, mid-second century BC. He is criticising Eudoxus, the astronomer of two centuries earlier.

On the passage where he explains through which stars each of the three parallel circles [the equator and tropics] passes, I refrain here from proving that he is completely astray – the circles cannot pass through the stars he says they do – because you have observed them, tracing them by dioptra.

19 Geminus, *Introduction to the Phenomena*

Greek astronomer, probably first century BC.

1.4. The twelfths [i.e. the signs of the zodiac] are equal in size, for the circle of the zodiac is divided by means of the dioptra into twelve equal parts.

5.10–11. Of the five circles mentioned, the greatest is the equator, next in size are the tropics, and the smallest, at least for our latitude, are the arctic circles. One should conceive these circles as having no width, visible only by reasoning and traceable only by the position of the stars, by observation with dioptras, and by our imagination. The only circle visible in the heavens is the Milky Way, but the rest are visible by reasoning.

12.3–4. That the movement [of the heavens] is circular is clear from that fact that all stars rise at the same point and set at the same point. All stars when observed through dioptras appear to describe a circular motion throughout the whole rotation of the dioptras.

20 Strabo, *Geography* II 1.35

Greek geographer, late first century BC.

[Differences of latitude are observed], if they are greater, by the evidence of our eyes, or of the crops, or of the air temperature . . . but if they are smaller, by means of sundials or dioptras.

21 Hesychius of Alexandria, *Lexicon*
Fifth or sixth century AD, a list of rare Greek words based on the lexicon of Diogenianus (second century AD), itself an epitome of one by Pamphilus (first century AD).

Astrabister: a device like a *dioptron.*
Diopter: the spy; the mechanical device.
Dioptra: a geometrical device.

22 *Corpus Glossariorum Latinorum* II 278.25
Greek–Latin glossary of Carolingian date.

Dioptra, the <geo>meters' <instrument>: *gruma.*

23 *Etymologicum Gudianum* 367
Greek lexicon compiled in ninth century.

Dioptra: mirror; also a geometrical instrument and a medical implement.

24. *Etymologicum Magnum*
Greek lexicon compiled in mid-twelfth century. Pseudo-Zonaras' *Lexicon,* of the thirteenth century, has an almost identical entry.

Gnomon is the mechanics' name for a bar (*kanonion*); . . . part of a dioptrical instrument, and of an astronomical one; but particularly applied to the [pointer] on sundials.

See also: **Dioptra**
Julius Africanus
Anonymus
Al-Karaji
Vitruvius, **Source 3**
Philoponus, **Source 32**
Severus Sebokht, **Source 33**
Kamateros, **Source 35**
Simplicius, **Source 69**
Theon of Smyrna, Theon of Alexandria and Simplicius, **Sources 74–6**

THE PLANE ASTROLABE (CHAPTER 3.D)

25 Ptolemy, *Planisphere* 14

Greek astronomer, mid-second century AD. This treatise on the theory of stereographic projection is lost in Greek but survives in a Latin translation from an Arabic translation.

The present section of our treatise contains the parallels to the zodiac in so far as they determine the positions of the fixed stars. For this reason it will contain what is called in the horoscopic instrument the spider (*aranea*, = Greek *arachne*).

26 Ptolemy, *Tetrabiblos* (*Astronomical Influences*) III 3.2–3

A treatise on astrology.

Problems often arise over the first and most important fact, namely the fraction of the hour of the nativity. In general only sighting with horoscopic [i.e. time-telling] astrolabes can provide scientific observers with the minute (*lepton*) of the hour, whereas almost all the other horoscopic instruments used by most of the more careful practitioners are liable to frequent error, sundials by the accidental displacement of their positions and their gnomons, water-clocks by various chance interruptions and irregularities in the flow of water.

27 Ibn al-Nadim, *al-Fihrist*

Iraqi bibliography compiled in 987.

21. Theon [of Alexandria] wrote . . . on the procedure with the astrolabe.

22. Hero [of Alexandria] wrote . . . on the procedure with the astrolabe.

[Most likely 'astrolabe' is merely the nearest available Arabic equivalent for 'dioptra'.]

41. Ptolemy was the first who made a plane astrolabe, though there are people who say that [plane astrolabes] were made before his time, though this cannot be stated with certainty.

[Dicks 1960, 207 doubts the reliability of this entry.]

THE SOURCES

28 Al-Ya'qubi, *History* 21–3

Ninth-century historian and geographer. He summarises the contents of a treatise on the astrolabe which he wrongly ascribes to Ptolemy; Neugebauer 1949, 242–5 shows that it was really by Theon.

The books on discs, that is the astrolabe. He begins by describing its manufacture, its shape and size and how its rim, discs, spider and alidade are joined . . . [Chapter headings include] 2. On checking both ends of the alidade.

29 Souda, *Lexicon*

Greek lexicon compiled *c.* 1000. Thumb-nail biography of Theon of Alexandria, who flourished *c.* AD 360–80.

Theon from the Museum, an Egyptian, a philosopher . . . lived under the emperor Theodosius the elder. He wrote . . . *Commentary on the Little Astrolabe*.

30 Paul of Alexandria, *Introduction* 29

Greek astrologer writing in AD 378, in this passage discussing horoscopes for nativities. See Neugebauer 1975, 956 and Segonds 1981, 22 for discussion.

If you have the hour from the astrolabe, if it is in daytime, multiply the above-mentioned hour-times for heliacal degrees . . . Both standard and seasonal hours are found by the astrolabe.

31 Heliodorus, *Commentary on the Almagest*, fragment

Alexandrian astronomer, brother of the more famous Ammonius. See Neugebauer 1975, 1040 and Segonds 1981, 22–3 for discussion.

In 219 [local era = AD 503], on the night of 27–28 Mechir, the moon occulted Saturn at very nearly the fourth hour. When the occultation ended, my dear brother and I determined the time with an astrolabe and found that it was $5\frac{3}{4}$ seasonal hours.

32 John Philoponus, *On the Astrolabe*

Alexandrian scientist and philosopher writing between 510 and 550. This treatise was based on the lost one by Theon of Alexandria (see above). Philoponus tells us (in chapter 1) that his own teacher Ammonius (see above) had written another. The bulk of the treatise concerns the front of

314

the astrolabe, the *arachne*, the discs engraved with coordinate lines, and how to use them. In chapter 3 the ring is also termed the suspension point (*artema*), and the alidade side of the instrument is once called the disc (*tympanon*). Only the chapters relevant to the back of the astrolabe are translated here, and much of the repetitive verbiage is pruned.

2. *On the markings on the face occupied by the alidade, and what each of the markings signifies.*

Of the two lines on the face occupied by the alidade (*dioptra*), which intersect each other at the centre, that coming down from the ring at the top by which the instrument is suspended corresponds to the meridian, and the other bisecting it at right angles corresponds to the horizon. The latter forms the diameter of the semicircle above, which corresponds to the hemisphere of the heavens above the earth. This semicircle is bisected by the meridian line. Each of the resulting quadrants is divided into 90 degrees on which the pointer (*moirognomonion*) of the alidade falls. By this means we can judge at each hour the altitude in degrees of the sun or another star above the horizon, whether eastern or western. The 90th degree mark indicates the zenith, the first degree mark the horizon. Not all astrolabes have both quadrants divided into 90 degrees; [some have] only one, which suffices because the altitude can be found from either of them. But to allow for easy sighting with the instrument suspended from either hand, some have both quadrants graduated.

5. *On the daytime sighting of the sun and how to conduct it systematically.*

If during the day we want to find out the time from the instrument, we hang it from the ring in such a way that the graduated quadrant is directed at the sun. Then little by little we turn the alidade up and down the quadrant until the sun's ray passes through the hole (*trypema*) in the alidade nearest the sun and falls on the hole nearest us. To avoid holding the instrument wrongly and getting annoyed with the alidade, remember to hold it so that the rim is lit by the sun while both faces are in shadow . . . [Philoponus explains why, and repeats the procedure] until the sun's ray passing through the hole in the sight (*systemation*, lit. 'little device') on that side falls on the hole in the sight nearest us. You will see a light of the same size and shape as the hole wandering around and falling now here, now there as you turn the alidade. You should turn it carefully until you see the light falling on the inner face of the sight nearest us and coinciding with that hole, at which point it becomes invisible because it is passing through a void. If you put your hand near the hole on our side, you will see the light fall on it. The light becomes totally invisible if the first hole (*ope*) it meets is smaller than, or exactly equal to, the second. If it is bigger, the light overlaps the other hole. When this has been done, mark with ink or something else the line marked by the pointer of the alidade, that is the tip of the bar (*kanonion*) which is sharpened to a point. Take the reading starting from the bottom at the horizon, and note if the sighting was taken before or after noon. The number of degrees above the horizon gives the altitude of the sun above its rising or setting. [Reference to the front of the astrolabe, or to tables, will convert the altitude for a given date and a given latitude into the time.]

8.   *On the night-time sighting of the fixed stars.*

[A similar procedure, but sighting through the alidade.]

33 Severus Sebokht, *Treatise on the Plane Astrolabe* 90
Syriac text. Syrian Bishop of Qenserin near Aleppo, died AD 665. The treatise, like Philoponus', is based on that of Theon of Alexandria. The present translation includes only the description of the back of the astrolabe, and omits repetitive matter.

Mark 90 degrees on one of the quarters of the external plate which encloses and carries all the rest [i.e. the back of the astrolabe]. These degrees give the altitude in the hemisphere above, which goes up to 90 degrees at the zenith. Divide this plate into four quarters by means of two lines, one running from top to bottom and the other from east to west in the revered shape of the cross. On the upper half of the plate's surface are inscribed the 90 degrees of which we spoke: the first degree mark is where the upper hemisphere begins, i.e. at the horizon, and the 90th degree mark is the top, i.e. the zenith. On this plate is fixed a blade or rule whose ends are sharpened to a point. On it are fixed two very small plates almost an inch square and each pierced by a hole. These two holes are exactly in line with each other so that if one sights the sun, moon, or a star, the line of sight passes directly through both holes. The length of the bar is the same as the diameter of the plate so that one of its ends is always over the degree marks on the quadrant, and its width is about one inch. The geometers call it a dioptra because it allows us to sight a ray of the sun or a star in a straight line. Its pointed ends are called degree-indicators [also the meaning of the Greek *moirognomonion*] because they show the altitude in degrees in the quadrant of the sky of the sun or star at the moment when we make the observation, when a line from the star passes through the dioptra.

At the centre of this dioptra, of all the discs described and of the *arachne* [on the front of the astrolabe] there is a hole, the same size in all of them, in which a pin is put after the plates have been exactly aligned with each other.

34 Pseudo-Stephen of Alexandria, *Treatise on the horoscope of Islam* 273

Written apparently in 775 and falsely ascribed to Stephen (early seventh century).

The merchant in question [one Epiphanes, supposedly reporting the rise of Mohammed] came to us at the third hour of the fifth day of Thoth. We found that the sun was at 9° 05′ in Virgo. Transferring these data to the astrolabe, we found for this hour of the day that the 20th degree of Libra was rising and the 22nd degree of Cancer was in the centre of the heavens.

35 John Kamateros, *Introduction to Astronomy* 2206–21, 2229–30, 2262–9

Byzantine astrologer, addressing Manuel Comnenus (1143–80). Lines 2153–2281 of the poem, describing the astrolabe, are largely drawn from ancient sources, but because the terminology differs Segonds 1981, 69 thinks the source is not Philoponus.

Attend to the method of taking the time. On its back the astrolabe has intersecting lines: regard them as the lines which delimit the quadrants. One quadrant carries up to 90 small engraved figures called degrees, which pertain to the sun by day and the stars by night: that is the stars inscribed on the *arachne*. Turning in the centre is the alidade (*kanonion*) with a hole (*trype*) at each end of it, called the dioptra and the suntaker. Face the sun with the astrolabe hanging from your finger, and balance the dioptra, moving it up and down, until the sun's ray passes clean through the [upper] hole and lights on the other lower hole.

Thus, by this balancing, you take the sun . . . Mark carefully where the pointed end of the dioptra falls, so that you do not lose it [and work out the time from the front of the astrolabe.] . . . If you now wish to take the time by night, . . . put your astrolabe on your finger and hold the alidade above your eye. Take an unobstructed sight through the two holes on the star of your choice, and then note the elevation at which the alidade is set.

The libra (Chapter 4)

36 Vitruvius, *On Architecture* VIII 6.3
Between 35 and 25 BC, on aqueduct building.

If there are hills between the city and the source of water, proceed as follows: dig tunnels underground and level them (*librentur*) to the gradient as described above [**Source 3**].

37 Palladius, *On Agriculture* IX 11.2
Latin treatise, *c.* AD 400, section on aqueducts derived indirectly from Vitruvius.

If a hill intervenes, either we lead the water indirectly round its flanks or we level (*librabimus*) tunnels through which the channel may pass to the source of the water.

38 Pliny, *Natural History* XXXIII 74–5
Roman encyclopaedist, died AD 79. On flushing away the waste rock engendered by mining for gold in the Asturias in Spain, where Pliny was procurator in 72–4.

To wash away this debris, an equally laborious and even more expensive task is that of bringing streams, often for a hundred miles along mountain ridges. They are called *corrugi*, a word derived, I think, from *conrivatio*, 'confluence'. They involve a thousand problems. Because the gradient (*libramentum*) must be steep to make the water rush, not flow, it is brought from very high ground. Gorges and crevasses are crossed on masonry bridges. Elsewhere impassable crags are cut away to hold wooden troughs. The workmen, hanging on ropes to cut the rock, look from a distance more like birds than beasts. It is usually suspended like this that they take the levels (*librant*) and mark out the route, and man brings water where there is not even room to plant his feet.

39 Frontinus, *On the Aqueducts of the City of Rome* 6
Aqueduct administrator writing in AD 97 on the Anio Vetus of 272 BC, which followed a very winding course. His location of the intake is not accurate, and some text may be missing: see Evans 1994, 16.

The Anio Vetus has its intake above Tibur at the twentieth milestone outside the [name corrupted] Gate. Because of the requirements of the gradient (*libramentum*), its conduit has a length of 43 miles. Of this, 42 miles 779 paces is underground channel, 221 paces is substructure above ground.

40 Frontinus, *Aqueducts* 18

All the aqueducts reach the city at a different height (*libra*). [Five more recent ones arrive at a high level] . . . but the ancients brought theirs in at a lower elevation, either because the science of levelling (*librandi*) was not yet developed or because they deliberately kept their aqueducts underground to avoid them being easily disrupted by enemies.

41 Pliny the Younger, *Letters*
In AD 112 Pliny, governor of Bithynia, is planning a navigable canal to connect Lake Sophon (Sapanca Gölü), which drained north-east towards the Black Sea, with a river flowing north-west into the Sea of Marmara near Nicomedia (Izmit). He writes to the emperor Trajan for approval and practical support. Shortly after this exchange of letters, Pliny died.

X 41. [Pliny to Trajan] It remains for you, should you see fit, to send a *librator* or engineer (*architectus*) who can make an accurate survey (*explorare*) to see whether the lake is above sea level. Local experts claim that it is 40 cubits higher.

X 42. [Trajan to Pliny] Linking that lake of yours to the sea might tempt me to action, but clearly it must be carefully surveyed to find how much water enters it and from where, otherwise an outlet to the sea might totally drain it. You may apply to Calpurnius Macer [governor of Lower Moesia] for a *librator*, and I will send you someone from here who is qualified for this kind of work.

x 61. [Pliny to Trajan. He assures him that the water supply is plentiful, and that the outflow through the canal could either be controlled by sluices or avoided altogether by leaving a barrier between canal and river and portaging goods across.] But these and other options can be much more expertly investigated and surveyed by a *librator*, whom you must send, Sir, as you promised. Meanwhile, as you instructed, I have written to the honourable Calpurnius Macer asking him to send the most suitable *librator*.

x 62. [Trajan to Pliny, patting him on the back.] I am sure Calpurnius Macer will see to it that you are provided with a *librator*, and the provinces in your part of the world are not short of such experts.

42 *Codex Theodosianus* XIII 4.2 = *Codex Justinianus* X 66.1
Imperial decree of AD 337, when skilled professionals were in short supply.

Emperor Constantine to Maximus, praetorian prefect. We decree that experts in all cities who practise the skills included in the appended list be immune from all compulsory services so that, their leisure being devoted to learning, they may desire to increase their own proficiency and to transmit it to their sons . . . [List includes] *architecti, aquae libratores.*

43 *Codex Theodosianus* XIII 4.3 = *Codex Justinianus* X 66.2
Imperial decree of AD 344.

Emperors Constantius and Constans to Leontius, praetorian prefect. On engineers (*mechanici*), geometers and architects (*architecti*) who preserve divisions and subdivisions of land and regulate building works with standard measures and practices, and on those who show by simple levelling (*libratio*) how to conduct and gauge water which they have found, we urge with our pronouncement an eagerness to teach and to learn. Let those who are competent to teach, take pupils and enjoy immunities.

44 Libra and compounds
In view of the paucity of direct references to the libra as a surveying instrument, it may be useful to list the shades of meaning of *libra* and its compounds. Only the senses – but it is hoped all the references – relevant to levelling are included.

Libra   height, level in the sense of 'elevation':
Caesar, *Civil War* III 40.1 (of towers, but reading dubious); Columella, *Husbandry* VIII 17.4 (of sea level); *CIL* V 8146 (of sewer, Pola).
ad libram = horizontal:
Vitruvius VIII 6.6; Frontinus, *Aq.* 36 (pipes).
level of aqueducts relative to each other or to the ground:
Frontinus, *Aq.* 18 (*ter*) (**Source 40**), 19, 23, 65, 91, 124; *CIL* X 4842.10 = *ILS* 4743 (Venafro aqueduct regulations).
procedure of levelling, or survey in general:
CIL VIII 2728 = *ILS* 5795 (Nonius Datus, **Source 104**).
libra aquaria, levelling instrument:
Vitruvius VIII 5.1 (**Source 3**).

Libella   diminutive of *libra*; mason's or builder's level:
Vitruvius VII 1.3, VII 4.5; Columella III 13.12, VIII 17.3; Lucretius IV 515; Pliny, *Nat. Hist.* VII 198, XXXVI 172, 188; Vegetius III 20.
ad libellam = horizontal:
Varro, *Husbandry* I 6.6; Vitruvius I 6.6, III 4.5, III 5.8, X 6.1.

Librare,   to equalise, as the width of a gap:
perlibrare   Vitruvius X 8.2.
to make level with, e.g. one part of a building with another:
Vitruvius IV 6.1, V 6.4.
to make horizontal, e.g. a pavement; in passive, to be flat:
Cato, *Agr.* 18.7, 22.1 (?); Vitruvius II 8.6, VI 1.5; *CIL* I 1687.3; Columella II 2.1, III 13.13; Seneca, *Natural Questions* III 28.5.
to make horizontal, in connection with surveying:
chorobates: Vitruvius VIII 5.1, 2 (**Source 3**);
water surface: Vitruvius VIII 5.3 (**Source 3**);
pipes in bottom of siphon: Vitruvius VIII 6.5, 6.8 (*bis*).
to adjust the gradient, of pipes up and down siphon:
Vitruvius VIII 6.9.
to level with an instrument, i.e. survey heights or gradients:
take levels of aqueduct: Vitruvius I 1.7, VIII 5.1, 2 (**Source 3**); Frontinus, *Aq.* 18 (**Source 40**); Pliny, *Nat. Hist.* XXXIII 75 (**Source 38**);
level tunnels to gradient: Vitruvius VIII 6.3 (**Source 36**);

Libramentum geometric plane, horizontal or otherwise, from Cicero onwards.

horizontal surface, floor:

Vitruvius III 4.2, VII 4.1, VII 4.5 (*bis*), IX praef. 8 (*bis*); Ulpian in *Digest* XLIII 11.1.1.

level in the sense of elevation, e.g. of a lintel or a water surface:

Vitruvius IV 6.4, V 6.6, VIII 3.3, VIII 6.5; VIII 6.14 (*bis*); Pliny, *Nat. Hist.* XXXVII 24, 127; Pliny, *Letters* IV 30.10; Festus 314; Faventinus 6 (*bis*); Palladius IX 9.2.

gradient of an aqueduct:

Vitruvius VIII 6.1 (**Source 96**), VIII 6.5, VIII 6.6, VIII 6.8; Pliny, *Nat. Hist.* XXXI 57 (*bis*) (**Source 97**), XXXIII 74 (**Source 38**); Frontinus, *Aq.* 6 (**Source 39**).

Libratio, use of the mason's level:
perlibratio Vitruvius I 1.4.

horizontal surface:

Vitruvius VI 1.5.

gradient of a staircase:

Vitruvius IX praef. 7.

taking of levels in surveying:

Vitruvius VIII 5.1, VIII 5.3 (both **Source 3**); *Cod. Theod.* XIII 4.3 (**Source 39**).

Librator surveyor, leveller:

Pliny, *Letters* X 41, 42, 61, 62 (**Source 41**); *Cod. Theod.* XIII 4.2 (**Source 42**); Frontinus, *Aq.* 105 (*bis*); *CIL* VI 2454 = *ILS* 2060, VI 2754 = *ILS* 2059, tombstones from Rome of *libratores* of praetorian guard; *CIL* VIII 2728 = *ILS* 5795, Nonius Datus *librator* (**Source 104**); *CIL* VIII 2934 = *ILS* 2422, tombstone of Lollius Victor, *librator* of Leg. III Augusta, Lambaesis; *Année Epigraphique* 1942/3, 93, trainee *librator* Clodius Septiminus (**Source 101**).

Greek words purporting to be equivalents of *libratio* (*litrasmos*) and *librator* (*zygostatai*, plural) in *Corpus Glossariorum Latinorum* III 454.6, 47 and 485.17 occur only in renaissance glossaries and have no authority.

The groma (Chapter 5)

The text of the *Corpus Agrimensorum* (**Sources 51–8**) is very confused, corrupt and often difficult to translate. The latest editions available are used: see Index of Ancient Authors. Bouma (see under Nipsus) has a full discussion of the manuscripts.

45 Souda
Greek lexicon compiled *c.* 1000.

Gnoma: just outside the general's tent [in a camp] there was designated an area like a market place (*agora*), which was also called the *gnoma*. Embassies and proclamations and everything took place there.

46 Nonius Marcellus, *On Compendious Learning* I 87
Roman lexicographer, early fourth century AD?, citing only republican authors. *Degrumare* is a verb found only here, 'to lay out with a gruma'.

Grumae are central locations, the targets and meeting-points of four roads. Gruma is also a surveying <device> used by land surveyors and suchlike. When it is set up it lays out roads in a straight line. Ennius Book XVIII [epic poet, *c.* 170 BC] speaks of laying out with the gruma: '*degrumare* the forum'. Lucilius Book III [satirist, late second century BC, here speaking of the Rome–Capua road]: 'and you will *degrumare* the road, as the surveyor (*mensor*) habitually does a camp'.

> For other uses of groma or gruma as the central point of a town or fort, see Souda (**Source 45**); pseudo-Hyginus (**Source 53**); Hyginus Gromaticus 135.4, 144.16; *Liber Coloniarum* 225.7 (a compilation of the fifth century AD, with reference to the Etruscan origins of land surveying).

47 Glossaria Latina
Other than *degrumare* in **Source 46**, the verb *grumare* is recorded only in glossaries of Carolingian date drawing on the classics. First, Philoxenus' Latin–Greek glossary:

II 159 GA 30. *Gauma: horaia tektonike* [corrupted from *gruma: horaia tektonike* <*mechane*>: gruma: craftsmen's <instrument> for boundaries?]

II 163   GR 85. Grumat: measures; makes equal (or level).
GR 86. Gruma: *gnomon* [from Festus, **Source 50?**].
GR 90. Grumari: to direct; to make straight.
GR 91. Gruma: royal *gnome*.

Carolingian Latin–Latin glossaries following Philoxenus:

V 67   GRO 16. Grumat: directs; makes equal (or level).
258   G 211. Grumare: to direct; to make equal (or level).

The Greek 'royal' (*basilike*) in GR 91 is unconvincingly explained by Lindsay (IV 217n.) as a misunderstanding of the Latin *regula*, 'ruler' or 'straight-edge'. More probably it relates to the Souda entry (**Source 45**) and the area outside the general's (or king's) tent.

48   *Corpus Glossariorum Latinorum* II 278.25
Greek–Latin glossary of Carolingian date, = **Source 22**.

Dioptra, the <geo>meters' <instrument>: *gruma*.

49   Scipio Africanus, *Fifth Oration against Claudius Asellus*
Quoted by Aulus Gellius, *Attic Nights* II 20.6. Roman general and politician, here speaking of his political opponent Asellus in 140 BC. The text is corrupt, but *gruma* is very plausibly restored.

When he had seen the admirably cultivated fields and well-kept farmhouses, he ordered a gruma to be set up on the highest point in the district, and from there a road to be driven straight through the middle of vineyards, through the stockyard and fishpond, through the farmhouse.

50   Festus, *On the Meaning of Words* 86.1–3
Latin scholar, late second century AD, abridging Verrius Flaccus' work of the same title compiled in the very early first century AD.

Groma is the name of a type of little instrument (*machinula*) by means of which land boundaries can be identified. The Greeks call this type a *gnomon*.

51   Frontinus, *On the Art of Surveying*, 16.6–17.9
Roman administrator writing in late first century AD, though the attribution of the work to him may be wrong (Campbell 1996, 76–7). On dividing land by grid.

[A total and accurate survey is needed. We must] first use the *ferramen-tum* and regulate all procedures by plumb-line, and so sight by eye the paired threads or cords (*fila seu nervias*) extended by weights from each arm (*corniculus*) until one sees only the nearer, the other being hidden from sight; then sight the markers and take a back sight on them, mean- while exchanging the furthest marker for the *ferramentum* by the same process by which it was reached; and continue the line that has been begun to an intersection or to the boundary. At all intersections the site of the right angle is located by plumb-line. Whatever place has to be measured, one must first of all go round it and place markers at each angle where the straight line is turned at right angles; then, setting up and plumbing the *ferramentum*, sight a second line on the next side, and after placing markers on the other side lay out the line which, when it reaches the end, will be parallel to the first line.

> Other passing references to the *ferramentum*, which add nothing to our understanding, occur in 16.3, 17.17, 18.9.

52 Pseudo-Hyginus, *On Fortifying a Camp* 12
Roman military surveyor dated variously from *c.* AD 89 to the 170s and generally agreed not to be the same man as Hyginus Gromaticus (see Campbell 1996, 78n). *Gromaticus* as a description of the science recurs in Cassiodorus, *Variae* III 52.2.

The entrance to the central part of the *praetorium* on the *via principalis* is called the *locus gromae*, either because the crowd assembles (*congruat*) there or because in sighting markers the groma is placed on the *ferra-mentum* which is located at the same point, so that the gates of the fort make a star (*stella*) in the sighting of the line. For the above reason, experts in this science are called *gromatici*.

53 Hyginus Gromaticus, *Establishment of Boundaries* 154.18–155.7
Roman land surveyor, between late first and third century AD (Campbell 1996, 77–8). Surveyors should set out the main right-angled roads (*decu-manus maximus* and *cardo*) and *quintarii* (every fifth intersection) to save embarrassing mistakes.

If there has been a fault either in the *ferramentum* or in sighting, bad sur- veying becomes immediately apparent in one *quintarius* and can readily be altered ... Many surveyors set out permanent boundaries and were wrong in insisting on their work, as we find in the boundaries of old *coloniae*, most often in the provinces, where they did not use the *ferramentum* except for intersections.

54 Hyginus Gromaticus, *Establishment of Boundaries* 155.17–156.15

For establishing a line parallel to two inaccessible points A and C by similar triangles. The manuscript diagram (Dilke 1971, 59) is corrupt.

Let the survey diagram be ABCD. From the base line BD we sight [the line] BA [at right angles]. Moving the *ferramentum* a little along the base line we sight a few marks at right angles from E. Moving the *ferramentum* again to F, we sight the mark [A] so that the line from E intersects it at G, and we obtain the distances. As FE is to EG, so FB is to BA. In the same way we sight on the other side [CD] and mark its excess of length [over BA] at H. The line joining this mark to B will be parallel to AC.

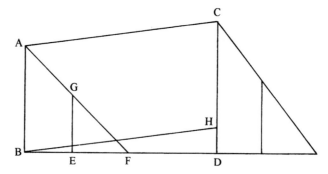

Other passing references to the *ferramentum*, which add nothing to our understanding, occur in 135.3, 147.5, 161.20.

55 M. Junius Nipsus (or Nypsus), *Measuring the Width of a River* 4–28

Roman land surveyor, most likely second century AD. Intrusive material in MSS F and N is omitted. The text of these short treatises or chapters is particularly difficult, and the diagram and reference letters (following Bouma) are added to aid comprehension.

If when dividing land into squares you encounter in your sighting a river whose width has to be measured, act as follows. The line which meets the river [AB]: make an angle from it. Make a right angle at the point where you reached it [C]. Then move the *ferramentum* along this line you have sighted [CD] from the line which meets the river [AB]. Then move the *ferramentum* again and by looking along the line you have sighted make a [right] angle to the right [D]. Then measure the intermediate line between right angle [C] and right angle [D] and divide it into two halves and set up a plumbed marker [E]. Then fix the *ferramentum* by the marker which divides the two halves you have divided <and plumb it>. When the *ferramentum* has been fixed and plumbed, and you have sighted along the line, and a plumb-line dropped from the *umbilicus soli* has centred on the marker, tap the croma until you sight the marker [F] which you had placed across the river. After you have carefully sighted, go to the other side of the *ferramentum* and with the croma remaining [unmoved] sight a line. Where your right-angled line [DG] intersects the line you have sighted [EH], place a marker [H], and measure the distance from the marker to the right angle [D]. Because the line you have divided in half [CD] carries two triangles and because the perpendiculars [CE and ED] are equal, the bases [CF and DH] will also be equal. The length of the base [DH] of the connected triangle which you have measured will be the same as the length of the [base] line [CF] of the other triangle which was previously laid out on the river. Therefore from this base [DH] which you have measured, subtract the distance which you measured from the right angle to the river [CB]. The remainder that is left will be the width of the river.

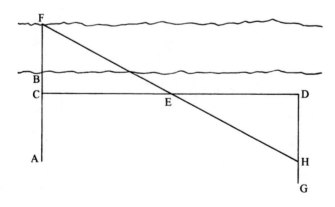

327

56 M. Junius Nipsus, *The Resighting of a Boundary Line* 7–18

Re-establishing an old boundary on centuriated land.

If you find the [boundary] stone to be incised with four lines at right angles, you fix the *ferramentum* a little further away from the stone so that you can see the centre of the *decumanus* or *cardo* line and can sight two poles which you carefully plumb on four sides, one beyond the stone, the other this side. Then you move the *ferramentum* to the other side of the stone and do as above described. Then remove the *ferramentum*, move it to the stone and fix it. When you have fixed it, plumb it. When you have plumbed it, carefully arrange that the plumb-line dropped from the *umbilicus soli* falls on the centre of the cross. When you have done this, sight the four poles and begin to sight the boundary in the direction you are going to follow.

57 M. Junius Nipsus, *The Resighting of a Boundary Line* 34–9

Bypassing an obstacle on a straight boundary AB. C is the beginning of the obstacle. To put it simply: lay out lines CE, EG and GI at right angles to each other. CE = EG, and GI = twice CE, with H at its centre. The obstructed length CH = EG. Again the diagram and letters are Bouma's additions.

When you have done this, fix the *ferramentum* at the stone [H] in such a way that you do not fix it on the line of the boundary. When the *ferramentum* is fixed, turn the *umbilicus soli* over the centre of the stone and thus plumb the *ferramentum*. When the *ferramentum* is plumbed, drop a plumb-line from the *umbilicus soli* so that it falls on the centre of the stone and you can sight on the four markers which you have placed on <the line perpendicular to> the boundary. And with the other arms (*corniculi*) you will be on the other [original] boundary.

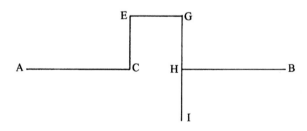

58   M. Junius Nipsus, *The Resighting of a Boundary Line* 190–1

[When the original survey was finished,] the bronze [map] was hung up and the *machina* removed.

> See also **Dioptra 33**
> Balbus, **Source 14**
> *Etymologicum Magnum*, **Source 24**

The hodometer (Chapter 6)

59   Vitruvius, *On Architecture* X 9
35–25 BC.

1.   Our treatise now turns to consider a matter handed down by our predecessors, which is not useless but highly ingenious. By its means we can tell, whether sitting in a carriage on the road or sailing the sea, how many miles we have travelled. It is as follows. The carriage wheels are four [*wrongly added by a copyist:* and a sixth] feet in diameter so that, if a wheel is marked at a certain point from which it begins to roll forward along the road surface, when it reaches the mark from which it started to roll it will have covered a distance of exactly twelve and a half feet.

2.   When this has been arranged, there is firmly attached to the inner side of the wheel hub a disc with one small tooth projecting beyond the rim of its circumference. Above it, firmly fixed to the carriage body, is a sleeve carrying on a small axle a rotating disc mounted vertically, on whose rim 400 equally spaced teeth are made which engage the tooth [MSS 'teeth'] of the lower disc. Moreover there is fixed to the side of the upper disc another small tooth projecting beyond its teeth.

3.   Above it, mounted in another sleeve, is a horizontal disc toothed in the same way, its teeth engaging the small tooth fixed to the side of the second disc. In this disc there are holes, as many as the number of miles the carriage can cover in a lengthy journey: more or less does not matter. Round pebbles are placed in all these holes, and in the casing or sleeve of this disc is a single hole with a tube. Through this, when they reach this point, the pebbles in the disc can drop one by one into the carriage body and into a bronze bowl placed below.

4. Thus as the wheel moves forward it takes with it the lowest disc, whose tooth impinges on and advances the teeth of the upper disc [by one tooth] per turn. The result is that when the lower disc has turned 400 times, the upper one turns once, and the tooth attached to its side advances one tooth of the horizontal disc. So when the upper disc has been turned once by 400 turns of the lower one, the distance covered will be 5000 feet, i.e. a mile. Hence each pebble, as it falls and produces a sound, marks the passage of a single mile. The number of pebbles collected below indicates the total number of miles travelled in the day.

5. A similar result is achieved for sea voyages by the same method but with a few changes. An axle is passed through the sides of the hull, its ends projecting outside the ship and carrying wheels four [*wrongly:* and a sixth] feet in diameter with projecting paddles fixed around its rim and touching the water. Further, the centre of the axle amidships has a disc with one small tooth projecting beyond its rim. At this point a sleeve is fixed containing a disc with 400 equally spaced teeth, engaging the tooth on the disc on the axle, and with another single tooth fixed to its side and projecting beyond its rim.

6. Above it is fixed another sleeve containing a horizontal disc toothed in the same way and engaging the single tooth fixed on the side of the vertical disc, so that the single tooth advances the teeth on the horizontal disc, one tooth per turn, and rotates the horizontal disc. In the horizontal disc are holes in which pebbles are placed. In the casing or sleeve of this disc there is drilled one hole with a tube down which a pebble, when it is free and unrestrained, falls into a bronze bowl and makes a sound.

7. So when the ship is propelled by oars or by wind, the paddles on the wheels touch the counterflowing water, are driven forcibly backwards, and turn the wheels. These rotate the axle, and the axle rotates the disc whose revolving tooth, advancing the teeth of the second disc by one tooth per turn, generates a slow rotation. Thus when the paddles have turned the wheels 400 times, the disc is rotated once, and with the tooth fixed to its side it advances one tooth on the horizontal disc. Therefore as often as the turning of the horizontal disc brings pebbles to the hole, it will drop them down the tube, and thus both by sound and by number it will indicate the miles traversed by the ship.

60 Historia Augusta, *Pertinax* VIII 6–7

Imperial biographies in Latin written *c.* AD 390. Pertinax, during his brief reign in AD 193, held an auction of the effects of his dissolute predecessor Commodus. The following items were included in the sale catalogue.

There were also carriages of an unusual technique of construction with meshing and branching gear trains and seats accurately designed to rotate, sometimes to face away from the sun, sometimes to take advantage of the breeze; and hodometers; and clocks; and other items appropriate to his vices.

61 Proclus, *Commentary on the First Book of Euclid's Elements* 63.6–19

Greek philosopher, *c.* AD 410–85. A list of the by-products of geometry which has a close correlation with the known mechanical work of Archimedes.

[Geometry] has generated a variety of sciences like geodesy, mechanics and optics which benefit the life of mortals. It has constructed machines of war and for defending cities, made familiar the cycles of the hours and the establishing of positions (*topon theseis*), shown how to measure routes by land and sea, manufactured scales and balances to establish standard municipal measures, explained the order of the universe by means of models, and revealed many things which men did not believe and made them universally credible. An example is the verdict attributed to Hiero of Syracuse on Archimedes [when single-handed he launched the great ship].

62 John Tzetzes, *Chiliads* XI 586–97

Byzantine polymath, twelfth century. This section of the poem, 'On Geometry and Optics', has some Archimedean features in common with Proclus' list above.

Geometry is useful for many mechanical works, for lifting of weights, launching ships, stone throwers and other machines of destruction, burning mirrors and other devices for defending cities; it is profitable for building bridges and harbours, and for wonderful lifelike machines of bronze or wood or iron or suchlike that drink and move and utter, and for measuring the stades of the sea by machine and the land by hodometers. A myriad other works are born of geometry, the ingenious art.

63   Tzetzes, *Chiliads* XII 964–71
On Archimedes' career and works. The implication, although Tzetzes is
not the most trustworthy of sources, is that Hero's titles were inspired by
Archimedes' work. The opening statement is a misrepresentation of
Pappus, *Collections* 1026, which quotes Carpus of Antioch to the effect
that Archimedes wrote only one book on machines.

Some say that Archimedes wrote one book; but I have read various
books of his: <*title missing*>, *Centre of Gravity*, *Burning Mirrors*,
Epistasidia and other books, on the basis of which Hero, Anthemius
and every writer on mechanics wrote on hydraulics, pneumatics, every
kind of *barulkos* and sea-hodometers (*thalassodometraî*).

See also **Dioptra 34, 38**
Simplicius, **Source 69**

Measurement of the Earth (Chapter 7)

64   Ptolemy, *Geography* I 2.2.
Mid-second century AD. In order to provide an accurate geographic
description of the earth, he says, it is necessary to take account of travellers' reports and of geometric and meteoroscopic (i.e. celestial) investi-
gations and traditions.

The geometric method consists of revealing the relationship of places
to each other by the simple measurement of distances; the meteoroscopic does so by observation with [armillary] astrolabes and gnomons
(*skiothera*). The latter method is self-sufficient and less disputable; the
former is cruder and needs the latter as well.

65   Ptolemy, *Geography* I 2.4
Measuring stades does not provide a secure knowledge of the true
figure because journeys, whether by road or sea, are rarely direct, but
involve many deviations. On journeys by land, to find the distance in a
straight line, one has to calculate the excess from the nature and number
of the deviations and subtract it from the total number of stades. On sea
voyages one has to take account of variations in the strength of the
wind, which does not often maintain the same force.

66 Ptolemy, *Geography* I 3.1–4

1. In order to make an arc of the greatest circle, our predecessors investigated a distance on earth that was not only direct but also aligned in the plane of a single meridian. By observing with sundials (*skiothera*) [this is impossible; for discussion, see Chapter 7] the points in the zenith at the two termini of the distance, they obtained the arc on the meridian which corresponded to the distance travelled. This is because these points lie, as we said, in a single plane and lines projected through the termini to the points in the zenith must meet, and because that meeting point is the common centre of the circles. (2.) Therefore the ratio of the arc between the points at the zenith to the circle through the poles is the same as the ratio of the terrestrial distance to the whole circumference.

3. But if we take a measured distance on a circle that does not pass through the poles but follows another of the greatest circles, the same thing can be shown by observing from the termini in the same way the meridian altitudes and the relationship of the [measured] distance to either meridian. This we showed by constructing a meteoroscope, with which we readily found much other useful information. For any day or night it gives us the altitude of the north pole from the position of the observer, and for any hour it gives us the position of the meridian and the angle which the greatest circle through the line of the [terrestrial] distance makes with the meridian at the zenith. (4.) In this way we can likewise show with the meteoroscope the required arc and also the arc intercepted between the two meridians, even on parallels other than the equator. Thus by this method, if we measure only one direct distance on earth, we can discover the total circumference in stades.

Following from this, we can obtain other terrestrial distances without measuring them, even if they are not direct nor aligned with a meridian or parallel, provided we carefully observe the angle [of the distance to the meridian] and the meridian altitude at the termini. To repeat: if we know the ratio between the greatest circle and the arc subtended by the distance, the number of stades can easily be calculated from the known circumference of the earth.

67 Scholiast on Ptolemy, *Geography* 1 3.3

As Hipparchus and Ptolemy himself bear witness, if we take stars at the zenith and the distance between them in degrees, we will find what proportion it is of the greatest circle. The proportion will also be the same on the earth, for the circle of the heavens and the circle drawn on the earth have the same circumferences. Let AB be a circle of the heavens and ΓΔ one on earth, and EZ be the given places, and HΘ be the points at the zenith whose positions we will find if we project [the radii through E and Z] to the line of the circle. For having discovered with the meteoroscope the distance in degrees between the stars, we will also know the distance in stades. If we stand at the given places and with the instrument take the stars at the zenith, we will also find that the distance on earth between them is the same, according to the number of stades to each terrestrial degree. There is no need to relate this figure to the circumference of the whole earth; and this will be true even if the given journey [between the places] is not straight and direct.

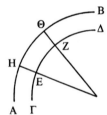

EZ = terrestrial distance
HΘ = stars at zenith

68 John Philoponus, *Commentary on the First Book of Aristotle's Meteorology* 15.5–8

Alexandrian philosopher writing AD 510–50. Reading *moiriaion*, 'one degree', rather than the *metriazon*, 'a moderate distance', of the MSS, transforms the statement from the vague to the precise, and brings it into line with Simplicius' almost identical wording (**Source 69**).

They also discovered its circumference. They took two stars one degree apart, measured the line they subtended on earth, and found it to be a distance of 500 stades. Dividing the greatest circle into 360 degrees and multiplying these by the 500 stades, they found the whole circumference of the earth to be 180,000 stades.

69 Simplicius, *Commentary on Aristotle's De Caelo* 548.27–549.10
Greek philosopher, mid-sixth century AD. The second sentence is apparently paraphrased from Ptolemy, *Almagest* I 6, which however mentions only the armillary astrolabe, not the meteoroscope. This is first recorded in the (later) *Geography* (**Source 66**).

If one compares the earth with the whole sphere of the fixed stars, it will indeed appear to have an invariable relationship to it as the fixed centre. This is clear from the fact that the centres of instruments used for astronomy – the meteoroscope and astrolabes – placed in every part of the earth are analogous to the centre of the universe.

Because Aristotle referred to the measurement of the earth, remarking that its circumference was said to be 400,000 stades, it would be a good thing to record briefly, especially on account of those who do not believe in the ingenuity of the ancients, the method of measurement that they used. They took by dioptra two fixed stars one degree apart, that is one 360th of the greatest circle in the fixed sphere, located with dioptras the places at which the two stars are at the zenith, and measured the distance between them by hodometer. They found it to be 500 stades. It follows that the greatest circle on earth has a circumference of 180,000 stades, as Ptolemy calculated in his *Geography*.

Mountain heights (Chapter 8)

70 Dicaearchus of Messana
Greek polymath, late fourth century BC. The Souda, s.v. Dicaearchus, lists among his works:

Measurement of the Mountains of the Peloponnese.

71 Xenophon (of Lampsacus?)
Cited by Alexander Polyhistor, Frag. 72. Geographer writing between early third and early first century BC.

Xenophon in his *Measurements of Mountains* says that Oropus lies near Amphipolis . . .

[But Capelle 1916, 23 suggested that *oron*, 'mountains', is a corruption of *horon*, 'boundaries'.]

72 Diodorus Siculus, *Historical Library* II 13.2
Greek historian, late first century BC, quoting Ctesias of Cnidus' *History of Persia* (early fourth century BC).

The mountain of Bagistanos has sheer cliffs rising to a height of 17 stades.

73 Pliny, *Natural History* II 162
Roman encyclopaedist, died AD 79.

It is amazing that a globe results from such a level expanse of sea and plain. This view is supported by Dicaearchus, a scholar of the first rank, who with the support of royal patrons measured the height of mountains and announced that the highest of them was Pelion, with a vertical altitude of 1250 paces, deducing that this was no [significant] proportion of the earth's overall sphericity. This seems to me a questionable hypothesis because I know that some peaks of the Alps rise over large expanses to not less than 50,000 paces.

74 Theon of Smyrna, *Useful Mathematical Hints* 124.7–125.3
Greek Platonist, first half of second century AD, here quoting from Adrastus of Aphrodisias, a contemporary Peripatetic philosopher.

The whole mass of the earth and the sea is spherical. Nobody would hold the projection of the mountains or the lowness of the plains to be adequate evidence of irregularity relative to the whole size [of the earth, which Eratosthenes shows to be about 252,000 stades in circumference or 80,182 stades in diameter . . .] The vertical difference between the highest mountains and the lowest land <is 10 stades> as Eratosthenes and Dicaearchus are said to have discovered: such observations are made instrumentally with dioptras that measure heights from distances. So the projection of the highest mountain is about one eight-thousandth of the whole diameter of the earth.

75 Theon of Alexandria, *Commentary on the Almagest* 394.10–395.2
Greek mathematician and astronomer writing *c.* AD 360–80. This passage and the next are drawn, whether directly or indirectly, from Adrastus but misquote him, since according to Theon of Smyrna's version he did not specifically state that Eratosthenes used a dioptra.

The whole size of the earth measured on its greatest circle is 180,000 stades, as Ptolemy himself concluded in his *Geography*. [The diameter is therefore 57,273 stades.] Eratosthenes shows by means of dioptras which measure [their heights] from their distances that the vertical drawn from the highest mountains to the lower land is 10 stades.

76 Simplicius, *Commentary on Aristotle's De Caelo* 549.32–550.4
Greek philosopher, mid-sixth century AD.

Set against such a size of the earth [180,000 stades circumference], the heights of mountains are not sufficient to detract from its spherical shape or to affect the measurements which imply its sphericity. For Eratosthenes shows by means of dioptras which measure [their heights] from their distances that the vertical drawn from the highest mountains to the lowest land is 10 stades.

77 Cleomedes, *On the heavens*, II 1.347–9
Greek astronomer, writing probably in the second century AD. This passage, unlike **Source 82**, is probably drawn from the Eratosthenean tradition.

. . . the highest mountains, some of which have a vertical height of even more than 10 stades.

78 Apuleius, *On Socrates' God* 8
Latin orator, second century AD.

No bird flies higher than the summit of Olympus. Although this is called the highest of all <mountains>, nevertheless if you measure its vertical altitude, as the geometers affirm, the height of its summit does not reach <ten> stades.

79 Martianus Capella, *Philologia* II 149
Roman encyclopaedist, late fifth century AD.

I am concerned not with the lowness of the air traversed by birds, which is exceeded by the peak of Mount Olympus that barely rises to an altitude of 10 stades, but with its height.

80 Geminus, *Introduction to the Phenomena* 17.2–5
Greek astronomer, probably first century BC. For the height of Atabyrios the text is probably corrupt.

The clouds do not extend 10 stades in height. [The ashes of sacrifices on the summit of Kyllene, the highest mountain in the Peloponnese (*sic*: Taygetus is higher), have been found a year later untouched by rain or wind, because the clouds and wind do not rise so high. Those who climb Atabyrios on Rhodes through the clouds often find the summit above the clouds.] The height of Kyllene is less than 15 stades, as Dicaearchus' measurement shows. The vertical height of Atabyrios is less than 4 (?) stades.

81 Strabo, *Geography*, VIII 8.1
Greek geographer, late first century BC.

The greatest mountain in it [Arcadia] is Kyllene: at all events, some say its vertical height is 20 stades, others 15.

82 Cleomedes, *On the heavens*, 1 7.121–5
This passage, unlike **Source 77**, is presumably drawn, like much of his material, from Posidonius of Rhodes, the philosopher of the first half of the first century BC.

The views of those who deny the sphericity of the earth, because of the hollows under the sea and the mountains that project, are unreasonable. For no mountain has a vertical height, and no sea has a depth, greater than 15 stades. The proportion of 30 stades to [the earth's diameter of] more than 80,000 stades is insignificant.

83 Arrian cited in Stobaeus, *Anthologia* 1 31.8
Greek philosopher and historian writing in first half of the second century AD.

The clouds extend upwards, but are not higher than 20 stades from the earth. For this reason such mountains as rise vertically to more than 20 stades (which at least in our parts are few) are never seen to be affected by rain or wind, and have no clouds standing on them or above them.

84 Plutarch, *Aemilius Paullus* 15.5–7
Greek writer and philosopher, second century AD. This passage is quoting from a letter written by the Roman general Scipio Nasica in 168 BC.

Above this point Olympus rises to a height of more than 10 stades, as witnessed by the following inscription by the man who measured it: 'The sacred peak of Olympus at Apollo's Pythion has a height in vertical measurement of ten full stades and in addition a plethron [100 feet] lacking four feet. Xenagoras son of Eumelus measured it. Hail, Lord [presumably Apollo], and give us prosperity.' Yet the geometers say that the height of no mountain and the depth of no sea is greater than 10 stades. However, Xenagoras seems to have taken his measurement not cursorily but systematically with instruments.

85 Apollodorus of Athens
Quoted in Eustathius, *Commentary on Homer's Odyssey* II 311.13–14. Greek grammarian, second century BC. This passage is also quoted in Stephen of Byzantium (s.v. *Kyllene*), but without the attribution to Apollodorus, whom Stephen frequently cites elsewhere.

Kyllene, a mountain in Arcadia, is 9 Olympic stades in height less 80 feet, as Apollodorus is said to record.

86 Strabo, *Geography* VIII 6.21
On Corinth.

The situation of the city, as described by Hieronymus [of Cardia, *c.* 300 BC], Eudoxus [the astronomer, *c.* 350 BC] and others, and as I myself saw after its recent restoration by the Romans, is something like this. A tall mountain with the great vertical height of 3½ stades and an ascent of 30 stades ends in a sharp peak. It is called Acrocorinth.

87 John Philoponus, *Commentary on the First Book of Aristotle's Meteorology* 26.32–27.12
Alexandrian philosopher writing between 510 and 550. He quotes from Geminus (**Source 80**) on sacrifices on Kyllene. Writings left by priests on top of Olympus were found untouched on their next visit. He himself was told by a man who had crossed Olympus that he climbed above the clouds and heard thunder and lightning below.

339

The highest points on mountains are above the clouds and above the wind . . . Even the highest of mountains do not rise much above the earth. Mechanical experts who discover their heights with the instruments they habitually use for measuring mountains say that the loftiest mountains have a vertical height of 12 stades.

> See also *Dioptra* 13
> Hero of Alexandria, **Source 13**
> Balbus, **Source 14**

Canals and aqueducts (Chapter 9)

88 Aristotle, *Meteorology* 353b
Greek philosopher writing *c.* 340s BC.

The whole [of Egypt] appears to be made ground, the work of the river. This is obvious when one looks at the land itself, and the country towards the Red Sea provides good evidence too. One of the kings tried to dig a canal through it, for it would be no small advantage to them to open up the whole region to shipping; the first ancient attempt is ascribed to Sesostris [Seti, thirteenth–twelfth century BC]. But the sea was found to be higher than the land. For this reason first Sesostris and later Darius [521–486 BC] stopped the cutting, to avoid sea water mixing with the river water and polluting it.

89 Diodorus Siculus, *Historical Library* I 33.9–10
Greek historian, late first century BC. On the Nile–Red Sea canal, begun by Necho (II: 610–595 BC). Information drawn probably from Agatharchides' *On the Red Sea* written in the mid-second century BC.

After him Darius the Persian made progress with the work for a while, but in the end left it unfinished. Some people told him that if he cut the canal through the isthmus he would be responsible for the drowning of Egypt, for they pointed out that the Red Sea was higher than Egypt. Later Ptolemy II completed it [in 270/69: Fraser 1972, I 177] and at the most convenient point devised an ingenious lock.

90 Strabo, *Geography* XVII 1.25

Quoting from Artemidorus, a geographer of *c*. 100 BC who in turn drew on Agatharchides, he gives much the same account as Diodorus: the canal was first attempted by Sesostris or by Necho, then by Darius.

But he too gave up the work when it was nearly completed, being persuaded by the false idea that the Red Sea was higher than Egypt and that, if the isthmus between them were cut through, Egypt would be inundated by the sea. [But, he continues, the Ptolemies did complete the canal with a lock on it.]

91 Pliny, *Natural History* VI 33

Roman encyclopaedist, died AD 79. On the Red Sea,

from which they led a navigable canal to the Nile at the point where it flows into what is called the Delta, 62½ miles long, which is the distance between the river and the Red Sea. Sesostris king of Egypt was the first to contemplate it, shortly followed by Darius the Persian, then by Ptolemy II, who did take the canal, 100 feet wide and 30 feet deep, for 34½ miles as far as the Bitter Lakes. What deterred him from taking it further was the fear of drowning Egypt, as the Red Sea was found to be 3 cubits higher. Others say the reason was not that, but the danger of polluting the Nile, the only supply of drinking water, by admitting the sea.

92 Strabo, *Geography*

He is criticising the opinions of Eratosthenes who claimed that the Mediterranean, though continuous, does not obey Archimedes' theorem that the surface of any liquid at rest is spherical and has the same centre as the earth.

I 3.11. As authorities for such an ignorant view, he cites engineers, even though mathematicians define engineering as a branch of mathematics. For he says that Demetrius attempted to cut through the Isthmus of Corinth to provide a passage for his fleets, but was prevented by the engineers who took measurements and reported that the sea in the Corinthian Gulf [to the west] was higher than at Cenchreae [to the east], so that if he cut through the land between, the whole sea around Aegina, Aegina itself, and the islands near by would be submerged, and the passage would moreover be unusable.

I 3.14. [Eratosthenes says] that it does not follow from the concept of one continuous sea that it has the same height and the same level; just as the Mediterranean does not, nor assuredly do the seas at Lechaeum and round Cenchreae.

93 Pseudo-Lucian, *Nero* 4
Probably written by the elder Philostratus, father of the next. The fictitious speaker in this extract had served in the chain-gang digging Nero's canal.

On the 75th day of our bondage to the Isthmus vague rumours came from Corinth that Nero had changed his mind about cutting the canal. They said that Egyptians who surveyed (*geometrein*) the features of the seas on either side found that they were not at the same level, but considered that the sea at Lechaeum was higher. They feared for Aegina, which they thought would be submerged and swept away if so great a sea poured over it.

94 Philostratus, *Life of Apollonius of Tyana* IV 24
Greek sophist, writing in AD 217.

The canal was begun at Lechaeum and had advanced about 4 stades by continuous excavation when Nero is said to have stopped the cutting. Some say that Egyptians investigated the sea for him and declared that the sea above Lechaeum would swamp Aegina and obliterate it, others that Nero feared a revolution in the empire.

AQUEDUCT SURVEYING (CHAPTER 9.B)

95 Philo of Byzantium, *Water Conducting*
See **Source 10**; *c.* 230s BC. On an irrigation channel.

The smallest slope to give it is 12 fingers [i.e. dactyls] per 100 cubits. That is the figure given by Aflimun in his *Book on Water Conducting*.

96 Vitruvius, *On Architecture* VIII 6.1
35–25 BC. On open channels in aqueducts.

Let the bed of the channel have a minimum gradient (*libramenta fastigata*) of half a foot per 100 feet (*in centenos pedes semipede*).

97 Pliny, *Natural History* XXXI 57
Written *c.* AD 70. On aqueducts.

The minimum gradient (*libramentum*) of the water shall be a quarter of an inch per 100 feet (*in centenos pedes sicilici*).

98 Faventinus, *On the Diverse Skills of Architecture* 6
Written *c.* AD 300. On aqueducts.

If there is a longish level area, let the structure fall at a rate of a foot and a half per 100 or per 60 feet (*pede semis inter centenos vel LX pedes*) so that the water flows briskly, not sluggishly.

99 Palladius, *On Agriculture* IX 11
Written *c.* AD 400. On aqueducts.

If it crosses a level area, let the structure fall gradually by one and a half feet per 100 or per 60 feet (*inter centenos vel sexagenos pedes . . . sesquipedem*) to give force to the current.

100 Tabula Contrebiensis
Année Epigraphique 1979, 377; Fatás 1980; further discussion and bibliography in Birks, Rodger and Richardson 1984. Bronze tablet dated 87 BC from Contrebia Belaisca (Botorrita), 18 km south-west of Zaragoza in Spain, recording a dispute between two local tribes, the Salluinenses and Sosinestani, over rights to water, presumably for irrigation. The case had been handed back by the Roman governor for settlement at Contrebia; the legal detail is irrelevant to us.

[Let the judges decide whether,] with regard to the land which the Salluinenses purchased from the Sosinestani for the purpose of making a channel (*rivus*) or conducting water, . . . the Sosinestani were within their rights in selling . . . [and] in the place most recently and officially staked out (*depalare*) by the Salluinenses . . . if it would be permissible for the Salluinenses within their rights to make a channel through the public land of the Sosinestani within those stakes (*pali*).

101 Clodius Septiminus
Année Epigraphique 1942/3, 93. Altar found near Ain Cherchar in Aurès Mountains in Algeria. Text as restored by Le Bohec 1986. Apronius was governor of Numidia and commander of Legion III Augusta at

Lambaesis in the mid-220s AD under Severus Alexander (Thomasson 1960, 210–11). I translate *discens librator* in its obvious meaning of 'trainee surveyor', but Le Bohec 1986 makes a good case for the opposite meaning, namely 'surveying instructor'.

Lucius Apronius Pius, the emperor's propraetorian governor, consul designate, [on the completion of the work] fulfilled the vow which [he had made] when work was begun on the aqueduct [of Alexander]. Clodius Septiminus, trainee surveyor, made this.

See also **Anonymus 1, 2**
    Dioptra 6
    Vitruvius, **Source 3**
    Philo, **Source 10**
    Sources 36–40, 42–4 on libra
    Nonius Datus, **Source 104**

THE CHALLENGES OF SURVEYING (CHAPTER 9.D)

102 Pliny the Younger, *Letters* x 37
Pliny, as governor of Bithynia, is writing in AD 112 to the emperor Trajan. Nicomedia was the largest city in the province.

The citizens of Nicomedia, Sir, have spent 3,318,000 sesterces on an aqueduct which they abandoned before it was finished, and then pulled down. A further 200,000 sesterces was granted towards another one which was also abandoned. Having wasted such huge sums, they must spend yet more money to obtain a water supply. I have myself visited the spring – its water is excellent – from which I think that water should be brought, as was originally attempted, by a raised arcade so as to supply not only the lower-lying parts of the city. Very few of the arches still survive; some could be built of blocks of stone taken from the earlier work, but some, I feel, should be made of brick, which would be easier and cheaper. But the first essential is for you to send out a surveyor (*aquilex*) or engineer (*architectus*) to prevent a repetition of what has happened.

103 Betilienus Varus
CIL x 5807 = I² 1529 = *ILS* 5348 = *ILLRP* 528. Inscription from Alatri, SE of Rome, c. 130/120 BC.

Lucius Betilienus Varus, son of Lucius, by decree of the senate oversaw the construction of what is listed below: all the pavements in the town, the portico leading to the citadel, the playing field, the clock [sundial], the market, the stucco on the basilica, the seats, the bathing pool, the reservoir by the gate, the aqueduct to the town to a height of 340 feet and its arches and its solid pipes [cast as pipes rather than rolled from sheets?]. For these things he was twice made censor, the senate decreed that his son be excused military service, and the people gave a statue to Censorinus.

Tunnels (Chapter 10)

ALIGNMENT (CHAPTER 10.B)

104 Nonius Datus

CIL VIII 2728 = *ILS* 5795. Hexagonal inscribed base at Lambaesis (Algeria) of which only three sides survive; above the inscription are busts of Patience, Virtue and Hope. Saldae (Bougie, Bejaia) is in Algeria. The letters were written by successive procurators of Mauretania Caesariensis to successive commanding officers of Legion III Augusta at Lambaesis: the letter first quoted dates from probably 153, the second from 147/9, and Celer was procurator in 137 or before. The aqueduct therefore took about 10 years from feasibility study to the beginning of construction, and another 4–6 years to completion (for chronology see Laporte 1997).

[The surviving text opens with a letter from]

. . . <Varius Clemens to M. Valerius> Etruscus. Saldae is a most splendid city, and I, together with the citizens of Saldae, ask you, Sir, to request Nonius Datus, retired surveyor (*librator*) of Legion III Augusta, to come to Saldae to complete the remainder of his work.

I set out and on the way was attacked by bandits; my staff and I were stripped and injured, but escaped. I came to Saldae and met Clemens the procurator who took me to the hill where they were bemoaning the poor quality of workmanship on the tunnel. It seemed that they were considering abandoning it, because the length of tunnel driven was longer than the width of the hill. The headings had evidently diverged from the straight line (*rigor*), so that the upper heading had swung right towards the south, and the lower one had likewise swung right towards the north, and thus the two parts had left the straight line and diverged. But the straight line had been staked out (*depalatus*) across the hill from east to west. To save the reader from confusion about the headings which are called 'upper' and 'lower', the 'upper' is understood to be the part of the tunnel where the water is admitted, the 'lower' that where it is discharged. When I allocated the labour, I organised a competition between the marines and the *gaesates* (Alpine troops) so that they could learn each others' method of tunnelling; and so they began driving through the hill. Therefore, since it was I who had first taken the levels (*libra*), marked out the aqueduct, and had a second copy of the plans (*forma*) made which I gave to Petronius Celer the [then] procurator, <I completed> the task. When it was done and the water admitted, Varius Clemens the procurator dedicated it.

5 *modii* [relevance unknown].

To clarify my work on this aqueduct at Saldae, I append a few letters.

Porcius Vetustinus to [L. Novius] Crispinus. Sir, you acted most generously and from your humanity and kindness in sending me Nonius Datus, retired, so that I could use him on the works whose supervision he undertook. So, though pressed for time and hurrying to Caesarea, yet I dashed to Saldae and saw that the aqueduct was well begun, though of great magnitude, and that it could not be completed without the superintendence of Nonius Datus, who handled the job both diligently and faithfully. For this reason I would have asked you to second him to us so that he could stay for a few months dealing with the matter, had he not succumbed to an illness contracted . . .

LEVEL (CHAPTER 10.C)

105 Bologna aqueduct tunnel
CIL xi 739. Graffiti on tunnel wall, representing memoranda on gradients by surveyor, *c.* 20–1 BC.

a. IIII above arrow = '4 [feet]', frequent.

b. RES P CCXXV ET P C

c. RERSVPIN [*sic*] II PS

d. RESVPIN I S

e. R P

    (b–e = '(gradient) sloping backwards, so many feet')

f. FASTIGIVM

g. INTER FA[st]IGIVM

    (f–g = 'gradient')

h. LIBRATVM

i. [li]BRATVM

    (h–i = 'levelled')

Roman roads (Chapter 11)

106 Ptolemy, Geography I 2.3 (between Sources 64 and 65)
Mid–second century AD. On locating places by terrestrial measurement or, preferably, by celestial observation with (armillary) astrolabe and gnomon.

If the need arises to establish, by either of these two methods, what part of the world the line between two places points to – for we need to know not only the distance between them but also its direction, whether to the north, say, or to the east, or to some smaller subdivision between them – it cannot be accurately determined without the instruments mentioned which will, anywhere and at any time, readily establish the direction of the meridian and hence the directions of the intervals obtained.

APPENDIX

UNCERTAIN DEVICES

A. THE U-TUBE LEVEL

This simple builder's level of recent times works on the principle of the U-tube in which water finds its own level. A long flexible tube of rubber or polythene is laid along the ground. One end is held vertical against the mark from which the level is to be taken, the other end is also held vertical, but initially rather higher, at the point to which the level is to be transferred. The tube is then filled until the water reaches the brim at the starting end, and the other end is slowly lowered until it coincides with the water surface. Because no sighting is involved, the result is extremely accurate. The question of whether the method was used in the ancient world has in the past been asked, but rejected on the grounds that making a U-tube of sufficient length would have been difficult.[1]

Flexible pipes, however, were not unknown. A leather pipe at least 50 cubits long, no doubt sewn and greased, was used to raise fresh water to the surface from a spring on the sea bed off the Phoenician coast,[2] and others for carrying steam were installed in a fiendish early Byzantine device.[3] A better material, because less prone to leakage and easier to make, would be animal intestine. Such a pipe of ox gut is attested about AD 100 by Apollodorus of Damascus as part of the fire-fighting equipment for lifting water to the top of a siege tower at least 40 feet high.[4] A cow's intestine is of the order of 40 m long[5] and can be tanned or similarly treated. Two or three could be joined together by tying the ends round short metal sleeves to make a U-tube around 100 m long. Although fragile, it could be protected from wear and tear by a leather or canvas cover. The Greek term for an inverted siphon on an aqueduct was *koilia*, 'intestine':[6] was this possibly because, as a sag-pipe with water finding its own level, a siphon was in effect the same thing as a gut U-tube for levelling?

---

[1] Smith 1990–91, 78. [2] Strabo, *Geography* XVI 2.13; Pliny, *Natural History* V 128.
[3] Agathias, *Histories* V 7.
[4] Apollodorus of Damascus, *Siegecraft* 174.2; height, 164.12.
[5] Vonk et al. 1946, 41.
[6] Vitruvius VIII 6.5. *Venter*, according to Vitruvius the Latin word for an inverted siphon, normally means 'belly', as sometimes does *koilia*; but *koilia* normally and *venter* sometimes means 'intestines'.

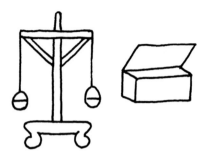

FIG. APP. 1. Control marks on denarius (after Crawford 1974,
Pl. LXVIII no. 74).

This note is banished to the appendix because there is no direct evidence
whatever that the U-tube was used in antiquity. But the principle, demonstrated by Archimedes, was well known (and was indeed applied by Hero in
his dioptra) and flexible tubing was available. This useful device should therefore not be rejected as a total impossibility.

B. THE DIOPTRA ON A COIN

In 50 BC L. Roscius Fabatus minted *denarii* with a huge variety of control
marks, one of which (Fig. App. 1) Schiöler takes to be a dioptra from its supposed similarity to the sketch of Hero's instrument in the Paris manuscript
(Fig. 3.8).[7] This seems most improbable. If the horizontal bar at the top is for
sighting, it is interrupted by the upward extension of the column; the diagonal struts have no known counterpart on the dioptra; and the plumb-lines (if
that is what Schiöler takes them to be) have nothing to register on. These
control marks come in pairs, one on the obverse and one on the reverse,
which are usually linked in subject matter, for example a spade and a rake, or
a shaduf and a well-head. The companion of the 'dioptra' is a box with the
lid open. The standard catalogue of control marks suggests that they are a
pair of scales and a box of weights,[8] which seems only marginally more plausible. I have no idea what is depicted, but I cannot see a surveying instrument
in it.

C. DODECAHEDRONS

At least 77 hollow bronze dodecahedrons, in every case with a circular hole of
different diameter in each face, are known from the north-western provinces

---

[7] Schiöler 1994, 54.   [8] Crawford 1974, pl. LXVIII no. 74 and p. 791.

of the Roman Empire. Their purpose remains unknown, but many suggestions, sometimes bizarre, have been put forward. One, most recently discussed by Thompson, is that they were for surveying.[9] Occasionally the difference in diameter between opposite holes bears a straightforward relationship to the distance between the two faces in question; in the example from Carnuntum three of these proportions are 1:10, 1:20 and 1:40. 'The Roman surveyor', it has been proposed, 'would sight through a pair of holes, holding the instrument far enough from his eye for the circles to coincide; he would then instruct his assistant, holding a rod of given length, to move far enough in the required direction for the rod to fill the visual aperture precisely. The distance between surveyor and assistant would then be the length of the rod multiplied by the figure (10, 20 or 40) appropriate to the pair of holes being used.' But there are many objections to this procedure. Most dodecahedrons do not yield such neat proportions; in not a single case is any dimension or scale inscribed against a hole; and it would be far simpler and more accurate to measure the distance directly by rope or rod. For these and other reasons Thompson rightly rejects the suggestion.

D. THE 'CROSS–STAFF'

This simple instrument remained in common use into the twentieth century, but despite its English name it had nothing in common with the medieval cross-staff or Jacob's staff. Its function, rather, was to set out right-angled offsets from a base line. A square or octagonal brass box, each side provided with a vertical slit and often with a vertical wire for more accurate sighting, was mounted on a pole (Fig. App. 2). The surveyor planted it on the base line, with which he aligned it by sighting through two opposite slits. He then looked through the two slits at right angles and directed an assistant to mark the offset with a pole.[10] What might be a Roman example was dredged from the Mosel at Koblenz a century ago.[11] It is an octagonal brass box 50 mm high excluding the socket at the bottom and the triple rings at the top, and 20 mm in diameter. Each side is 8–9 mm wide and carries a vertical slot, alternately tall (36 mm high) and short (varying from 16 to 25 mm), and all 4 mm wide. The tall slots have a square notch at the top as if to hold a vertical wire or thread. Just like the modern cross-staff, it could be mounted on a pole and the tall slots could set out right angles and the short slots angles of 45°. The function of the rings is not clear. The main difficulty with this identification is the microscopic size, which is hardly conducive to accuracy.

[9] Thompson 1970. See Hill 1994 for an update on the subject.
[10] Merrett 1893, 241.   [11] Günther 1931.

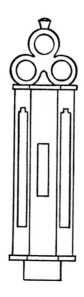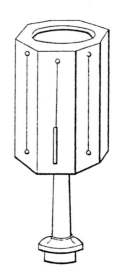

FIG. APP. 2. Roman cross-staff (?) from Koblenz and a nineteenth-century example (after Günther 1931, Abb. 1 and Merrett 1893, Pl. 36 Fig. 60).

E. SAGUI'S INSTRUMENTS

Seventy years ago Cornelio Sagui published reconstructions of fragments of what he considered to be two surveying instruments found at the Pangaeus gold mines in Macedon. One consisted of 'two metallic rods joined by a hinge and peculiarly bored' which he did not illustrate as such, but likened to an E-shaped carving on the wall of the Byzantine church of St Eleutherius (the Little Metropolis) in Athens which incorporates many stones reused from earlier monuments. He interpreted the rods and carving as what he called a surveying table (Fig. App. 3). Although he gave no explanation of how it might have worked, his drawing implies that the central arm of the E carried an alidade adjustable for altitude and the outer arms carried sights (floating?) for determining distance by parallax. With it, he thought, Dicaearchus probably measured the height of 'Peloponnesus Mount'.[12]

The other find from Pangaeus was a broken and corroded iron bar with a hole and a hook, which Sagui thought was part of an instrument for measuring vertical angles in mine surveying (Fig. App. 4, where the broken bar is the outer end of R, and both hooks were attached to the ends of cords stretched along the workings): 'Let O be the station and RR' two rods of equal length

[12] Sagui 1930, 82–3.

352

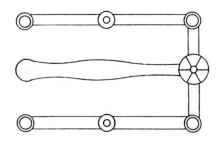

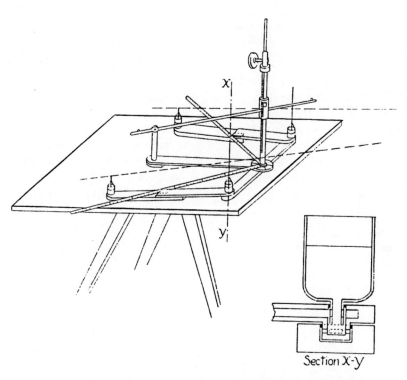

Section X-Y

FIG. APP. 3. Carving at Little Metropolis, Athens, and Sagui's surveying table (Sagui 1930, Figs. 9, 7, courtesy Economic Geology Publishing Co.).

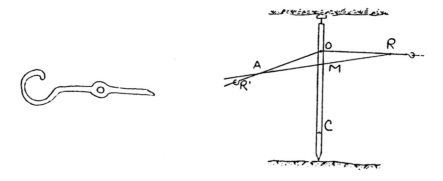

FIG. APP. 4. Sagui's mine inclinometer (Sagui 1933, Fig. 7, courtesy Economic Geology Publishing Co.).

hinged in O. An adjustable rod M would measure the chord of the angle AOR; M, being movable, could also be used in measuring the sides AC and RC.'[13] Sagui's reconstructions, possibly because they appeared in a journal rarely read by historians of technology, have stimulated no debate. It seems right to rescue them from oblivion, but to restrict comment to reporting another of his conclusions. Since, he claimed, Hesiod was approximately correct in stating that 'an anvil set free at the sky's vault [that is, he says, at the moon's orbit] would reach the earth in nine days and nine nights',[14] the Greeks had by 700 BC evidently calculated the distance of the moon and discovered the laws of gravity.[15]

[13] Sagui 1933, 38.
[14] Hesiod, *Theogony* 722–5; the Greek actually speaks of a meteorite taking nine days to fall from heaven to earth, and (what Sagui ignores) another nine days to fall to Tartarus, the nethermost pit of Hell.   [15] Sagui 1930, 84.

BIBLIOGRAPHY

Adam, J.-P. 1982. 'Groma et Chorobate, exercices de topographie antique', *Mélanges de l'école française de Rome: Antiquité* 94: 1003–29.

1994. *Roman Building* (London).

Andrieu, J.-L. and G. Cazal 1997. 'L' aqueduc gallo-romain de Caberzac près de Narbonne (Aude)' in Bedon 1997: 109–32

Arnaldi, M. and K. Schaldach 1997. 'A Roman cylinder dial: witness to a forgotten tradition', *Journal for the History of Astronomy* 29: 107–17.

Arvanitopoulos, A. 1924. 'Thessalikai Epigraphai', *Archaiologike Ephemeris*, 142–93.

Ashby, T. 1935. *The Aqueducts of Ancient Rome* (Oxford).

Aujac, G. 1966. *Strabon et la science de son temps* (Paris).

1975. *Géminos: Introduction aux Phénomènes* (Paris).

1993. *Claude Ptolémée, astronome, astrologue, géographe: connaissance et représentation du monde habité* (Paris).

Baatz, D. 1975. *Der römische Limes*, 2nd ed. (Berlin).

Beaumont, P. 1968. 'Qanats on the Varamin Plain, Iran', *Transactions of Institute of British Geographers* 45: 169–79.

Bedon, R. (ed.) 1997. *Les aqueducs de la Gaule romaine et des régions voisines*, Caesarodunum 31 (Limoges).

Behrends, O. and L. Capogrossi Colognesi (eds.) 1992. *Die römische Feldmesserkunst*, Abhandlungen der Akademie der Wissenschaften in Göttingen, phil.-hist. Klasse, 3 Folge 193 (Göttingen).

Belvedere, O. 1986. *L'Acquedotto Cornelio di Termini Imerese*, Studi e Materiali, Istituto di Archeologia, Università di Palermo, 7 (Rome).

Bessac, J.-C. 1991. 'Le chantier du creusement des galeries du vallon des Escaunes à Sernhac', in Fabre, Fiches and Paillet, 1991: 289–316.

Birebent, J. 1964. *Aquae Romanae: recherches d'hydrologie romaine dans l'Est algérien* (Algiers).

Birks, P., A. Rodger and J. S. Richardson 1984. 'Further aspects of the *Tabula Contrebiensis*', *Journal of Roman Studies* 74: 45–73.

Blackman, D. R. 1978. 'The volume of water delivered by the four great aqueducts of Rome', *Papers of the British School at Rome* 46: 52–72.

1979. 'The length of the four great aqueducts of Rome', *Papers of the British School at Rome* 47: 12–18.

Boardman, J. 1964. *The Greeks Overseas* (Harmondsworth).

Bonneau, D. 1986. 'Le Nilomètre: aspect technique', in P. Louis (ed.), *L'Homme et l'Eau en Méditerranée et au proche Orient* III (Lyon), 65–73.

Borchardt, L. 1899. 'Ein altägyptisches astronomisches Instrument', *Zeitschrift für ägyptische Sprache und Altertumskunde* 37: 10–17.

1906. *Nilmesser und Nilstandsmarken* (Berlin).

Bouma, J. 1993. *Marcus Junius Nipsus – Fluminis Varatio, Limitis Repositio*, Studien zur klassischen Philologie 77 (Frankfurt am Main).

Bourdon, C. 1925. *Anciens canaux, anciens sites et ports de Suez*, Mémoires de la Société royale de Géographie d'Egypte 7 (Cairo).

Bradford, J. 1957. *Ancient Landscapes* (London).

Bubnov, N. 1899. *Gerberti Opera Mathematica* (Berlin).

Burdy, J. 1991. 'Some directions of future research for the aqueducts of Lugdunum (Lyon)', in Hodge 1991: 29–44.

Burns, A. 1971. 'The tunnel of Eupalinus and the tunnel problem of Hero of Alexandria', *Isis* 62: 172–85.

1974. 'Ancient Greek water supply and city planning: a study of Syracuse and Acragas', *Technology and Culture* 15: 389–412.

Butzer, K. W. 1976. *Early Hydraulic Civilization in Egypt: a Study in Cultural Ecology* (Chicago and London).

Cahen, C. 1951. 'Le service de l'irrigation en Iraq au début du XIᵉ siècle', *Bulletin d'Etudes Orientales* 13: 117–43.

Cajori, F. 1929. 'History of the determinations of the height of mountains', *Isis* 12: 483–514.

Callebat, L. (ed.) 1973. *Vitruve, de l'architecture, Livre* VIII (Paris).

1974. 'Le vocabulaire de l'hydraulique dans le Livre VIII du *de architectura* de Vitruve', *Revue de Philologie* 48: 313–29.

Campbell, B. 1996. 'Shaping the rural environment: surveyors in ancient Rome', *Journal of Roman Studies* 86: 74–99.

Capelle, W. 1916. *Berges- und Wolkenhöhen bei griechischen Physikern*, Stoicheia 5 (Leipzig–Berlin).

Carpenter, R. 1970. *The Architects of the Parthenon* (Harmondsworth).

Castellani, V. and W. Dragoni 1991. 'Italian tunnels in antiquity', *Tunnels and Tunnelling*, 23 no. 3 (March): 55–7.

Caton-Thompson, G. and E. W. Gardner 1929. 'Recent work on the problem of Lake Moeris', *Geographical Journal* 73: 20–60.

Çeçen, K. 1996. *The Longest Roman Water Supply Line* (Istanbul).

Chevallier, R. 1974. 'Cité et territoire. Solutions romaines aux problèmes de l'organisation de l'espace', *Aufstieg und Niedergang der römischen Welt*, Teil 2, 1 (Berlin), 649–788.

Cichorius, C. 1922. *Römische Studien* (Berlin–Leipzig).

Clancy, J. 1991. *Site Surveying and Levelling* (London).

Collinder, P. 1956. 'On the oldest earth-measurements', *Actes du VIIIe Congrès International d'Histoire des Sciences*, 456–62.

——— 1964. 'Dicaearchus and the "Lysimachian" Measurement of the Earth', *Ithaca I, Actes du 10e Congrès International d'Histoire des Sciences*, 475–7.

Coulton, J. J. 1975. 'Towards understanding Greek temple design: general considerations', *Annual of British School at Athens* 70: 59–99.

——— 1982. *Greek Architects at Work* (London).

——— 1987. 'Roman aqueducts in Asia Minor', in S. Macready and F. H. Thompson (eds.), *Roman Architecture in the Greek World*, Society of Antiquaries Occasional Papers n.s. 10 (London), 72–84.

Crawford, M. H. 1974. *Roman Republican Coinage* (Cambridge).

Dain, A. 1933. *La tradition du texte d'Héron de Byzance* (Paris).

Dalton, O. M. 1926. 'The Byzantine astrolabe at Brescia', *Proceedings of British Academy* 12: 133–46.

Daremberg, C. and E. Saglio, *Dictionnaire des antiquités grecques et romaines d'après les textes et les monuments* (Paris, 1877–1919).

Davies, H. E. H. 1998. 'Designing Roman roads', *Britannia* 29: 1–16.

Davies, O. 1935. *Roman mines in Europe* (Oxford).

Delatte, A. 1939. *Anecdota Atheniensia et alia*, 2 (Paris).

Della Corte, M. 1922. 'Groma', *Monumenti Antichi* 28: 5–100.

Dicks, D. R. 1954. 'Ancient astronomical instruments', *Journal of British Astronomical Association* 64: 77–85.

——— 1960. *The Geographical Fragments of Hipparchus* (London).

——— 1966. 'Solstices, equinoxes and the Presocratics', *Journal of Hellenic Studies* 86: 26–40.

——— 1970. *Early Greek Astronomy to Aristotle* (London).

Dilke, O. A. W. 1971. *The Roman Land Surveyors* (Newton Abbot).

——— 1974. 'Archaeological and epigraphical evidence of Roman land surveys', *Aufstieg und Niedergang der römischen Welt*, Teil 2, 1 (Berlin), 564–92.

——— 1985. *Greek and Roman Maps* (London).

——— 1987a. *Mathematics and Measurement* (London).

——— 1987b. 'Roman large-scale mapping in the Early Empire', in Harley and Woodward 1987: 212–33.

——— 1992. 'Insights in the Corpus Agrimensorum into surveying methods and mapping', in Behrends and Capogrossi Colognesi 1992: 337–47.

Dirimtekin, F. 1959. 'Adduction de l'eau à Byzance dans la région dite "Bulgarie"', *Cahiers Archéologiques* 10: 217–43.

Dodgeon, M. H. and S. N. C. Lieu 1991. *The Roman Eastern Frontier and the Persian Wars (AD 226–363)* (London).

Dölger, F. 1927. *Beiträge zur Geschichte der byzantinischen Finanzverwaltung, besonders des 10. und 11. Jahrhunderts*, Byzantinisches Archiv 9 (Leipzig– Berlin).

Domergue, C. 1990. *Les mines de la péninsule ibérique dans l'antiquité romaine*, Collection de l'Ecole Française de Rome 127 (Paris).

Donaldson, G. H. 1988. 'Signalling communications and the Roman imperial army', *Britannia* 19: 349–56.

Downey, G. 1951. 'The water supply of Antioch on the Orontes in antiquity', *Annales Archéologiques de Syrie* 1: 171–87.

Drabkin, I. E. 1943. 'Posidonius and the circumference of the earth', *Isis* 34: 509–12.

Drachmann, A. G. 1935. 'Dioptra', *RE* Supp. 6: 1287–90.

— 1948. *Ktesibios, Philon and Heron, a Study in Ancient Pneumatics*, Acta Historica Scientarum Naturalium et Medicinalium 4 (Copenhagen).

— 1954. 'The plane astrolabe and the anaphoric clock', *Centaurus* 3: 183–9.

— 1957. 'Hero's dioptra and levelling-instrument', in C. Singer et al. (eds.), *A History of Technology* III (Oxford), 609–12.

— 1963. *The Mechanical Technology of Greek and Roman Antiquity* (Copenhagen).

— 1968. 'A physical experiment in Heron's dioptra?' *Centaurus* 13: 220–7.

— 1969. 'A detail of Heron's dioptra,' *Centaurus* 13: 241–7.

DSB: C. C. Gillespie (ed.), *Dictionary of Scientific Biography* (New York, 1970–80).

Duffaud, —. 1854. 'Notices sur les aqueducs romaines de Poitiers', *Mémoires de la Société des Antiquaires de l'Ouest*, 55–83.

Edwards, I. E. S. 1985. *The Pyramids of Egypt* (Harmondsworth).

Eisler, R. 1949. 'The polar sighting-tube', *Archives internationales d'histoire des sciences* 2: 312–32.

Eitrem, S. 1933. 'Fragment of astronomy on an Oslo papyrus', *Aegyptus* 13: 479–86.

Evans, H. B. 1994. *Water Distribution in Ancient Rome* (Ann Arbor).

Evenari, M., L. Shanan and N. Tadmor 1982. *The Negev: the Challenge of a Desert*, 2nd ed. (Cambridge, Mass.).

Fabre, G., J.-L. Fiches and J.-L. Paillet 1991. *L'Aqueduc de Nîmes et le Pont du Gard: Archéologie, Géosystème et Histoire* (Nîmes).

— 1997. 'L'aqueduc antique de Nîmes et le drainage de l'étang de Clausonne: hypothèses sur le financement de l'ouvrage et sur l'identité de son concepteur', in Bedon 1997: 193–219

Fabre, G., J.-L. Fiches, P. Leveau and J.-L. Paillet 1992. *The Pont du Gard: Water and the Roman Town* (Paris).

Fabricius, E., F. Hettner and O. von Sarwey (eds.) 1933. *Der Obergermanisch-*

Raetische Limes der Römerreiches, Abt. A. Bd IV, *Die Strecken* 7–9 (Berlin–Leipzig).

Fatás, G. 1980. *Contrebia Belaisca II: Tabula Contrebiensis* (Zaragoza).

Field, J. V. 1990. 'Some Roman and Byzantine portable sundials and the London sundial-calendar', *History of Technology* 12: 103–35.

Fischer, I. 1975. 'Another look at Eratosthenes' and Posidonius' determinations of the earth's circumference', *Quarterly Journal Royal Astronomical Soc.* 16: 152–60.

Folkerts, M. 1992. 'Mathematische Probleme im Corpus agrimensorum', in Behrends and Capogrossi Colognesi 1992: 310–36.

Forbes, R. J. 1955. *Studies in Ancient Technology* I (Leiden).

Frankel, R. 1985. 'The Hellenistic aqueduct of Acre-Ptolemais', *'Atiqot*, English series 17: 134–8.

Fraser, P. 1972. *Ptolemaic Alexandria* (Oxford).

Froriep, S. 1986. 'Ein Wasserweg in Bithynien', *Antike Welt* 17, 2. Sondernummer: 39–50.

Gandz, S. 1933. 'Der Hultsch-Cantorsche Beweis von der Reihefolge der Buchstaben in dem mathematischen Figuren der Griecher und Araber', *Quellen und Studien zur Geschichte der Mathematik, Astronomie und Physik*, Abt. B: Studien, 2: 81–97.

Garbrecht, G. 1978. 'Die Madradag-Wasserleitung von Pergamon', *Antike Welt* 4: 40–9.

1987. 'Die Wasserversorgung des antiken Pergamon,' in *Die Wasserversorgung antiker Städte*, II (Mainz), 11–47.

Garbrecht, G. and J. Peleg 1989. 'Die Wasserversorgung geschichtlicher Wüstenfestungen am Jordantal', *Antike Welt* 20.2: 3–20.

Gerster, B. 1884. 'L'Isthme de Corinthe: tentatives de percement dans l'antiquité', *Bulletin de Correspondance Hellénique* 8: 115–32.

Gibbs, S. L. 1976. *Greek and Roman Sun-dials* (New Haven and London).

Giorgetti, D. 1988. 'Bologna', in *Die Wasserversorgung antiker Städte*, III (Mainz), 180–5.

Glanville, S. R. K. (ed.) 1942. *The Legacy of Egypt* (Oxford).

Goblot, H. 1979. *Les qanats: une technique d'acquisition de l'eau* (Paris).

Goodfield, J. and S. Toulmin 1965. 'How was the tunnel of Eupalinus aligned?', *Isis* 56: 46–55.

Goodyear, F. R. D. 1981. *The Annals of Tacitus, Books 1–6*, vol. II (Cambridge).

Gough, J. W. 1964. *Sir Hugh Myddelton* (Oxford).

Gounaris, G. 1980. 'Anneau astronomique solaire portative antique, découvert à Philippes', *Annali dell' Istituto e Museo di Storia della Scienza di Firenze* 5(2): 3–18.

Gräber, F. 1913. 'Die Wasserleitungen', in *Altertümer von Pergamon* Bd 1 Teil 3: *Stadt und Landschaft* (Berlin).

Grenier, A. 1960. *Manuel d'Archéologie Gallo-romaine*, 4.1 (Paris).

Grewe, K. 1986. *Atlas der römischen Wasserleitungen nach Köln* (Köln).

1998. *Licht am Ende des Tunnels: Planung und Trassierung im antiken Tunnelbau* (Mainz).

Günther, A. 1931. 'Römisches Landmesserinstrument bei Koblenz', *Germania* 15: 271–2.

Hadfield, C. 1986. *World Canals* (Newton Abbot).

Hadot, I. (ed.) 1987. *Simplicius: Sa vie, son œuvre, sa survie* (Berlin).

Hamey, L. A. and J. A. 1981. *The Roman Engineers* (Cambridge).

Hammer, J. von 1838.'Extracts from the Mohit, that is the Ocean, a Turkish work on navigation in the Indian Seas', *Journal of the Asiatic Society of Bengal* 7: 767–80.

Hargreaves, G. H. 1990. 'Road planning operations of Roman surveyors', BA dissertation, Institute of Archaeology, University College London.

1996. 'Roman surveying on continuous linear features', PhD thesis, London.

Harley, J. B. and D. Woodward (eds.) 1987. *History of Cartography*, 1: *Cartography in Prehistoric, Ancient, and Medieval Europe and the Mediterranean* (Chicago).

Hartner, W. 1960. 'Asturlab', *Encyclopaedia of Islam*, new ed. 1 (Leiden and London), 722–8.

Hauck, G. 1988. *The Aqueduct of Nemausus* (Jefferson).

Heath, T. 1913. *Aristarchus of Samos* (Oxford).

1921. *A History of Greek Mathematics* (Oxford).

Heiberg, J. L. 1912. *Heronis Alexandrini Opera quae supersunt omnia*, IV (Leipzig).

1914. *Heronis Alexandrini Opera quae supersunt omnia*, V (Leipzig).

1919. 'Karpos 3', *RE* II: 2008–9.

Hill, C. 1994. 'Gallo-Roman dodecahedra: a progress report', *Antiquaries Journal* 74: 289–92.

Hill, D. R. 1979. *The Book of Ingenious Devices (Kitab al-Hiyal) by the Banu (sons of) Musa bin Shakir* (Dordrecht).

Hill, D. 1984. *A History of Engineering in Classical and Medieval Times* (London).

Hill, D. R. 1993. *Islamic Science and Technology* (Edinburgh).

Hinrichs, F. T. 1974. *Die Geschichte der gromatischen Institutionen* (Wiesbaden).

Hinz, W. 1955. *Islamische Masse und Gewichte*, Handbuch der Orientalistik, Ergänzungsband 1 Heft 1 (Leiden).

1965. 'Dhira'', *Encyclopaedia of Islam* 2 (Leiden and London), 231–2.

Hodge, A. T. (ed.) 1991. *Future Currents in Aqueduct Studies* (Leeds).

1992. *Roman Aqueducts and Water Supply* (London).

Hultsch, F. 1866. *Metrologicorum Scriptorum Reliquiae* II (Leipzig)

1882. *Griechische und Römische Metrologie*, 2nd ed. (Berlin).

1899. 'Winkelmessungen durch die Hipparchische Dioptra', *Abhandlungen zur Geschichte der Mathematik* 9: 193–209.

Irving, C. 1979. *Crossroads of Civilization* (London).

Isager, S. and J. E. Skydsgaard 1992. *Ancient Greek Agriculture, an Introduction* (London).

Jacobsen, T. and S. Lloyd 1935. *Sennacherib's Aqueduct at Jerwan*, University of Chicago Oriental Institute Publications 24 (Chicago).

Johnston, D. E. 1979. *Roman Roads in Britain* (Bourne End).

Jones, A. 1991. 'The adaptation of Babylonian methods in Greek numerical astronomy', *Isis* 82: 441–53.

Jones, L. 1927. Discussion of Lyons 1927, q.v.

Judson, S. and A. Kahane 1963. 'Underground drainageways in Southern Etruria and Northern Latium', *Papers of the British School at Rome* 31: 74–99.

Kalcyk, H. and B. Heinrich 1986. 'Hochwasserschutzbauten in Arkadia', *Antike Welt* 17, 2 Sondernummer: 2–14.

Kambanis, M. L. 1893. 'Le dessèchement du Lac Copaïs par les anciens', *Bulletin de Correspondance Hellénique* 17: 322–42.

Kidd, I. G. 1988. *Posidonius*, II: *The Commentary* (Cambridge).

Kiely, E. R. 1947. *Surveying Instruments* (New York).

Kienast, H. J. 1987. 'Samos', in *Die Wasserversorgung antiker Städte*, II (Mainz), 214–17.

1995. *Die Wasserleitung des Eupalinos auf Samos*, Samos Band 19 (Bonn).

King, H. C. 1955. *The History of the Telescope* (London).

Kirk, G. S., J. E. Raven and M. Schofield 1983. *The Presocratic Philosophers*, 2nd ed. (Cambridge).

Koldewey, R. 1890. *Die antiken Baureste der Insel Lesbos* (Berlin).

KP: K. Ziegler and W. Sontheimer (eds.), *Der Kleine Pauly Lexicon der Antike* (Munich 1964–).

Krenkow, F. 1947–9. 'The construction of subterranean water supplies during the Abbaside Caliphate', *Transactions Glasgow University Oriental Society* 13: 23–32.

Kurz, M. 1923. *Le Mont Olympe* (Paris).

Laporte, J.-P. 1997. 'Notes sur l'aqueduc de *Saldae* (= Bougie, Algérie)', in Bedon 1997: 747–79

Lauffray, J. 1977. 'Beyrouth Archéologie et Histoire, époques gréco-romaines I. Période hellénistique et Haut-Empire romain,' *Aufstieg und Niedergang der römischen Welt*, Teil 2, 8 (Berlin), 135–63.

Le Bohec, Y. 1986. 'Les "Discentes" de la IIIème Légion Auguste,' in A. Mastino (ed.), *L'Africa romana*, Atti del IV convegno di studio (Sassari), 235–52.

1987. 'Le mystère des libritores de Tacite (Ann. II, 20 et XIII, 39)', *Kentron* 3: 21–9.

Lehmann-Haupt, F. 1929. 'Stadion', *RE* 2 Reihe, III: 1930–63.

Lehner, M. 1983. 'Some observations on the layout of the Khufu and Khafre Pyramids', *Journal of American Research Center in Egypt* 20: 7–25.

Lemerle, P. 1986. *Byzantine Humanism* (Canberra).

Lendle, O. 1975. *Schildkröten: antike Kriegsmaschinen in poliorketischen Texte*, Palingenesia 10 (Wiesbaden).

1983. *Texte und Untersuchungen zum technischen Bereich der antiker Poliorketiker*, Palingenesia 19 (Wiesbaden).

Leveau, P. 1991. 'Research on Roman aqueducts in the past ten years', in Hodge 1991: 149–62.

Levy, R. (trans.) 1990. *The Epic of the Kings* (London).

Lewis, M. J. T. 1984. 'Our debt to Roman engineering: the water supply of Lincoln to the present day', *Industrial Archaeology Review* 7: 57–73.

1992. 'The south-pointing chariot in Rome', *History of Technology* 14: 77–99.

1997. *Millstone and Hammer: the Origins of Water Power* (Hull).

1999a. 'When was Biton?', *Mnemosyne* 52: 159–68.

1999b. 'Vitruvius and Greek aqueducts', *Papers of the British School at Rome* 67: 145–72.

2000. 'Theoretical hydraulics, automata, and water clocks', in Ö. Wikander (ed.), *Handbook of Ancient Water Technology* (Leiden), 343–69.

Lewis, N. 1986. *Greeks in Ptolemaic Egypt* (Oxford).

Lindner, M. 1987. 'Nabatäische Talsperren', in G. Garbrecht (ed.), *Historische Talsperren* (Stuttgart), 147–74.

LSJ: H. G. Liddell, R. Scott and H. S. Jones, *A Greek–English Lexicon*, 9th ed. (Oxford, 1990) and revised supplement (1996).

Lyons, H. 1927. 'Ancient surveying instruments', *Geographical Journal* 69: 132–43.

Mango, C.-A. 1949. 'L'Euripe de l'Hippodrome de Constantinople', *Revue des Etudes Byzantines* 7: 180–93.

Margary, I. D. 1965. *Roman Ways in the Weald* (London).

1973. *Roman Roads in Britain*, 3rd ed. (London).

Marlowe, J. 1964. *The Making of the Suez Canal* (London).

Marsden, E. W. 1969. *Greek and Roman Artillery: Historical Development* (Oxford).

1971. *Greek and Roman Artillery: Technical Treatises* (Oxford).

Martin, R. E. 1965. *Manuel d'architecture grecque, I. Matériaux et techniques* (Paris).

Maula, E. 1975–6. 'The spider in the sphere. Eudoxus' *Arachne*', *Philosophia* 5–6: 225–57.

Mazaheri, A. 1965. 'Le traité de l'exploitation des eaux souterraines de Al-Karagi', *Archives internationales d'histoire des sciences* 18: 300–1.

Merrett, H. S. 1893. *A Practical Treatise on the Science of Land & Engineering Surveying, Levelling, Estimating Quantities, &c, with a Description of the Various Instruments Required, &c* (London and New York).

Michon, E. 1899. 'Libra', in Daremberg and Saglio, III: 1222–31.

Millard, A. R. 1987. 'Cartography in the ancient Near East', in Harley and Woodward 1987: 107–116.

Mitchell, B. M. 1975. 'Herodotus and Samos', *Journal of Hellenic Studies* 95: 75–91.

Mitchell, S. 1995. *Cremna in Pisidia: an Ancient City in Peace and in War* (London).

Montagu, C. F. 1909. 'Survey of the boundary stelae of Tel-el-Amarna', *Cairo Scientific Journal* 3: 80–1.

Montauzan, C. G. de 1909. *Les aqueducs antiques de Lyon* (Paris).

Moraux, P. 1984. *Der Aristotelismus bei den Griechen*, II (Berlin).

Müller, K. K. 1883. 'Handschriftliches zu den Poliorketika und der Geodäsie des sogenannten Hero', *Rheinisches Museum für Philologie* NF 38: 454–63.

Nasr, S. H. 1976. *Islamic Science* (London).

Needham, J. 1959. *Science and Civilisation in China*, III: *Mathematics and the Sciences of the Heavens and the Earth* (Cambridge).

1965. *Science and Civilisation in China*, IV: *Physics and Physical Technology*, part 2: *Mechanical Engineering* (Cambridge).

1971. *Science and Civilisation in China*, IV: *Physics and Physical Technology*, part 3: *Civil Engineering and Nautics* (Cambridge).

Neugebauer, O. 1938–9. *Über eine Methode zur Distanzbestimmung Alexandria-Rom bei Heron*, Kgl. Danske Videnskabernes Selskab, historisk-filologiske Medelesler 26.2 and 26.7 (Copenhagen).

1949. 'The early history of the astrolabe', *Isis* 40: 240–56.

1955. *Astronomical Cuneiform Texts* (London).

1969. *The Exact Sciences in Antiquity* (New York).

1975. *A History of Ancient Mathematical Astronomy* (Berlin etc.).

Noble, J. V. and D. J. de Solla Price 1968. 'The water clock in the Tower of the Winds', *American Journal of Archaeology* 72: 345–55.

Nowotny, E. 1923. 'Groma', *Germania* 7: 22–9.

Oberhümmer, E. 1939. 'Olympos IA', *RE* XXXV: 259–72.

OCD: S. Hornblower and A. Spawforth (eds.), *Oxford Classical Dictionary*, 3rd ed. (Oxford 1996).

Oertel, F. 1964. 'Das Problem des antiken Suezkanals', in K. Repgen and S. Skalweit, *Spiegel der Geschichte. Festgabe für Max Braubach* (Münster), 18–51.

Ogilby, J. 1675. *Britannia* (London).

Olami, Y. and Y. Peleg 1977. 'The water supply system of Caesarea Maritima', *Israel Exploration Journal* 27: 127–37.

Oleson, J. P. 1984. *Greek and Roman Mechanical Water-Lifting Devices: the History of a Technology*, Phoenix supp. vol. 16 (Toronto).

—— 1991. 'Aqueducts, cisterns, and the strategy of water supply at Nabataean and Roman Auara (Jordan)', in Hodge 1991: 45–62.

—— 2000. 'Irrigation', in Ö. Wikander (ed.), *Handbook of Ancient Water Technology* (Leiden), 183–215.

Owens, E. J. 1991. *The City in the Greek and Roman World* (London).

Pannekoek, A. 1961. *A History of Astronomy* (London).

Paret, O. 1933. 'Die Absteckung der geraden Limesstrecke Walldürn-Haghof', *Germania* 17: 263–6.

Parke, H. W. 1944. 'A note on the topography of Syracuse', *Journal of Hellenic Studies* 64: 100–2.

Pattenden, P. 1983. 'The Byzantine early warning system', *Byzantion* 53: 258–99.

Pederson, O. 1986. 'Some astronomical topics in Pliny', in R. French and F. Greenaway (eds.), *Science in the Early Roman Empire: Pliny the Elder, his Sources and Influence* (London), 162–96.

Penrose, F. C. 1888. *An Investigation of the Principles of Athenian Architecture*, 2nd ed. (London).

Piganiol, A. 1962. *Les documents cadastraux de la colonie romaine d'Orange, Gallia* Supplément 10 (Paris).

Pingree, D. 1963. 'Astronomy and astrology in India and Iran', *Isis* 54: 229–46.

Posener, G. 1938. 'Le Canal du Nil à la Mer Rouge avant les Ptolémées', *Chronique d'Egypte* 13: 258–73.

Powell, M. A. 1987–90. 'Masse und Gewichte', in D. O. Edzard (ed.), *Reallexicon der Assyriologie* VII (Berlin–New York), 457–517.

Prager, F. 1974. *Philo of Byzantium: Pneumatica* (Wiesbaden).

Price, D. J. 1957. 'Precision instruments: to 1500', in C. Singer et al. (eds.), *A History of Technology* III (Oxford), 582–619.

Price, D. J. de Solla 1969. 'Portable sundials in antiquity, including an account of a new example from Aphrodisias', *Centaurus* 14: 242–66.

Price, D. de Solla 1974. 'Gears from the Greeks', *Trans. American Philosophical Soc.* NS 64 part 7 (Philadelphia).

Prinsep, J. 1836. 'Note on the nautical instruments of the Arabs', *Journal of the Asiatic Society of Bengal* 5: 784–94.

Provost, A. and B. Lepretre 1997. 'L'aqueduc gallo-romain de Carhaix (Finistère). Rapide synthèse des recherches en cours', in Bedon 1997: 525–46

Putnam, W. 1997. 'The Dorchester Roman aqueduct', Current Archaeology 154: 364–9

Rashed, R. 1973. 'Al-Karaji', in DSB VII: 240–6.

RE: A. Pauly, G. Wissowa and W. Kroll (eds.), Real-Encyclopädie der klassischen Altertumswissenschaft (Stuttgart, 1893–).

Rivet, A. L. F. 1982. 'Viae aviariae?', Antiquity 56: 206–7.

Rivet, A. L. F. and C. Smith 1979. The Place-Names of Roman Britain (London).

Rodriguez Almeida, E. 1980. Forma Urbis Marmorea, Aggiornamento generale (Rome).

    1988. 'Un frammento di una pianta marmorea di Roma', Journal of Roman Archaeology 1: 120–31.

Rodwell, W. 1975. 'Milestones, civic territories and the Antonine Itinerary', Britannia 6: 76–101.

Rosenthal, F. 1992. The Classical Heritage in Islam (London).

Rossi, G. B. de 1857–61. Inscriptiones Christianae Urbis Romae I (Rome).

Rouanet, G. 1974. 'Etude de quatre pompes à eau romaines,' Cahiers d'Archéologie Subaquatique 3: 49–79.

Sackur, W. 1925. Vitruv und die Poliorketiker (Berlin).

Sáez Fernández, P. 1990. 'Estudio sobre una inscripcion catastral colindante con Lacimurga', Habis 21: 205–27.

Saglio, E. 1899. 'Libella', in Daremberg and Saglio, III: 1174.

Sagui, C. L. 1930. 'Economic geology and allied sciences in ancient times', Economic Geology 25: 65–86.

    1933. 'Economic geology and its allied sciences in ancient times', Economic Geology 28: 20–40.

Salmon, J. B. 1984. Wealthy Corinth, a History of the City to 338 BC (Oxford)

Sambursky, S. 1987. The Physical World of Late Antiquity (London).

Saprykin, S. J. 1994. Ancient Farms and Land-plots on the Khora of Khersonesos Taurike (Research in the Herakleian Peninsula 1974–1990), McGill University Monographs in Classical Archaeology and History 16 (Amsterdam).

Scarborough, J. 1969. Roman Medicine (London).

Schilbach, E. 1970a. Byzantinische Metrologische Quellen (Düsseldorf).

    1970b. Byzantinische Metrologie, Byzantinisches Handbuch 4 (Munich).

Schiöler, T. 1994. 'The Pompeii-groma in new light', Analecta Romana 22: 45–60.

Schönberger, H. 1969. 'The Roman Frontier in Germany: an archaeological survey', Journal of Roman Studies 59: 144–97.

Schöne, H. 1899. 'Die Dioptra des Heron', *Jahrbuch des deutschen archäologischen Instituts* 14: 91–103.

1901. 'Das Visirinstrument der römischen Feldmesser', *Jahrbuch des deutschen archäologischen Instituts* 16: 127–32.

Schulten, A. 1912. 'Groma', *RE* VII.2: 1881–6.

Segonds, A. P. 1981. *Jean Philopon, Traité de l'astrolabe*, Astrolabica 2 (Paris).

Sharples, R. W. 1987. 'Alexander of Aphrodisias: scholasticism and innovation', *Aufstieg und Niedergang der römischen Welt*, Teil 2, 36.2 (Berlin), 1176–1243.

Shaw, B. 1984. 'Water and society in the ancient Maghrib: technology, property and development', *Antiquités Africaines* 20: 121–73.

Shelton, J. 1981. 'Mathematical problems on a papyrus from the Gent collection', *Zeitschrift für Papyrologie und Epigraphik* 42: 91–4.

Sherk, R. K. 1974. 'Roman geographical exploration and military maps', *Aufstieg und Niedergang der römischen Welt*, Teil 2, 1 (Berlin), 534–61.

Sherwin-White, A. N. 1966. *The Letters of Pliny: a Historical and Social Commentary* (Oxford).

Sleeswyk, A. W. 1979. 'Vitruvius' waywiser', *Archives internationales d'histoire de science* 29: 11–22.

1981. 'Vitruvius' odometer', *Scientific American* 245: 158–71.

1990. 'Archimedes' odometer and water clock', in Finnish Institute at Athens, *Ancient Technology*, Tekniikan museon julkaisuja 5 (Helsinki), 23–37.

Smiles, S. 1862. *Lives of the Engineers*, III (London).

Smith, N. 1971. *A History of Dams* (London).

Smith, N. A. F. 1990–91. 'The Pont du Gard and the Aqueduct of Nîmes', *Transactions of Newcomen Society* 62: 53–80.

1991. 'Problems of design and analysis', in Hodge 1991: 113–28.

1998–99. 'Edward Wright and his perspective glass: a surveying puzzle of the early 17th century', *Transactions of Newcomen Society* 70: 109–22.

Sorabji, R. (ed.) 1987. *Philoponus and the Rejection of Aristotelian Science* (Ithaca).

Southern, P. 1990. 'Signals versus illumination on Roman frontiers', *Britannia* 21: 233–42.

Sperber, D. 1986. *Nautica Talmudica* (Ramat-Gan).

Steinschneider, M. 1896. 'Die arabischen Übersetzungen aus dem Griechischen, zweiter Abschnitt: Mathematik', *Zeitschrift der deutschen morgenländischen Gesellschaft* 50: 161–219 and 337–417.

Stenton, E. C. and J. J. Coulton 1986. 'Oenoanda: the water supply and aqueduct', *Anatolian Studies* 36: 15–59.

Stillwell, R. 1938. *Antioch-on-the-Orontes: II, The Excavations 1933–36* (Princeton).

Stone, E. N. 1928. 'Roman surveying instruments', *University of Washington Publications in Language and Literature* 4.4 (Seattle), 215–42.

Struik, D. J. 1972. 'Gerbert', in *DSB* v, 364–6.

Taisbak, C. M. 1973–4. 'Posidonius vindicated at all costs? Modern scholarship versus the Stoic earth measurer', *Centaurus* 18: 253–69.

Tannery, P. 1887. *La géométrie grecque* (Paris).

1893. *Recherches sur l'histoire de l'astronomie ancienne* (Paris).

Taylor, C. 1979. *Roads and Tracks of Britain* (London).

Taylor, E. G. R. 1956. *The Haven-finding Art: a History of Navigation from Odysseus to Captain Cook* (London).

Théry, G. 1926. *Alexandre d'Aphrodise: aperçu sur l'influence de sa noétique*, Bibliothèque Thomiste 7 (Le Saulchoir).

Thomasson, B. E. 1960. *Die Statthalter der römischen Provinzen Nordafrikas von Augustus bis Diocletianus*, Skrifta utgivna av Svenska Institutet i Rom IX 2 (Lund).

Thompson, F. H. 1954. 'The Roman aqueduct at Lincoln', *Archaeological Journal* 111: 106–28.

1970. 'Dodecahedrons again', *Antiquaries Journal* 50: 93–6.

Tittel, K. 1913. 'Heron von Alexandreia', *RE* VIII: 992–1080.

TLL: Thesaurus Linguae Latinae (Berlin, 1900–).

Tölle-Kastenbein, R. 1994. *Das archaische Wasserleitungsnetz für Athen* (Mainz).

Toomer, G. J. 1973. 'The Chord Table of Hipparchus and the early history of Greek trigonometry', *Centaurus* 18: 6–28.

1975. 'Ptolemy', in *DSB* XI: 186–206.

1978. 'Hipparchus', in *DSB* XV: 207–25.

1996. 'Astronomical instruments' and 'Astronomy', in *OCD* 195–8.

Ulrix, F. 1963. 'Recherches sur la méthode de traçage des routes romaines', *Latomus* 22: 153–80.

Van der Waerden, B. L. 1954. *Science Awakening* (Groningen).

Van Hee, P. L. 1933. 'Le classique de l'île maritime, ouvrage chinois du IIIᵉ siècle', *Quellen und Studien zur Geschichte der Mathematik Astronomie und Physik*, Abt. B, 2: 255–80.

Venturi 1814: see Hero, *Dioptra* in author index.

Vernat, J. 1978. 'Al-Karadji', *Encyclopaedia of Islam*, 2nd ed., 4 (Leiden), 600.

Viedebantt, O. 1917. *Forschungen zur Metrologie des Altertums*, Abhandlungen der phil.-hist. Klasse der königl. Sächsischen Gesellschaft der Wissenschaften, Bd 34 No. 3 (Leipzig).

Vieillefond 1932, 1970: see Julius Africanus in author index.

Vincent 1858: see Hero, *Dioptra* and Anonymus Byzantinus in author index.

Vita-Finzi, C. 1961. 'Roman dams in Tripolitania', *Antiquity* 35: 14–20.

Vonk, H. J. et al. (eds.) 1946. *Digestion*, Tabulae Biologicae vol. 21 pars 1 (Amsterdam).

Wacher, J. 1974. *The Towns of Roman Britain* (London).

Walbank, F. W. 1957–79. *A Historical Commentary on Polybius* (Oxford).

Ward-Perkins, J. B. 1962. 'Etruscan engineering: road-building, water-supply and drainage', *Collection Latomus* 58: 1636–43.

Ward-Perkins, J. B. 1974. *Cities of Ancient Greece and Italy: Planning in Classical Antiquity* (London).

Wartnaby, J. 1968. *Surveying Instruments and Methods* (London).

Weber, G. 1898. 'Die Hochdruck-Wasserleitung von Laodicea ad Lycum', *Jahrbuch des deutschen archäologischen Instituts* 13: 1–13.

— 1899. 'Die Wasserleitungen von Smyrna', *Jahrbuch des deutschen archäologischen Instituts* 14: 4–25 and 167–88.

— 1904. 'Wasserleitungen in Kleinasiatischen Städten', *Jahrbuch des deutschen archäologischen Instituts* 19: 86–101.

Wehrli, F. 1944. *Die Schule des Aristoteles, Texte und Kommentar*, 1: *Dikaiarchos* (Basel).

Weidner, E. F. 1915. *Handbuch der babylonischen Astronomie*, 1 (Leipzig).

White, K. D. 1984. *Greek and Roman Technology* (London).

Wiedemann, E. 1970. *Aufsätze zür arabischen Wissenschaftsgeschichte* (Hildesheim).

— 1993. 'Al-Mizan', in *Encyclopaedia of Islam*, new ed., 7 (Leiden and New York), 195–204.

Wiedemann, E. and F. Hauser 1918. 'Übervorrichtungen zum Heben von Wasser in der islamischen Welt', *Beiträge zür Geschichte der Technik und Industrie* 8: 121–54.

Williamson, J. 1915. *Surveying & Field Work: a Practical Text-book on Surveying Levelling & Setting Out* (London).

Wilson, R. J. A. 1990. *Sicily under the Roman Empire: the Archaeology of a Roman Province 36 BC – AD 535* (Warminster).

— 1996. '*Tot aquarum tam multis necessariis molibus* . . . Recent studies on aqueducts and water supply', *Journal of Roman Archaeology* 9: 5–29.

Wiseman, T. P. 1970. 'Roman Republican road-building', *Papers of the British School at Rome* 38: 123–52.

Woolley, C. L. 1925. 'The excavations at Ur, 1924–1925', *Antiquaries Journal* 5: 347–402.

Wright, R. R. 1934. *Al-Biruni, The Book of Instruction in the Elements of the Art of Astrology* (London).

Würschmidt, J. 1912. 'Geodätische Messinstrumente und Messmethoden bei Gerbert und bei den Arabern', *Archiv der Mathematik und Physik*, 3 Folge, 19: 315–20.

INDEX

Note: page references to figures are in *italic*.

Abdaraxos 102
Acrocorinth 161, 165, 166, 339
Adrastus 151, 159, 162, 165, 336
Aegina 169, 341, 342
Aflimun (Philo) 49, 307, 308, 342
Africanus, Julius 56, 63–6, 71–3, 78, 98,
    286–8
Agatharchides 340, 341
Agesistratus 309
agrimensor 3, 4, 5, 21, 122
akaina 21
Alatri aqueduct 115, 174, 195, 344
Albano, lake emissary 113, 197, 200, 202,
    203, 215
Alexander of Aphrodisias 65, 150, 151,
    155
Alexandreion aqueduct 173
Alexandria 33, 149, 165
    astronomy at 39, 43, 44
    latitude of 45, 144, 145, 147, 153, 154
    mechanics at 48, 53, 102, 136
    Museum of 2, 102, 314
    science at 2, 102, 104
    surveying at 17, 62, 63, 101
algebra 17, 59, 247–8, 251, 254
alidade 39, 47, 50, 51, 72–5, 92
alignment by dead reckoning 224–32,
    225, *230–1*
    by extrapolation *219*, 220
    by geometrical construction 232–3,
        233, 237–8, 240–1
    by interpolation 99, 202, 218–20, *219*
    by successive approximation 220–3,
        223
alpharion 29, 33
Alps 157, 158, 160, 336

Ammonius 70, 149, 314
amphitheatres 99
Anaximander 17
Andrias 40
Anna Comnena 67, 105, 250, 310
Anonymus Byzantinus 56–8, 63–6,
    71–82, 98, 289–98
Antikythera mechanism 8, 9, 136, 154
Antioch in Pisidia aqueduct 173
Antioch on Orontes aqueduct 173, 188
Apollodorus of Athens 103, 162, 165–6,
    339
Apollodorus of Damascus 57, 349
Apollonius of Perge 34, 64, 65
Apollonius, engineer 309
Apuleius 337
aqueducts 17, 31, 35, 100, 250
    arcades on 171, 189
    bridges on 183, 185, 188–9, 191, 194
    builders of 114, 180, 187
    cascades on 174, 175
    discharge of 99
    gradients on 50, 96–7, 113–15, 119,
        172–96 *passim*, 214–15, 253
    inverted siphons on 104, 171, 174, 183,
        195, 349
    pipelines on 171–2, 174, 180, 193,
        194
    reverse gradients on 114, 187, 189,
        193, 206
    surveying of 55, 103–4, 106, 109,
        113–15, 170–96 *passim*
    surveying errors on 187–8, 194–5,
        207–11
    and see under name of city served
Aquileia sundial 70

Arabic, reference letters in, 61, 302
terminology in, 50, 249, 251, 253
translations into 48–9, 59, 60, 250, 313
arachne 47, 69
Archimedes
on astronomy, 40–2
on circumference of earth, 143–4
on geometry, 44, 63, 295, 297
on mechanics, 34, 48–9, 135–6, 331, 332
on water surface, 35, 305, 341, 350
reference letters, 64–5
Aristarchus 40
Aristotle 36, 65, 143, 216, 340
Aristyllus 44
Arrian 159, 338
Artemidorus 341
Ashurbanipal 68
asl, aslu 60
Assyria 14, 17, 199
asteriskos 55, 126
astrabister, astraphister 67
astrolabe, armillary 39–40, 68, 69, 81,
152–3, 228
plane 47, 67–71, 82, 250, 253–5
name synonymous with dioptra
49–50
shadow square on 69, 254
astrology 67, 70, 71, 250, 255
astronomical instruments 8, 38–46, 81,
82, 103
and see names of instruments
astronomy 4, 8, 16–17, 38–46, 67–71, 251
Atabyrios 160, 338
Athenaeus Mechanicus 57, 66, 104,
308–9
Athens 30, 104, 146, 149, 165, 352
aqueduct 18, 173, 198, 199, 215
Attalus, astronomer 67, 79, 103, 311
Attalus II 64–5
augeion 73
Avienus 44

Babylon, science in 17–18, 40–1, 42–3,
45, 68

surveying in 18, 21–2, 60, 62, 251, 253
Bahr Yusuf canal 101
balance 110–12, *111*, 253, 350
Balbus 23, 55, 67, 122, 165, 309–10
al-Battani 254
beacons 220–3, 240, 243
Beirut aqueduct 188
bematistai 22
L. Betilienus Varus 195, 344–5
al-Biruni 255
Bisitun (Bagistanos) 157
Bithynia 40, 125, 319, 344
Biton 57, 64–5, 66, 103, 104, 308, 309
Bohemond 104, 310
Bologna aqueduct 198, 205–6, 210, *210*,
212, 346–7
boning boards 180, 187, 193, 205
Brescia astrolabe 71, 82
bridges 98, 249
and see aqueducts *and* river, width of
Briord tunnel 209, *209*
Byzantium, astronomy in 71, 80–1, 105
surveying in 20, 21, 63, 250
technology in 249, 349

Caesarea 306
aqueduct 174, 175
Caligula 169, 173
Cambyses II 199
canals 15, 18, 101, 167–70, 178, 246, 256
Canterbury 236, 237
Cardan suspension 75
Carhaix aqueduct 175, 187
Carpus of Antioch 33–5, 103, 305, 332
Cassiodorus 14, 26, 325
catapults 36, 65, 67, 76, 104, 112
centuriation 121–2
Chagnon tunnel 212, *213*
chains, measuring 20–1, 59–60, 246
Chaireas son of Damon 121
Chichester 226, 228, 238, 240–2
China 46, 137, 138, 246–8, *247–8*, 254
Chios 308, 309
chord tables 6, 39, 45

chorobates 31–5, *31*, 89, 103, 109, 189
Cicero 123, 154
circle, division of 27, 40–1, 42–6, 144
Cleomedes 41, 45, 144, 146, 158–9, 337, 338
Cleon 102
clocks 48, 49, 68, 124, 125, 135
Clodius Septiminus 322, 343–4
clouds, height of 157, 159
Cologne aqueduct 180
Commodus 137, 138–9, 331
Constantine VII Porphyrogennetos 57
Constantinople 57, 221, 250
  aqueduct 188, 193
  hippodrome 57, 58, 290–8
Contrebia Belaisca inscription 343
Copais tunnel 173, 199, 215
cords, measuring 18, 19–21, 138, 226, 246
Corinth 200, 339
  aqueduct 173
  canal 8, 168–70, 341–2
corniculi 126
Corpus Agrimensorum 109, 122–3, 126, 255, 303, 323
Crates of Mallos 123, 124
Cremna aqueduct 194
Crimea 121
cross-staff (Jacob's staff) 46, 255, 351
  so-called, for right angles 351, *352*
Ctesias 157
Ctesibius 48, 102, 104
cultellatio 125
cuniculi 199–200, 205, 209, 215
Cyrus I 18, 199

Dagon aqueduct 173
Darius I 157, 340, 341
decempeda 21
degree, value of 144–5, 146–50, 153, 156
  and see circle, division of
Demetrius Poliorcetes 169
diabetes 29, 30, 33
diagrams in treatises 56, 58, 84, 88, 123, 201, 258

diaugeion 73
Dicaearchus 143–4, 158–62, 166, 335, 336, 338
Diodorus Siculus 157, 336, 340
Dionysius 43–4
dioptra, as sighting tube 36–8
  Hero's 54–5, 82–9, *83–7*, 227
  Hipparchan (four-cubit) 42, *43*, 67, 78, 81, 153
  standard 51–108 *passim*, 153, 165–6, 216, 253–4, 299
  chronology of 101–5, 154, 159
  degree scale on 51, 69, 73, 97, 227
  material of 82
  not used in West? 67, 100, 109
  reconstruction of *52–3*, 105–8
  size of 82
  stand of 71–3, 78–9, 84, *299*
  universal joint on 51, 75
direction (bearing) 218, 226–9, 232–3
  and see orientation
dodecahedrons 350–1
Dorchester, aqueduct 194
Dyrrhachium (Durazzo) 104, 310

earth, circumference of 22, 67, 138, 143–56
  curvature of 108, 243
ecliptic circle 41, 68, 69
  coordinates 40
  obliquity of 27, 39
  plane of 79
Egypt 18, 24, 136, 199, 250
  science in 2, 16–17
  surveying in 14–17, 19–21, 101–2, 120, 167–9
Ephesus aqueduct 171
equator, plane of 39, 79
equatorial armillary 39
  coordinates 40, 45, 149
Eratosthenes 40, 165, 169, 341–2
  on circumference of earth 22, 143–8, 154–6
  on mountain heights 158–9, 162, 166, 336–7

Ermine Street 234, *235*, 243
Etruscans, surveying by 113, 115, 120,
    125, 323
    tunnels of 18, 31, 199–200, 205, 213,
    215–6
Euclid 23, 37, 41, 60, 63, 97
Eudoxus 44, 45, 166, 311, 339
Eumenes II 104
Eupalinus 170, 197, 199, 201, 204, 207
exercises, surveying 55, 63, 97–100, 254,
    255
Ezekiel 22

Faventinus 176, 343
Fayum, groma from 130, *131*, 132
    irrigation of 101–2
ferramentum 67, 123, 126–7, 131–2
Festus 125, 126, 324
Firdausi 249
Fontvieille tunnel 210
Forma Urbis Romae 100, 109
Foss Way 233
Frontinus 100, 122, 133, 319, 324–5
Fucino, lake emissary 198

Gadara aqueducts 173
Galen 217
Gamaliel II, Rabbi 46, 47, 305, 306
Gardon, river 182, 183, 188
Gartree Road 242
gears 8, 76, 83–4, 88, 134–7, 154
Geminus 34, 67, 79, 145, 155, 311, 338
Geneva aqueduct 174
geometry 6, 8, 13–14, 26, 34, 97, 123
Gerbert d'Aurillac 255
gnoma, gnome 125
gnomon (shadow stick) 14, 17, 246
    for orientation 22, 123, 228
    for sun altitude 24, 26–7, 143–4, 147,
    229
Goths 24
C. Gracchus 217
gradients xviii
    and see aqueducts

Greece, influence of on Roman surveying
    122–4, 233
grids 22, 120–2, 125
groma 15, 67, 120–33, *127–32*, 218–45
    passim
gromaticus 3, 122
gruma, *see* groma

halysis 20
hamma 19
harbours 58, 99
Heliodorus 41, 70, 314
Heraclea, Italy 121
Hero of Alexandria *passim and*
    asteriskos 126, 131–2, 282–3
    dioptra 53–6, 62–3, 82–9, *85, 87–8*, 96,
    259–63
    hodometer 136–7, 283–5
    levelling 89, 93, 180, 263–5
    other procedures 99, 201, 211, 224,
    228–9, 265–82
Herod the Great 174
Herodes Atticus 169
Herodotus 13, 17, 120, 197, 199
Hieronymus of Cardia 166, 339
Hipparchus and astronomy 6, 17, 38–45,
    68, 103, 334
    and circumference of earth 144–5,
    147, 148, 152, 154
    and see dioptra
Hippodamus of Miletus, 120
Hippolytus 143
Hisdai, Rabbi 47, 306
hodometer 8, 134–9, *135*, 153, 154–5, 226
Humeima aqueduct 173
Hyginus Gromaticus 23, 122, 123, 126,
    325–6
Hypsicles 41

Ibn al-'Awwam 49, 50, 251, 307–8, 342
Ibn al-Nadim 50, 313
Ibn al-Saffar 253, 254
Ibn Lujun 253
India 46, 249, 251

Iran, *see* Persia
Iraq 18, 156, 251
irrigation 30, 91, 92
  channels 31, 49, 89, 176, 191, 249
  in Egypt 15, 101–2, 167
  in Mesopotamia 18
Islam, surveying in 60, 156, 249, 250–5
  surveying instruments in 18, 59, 71,
    105, 251–5
Isthmus, *see* Corinth
Ivrea, relief of groma from 129, *129*

Jacob's staff, *see* cross–staff
Joshua, patriarch 33
Joshua ben Hananiah, Rabbi 20, 305
Julian of Ascalon 60
Julius Caesar 151, 169
Justinian 149, 250
Juvenal 124

Kaikos, river 191
  and see Pergamon, aqueducts
kamal 46
Kamateros, John 71, 80, 317–18
al-Karaji, date of source of 64–6
  on dioptra 59, 71–3, 78, 82, 299, *299*
  on levelling 19, 91, 93–4, 102, 107,
    299–302
  on staff 59, 62, 299, *299*
  on suspended sighting tube 38, 101,
    214–16, *214*
  on tunnel surveying 59, 199, 203,
    212–14, *212*
karchesion 76, *77*, 79
Karun, river 249
Kharga oasis 18, 199
al-Khuwarizmi 254
koilia 349
Kyllene, Mount 103, 159, 165, 166, 338,
  339

Lambaesis 322, 344, 345
Laodicea ad Lycum aqueduct 173
latitudes 26–7, 39, 143–7, 153

Leicester 242
  aqueduct 194
length, units of xviii–xx, 19–21, 60, 62–3,
  137
Lepcis Magna aqueduct 194
lepta 82
level, gunner's 113
  Hero's water 54, 82, 83–9, 96
  plumb-line (A-frame, builder's) 6, 29–30
    Egyptian 16, 27, *28*
    Greek 27–30, 33, 35, 49, 92
    Islamic 214, 251
    Roman 29, 112
  spirit 6, 256
  U-tube 349–50
  water 6, 32, 109–10, 246, 251, 253, 255
  and see individual names of levels
levelling 15, 27–35, 49–50, 170, 204–6,
  251–4
  with dioptra 51, 60, 62, 72, 89–97, *90*,
    105–6
  with libra 111–15
  with water 15, 16, 27, 191–3
Levi ben Gerson 46, 255
libella 29, 112
libra 5, 18, 97, 109–19, 216, 253
  reconstruction of 116–19, *117–18*
librator 3, 169, 195
libritor 112–13
limes, German 133, 242–5, *244*
Lincoln 233, 234, 236
  aqueduct 180, 194
linee 19
Little St Bernard Pass 206
Liu Hui 247
London 226, 228, 236, 238, 240–2
  and see New River
Lorch 243
Lupitus 255
lychnia 58, 72
Lyon aqueducts 174, 175, 194, 212

Main, river 243
al-Mamun, caliph 156, 251

Mappae Clavicula 26, 27, 76, 303–4
maps 3, 18, 99–100, 224–6
  Agrippa's 137, 139
  of Rome 100
  Ptolemys's 4, 137, 242
Marcellus, M. Claudius 24, 42, 103
Marinus of Tyre 137, 148, 241
markers 126–7, 132, 202, 218, 221, 238
  and see stakes
Marseille 26, 27, 43
Martianus Capella 143, 144, 337
Masha'allah 254
mathematics 8, 16, 17
measurement of distances 15, 19–22, 145,
  148, 150, 226, 241
  and see chains, cords, pacing *and* rods
'measuring rod', astronomical 42–6, 159
Medway, river 236–8
mensor 3, 122, 129
meridian 144, 145, 148, 151, 152, 228, 232
  plane of 39, 79
meridional altitudes 39, 45
  armillary (ring) 39, 73, 81, 82
merkhet 15, 16
Mesopotamia 17, 30, 120
meteoroscope 40, 73, 82, 148, 152
Meton 120
mezupit 46–7
Middle Ages, surveying in 246, 255
milestones 135, 138, 242
Miletus 14, 24, 120
Miltenberg-Altstadt 243
mining 110, 197, 200, 211, 318, 352
Mithridates VI 309
mizan 18, 59–60, 91, 214–15, 251–3, *252*
Moeris, lake 101, 102
mountains, heights of 66, 98, 103, 122,
  150, 157–66
murjiqal 253
Mynas Codex 55, *85*, 87, *87–8*, 202
Mytilene aqueduct 173

Narbonne aqueduct 175
Naucratis 14, 24

Necho 169, 341
Nemi, lake emissary 113, 197, 200, 202,
  203, 208–9, 215
Nero 169, 342
New River 79, 193, 256
Nicomedes 34
Nicomedia, Bithynia 195, 319, 344
Nile, river 13–15, 101, 143, 167–8
Nile–Red Sea canal 167–70, *168*, 340–1
Nîmes aqueduct 175, 181–93, *182*, *184*,
  186, 210
Nineveh aqueduct 17, 172
Nipsus, M. Junius 107, 123, 125, 132,
  326–9
Nonius Datus 180, 207, 345–6

Oenoanda aqueduct 173
Ogilby, John 138
Olympiodorus 37, 65
Olympus, Mount 103, 160–5, *164*, 337,
  339
orientation 13, 15, 22–3, 100, 120–1, 123
  and see direction

pacing 22, 138, 144, 226
paddle wheel 136, 139
Palladius 26, 176, 318, 343
Pangaeus mines 352
Pappus 34, 40, 42, 65, 332
parallactic instrument 39, 74, 81
Parthenon 29–30, 79
Paul of Alexandria 70, 314
Paul, Saint 227
Pelion, Mount 160, 336
Pergamon 64, 124, 165
  aqueducts 104, 172, 173, 175, 188, 191,
  195
  nursery of surveying 2, 104, 166
Periander 169, 170
Persia 59, 149, 248–9, 250, 252
  tunnels and surveying in 18, 31, 38,
  198–9, 213
pertica 21
Pfünz groma 129, *130*

Pheneos 103, 166
Philo of Byzantium, and Archimedes 136
    on aqueduct gradient 96, 176, 342
    on levelling 31–2, 48–50, 92–3, 101–2,
        307–8
    reference letters 61
Philoponus, John 149–51, 155, 166,
    314–16, 334, 339–40
Philostratus 169, 342
pigeons, homing 218
planetarium 34, 154
planisphere 8, 68–9
Plataea 23
platforms for instruments 243
plethron 60
plinth 39, 305
Pliny 37, 341
    on aqueduct gradients 176, 343
    on circumference of earth 144–7
    on levelling aqueducts 110, 318–19
    on mountain heights 157–8, 159, 336
Pliny the Younger 195, 319–20, 344
Plutarch 45, 163, 217, 339
Poitiers aqueducts 175, 189, *190*, 191, *192*
Pola 99, 321
Polybius 24, 37, 76, 158, 222
Polycrates 18, 197, 199
Pompeii 21, 137
    groma from 127–9, *128*
    relief of groma from 129, *129*
Pond, Edward 79, 256
Pont du Gard 181, 183, 185, 187, 188
Portus, Trajan's harbour 99
Portway, The 234, *235*
Posidonius 41, 143–55, 158–62, 166
Posilipo aqueduct 207
precession of equinoxes 45, 57
precision 6–7, 8, 15, 20–1, 253, 256
    in alignment 243–5
    in levelling 177–8, 189
    in measuring mountains 165–6
    in surveying tunnels 215
    of A-frame level 29–31
    of chorobates 31–5, 189

of dioptra 93–7, 100, 106–8
of groma 131–3
of Hipparchan dioptra 42
of libra 117–19
Proclus 82, 135, 310–11, 331
Psammetichus I 14
Psammetichus II 169
pseudo-Hero 57
pseudo-Hyginus 325
pseudo-Lucian, *see* Philostratus
pseudo-Stephen of Alexandria 71, 317
Ptolemais (Acre) aqueduct 174
Ptolemy 3, 37
    on circumference of earth 143–55, 333
    on instruments 38–40, 42, 68, 74,
        152–3, 332
    on map-making 4, 137, 241, 242, 332
    on plane astrolabe 69, 313
    on terrestrial direction 227, 228, 229,
        232, 347
    star map 45, 57
Ptolemy I Soter 169
    II Philadelphus 101, 168, 340–1
    II Euergetes I 101
    VIII Euergetes II 165
    dynasty 2, 22, 102, 167
pumps 8, 249
pyramids of Egypt 14, 23, 24, 27
Pytheas 26, 27, 43
Pythion 103, 163, 339

qanats 18, 197–200, 203, 205, 213–15
quadrant 254
qubtal 251

railways 6, 178, 179, 203
Rashi 47, 306
reference letters 60–2, 64–6, 102, 123
Rems, river 243
Rhodes 147, 153, 154, 227, 309, 338
    astronomical school 2, 41, 103, 144,
        145, 155
Ripoll, abbey 255
rivers, finding width of 56, 98, 107, 123

roads, aligning 99, 120, 124, 206, 217–45
  measuring 135, 137–8, 242
rods, measuring 18, 21–2, 125, 138, 226
Rome 24, 100, 124
  aqueducts 114–15, 174, 175, 197, 319
  inscriptions 110, 322
L. Roscius Fabatus 130, 350

Sabbath limits 21, 46, 306
Saldae (Bougie) aqueduct 202, 207,
  345–6
Samos tunnel 18, 115, 170, 173, 197–209,
  201, 203, 208, 215
Sardinian Sea 159
schiste sight 75
schoinion 19, 60, 102
scholiast
  on Homer 29
  on Ptolemy 147, 151, 334
science, influence of on surveying 2, 7–9
Scipio Africanus 324
Scipio Nasica 124, 163, 339
screw, Archimedean 48, 135, 136
  on dioptra 77, 136
  on hodometer 136–7
sea
  depth of 159
  level of 167–70
sefoforet 46–7
Segovia aqueduct 174
Seleucia tunnel 206
Sennacherib 17, 172
Sernhac tunnels 210, 210
Sesostris 14, 340, 341
Severus Sebokht 70, 316–17
shadow stick, see gnomon
shadows 22, 24, 39–40, 159
Shapur I 249
Shushtar 249
Siga aqueduct 180
sighting tube, see tube
sights
  floating 246, 247
  lack on chorobates 32–3, 35

on astronomical instruments 39, 42
on dioptra etc 50, 72–6, 74, 76, 105
on libra 112, 116, 118
on merkhet 15, 16
signalling 37, 219–20, 222
Silchester 234
Simplicius 137, 138, 149–55, 159, 335,
  337
Smyrna aqueduct 172, 173
Sophon, lake 195, 319
Sosigenes 45, 151
Sotiel Coronado mine 211
Souda 70, 310, 314, 323
Spain, Islamic 251, 253, 255
spartos, sparton, spartion 19
speculum, gynaecological 36, 136
square 15, 23, 121, 125
  geometric 254–5
stade, value of xix, 144, 149, 153, 156, 162
staff, surveyor's
  Chinese 246, 247
  Greek, cursor on 59, 92, 93
  Hero's 55, 93, 94, 262
  al-Karaji's 59–60, 91–3, 299, 299
  lack of for chorobates 32, 33, 35
  Philo's 49, 50, 92, 307
  Islamic 18, 59, 251–3
  sexagesimal division of 59, 60, 62, 91,
    253
stakes 180, 202
Stane Street 226, 233, 238–42, 239
staphyle 27–9
star intervals 43–4, 67, 78
stars
  Canopus, 145, 151
  Polaris, 22, 47, 156
  Kochab, 22
Stephenson, Robert 179
stereographic projection 68
Strabo 36, 67, 125, 167, 172, 311, 341–2
  on circumference of earth 146, 153,
    154, 155
  on mountain heights 159–62, 166, 338,
    339

Suez 167–8
sun and moon, apparent diameter of
41–2, 44, 45, 78
sun and stars, altitude of 39, 43, 46, 67,
69, 70, 78
sundial 14, 17, 40, 56, 124, 125, 152
portable 40, 70, 228
Syene (Aswan) 143, 144
Syracuse 2, 24, 42, 103, 135, 200
aqueducts 173, 199

Tacitus 112–13
Talmud 19, 21, 46, 305–6
Termini Imerese aqueduct 175
Thales of Miletus 24, 25, 26, 26
Thames, river 236, 240
Themistius 37
Theodorus 102
Theodosius 40
Theon of Alexandria, on astrolabe 69,
70, 313, 314
on builder's level 29, 33, 35, 305
on mountain heights 150–1, 159,
336–7
Theon of Smyrna 151, 159, 336
Tiber, river 99, 100
Timocharis 44, 45
Trajan 138, 195, 217, 319–20, 344
triangles, for determining heights 26, 27
right-angled 23, 63, 228–9, 255
similar 25–6, 25, 97, 123, 232, 247
trigonometry 6, 41, 51, 68, 251, 254
tube, sighting, on dioptra 47, 59–60, 62,
73, 91, 102, 299
simple 36–8, 46–7, 246
suspended 38, 62, 101, 115, 214–16,
214
tunnels 18, 38, 59, 99, 173, 191, 197–216
levelling in 18, 31, 38, 59, 97, 115,
204–6, 213–16

shafts on 174, 197–9, 201–5, 207–14
Tzetzes, John 135, 331–2

umbilicus soli 126–7, 132
Uzès 181

Valerian 249
Vegetius 24
Venafro aqueduct 321
venter 349
Via Appia 135, 217
Virgil 44
Vitruvius 26, 40, 66, 146, 255, 309
on aqueducts and gradient 50, 176,
180, 342
on chorobates 5, 31–5, 304–5
on hodometer 7, 48, 134–7, 135,
329–30
on libra 109–11, 113, 318
Vitruvius Rufus 26, 27, 303

Walferdingen tunnel 210
walls, finding height of 23–4, 58, 66, 72,
98, 107, 108
water-lifting devices 48, 49, 102, 171,
176, 194
Watling Street 235, 236–8
Welzheim 243, 245
Winchester 234, 237
wind, disturbance by 29, 32, 79, 105–6,
116, 132, 246
wind rose 227–8
Wright, Edward 256

Xenagoras son of Eumelus 103, 158, 163,
165, 166, 339
Xenophon of Lampsacus 158, 335

al-Ya'qubi 49, 70, 314

INDEX OF ANCIENT AUTHORS CITED

For inscriptions and papyri, see end of index.
Editions used not cited for 'standard' classical authors.
★ indicates citation by page and line.
References (page numbers and source numbers) to sources in Part III are in **bold**.

ABBREVIATIONS FOR COLLECTIONS OF AUTHORS

FHG   *Fragmenta Historicorum Graecorum*, ed. C. Müller (Paris 1848-83)
Lachmann   K. Lachmann, *Die Schriften der römischen Feldmesser* (Berlin 1848)
Marsden   E. W. Marsden, *Greek and Roman Artillery: Technical Treatises* (Oxford 1971)
Thulin   C. Thulin, *Corpus Agrimensorum Romanorum* (Leipzig 1913)
Wescher   C. Wescher, *Poliorcétique des Grecs* (Paris 1867)

AUTHORS

ACTS OF THE APOSTLES
27.14   227

AFRICANUS
Cesti, ed. J.-R. Vieillefond (Paris 1932
and Florence-Paris 1970)
115   **286–8**
115.1   64
115.2   63, 64, 65, 73, 75, 78, 97, 165
115.3   73, 97, 107, 290
115.4   50, 63, 71, 72, 78, 98, 107, 123,
                              165, 290

AGATHIAS
Histories, ed. R. Keydell (Berlin, 1967)
V 7   349

ALEXANDER POLYHISTOR
ed. F. Jacoby, *Fragmente der griechischen
Historiker* 3A (Leiden 1954)
Frag. 72   **Source 71**, 158

ANNA COMNENA
Alexiad, ed. A. Reifferscheid (Leipzig 1884)
XIII 3   **Source 16**, 67, 98, 104, 250

ANONYMUS BYZANTINUS
Geodesy, ed. A. J. H. Vincent, 'Extraits
des MSS relatifs à la géometrie pratique
des grecs', *Notices et Extraits des MSS de
la Bibliothèque Impériale*, 19 part 2
(1858), 157–431
1–11   **289–98**
1   57, 58, 65, 71, 98
2   58, 63, 71, 72, 98, 165
3   73, 97
4   58, 73, 97, 123
5   73, 97, 123
7   58, 63, 73, 75, 77, 97
10   63
11   56, 57, 63, 67, 73, 78, 79, 82, 227

Siegecraft, ed. Wescher★
268.2–9 309
271.4 77
271.7 66

APOLLODORUS OF ATHENS, *see*
EUSTATHIUS

APOLLODORUS OF DAMASCUS
Siegecraft, ed. Wescher★
164.12, 174.2 349

APOLLONIUS OF PERGE
Conics, ed. J. L. Heiberg (Leipzig 1891)
II 52 64

APPIAN
Mithridates 26–7 309

APULEIUS
On Socrates' God, ed. P. Thomas (Leipzig 1921)
8 **Source 78**, 158

ARCHIMEDES
Method, ed. J. L. Heiberg (Leipzig 1913)
12 64
On Conoids and Spheroids, ed. J. L. Heiberg (Leipzig 1910)
20, 30 64
Sand-reckoner, ed. J. L. Heiberg (Leipzig 1913)
1.8 143
1.12–13 42

ARISTOPHANES
Birds 995–1009 120

ARISTOTLE
De Caelo 298a.15–20 143
Generation of Animals 780b.19–22, 781a.9–12 36
Meteorology 353b **Source 88**, 167
Physics VI 2 64

ARRIAN, *see* STOBAEUS

ATHENAEUS
Learned Banquet
42B 125
442B 22

ATHENAEUS MECHANICUS
On War Engines, ed. Wescher★; part ed. O. Lendle, *Texte und Untersuchungen zum technischen Bereich der antiker Poliorketiker* (Wiesbaden 1983)
8.9–13 309
27.9–28.6 **Source 12**, 66, 98
35.4–36.5 76

ATTALUS, *see* HIPPARCHUS

AULUS GELLIUS
Attic Nights II 20.6 **Source 49**, 125, 218

AVIENUS
Aratus' Phenomena, ed. J. Soubiran (Paris 1981)
53 44

BALBUS
Explanation and System of Measuring, ed. Lachmann★
92.11–93.3 **Source 14**, 55, 67, 98, 109, 142, 165
95.6–7 21
107.12–108.8 23

BITON
Construction of War Engines and Artillery, ed. Marsden
52.5–53.3 **Source 11**, 66, 98, 309
58.12 77

CAESAR
Civil War III 40.1 321

CASSIODORUS
Variae, ed. Å. J. Fridh (Turnhout 1973)
III 52.2   14, 325
III 53   26

CATO
Agriculture 18.7, 22.1   321

CICERO
On the Nature of the Gods II 34.88   154
Philippics XIII 37   21
Tusculan Disputations
I 2.5   123
V 23.64   44

CLAUDIAN
Panegyric on the Consulship of Fl. Manlius Theodorus 274–5   44

CLEOMEDES
On the Heavens, ed. R. Todd (Leipzig 1990)
I 5.57–75   143
I 7.8–47   146
I 7.48–120   144
I 7.121–5   **Source 82**, 158, 159, 337
II 1.347–9   **Source 77**, 158
II 3.18–20   41, 45

CODEX JUSTINIANUS
ed. T. Mommsen et al. (Berlin 1928)
X 66.1–2   **Sources 42–3**

CODEX THEODOSIANUS
ed. T. Mommsen (Berlin 1905)
XIII 4.2   **Source 42**, 322
XIII 4.3   **Source 43**, 111, 322

COLUMELLA
Husbandry II 2.1, III 13.12, 13, VIII 17.3, 4   321

CONSTANTINE PORPHYROGENNETOS
De cerimoniis, ed. J. J. Reiske (Bonn 1829–30)
II 151.14   77

CORPUS GLOSSARIORUM LATINORUM
ed. G. Goetz (Leipzig 1888)★
II 278.25   **Sources 22, 48**, 67, 125, 126
III 454.6, 47, 485.17   322

DICAEARCHUS, *see* SOUDA

DIGEST
ed. T. Mommsen (Berlin 1905)
XLIII 11.1.1   322
L 6.7   195

DIO CASSIUS
Roman History LXXIII 5.5   139

DIODORUS SICULUS
Historical Library
I 33.9–10   **Source 89**, 167
II 13.2   **Source 72**, 157
II 13.7   158

ENNIUS, *see* NONIUS MARCELLUS

ERATOSTHENES
Geography, ed. H. Berger (Leipzig 1880)
Frags. II.B.1–42   144

ETYMOLOGICUM GUDIANUM
ed. A. de Stefani (Leipzig 1920)★
367   **Source 23**, 67

ETYMOLOGICUM MAGNUM
ed. T. Gaisford (Oxford 1848)
s.v. *gnomon*   **Source 24**, 67, 125

EUCLID
Phenomena, ed. H. Menge (Leipzig 1916)
I   37

EUSTATHIUS
Commentary on Homer's Odyssey II (Leipzig 1826)★
311.13–14   **Source 85**, 103, 162, 165

EUSTRATIUS
Commentary on the Nicomachean Ethics, ed.
G. Heylbut (Berlin 1892)★
74.2, 322.18   29

FAVENTINUS
On the Diverse Skills of Architecture, ed. W.
Plommer, *Vitruvius and Late Roman
Building Manuals* (Cambridge 1973)
6   **Source 98**, 176, 322

FESTUS
On the Meaning of Words, ed. W. M.
Lindsay (Leipzig 1913)★
86.1–3   **Source 50**, 125
314   322
476.26–9   126

FRONTINUS
On the Aqueducts of the City of Rome
6   **Source 39**, 322
17   100
18   **Source 40**, 114, 321
19, 23, 36, 65, 91   321
105   322
124   321
On the Art of Surveying, ed. Thulin★
16.3   325
16.6–17.9   **Source 51**, 126, 133
17.17, 18.9   325
18.12–16   125
Stratagems II praef.   54

GAIUS
On Boundary Stones, ed. Lachmann★
307.7, 346.9   126

GALEN
On the Therapeutic Method, ed. C. G.
Kühn (Leipzig 1821–33)★
x 632–3   217

GEMINUS
Introduction to the Phenomena, ed. G. Aujac
(Paris 1975)

1.4, 5.10–11, 12.3–4   **Source 19**,
                                     67, 79
16.6   145
16.22   124
17.2–5   **Source 80**, 159, 339

GEOPONICA
ed. H. Beckh (Leipzig 1895)
II 5.11   26

GEORGE OF PISIDIA
Heracliad, ed. A Pertusi (Ettal 1959)
Frag. 8   36

GLOSSARIA LATINA
ed. W. M. Lindsay et al. (Paris 1926–31)★
II 159, 163, V 67, 258   **Source 47**, 125

HELIODORUS
Commentary on the Almagest, ed. J. L.
Heiberg, *Ptolemaeus II* (Leipzig 1907),
xxxv-vii★
xxxvi-vii   **Source 31**, 41, 71

HERO OF ALEXANDRIA
Artillery, ed. Marsden
86.7   36
88   76
Automata, ed. W. Schmidt (Leipzig, 1899)
II 4–5   20
Catoptrics, ed. W. Schmidt (Leipzig
1900)★
354.20   37
Definitions, ed. J. L. Heiberg (Leipzig
1912)★
135.8   **Source 13**, 8, 66, 98
Dioptra, ed. G. Venturi, *Commentario sopra
la Storia e le Teorie dell'Ottica*, I
(Bologna 1814); ed. A. J. H. Vincent,
'Extraits des MSS relatifs à la géometrie
pratique des grecs', *Notices et Extraits
des MSS de la Bibliothèque Impériale*, 19
part 2 (1858), 157–431; ed. H. Schöne
(Leipzig 1903)
1–38   **259–86**

I	54	*Stereometry*, ed. J. L. Heiberg (Leipzig
2	54, 78, 98	1914)
3	55, 77	2.27 25
4, 5	55	
6	55, 64, 88, 93, 123, 180	HERODOTUS
7	22, 99, 218, 224, 228	*Histories*
8	88, 98, 123, 165, 287	II 109 13
9	88, 287	III 26 199
10	97, 123, 220, 291, 293	III 60 197
11	97, 220	
12	33, 55, 88, 89, 97, 98,	HESIOD
	99, 107, 165, 290	*Theogony* 722–5 354
13	98, 162, 165	
14	55, 88, 97, 99	HESYCHIUS
15	99, 201, 207, 224	*Lexicon*, ed. M. Schmidt (Jena 1858–68);
16	99, 202, 220	(partial) K. Latte (Copenhagen
17	99	1953–66)
18	64, 99	s.vv. *astrabister, diopter*, dioptra
19	99	**Source 21**, 67
20	20, 64, 203, 211	s.v. *chorobatein* 33
21	88, 97, 123	
22	97	HIPPARCHUS
23, 25	20	*Commentary on Aratus*, ed. K. Manitius
28	295	(Leipzig 1894)
31	55, 63, 99, 297	I 10.24 **Source 18**, 67, 79, 103
32	55, 63, 67, 78, 227, 297	*Geography*, ed. D. R. Dicks (London
33	35, 55, 126, 131, 132	1960)
34	20, 35, 55, 136	Frags. 35–9 144, 145
35	54, 55	
37	55	HIPPOLYTUS OF THEBES
38	55, 137	ed. F. Diekamp (Münster 1898)
Geodesy, ed. J. L. Heiberg (Leipzig 1914:		Frag. 7.1 77
see *Stereometry*, LXX–CXI)★		
lxxii 9–18, cvii	14	HISTORIA AUGUSTA
Geometry, ed. J. L. Heiberg (Leipzig 1912)		*Pertinax* VIII 6–7 **Source 60**, 137
2	14	
4.11	21	HOMER
4.12	19, 21	*Iliad* II 765 29
23.1	14	
23.13	21	PSEUDO-HYGINUS
23.14	19	*On Fortifying a Camp*, ed. M. Lenoir
Metrics, ed. H. Schöne (Leipzig 1903)		(Paris 1979)
I 14	295	12 **Source 52**, 126

HYGINUS GROMATICUS
Establishment of Boundaries, ed. Thulin★

135.3	326
135.4, 144.16	323
147.5	326
152.4–22	23
153.1–154.11	123
154.18–155.7	**Source 53**, 323
155.17–156.15	**Source 54**, 123
161.20	326

IBN AL-'AWWAM
Kitab al-Filaha, trans. J.-J. Clément-
Mullet (Paris 1864)★

I 130–1	251
I 131–3	**Sources 10, 95**, 31, 49, 92, 96, 176

IBN AL-NADIM
Al-Fihrist, trans. H. Suter, *Zeitschrift für Mathematik und Physik* 37 Supp. (1892), 1–88★

21, 22, 41	**Source 27**, 50, 70

JOSEPHUS
Jewish War III 118   217

JUVENAL
Satires 3.74–8   124

KAMATEROS
Introduction to Astronomy, ed. L. Weigl
(Leipzig-Berlin 1908)

2206–21, 2229–30, 2262–9	**Source 35**, 71

AL-KARAJI
The Search for Hidden Waters (*Inbat al-miyah al-khafiyya*); Arabic ed., Dept. of Ottoman Studies, Islamic University, Hyderabad 1940; ed. with French trans. A. Mazaheri, *La civilisation des eaux cachées* (Nice 1973) (which I have not seen); summaries Mazaheri 1965, Goblot 1979, 75–7, Hill 1993, 189–98

XXI-II	59, 61
XXIII	**298–302**, 61
XXIII 1	19, 59, 60, 73, 91
XXIII 2	59
XXIV	61
XXVI	212, 214

LIBER COLONIARUM
ed. Lachmann★

225.7	323
244.13	180

PSEUDO-LUCIAN
Nero 4   **Source 93**, 169

LUCILIUS, see NONIUS MARCELLUS

LUCRETIUS
On the Nature of Things IV 515   321

MAPPAE CLAVICULA
facsimile and English trans. C. S. Smith and J. G. Hawthorne, *Trans. American Philosophical Soc.* n.s. 64 part 4 (Philadelphia 1974)

213	**Source 2**, 26
288-O	76

MARTIANUS CAPELLA
Philologia, ed. J. A. Willis (Leipzig 1983)

II 149	**Source 79**, 158
VI 596–8	144

NIPSUS
Measuring the Width of a River, ed. J. Bouma (Frankfurt am Main 1993)

4–28	**Source 55**, 123, 125, 126

The Resighting of a Boundary Line, ed. J. Bouma (Frankfurt am Main 1993)

7–18	**Source 56**, 132
34–9	**Source 57**, 126

51–76   125
190–1   Source 58, 125

NONIUS MARCELLUS
On Compendious Learning, ed. W. M.
Lindsay (Leipzig 1903)
187   Source 46, 125, 218

OLYMPIODORUS
Commentary on Aristotle's Meteorology, ed.
W. Stüve (Berlin 1900)★
265.29   37

PALLADIUS
On Agriculture, ed. R. H. Rodgers
(Leipzig 1975)
IX 8   26
IX 9.2   322
IX 11.2   Sources 37, 99, 176, 322

PAPPUS
Collection, ed. F. Hultsch (Berlin 1878)★
1026   34
Commentary on the Almagest, ed. A. Rome
(Rome 1931)★
3–16   40
6   82
69–77   39
90–5   42

PATRIA OF CONSTANTINOPLE
ed. T. Preger, Scriptores Originum
Constantinopolitanarum (Leipzig
1902–7)
III 203, 213   77

PAUL OF ALEXANDRIA
Introduction, ed. E. Boer (Leipzig 1958)
29   Source 30, 71

PHILARGYRIUS
Explanation of the Bucolics, ed. H. Hagen,
Appendix Serviana (Leipzig 1902)
Ad Ecl. 3.41   44

PHILO OF BYZANTIUM
Artillery, ed. Marsden
59–67   35
64.9, 76.31   36
Pneumatics, ed. B. Carra de Vaux, 'Le livre
des appareils pneumatiques et des
machines hydrauliques par Philon de
Byzance', Notices et Extraits des MSS de
la Bibliothèque Nationale 38.1 (1903),
27–235
56   76
65   49
Siegecraft, ed. Y. Garlan, Recherches de
poliorcétique grecque (Athens–Paris 1974)
111   98
Water Conducting, see IBN AL-'AWWAM

PHILOPONUS
Commentary on the First Book of Aristotle's
Meteorology, ed. M. Hayduck (Berlin
1901)★
15.5–8   Source 68, 150
26.32–27.12   Source 87, 162, 166
On the Astrolabe, ed. H. Hase (Bonn
1839), repr. A. P. Segonds, Jean
Philopon, Traité de l'Astrolabe (Paris
1981)
1–3, 5, 8   Source 32, 50, 70
On the eternity of the universe, ed. H. Rabe
(Leipzig 1899)
212–22   150

PHILOSTRATUS
Life of Apollonius of Tyana
IV 24   Source 94, 169

PLINY
Natural History
II 85   153, 159
II 162   Source 73, 157, 158
II 176   37
II 178   146
II 224   159
II 247   144, 153

III 66–7	100
IV 41	158
V 128	349
V 132	147
VI 33	Source 91, 167
VI 61	22
VI 121	153
VII 198	321
VII 214–5	124
XXXI 44	26
XXXI 57	Source 97, 176, 322
XXXIII 74–5	Source 38, 110, 321, 322
XXXVI 172, 188, XXXVII 24,	
127	321–2

PLINY THE YOUNGER
Letters

IV 30.10	322
X 37	Source 102, 195
X 38	195
X 41–2, 61–2	Source 41, 195, 322

PLUTARCH

Aemilius Paullus 15.5–7	Source 84, 103, 158, 162–3
C. Gracchus 7.1	217
Marcellus 19.6	42
Moralia	
935d	45
1093e	37

POLYBIUS
Histories

VIII 5.10	76
VIII 37.2, IX 19.8	24
X 43–47	222
X 45.6–47.11	37
XXXIV 10.15	158

POSIDONIUS
ed. L. Edelstein and I. G. Kidd
(Cambridge 1972)

Frag. 202	146

PROCLUS
Commentary on the First Book of Euclid's Elements, ed. G. Friedlein (Leipzig 1873)*

41.24–43.6	Source 17, 40, 67
63.6–19	Source 61, 135
125.25, 241.19–243.11	34

Commentary on Plato's Republic, ed. W. Kroll, II (Leipzig 1901)*

218.22	34

Outline of Astronomical Positions, ed. K. Manitius (Leipzig 1909)

III 5–29	39
III 5, 9	82
III 16	73
III 19–20	78
III 23–4	23
III 25	73
IV 72–3	42
IV 74	78
IV 87–99	42
VI 2–25	40
VI 11	73
VI 15	78

PROCOPIUS

Gothic Wars I 21.3–4	24

PTOLEMY
Almagest, ed. J. L. Heiberg (Leipzig 1898–1903)

I 6	335
I 12	39
III 4	65
V 1	39, 40
V 12	39
V 14	42
VII 3	44, 45
IX 7, 10	43, 44
XI 7	43

Geography, I–V ed. C. Müller (Paris 1883–1901); whole ed. C. Nobbe (Leipzig 1843–5)

I 2.2	Source 64, 152

12.3   Source 106, 228, 232
12.4   Source 65, 149
13.1–4   Source 66, 148, 335
111.2   148
115.7   241
II 1.2   4
IV 5, V 2   153
VII 5.12   148
Optics, ed. A. Lejeune (Louvain 1956)
II 65, III 10–11   37
V 8–11   227
Planetary Hypotheses (Arabic version), ed.
B. R. Goldstein, *Trans. American
Philosophical Soc.*, n.s. 57 part 4
(Philadelphia 1967)★
7   148
Planisphere, ed. J. L. Heiberg (Leipzig
1907)
14   Source 25, 69
Tetrabiblos, ed. F. Boll and E. Boer
(Leipzig 1954)
III 3.2–3   Source 26, 69

SCHOLIA IN ILIADEN
ed. W. Dindorf (Oxford 1875)★
I 130   29

SCHOLIAST ON PTOLEMY
in Ptolemy, *Geography*, ed. Nobbe
I 3.3   Source 67, 145, 148

SCIPIO AFRICANUS, *see* AULUS GELLIUS

SENECA
Natural Questions III 28.5   321

SEPTUAGINT
Joshua 18.8   33
Ezekiel 40.3   22

SERVIUS
Commentaries, ed. G. Thilo and H. Hagen
(Leipzig 1923–7)
Ad Ecl. 3.41   44

SEVERUS SEBOKHT
Treatise on the Plane Astrolabe, ed. F. Nau,
Journal Asiatique 9th series, 13 (1899),
56–101, 238–303★
90   Source 33, 70

SIMPLICIUS
Commentary on Aristotle's De Caelo, ed. J.
L. Heiberg (Berlin 1904)★
504.33–5   45
548.27–549.10   Source 69, 67, 137,
                                150, 334
549.32–550.4   Source 76, 66, 150,
                                158, 159, 338
Commentary on Aristotle's Categories, ed. C.
Kalbfleisch (Berlin 1907)★
192.19   34
Commentaries on Aristotle's Physics, ed. H.
Diels (Berlin 1882)★
60.15   34

SOUDA (SUIDAS)
Lexicon, ed. A. Adler (Leipzig 1928–38)
s.v. *Dicaearchus*   Source 70, 158
s.vv. *diopter*, dioptra   Source 15,
                                67, 98
s.v. *gnoma*   Source 45, 125, 324
s.v. Theon   Source 29, 70

PSEUDO-STEPHEN OF ALEXANDRIA
Treatise on the Horoscope of Islam, ed. H.
Usener, *Kleine Schriften* III
(Leipzig–Berlin 1914) 247–322★
273   Source 34, 71, 250

STEPHEN OF BYZANTIUM
Ethnics, ed. A. Meineke (Berlin 1849)
s.v. *Kyllene*   339

STOBAEUS
Anthologia, ed. C. Wachsmuth (Berlin
1958)
I 31.8   Source 83, 159

INDEX OF ANCIENT AUTHORS CITED

STRABO
Geography

I 3.9	159
I 3.11, 14	**Source 92**, 8, 169
I 4.1	144, 146
I 4.4	27
I 4.6	146
II 1.12	27
II 1.18	43
II 1.35	**Source 20**, 67
II 2.2, 3.6	146
II 5.6	147
II 5.7	144, 145
II 5.8	27
II 5.10	124
II 5.24	147
II 5.34	144
II 5.39	147
II 5.41	27
III 1.5	36
IV 6.12	158
V 3.8	172
VII 7.4	153
VIII 6.21	**Source 86**, 162, 166
VIII 8.1	**Source 81**, 159
XII 4.7	125
XVI 2.13	349
XVII 1.25	**Source 90**, 167

SUETONIUS

| *Grammarians* 2 | 124 |

SYLLOGE TACTICORUM
ed. A. Dain (Paris 1938)★

| 43.11 | 98 |

TACITUS

| *Annals* II 20, XIII 39 | 112 |

TALMUD (BABYLONIAN)
'Erubin, trans. I. Epstein, *Seder Mo'ed* IV
(London 1938)

| 43b | **Sources 6, 8**, 46–7 |
| 58a | 19, 21 |

TALMUD (JERUSALEM)
'Erubin, see D. Sperber, *Nautica Talmudica*
(Ramat-Gan 1986), 107–8

IV 2	**Source 5**, 46
IV 2.21d	**Source 7**, 46
V 3.22d	**Source 9**, 47

THEMISTIUS
Paraphrase of Aristotle's Physics, ed. H.
Schenkl (Berlin 1900)★

| 41.26 | 37 |

THEON OF ALEXANDRIA
Commentary on the Almagest, ed. A. Rome
(Vatican 1936 and 1943)★

394.10–395.2	**Source 75**, 66, 150, 158, 159
513–22, 522–5	39
523.24–524.3	**Source 4**, 29, 33
527	65

THEON OF SMYRNA
Useful Mathematical Hints, ed. E. Hiller
(Leipzig 1878)★

| 124.7–125.3 | **Source 74**, 66, 150, 158, 159, 162 |

THUCYDIDES

| *History* III 20.3–4 | 24 |

TZETZES
Chiliads, ed. P. A. M. Leone (Naples 1968)

| XI 586–97 | **Source 62**, 135 |
| XII 964–71 | **Source 63** |

VARRO

| *Husbandry* I 6.6 | 321 |

VEGETIUS
Epitome of Military Science, ed. C. Lang
(Leipzig 1885)

| III 20 | 321 |
| IV 30 | 24 |

VETTIUS VALENS
Anthologies, ed. D. Pingree (Leipzig 1986)
II 41   36

VIRGIL
Aeneid VI 849–50   44
Eclogues 3.41   44

VITRUVIUS
On Architecture
I 1.4   322
I 1.7   321
I 6.6   23, 321
I 6.11   146
II 8.6, III 4.2, 5, 5.8, IV 6.1, 4,
V 6.4, 6, VI 1.5, VII 1.3, 4.1, 5   321–2
VIII 1.1   26
VIII 3.3   322
VIII 5.1–3   **Source 3**, 31, 66,
     109, 318, 321, 322
VIII 6.1   **Source 96**, 176, 322
VIII 6.3   **Source 36**, 321, 326
VIII 6.5   321, 322, 349
VIII 6.6, 8, 9, 14, IX praef. 7, 8   321–2
IX 8.1   40
IX 8.8–15   68
X 2.10   76

X 3.4   111
X 6.1, 8.2   321
X 9   **Source 59**, 134
X 16.3   76
X 16.9   309

VITRUVIUS RUFUS
ed. N. Bubnov, *Gerberti Opera*
Mathematica (Berlin 1899)
43   **Source 1**, 26

XENAGORAS
FHG IV 526   163

XENOPHON OF LAMPSACUS, *see*
ALEXANDER POLYHISTOR

AL-YA'QUBI
History (*Ta'rikh*), trans. M. Klamroth,
*Zeitschrift der deutschen morgenländischen
Gesellschaft* 42 (1888), 1–44*
21–3   **Source 28**, 70

PSEUDO-ZONARAS
Lexicon, ed. I. A. H. Tittmann (Leipzig
1808)
s.v. *gnomon*   312

INSCRIPTIONS AND PAPYRI

ANNÉE ÉPIGRAPHIQUE
1942/3, 93   **Source 101**, 322
1969/70, 589   138
1979, 377   **Source 100**, 180

CIL
Corpus Inscriptionum Latinarum (Berlin
1862–1989)
I² 1529   344
I 1687, V 8146   321
VI 1268   180
VI 2454, 2754   322
VIII 11   194
VIII 2728   **Source 104**, 180, 202, 207,
     321, 322

VIII 2934   322
X 4842   321
X 5807   **Source 103**, 195
XI 739h   **Source 105**, 206, 322
XI 3932   180

IG
Inscriptiones Graecae (Berlin 1873–)
II² 1627.349, 1628.522, 1629.998,
1631.229–30   67
II² 1668.10   29
VII 3073.128   19
XIV 645   121

ILLRP
Inscriptiones Latinae Liberae Rei Publicae,
ed. A. Degrassi (Firenze 1957–63)
528   344

ILS
Inscriptiones Latinae Selectae, ed. H. Dessau
(Berlin 1892–1916)
2059, 2060, 2422 322
4743 321
5348 **Source 103**, 195
5754 194
5795 **Source 104**, 180, 202, 207,
   321, 322

INSCRIPTIONES CRETICAE
ed. M. Guarducci (Rome, 1935–50)
IV 411 110

MAMA
Monumenta Asiae Minoris Antiquae
(Manchester etc, 1928–)
III 694 33

P. CAIR. ZEN.
ed. C. Edgar, Zenon Papyri III (Cairo
1928)
59329 33

P. OSLO
ed. S. Eitrem and L. Amundsen, Papyri
Osloenses III (Oslo 1936)
73 42

P. OXY.
ed. B. P. Grenfell and A. S. Hunt,
Oxyrhynchus Papyri I (London 1898)
100.10 227

P. PETRIE
ed. J. P. Mahaffy and J. G. Smyly, The
Flinders Petrie Papyri (Dublin
1891–1905)
general 102

RIB
Roman Inscriptions of Britain, ed. R. G.
Collingwood and R. P. Wright, new
ed. (Stroud 1995)
503 126

TABLETTES ALBERTINI
ed. C. Courtois et al. (Paris 1952)
XXII 6 228

LaVergne, TN USA
28 September 2009

159102LV00003B/7/P